W9-DHM-875

THE NEW WORLD OF SOUTHEAST ASIA

THE
NEW WORLD
OF
SOUTHEAST ASIA

Lennox A. Mills and Associates

THE UNIVERSITY OF MINNESOTA PRESS · MINNEAPOLIS
LONDON · GEOFFREY CUMBERLEGE · OXFORD UNIVERSITY PRESS

W 3509/55

THE CHINESE-JAPANESE LIBRARY
OF THE HARVARD-YENCHING INSTITUTE
AT HARVARD UNIVERSITY
JAN 19 1950

Copyright 1949 by the

UNIVERSITY OF MINNESOTA

All rights reserved. No part of this book
may be reproduced in any form without
the written permission of the publisher.
Permission is hereby granted to review-
ers to quote brief passages in a review to
be printed in a magazine or newspaper.

MANUFACTURED BY THE GEORGE BANTA PUBLISHING
COMPANY, MENASHA, WISCONSIN

DS 503.4 .M5

Mills, Lennox Algernon.

The new world of southeast
Asia

Preface

❖

SOUTHEAST ASIA has been the preserve of a few specialists who write articles and books for one another. When events there affect the United States, it is very hard for the average American to discover what is really happening. Few universities have given much attention to the area in their programs of Asiatic studies, although there are indications that this attitude is changing. The purpose of this book is to explain the present situation to the university student and the general reader. The main problems are similar throughout the whole area, and they are dealt with in the four final chapters. They discuss such questions as the place of Southeast Asia in American, British, and Russian foreign policy; its importance in international trade and investment; and the setting up of democratic governments. There are marked differences between the countries, and each is described in a separate chapter. Stress is laid on the present political and economic situation, set against the background of the prewar position and the effects of the Japanese conquest. Southeast Asia is so complicated a subject that no single specialist pretends to know everything about everything. The authors hope that by each writing on his own specialty they will help the university student to fill a gap in his knowledge of Asia. They also trust that they will enable the general reader to understand the news in the papers better.

Between 1929 and 1945 Claude A. Buss was an official of the United States foreign service in China and the Philippines, where he spent two years in a Japanese internment camp. He was also a professor and a member of the staff of the Office of War Information. In 1948 he was a visiting expert at General Headquarters, Tokyo. Since 1946 he has been professor of history at Stanford University, and is the author of *War and Diplomacy in Eastern Asia*.

Before the war John F. Cady was a professor of history in the United States and at the University of Rangoon (1935–1938). During the war he was Burma desk officer in the Office of Strategic Services and the Department of State, and in 1945–1946 he was on the staff of the consulate general in Rangoon. At present Dr. Cady is chief of the Department of State's South Asian branch.

Kenneth P. Landon lived in Siam from 1927 to 1937, and was at various times missionary, schoolteacher, and editor of a monthly magazine which was published in Siamese and Chinese. After a few years on the faculty of Earlham College, Indiana, he became an official of the Department of State dealing with Siamese affairs. He is the author of *Siam in Transition* and *The Chinese in Thailand*; and Mrs. Landon wrote *Anna and the King of Siam*.

Charles A. Micaud was born and educated in France, came to the United States in 1936, and is now assistant professor at the Woodrow Wilson School of Foreign Affairs at the University of Virginia. He is the author of various articles and of *The French Right and Nazi Germany, 1933 to 1939* and *A Study of Public Opinion*.

Lennox A. Mills is professor of political science at the University of Minnesota, and has traveled extensively in Southeast Asia and Ceylon. In addition to numerous articles he is the author or part author of five books on this part of the world. His latest book, *British Rule in Eastern Asia*, is a description of Malaya and Hong Kong during the interwar period, with comparisons drawn from American and Dutch experience in the Philippines and Indonesia. Dr. Mills has also been a radio commentator and columnist on international affairs.

Victor Purcell, C.M.G., was a member of the Malayan civil service from 1921 to 1946, and held various appointments including that of protector of Chinese. He traveled widely in southern and eastern Asia before and after the war, and was a member of the United Nations commission that investigated postwar conditions and reported on the needs for reconstruction. Dr. Purcell has written widely on Southeast Asian and Chinese subjects, his books including *The Chinese in Malaya.* He is at present writing *A Survey of Southeast Asia,* the first volume of which will deal with the Chinese.

Roland S. Vaile is professor of economics at the University of Minnesota, the author or part author of six books, and a consultant of the National Resources Commission. In 1918–19 he was a member of the American-Persian Commission, and during World War II he was branch chief of the division of civilian supply of the War Production Board.

Amry Vandenbosch is professor and head of the department of political science at the University of Kentucky. He has traveled and studied colonial policy in Southeast Asia, and is the author of numerous articles and three books, including *The Dutch East Indies, Its Government, Problems, and Politics.* From 1942 to 1945 he served in the Department of State and the Office of Strategic Services, first in Washington and later in Ceylon and India. In 1945 he was one of the secretaries of the United Nations Trusteeship Committee at the San Francisco Conference.

Jan O. M. Broek, professor and head of the department of geography at the University of Minnesota, drew the base map from which the map in this book was prepared.

LENNOX A. MILLS

July 1949
University of Minnesota

Table of Contents

ix

THE NEW WORLD OF SOUTHEAST ASIA

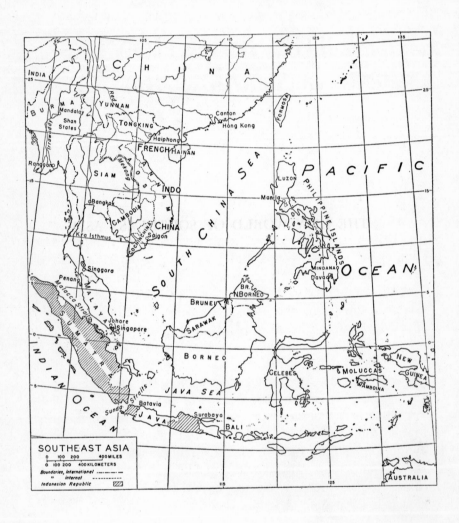

SOUTHEAST ASIA

0 100 200   400 MILES
0 100 200   400 KILOMETERS
Boundaries, international
      "   internal
Indonesian Republic

THE SITUATION
in Southeast Asia

Western Interests

SOUTHEAST ASIA is the forgotten zone of the continent. Americans and British living in Malaya sometimes receive letters addressed "Singapore, China." China and Japan are familiar and likewise India, but all that lies between is a vague and indeterminate limbo. So at the very beginning of this book it seems wise to take warning from the Roman emperor Claudius, who after speaking for three hours suddenly said, "And now, O Claudius Caesar, it is time you told the senators what on earth you have been talking about." Southeast Asia, then, is the portion of the continent that lies between India on the west and China on the north, and also includes the islands in the adjacent part of the Pacific Ocean. Politically the area is divided between Burma, French Indochina, Siam, Malaya, Indonesia (formerly known as the Dutch East Indies), and the Philippines. Geographically India, China, and Australia lie outside Southeast Asia, but because of their strategic, economic, and political interests in the area it is impossible to ignore them.

World War II impressed on the Western world the importance of this little known region. The shortage of automobile tires and the disappearance of beer in cans were results of losing control of 90 per cent of the world's rubber and 66 per cent of its tin. Along with them disappeared most of the world's quinine and a substantial part of its sugar, coconut oil, and hemp. The effects of this wartime dislocation persisted long after V-J day. One

3

reason for the continuing shortage of raw materials in western Europe is that it has been unable to obtain them from Southeast Asia in as large quantities as before 1941. Alternative sources of supply have had to be sought in the dollar areas, and a great part of the purchase has been financed by American funds. To some extent Marshall aid was made necessary because western Europe was unable to obtain its accustomed imports from Southeast Asia.

The area has had a further effect upon American trade. Before the war the United States habitually sold to Europe about $500,000,000 a year more than it bought from there. Europe was able to pay part of its debt by such items as American tourist expenditures and receipts for shipping services. To a large extent, however, it was Southeast Asia that provided the funds needed to balance the accounts. American purchases from Southeast Asia, especially tin and rubber, were far larger than sales to it, thus providing the area with a surplus of dollars. Southeast Asia used this money to buy from Europe much more than it sold to it, and Europe in turn used these dollars to pay its annual debt to the United States. This was one of the most important examples of triangular trade in the world, and in part, at least, it has been a war casualty.

There is no lack of demand for goods everywhere in Southeast Asia. Warfare still continues, however, in Burma, the Indonesian Republic, and a good part of French Indochina, with the result that production is only a fraction of what it was, and there is correspondingly less money to pay for imports. European production, moreover, has not yet recovered to the point where it can supply the needs of the area, and so obtains fewer dollars to pay for its purchases from the United States. At present the Marshall Plan disguises the situation as regards American-European trade; but the real position will become plain when the assistance comes to an end. Europe will then be compelled sharply to curtail its American purchases unless the former triangular trade with Southeast Asia can be restored. Failure to do so will have serious consequences for the United States as well as for Europe.

The importance of this market is not so surprising when one remembers that it is the home of some 155,000,000 people. It is true that about 90 per cent of them are subsistence farmers or fishermen with a low standard of living, which means that they have only a few dollars apiece to spend each year. Still, even a few dollars can become quite an impressive total when multiplied by so large a number of people. Moreover, the population includes a tiny minority of Europeans and Americans and a much larger number of well-to-do Chinese, the owners or employees of the rubber, sugar, and other plantations, tin mines, oil fields, shipping firms, and import-export companies. They have a high standard of living and the income to gratify it; and the business enterprises with which they are connected are heavy purchasers of machinery and other goods. It was estimated that before the war about $4,370,000,000 was invested in Southeast Asia. Practically all of it belonged to foreign investors, for, apart from the Philippines to some extent, there are virtually no wealthy men among the peoples of Southeast Asia. It is impossible to determine the nationality of owners of government bonds, but the American share of the capital invested in business enterprises was roughly about $330,000,000, the British $860,000,000, the European (principally Dutch in Indonesia and French in Indochina) $1,943,000,000, the Japanese $60,000,000, and the Chinese $640,000,000.

The colonial powers are surrendering political control of their former dependencies; but none of them propose to forego their economic interests if they can avoid it. An investment of over $4,000,000,000 is more money than anyone wants to lose. In Holland particularly so much of the national savings were invested in Indonesia that the annual dividends were an important element in maintaining the prewar high standard of living. The industrialized states need the Asiatic market for their exports, and they are vitally dependent upon raw materials. Some of these, like rubber and coconut oil, can be obtained only in the tropics. When one considers the various enterprises that are in some way connected with Southeast Asia—factories, exporters, importers, shipping companies, mines, plantations, and so on— one realizes that in the aggregate an impressive total of Europeans directly or indirectly depend upon tropical enterprise for their living.

The Western powers expect to expand their existing economic interests in Southeast Asia. The Trade Act of 1946, for instance, which provided for mutual free trade between the United States and the Philippines, stipulated that American businessmen must be given wider opportunities than they had before 1941. They must be allowed to take part in all forms of business activity, including the development of natural resources, on terms of complete equality with citizens of the Philippines. This necessitated a change in the Philippine constitution, which had required that only corporations of which Filipinos owned at least 60 per cent could exploit natural resources. Another indication of the same trend is that American companies own 60 per cent of the new oil field in Dutch New Guinea, and British and Dutch the rest. If carried out on proper principles the expansion of Western interests can be a benefit to all concerned. Apart from its return to investors it will expand the market for Western exporters, and it is a truism that enlarged markets are necessary for the economic well-being of the Western world. The peoples of Southeast Asia will benefit by a higher standard of living, which is very necessary for political stability and to combat the appeal that Asiatic Communists can make to poverty and discontent.

President Truman announced in January 1949 that American financial and technical help would be available for the improvement of backward and undeveloped areas. A very significant point in his policy was that government loans could meet only a small part of the cost, and that private investors must play the largest role. The president warned that unless the governments of the tropics create conditions under which investors can fairly and profitably invest their money, it will not be forthcoming. In this case there will be no raising of the native standard of living, for the tropics do not themselves have the capital to improve their own condition.

Strategically Southeast Asia is of far more than local importance. Whoever controls the Straits of Malacca and Singapore dominates a sea route and strategic key point that is comparable in importance with the Panama Canal. It is not only one of the great trade routes of the world, but also—for peace or war—the principal entrance into the Pacific from the west. The alternative passage

through the Straits of Sunda between Sumatra and Java is longer
and less direct, but also of major importance. Indonesia is a
barrier which separates the Pacific from the Indian Ocean. Its
significance was revealed by what followed the conquest of the
islands by the Japanese in 1942. They were able to break out of
the Pacific and extend their operations as far west as Ceylon.
This virtually cut communications between Great Britain and
Australia.

Southeast Asia cannot be considered in isolation from the
American naval and air bases in the western Pacific. Those in the
Philippines are only about a thousand miles from Saigon in French
Indochina, and the distance is even shorter if measured from
southern China or Hainan Island. The port of Davao in the
Philippines was an advanced base for the Japanese attack on
the eastern part of Indonesia. The former Japanese mandate in
the Caroline Islands was the base for the invasion of Australian
New Guinea, just as at a later stage of the war General Mac-
Arthur repeated the operation in reverse. He used recaptured New
Guinea as the base for his attack on the Carolines. The whole
area of the mainland and the western Pacific, including Australia,
is an interconnected strategic unit, from which the United States
cannot disinterest itself. It is to American interest that the various
countries shall be controlled by friendly governments, and that
there shall be stable and prosperous conditions which will afford
no opening to the forces of disorder.

Communism in Southeast Asia

This situation is very far from realization in the summer of 1949.
The disorder is worst in Burma and in a large part of French
Indochina; in Malaya a few thousand Chinese Communists are
carrying on a campaign of ambush and assassination against the
British and Kuomintang Chinese; and troops of the Indonesian
Republic are making guerrilla attacks both in their own territories
and in those states of Java and Sumatra that have sided with
the Dutch. Fighting still continues in Luzon between government
troops and the Huks, or peasant guerrillas. Siam is an oasis of
calm, despite rumors of an uprising by the local Chinese Communists. Confidence that peace will continue there, however, is

not increased by the knowledge that Russia has recently opened
an embassy in Bangkok, which is said to have a staff of fifty-nine
to look after a negligible trade and to protect the interests of the,
at most, forty Soviet citizens in the country. Premier Field
Marshal Phibun Songgram, the chief oligarch of Siam, probably
reflects that it is an ill wind that blows no one any good. As the
wartime arch-collaborator with Japan, he was decidedly unpopular with Washington and London a few years ago. His views on
Communists, however, are above reproach, and in the present
state of the world there is no disposition to look gift horses in the
mouth. The British Labor government has agreed to supply
Phibun with equipment for eight additional battalions, and has
promised more if necessary.

There is not a great deal of conclusive evidence that the
Cominform is connected with the disorders in Southeast Asia,
even though local Communists are concerned in all of them and
are especially prominent in Burma. It has been said, however,
that "Once is nothing; twice may be a coincidence; but three times
is a moral certainty." There are altogether too many coincidences
in Southeast Asia to be a coincidence, particularly when one
considers the simultaneous Communist activities which worry the
governments of India and Pakistan, and the situation in China.

One is inclined to wonder whether recent events are an example
of what nineteenth-century Europe called the swing of the
pendulum. Tsarist Russia, like Soviet Russia, was a predatory
state, and whenever her ambitions were blocked at one point she
tried to expand somewhere else along her thousands of miles of
land frontiers. For example, the main trends of tsarist foreign
policy from the 1870's to 1914 could be summarized as expansion
and stalemate in the Balkans; conquest in central Asia and
Afghanistan, which almost led to war with Great Britain; advance
in Manchuria and Korea, which was halted by the Russo-Japanese
war of 1904; and a renewed drive in the Balkans, which was one
cause of World War I.

The issue of the cold war in western Europe is still in doubt at
the time of writing; but at the most conservative estimate it
looks as though Soviet ambitions will be frustrated by a combination of Marshall aid, the Brussels Pact, the North Atlantic alliance,

and Western union. Since Soviet foreign policy is similar to that of the tsars with Marxist additions, one would rather expect what two generations ago would have been called a swing of the pendulum. Clearly the Western powers would be weakened strategically and economically if important parts of Asia could be brought into the Russian orbit. The West would also suffer a serious setback even if the only result were that disorders became so serious that the area was put out of action as a market and as a source of raw materials and income from investments.

The troubled state of Southeast Asia is not of course due solely to the Communists; such a statement would be a gross oversimplification of a very complex question. The underlying causes of the present situation extend far back into the early twentieth or late nineteenth century. What the Communists have done is to seize upon and aggravate a state of unrest, twisting it so as to realize their own purposes. The prime cause of the present conditions is the revolt of Asia against Western rule. This in turn is the product of political, racial, educational, and economic causes, which are analyzed in a later chapter. By 1939 this revolt was well established in all the colonial dependencies with the sole exception of Malaya, where it did not appear until after the war. The Japanese conquest strengthened the feeling of rebellion in several ways. The prewar standard of prosperity was seriously lowered by the destruction caused during the initial Japanese victory and—in Burma and the Philippines—during the eventual campaign of liberation. During the enemy occupation native life was disrupted by looting, military exactions, misrule, and anti-Western propaganda. The Japanese conquest gave Western prestige a blow from which it cannot recover. The chapter on the Philippines points out that this was apparent even among the Filipinos. The combined result was that the desire for independence was much stronger after the war than it had been before.

Policies of the Colonial Powers

The colonial powers met the problem in different ways. The Americans carried out their prewar program of establishing the Philippine Republic. In Burma, the British government abandoned its original intention of restoring law and order and material prosperity before completing the prewar policy of giving the Burmese self-government. Instead it recognized the independent Republic of Burma and withdrew its officials and troops. In Malaya the British set about creating democracy so quickly that they roused opposition from all three Asiatic races—for diametrically different reasons. The French insisted on retaining a considerable degree of control in Indochina, although the Viet Minh insurgents declared that they wanted the same position as Eire in the British Commonwealth. Since Eire is an independent republic there is a considerable gap between the French and Viet Minh positions, and the result has been war.

The Dutch followed a policy midway between those of the British and French. They were determined to save all they could of the large Dutch, American, and British economic interests, but they were willing to resign political power to Indonesian nationalist leaders. The Dutch, however, held that the policy of the British in Burma was an example of how not to do it: the British withdrew before they re-established settled government. The result has been that the Republic of Burma is in a condition of near anarchy, and it is anyone's guess whether the result of liberty will be a Communist dictatorship. The Dutch insisted that the Indonesian leaders must accept their advice and assistance while establishing themselves in power, and that the authority of Holland would not be finally abolished until law and order and security for Western economic interests had been assured. These terms were accepted in about two-thirds of Indonesia, and there the Dutch expect to give up their remaining powers in 1950. There too economic production is recovering fairly fast. The Indonesian Republic of Java and Sumatra refused the Dutch terms, with results that are described in a later chapter.

The general situation in Southeast Asia does not seem to support the widely held belief that freedom from foreign control automatically leads to democracy. It is argued in a later chapter that the self-governing countries of Southeast Asia are really oligarchies, and there is not too much reason for an easy optimism that they will inevitably and quickly change into Western-style democracies. Another conclusion appears to be that the British were perhaps precipitate in withdrawing so rapidly from Burma.

Possibly they did not make sufficient allowance for such factors as the inexperience of the nationalist leaders, the absence of political parties in the Western sense, the existence in their place of factions that are the personal followings of rival politicians, and the ignorance and indifference toward national government of the peasant 90 per cent of the population.

India, China, and Australia have their own special and important interests in Southeast Asia. Australia is aware that she is a numerically small outpost of Western civilization, close to the overcrowded countries of Asia. The West's "Far East" is Australia's "Near North." She realizes that her refusal to admit Oriental immigrants presents Asia with the tantalizing spectacle of wide areas which the Australians are too few to settle. Someday the Dominion may have to fight for its "white Australia" policy. In addition there is a growing trade with Asia which Australia hopes to expand. Her sea communications with Great Britain compel her to interest herself in Indonesia and Malaya. For all these reasons it is Australia's policy to cultivate friendly relations with her Asiatic neighbors.

The outstanding example of this policy has been Australia's vigorous support of the Indonesian Republic, and her strong opposition to Dutch military action. An Australian delegate attended the conference of Asiatic states in Delhi, which in January 1949 passed a resolution demanding that the United Nations take prompt and effective measures to re-establish the Indonesian Republic and remove Dutch control. There is an inconsistency between championing the rights of Asiatics abroad while barring them from Australia; but perhaps in this way the government hopes to reconcile its neighbors to its "white Australia" policy. It is inconceivable however that the peoples of Southeast Asia will accept Australia, a Western nation, as their leader.

Chinese Interests

Southeast Asia has been the borderland between the two great civilizations of India and China. Their influence began over 2,000 years ago, and has had a profound effect upon forms of government, religion, architecture, and literature. The Chinese completed their conquest of Annam in Indochina in 186 A.D., and ruled it until the successful revolt of 931 A.D. During these seven centuries the civilization of the conqueror was so effectively imposed upon the Annamites that to this day they bear the indelible print of Chinese culture. In the other countries of Southeast Asia the Chinese appeared as traders rather than conquerors, although occasionally an admiral or general imposed a brief acknowledgment of the emperor's overlordship. Indian influence came to Southeast Asia by sea, in the persons of Hindu and Buddhist missionaries, merchants, adventurers, and political exiles. The effect of Indian civilization was marked in Burma, Siam, Cambodia, Malaya, and the East Indies. Bali is the last survival of the Hindu period in Indonesia. Beginning in the thirteenth century Indian merchants brought the Moslem religion to Sumatra, and from there it spread through Indonesia and Malaya to Mindanao, the southern island of the Philippines. The arrival of the Portuguese probably prevented the rise of a great Moslem empire, and inaugurated the period of European control.

In view of the wide prevalence of Indian cultural influences, it is remarkable that in modern times Indian settlers have been far less numerous than Chinese in every country of Southeast Asia except Burma. The Chinese are found in every walk of life from manual laborers to millionaire bankers and businessmen. They largely control retail trade, produce buying, and moneylending. They own tin mines, plantations, shipping lines, rice mills, and factories, and are very effectively organized in chambers of commerce. They insist that their children shall be taught the Chinese language and culture, and for this purpose maintain their own private vernacular schools. They have close relations with their families in China, and most of them eventually return there. Politically the majority are strong supporters of Chiang Kai-shek, and his Kuomintang party has wide membership.

The Chinese abroad are a closely knit and economically powerful foreign community which stands apart from the bulk of the population. The Chinese community has aroused the ill will that always descends upon an alien group that seems to have gathered to itself an undue share of the wealth of the country where it lives. During the present century the gulf has widened with the development of nationalism in China and in the countries of Southeast Asia. For this reason the Chinese abroad cannot serve as agents for the spread of China's influence. On the contrary, the governments of Southeast Asia intend to curb Chinese economic power for the benefit of their own nationals. It seems inevitable that this trend will become stronger as nationalism develops.

The Chinese in Southeast Asia have a strong vested interest, and before the war they could count on the support of the National government of China. Chiang Kai-shek made it clear that he would oppose any attempt to interfere with them, and that he would press for further rights—for example, immigration into the Philippines—which would enable them to strengthen their position. This brought up the possibility of diplomatic conflict between China and the United States, Britain, and Holland as the protectors or rulers of countries in Southeast Asia. At the end of the war all signs pointed to a vigorous assertion of Chinese claims.

The civil war and the defeat of Chiang Kai-shek have made any intervention by the National government impossible. At the moment of writing it is not profitable to speculate about the attitude of a Communist government of China. It can count on the assistance of local Communist parties; and if it succeeds in conquering southern China, it will be in immediate contact with the Viet Nam Republic of Indochina, the leadership of which is to a considerable extent dominated by Communists. It will also have a common frontier with the Republic of Burma, where the weak Socialist government of Thakin Nu is struggling to maintain itself against its many enemies. There are all the elements of a serious situation.

General Romulo has suggested a federation of Southeast Asia under Filipino leadership. The differences between the peoples are so great, however, that a federation seems improbably remote; and so far as leadership goes, India is in a much stronger position than the Philippines. Apart from the great prestige which the attainment of self-government has brought, India's size and resources are immensely greater, and she too has upheld the claims of the colonial peoples in the United Nations.

India and Southeast Asia

There are many reasons why the predominantly Hindu Dominion of India should interest herself in Southeast Asia. Well over a million Indians live in Burma and Malaya, the majority being laborers and the rest business and professional men and money-lenders. Small numbers are found in other countries of Southeast Asia. The Indian government has been very solicitous in protecting their interests. Before the war Indian manufacturers had a substantial and growing market in this part of Asia, and they hope to increase it. They have ambitious plans for a great expansion of industrialization, and in addition to supplying the Indian domestic demand, foreign markets are sought. Southeast Asia is a logical outlet because its geographic propinquity gives the Indian exporter an advantage in low freight rates over competitors. Owing to the limited purchasing power of its peoples, it is a market where the cheapness of a product is a greater recommendation than its quality, and this again favors the Indian manufacturer as against his Western competitor.

India is open to attack from three directions, one of which is Southeast Asia. The traditional road of invasion, overland from the north through Afghanistan or possibly Persia, is the concern of the Moslem Dominion of Pakistan, now that the country is divided into two states. This is a burden it is incapable of sustaining, since it is financially the poorest and least developed part of the subcontinent. If Pakistan were overrun, India, which has no defensible frontier, would be invaded. Elementary prudence would dictate the closest cooperation between the two Dominions in their joint defense; but until their relations are much improved this is not possible. Even a united India would probably be incapable of affording the cost of modern military equipment; certainly it was never able to do so during the British regime. This is one reason why Pakistan and an influential school of thought in India favor close relations with Great Britain and the United States.

All the European invaders of India came by sea. From the eighteenth century onward the British navy protected India from sea-borne attack; but this duty would cease—except in so far as there is an obligation to supply aid through the United Nations—if India decided to become an independent republic. Oceanic defense would then be her own responsibility, a burden she could not carry in addition to the cost of maintaining an army and air force. Great Britain, for her own sake, is vitally interested in safeguarding the sea route through the Indian Ocean, since this is necessary to keep open communications between herself and her Dominions and dependencies in the Pacific. At present she holds nothing except Aden at the entrance to the Red Sea and Trincomalee in the British, self-governing Dominion of Ceylon, and these are not enough. Bases in India herself are the most important means of controlling the Indian Ocean. A defensive alliance between India and Britain would be in the interests of both. India realizes her weakness, but at present she seems to have a strong inclination to remain neutral in the cold war and not align herself with either the Western powers or Russia. In April 1949 India decided to become a sovereign, independent republic, but at the same time continue her full membership in the British Commonwealth. She thus retained the privileges of membership, although no specific arrangements were made for mutual defense. The decision not to sever connections leaves open the possibility that such a treaty may eventually be made.

A sea-borne attack on India from the Pacific would come through the Straits of Malacca or the Sunda Straits; and the only way to prevent this is to make certain that Malaya and at least the western part of Indonesia are in friendly hands. Burma was the immediate base for a land attack on India in World War II; but this was possible only after the Japanese had conquered Burma from their base in Siam, which in turn required the prior occupation of French Indochina. Southeast Asia is India's first line of defense on the Pacific side, though Burma and Malaya are of greater importance than the other countries. However, one may be permitted to wonder how India can defend these countries, when she has not the developed resources to protect herself.

The Indian government has denied any wish to form a South Asian bloc under its leadership, though this has been advocated by influential individuals. Some of them have gone further and

advised the annexation of Ceylon on account of its proximity
to India. The Indian attitude toward Pakistan has made the
Pakistanis doubtful whether India genuinely accepts the independence of this Moslem state. They believe that there are powerful forces in Nehru's cabinet which hope to force them to join
India through economic coercion. The determined attempt to
annex Kashmir, a princely state whose population is 80 per cent
Moslem, has strengthened their suspicion that Hindu India is
not willing to concede to others the freedom she demands for
herself. Cultural ties and historical relationships with Southeast
Asia have been stressed; and two conferences of Asiatic nations
have been held in Delhi to discuss common problems and ascertain
how wide an area of agreement could be found for cooperation.
A permanent Asian Relations Organization was created to further
the aims of the conference. India has taken the lead in Asia in
supporting the Indonesian Republic against Holland, and summoned the second Delhi conference of nineteen Asiatic states
for this express purpose. The Indian government reaffirmed its
opposition to the existence or reimposition of colonial rule anywhere in Asia. Nehru, the prime minister, declared that "Asia,
too long submissive and dependent, and a plaything of other
countries, will no longer tolerate interference with her freedom."
He denied that his aim was to acquire some form of leadership
in Asia, but the tone of his speeches was not inconsistent with
such an ambition.

The idea of Asiatic unity originated as a phase of nationalism.
A great part of the continent was under varying degrees of foreign
control, and the wish for freedom led to the feeling that Asiatic
unity would be desirable. Today most Asiatic countries either
have self-government or are within measurable distance of it.
Nationalism, which previously had been a unifying agent, at the
moment of achieving its purpose reveals its inherent tendency to
separation. It bids fair to divide the continent of Asia just as it did
Europe during the past hundred years.

The price of freedom in India itself was the division of the
subcontinent into two separate states in order to avoid the
alternative of civil war. Strong hostility has arisen in Burma to
Indian economic penetration, and no settlement has yet been

reached. Elsewhere in Southeast Asia, Indian traders and money-lenders have not been liked, though because they are few they have not been as unpopular as the more numerous Chinese. Ceylon has come into conflict with India over the rights of Indian immigrants. During the Asian Conference held at Delhi in 1947 there emerged more and more clearly great mistrust of Indian and Chinese expansion in Southeast Asia. The delegates from Burma, Malaya, Indonesia, and Ceylon voiced their fears of an Indian and Chinese economic strangle hold. The new nations of Asia want to manage their own affairs, and not exchange one foreign control for another.

They cannot do this by their own unaided resources. Their political leaders lack experience in administration, and there is a great dearth of technical experts—doctors, engineers, agricultural specialists, and the like—to staff their social services. In the economic field there are very few native business executives, bankers, and mine and plantation managers to carry on the exploitation of natural resources. There is equally a lack of capital to finance development. For a long time to come Southeast Asia will be unable to defend itself. A federation is not practical politics, and even if it were, it would not solve these problems. The union of six weak countries with identical wants does not create a strong one. India cannot supply what is required, for she herself needs the same sort of assistance, though to a lesser degree. The only source to which Southeast Asia can look for help is the Western powers, and particularly the United States and Great Britain.

THE PHILIPPINES

❖

THE international airport in Manila is the finest in the Far East. It is at the aerial crossroads between Guam, 1,600 miles to the east, and Singapore, 1,500 miles to the west, and it is the terminus for the long hop from Tokyo, 1,900 miles to the north. The harbor at Manila Bay, although horribly battered by bombs and shells and scarred by the half-submerged wrecks of a hundred ships, is one of the busiest in East Asia. Merchantmen flying the flags of the United States, Panama, Great Britain, the Netherlands, Norway, Sweden, and Denmark—and an occasional Russian—bring their cargoes from distant ports or take on new loads for not-too-distant Batavia, Saigon, Hong Kong, Singapore, Bangkok, or Shanghai.

Manila dominates the political and commercial life of the Philippines. The Philippines consist of 7,000 islands which stretch for some 1,100 miles off the coast of Asia. Their northernmost point is 65 miles south of Formosa, and their southernmost tip is only 43 miles north of the Dutch East Indies. On the map the Philippines range themselves into an imaginary donkey's head: Luzon forms the exaggerated ears; Mindanao, the mouth; Palawan and the Sulu Archipelago, the outline of the neck; and the Visayan Islands look like splotches on the face and forehead.

It is usually hot in the Philippines. Bataan brings memories of dust, and Leyte in the rainy season is a sea of mud. On the lowlands it is uncomfortable, but in the mountains, particularly near Baguio, the summer capital, it is cool and pleasant.

The Islands are home to 19,000,000 people. The inhabitants are descendants of Malay pioneers who overpowered the

18

indigenous Negritos and Indonesians, and were themselves conquered by the conquistadors of Spain, and later by the United
States. Each population stratum has made its peculiar contribution
to the national melting pot. The Malays, enriched by infiltrations
of Chinese, supplied the mysticism and the endurance of the
Orient, and the Spanish brought the Cross and the civilization
of the West. The Americans added their distinctive flavor of
politics and economics.

There are 43 identifiable ethnic groups in the Philippines,
speaking 87 languages, of which eight or nine are spoken by 90
per cent of the people. There are 7,500,000 Visayans, 3,500,000
Tagalogs, and 1,650,000 Ilocanos. A half-million pagans dwell in
mountains and forests, and 700,000 Moros, non-Christian and
independent, live in the Sulu Archipelago and Mindanao. Five
million Filipinos speak English, and one-tenth that number still
speak Spanish. Of all the people, 90 per cent are Christian and
80 per cent are Catholic. Two-thirds of all adults have had no
schooling at all, and two-fifths of those who went to school never
got beyond the fourth grade. Half the people are unable to read
or write any language.

It has been alleged that the Filipinos are passive, indolent, and
sometimes fawning as a result of the natural languor of the tropics,
disease, and the patronizing attitude of Spain and the United
States. Filipinos were supposed to be without a sense of responsibility or personal dignity, and incapable of making a decision without looking to the landlord, the political boss, or the
priest. Filipino society was said to be dependent upon foreign
elements for vigor and sustenance. These judgments must be
recast and remolded. In their years of travail under the Japanese
occupation, the Filipinos displayed an unsuspected inner strength.
They demonstrated beyond doubt an individual and social vitality
in their resistance to the Japanese challenge to their way of life—
a way of life that had become theirs by choice and not by force.

The impressive thing about the Filipinos is their unity, not
their diversity. They take a fierce pride in their local origins:
Manuel Quezon loved to refer to himself as the boy from Baler.
Unity against Spain instilled the consciousness of solidarity,
America fostered it, and fighting against Japan erased the last

vestiges of any tendencies toward separatism. The Filipinos take pride in their history. They have their own heroes, their martyrs, and their flag.

The Philippines are rich in the products of the land and the sea. Their agricultural prosperity has been based on rice, sugar, coconuts, hemp, lumber, and tobacco. They can develop rubber, quinine, coffee, kapok, and lumbang nuts (from which tung oil is extracted); and if it is necessary to produce for subsistence instead of profit, they can meet their own needs in rice, corn, *camotes* (sweet potatoes), vegetables, and fruit. Only one-fourth of their arable land was in production at the outbreak of the war. Their population problems are those of maldistribution, not over-population. It has been estimated that the Islands could provide a reasonable living for three times the present population.

The forest, pastoral, and mineral resources have never been completely developed. Lumber companies have never reached the point where they felt obliged to consider the necessity of re-forestation. Large ranches in Mindanao were just beginning to offer competition to American and Australian beef at the begin-ning of the war. Gold production has passed that of Alaska, and the current demand for strategic materials has just uncovered the possibilities of chrome, copper, iron, and manganese. Two large companies are drilling for oil, and industrial plans call for large-scale development of water power.

Economic development or trade has brought riches to the favored few at the top of the social scale. The aristocrats live like aristocrats anywhere. They have their beautiful homes, motorcars, racing stables, and fantastic parties. The *taos,* or peasants, at the bottom of the social structure still live in their *nipa* huts and eat their simple meals of rice and sardines. They work in the fields for a pittance and pay over a good share of their wages to the land-lord or usurer. Not the least of their debts are created by fiestas or cockfights. Even in their poverty they seek fun and enjoyment in the simple but expressive life of the tropics.

A middle class is gradually coming into existence. Six million Filipinos live in towns or cities of over 15,000. Among them are the poor workers, the *calesa* drivers, the servants, and the fisher-folk; but there are also the lawyers (too many of them), businessmen, doctors, dentists, teachers, and government employees and officials who make up the middle class. These include a large proportion of Spanish and Chinese mestizos, as well as growing numbers of those who are Filipino both in heart and face. For some unaccountable reason, the children of mixed marriages between Spanish and Filipinos (like Quezon), or between Chinese and Filipinos (like Sergio Osmena) have come to be regarded as distinct social assets, while children of mixed marriages between Americans and Filipinos, or illegitimate children "of the liberation," are often faced with unpleasant social barriers.

The Filipino way of life is an interesting composite of diverse cultural influences. Indonesian characteristics are manifest everywhere—in the style of houses, utensils, and tools, in language patterns, in local customs and beliefs. Hindu and Arabic influences have persisted through the centuries, and Spanish customs and traditions underlay the entire process of Westernization.

The Philippines under Spanish Rule

For more than three centuries Spain was the political mistress of the Philippines. She left in the Philippines a heritage that is completely comparable to the Spanish legacy in Latin America or the southwestern part of the United States. Spanish names are common in the Philippines. The cross of Magellan, enshrined in Cebu, is a poignant reminder that Magellan persisted even after Columbus failed to find the westward route to the Indies. Braggart that he was, Magellan met his death when he determined to teach the native ruler of the little island of Mactan that no infidel could blaspheme the Christian God and expect to get away with it.

The Legaspi peninsula preserves the memory of the cavalier who extended the power of Spain from the southern islands to Luzon, and who founded the city of Manila in 1571. Place names like Dasmarinas, Dumaguete, Plaza Goiti, and San Fernando keep alive the historic role of various grandees or their patron saints in the Spanish era in the Philippines. Spanish and Basque family names are distinguished in the Philippines, and the older generation has as its most common Christian names Miguel, Felipe, Tomas, and Jesus.

Spain extended her dominion by the power of the sword.

Expeditions from the mother-country, or from Mexico, fought against Portuguese, Dutch, and British to maintain their foothold in the East. On certain occasions the Chinese in Manila were massacred, and Chinese pirates attacked the city in vain efforts for revenge. Blake, Cavendish, and Sir Francis Drake at one time or another clashed with Spanish steel, and in 1762 the British actually occupied Manila. In less than a year, however, it was returned by the Treaty of Paris to the Spanish crown. The Spanish were unable completely to conquer the Mohammedans, whom they scornfully called Moros, reminiscent of their traditional enemies in North Africa. Moro hatred of the Christians—that is, of the Spanish and their protégés, the Filipinos, but not of the Americans—stems from these centuries of wars of subjugation.

When Spain colonized the Philippines, the native peoples were living in *barrios,* or villages, under a loose but fairly well-crystallized form of government, the prime unit of which was the *barangay,* or group of fifty to one hundred families. Society was composed of three classes—serfs, freemen, and nobles—and distinct rules governed each class. The Spaniards organized their government partly on the native structure, with a governor-general as supreme political chief, an *audiencia* or supreme court, and a treasury official in Manila as direct representatives of the Crown. The governor-general was supposed to be a paragon of virtue, neither too old nor too young, unmarried, neither in debt nor a creditor, neither avaricious nor profuse, but courageous and prudent, a frank and humane cavalier, and above all a man of piety. Judging from the contemporary accounts of the bishop, such good men were hard to find.

Provinces, districts, and municipalities were ruled over by inspectors or magistrates (*alcaldes mayores* or *corregidores*). They kept an eye on the tributes and revenues as reported by the *encomenderos,* or lords of the feudal manors. They administered the police and the militia, and as such were the objects of particular hatred by the native Indios. They were responsible for roads, bridges, and public works, and were charged with assisting to propagate the faith. This centralized administrative system lasted until the Americans came in 1898, and in its rigid centralization set the style for the Commonwealth and the Republic that followed.

The landholding system and the church also bear the indelible marks of the stamp of Spain. Improvident kings had little with which to reward the dashing conquistadors. Since all land in the Philippines was in the king's name, however, he signed over vast estates to his nobles and to the friars. The landlord might receive ten thousand hectares (one hectare equals two and one-half acres) and a thousand families in *encomienda,* as serfs. He would collect rents and taxes, he would pay wages as he pleased, and he was the final arbiter in disputes and quarrels. His was the practical power of life and death over his peasants, subject only to his own conscience, the avaricious inspectors of the governor-general, and the prying eyes of the priests, who insisted upon the tithe to which the church was entitled. The landlord was the original *cacique,* or political boss, the complete master of his estate and his community.

The friars came with the explorers—first the Augustinians, then the Franciscans, the Jesuits, the Dominicans, the Benedictines, and others in rapid succession. They were given tremendous land grants for their monasteries and religious activities. The bishopric of Manila was established in 1578, and the real authority of the bishop, and later of the archbishop, was equal to that of the governor-general. The friars were in charge of hospitals and schools. They studied the native dialects and reduced them to writing, but made little effort to teach Castilian or to change the Indios into Spaniards. They brought new methods of agriculture but satisfied themselves with very modest improvements in the native standard of living. The friars rather resisted the efforts to secularize the clergy. Parish priests have always been very popular with the Filipinos, and the humble churches are the most familiar sights in the *barrios.* Religion is an important part of the life of the average Filipino.

When the Spaniards discovered to their dismay that there was no wealth to be had in gold or spices, they turned to the possibilities of trade. The Indies were closed, and China and Japan were isolated. (The Japanese feared that monks and merchants

would conspire to incorporate Japan into the empire of Spain.)
The Spaniards conceived the idea of making Manila the emporium
of the Orient. Teas from Ceylon, teak from Siam, velvets, silks,
and brocades from China, and spices from the Indies were free-
lanced into Manila, stacked high in the warehouses, and loaded
on the annual galleon for Mexico. When the traffic was particularly
good, the Crown gave its gracious permission to the Royal Company of the Philippines to trade directly between Manila and
Cadiz.

Mexican independence put an end to the galleon trade. The
last Manila galleon left the Philippines in 1811 and returned four
years later. Then the trade was taken over by private persons.
Foreign companies entered the Philippines in spite of reactionary
and discriminatory decrees against them. By 1842 there were a
dozen foreign houses in Manila, and various governments maintained consuls there, among them the United States and Great
Britain.

At that time, 1842, China was opened to the traders of the
West. The monopoly of the English East India Company had
been broken, and the clipper ships passed Manila by for the
more lucrative profits of Canton. As profits tobogganed, Spanish
political power and the prestige of Spain also declined. Spain
could not keep pace with her more progressive rivals, and as a
result the political system in the Philippines tottered and threatened to collapse at any time after the middle of the nineteenth
century. There were only two thousand to five thousand Spaniards
in the Philippines, and the annual budget totaled in the neighborhood of $10,000,000. Most of this went to the army, the administra-
tive officials, and the church; but even this tiny amount proved too
heavy for the natives to bear. As Spanish exploitation increased,
native resistance strengthened. By the time the Americans came
in 1898, the Filipinos were in revolt.

Spain tried to prevent the entry and spread of dangerous
thoughts, but it was impossible. The heresies of the French
Revolution found their way into Asia, often by way of the
sailors, who had plenty of time to think and to talk on the
journey out. More and more of these merchant seamen came to
the Philippines after the opening of the Suez Canal in 1869.

Sons of the intellectual classes of the Philippines sometimes completed their education in Europe, and an occasional scion of the nobility took up the cause of the ignorant and illiterate masses on his return.

The first daily newspaper in Manila, *La Esperanza,* was established in 1847. Another paper, *La Solidaridad,* was founded in 1888 in Barcelona by Graciano Lopez Jaena in the interest of Filipino propaganda, and throughout its course urged reforms both in religion and government. A premature revolt of some two hundred native soldiers at the Cavite arsenal in 1872 had resulted in the deaths of their officers and in lusty shouts for independence. These in turn had led to harsh measures of repression and persecution. *La Solidaridad* was an excellent outlet for fervent young writers, prominent among whom was the brilliant Chinese mestizo, the foremost hero of the Philippines, José Rizal y Mercado.

The idea of Filipino nationalism grew rapidly during the decade 1890 to 1900. Rizal, del Pilar, and A. Mabini formed a Young Filipino party as a protest against both the domination of the friars and economic and administrative *caciquism.* Several Spanish governors were sympathetic, but other Spaniards, particularly the friars, were diametrically opposed. Rizal's books, *The Social Cancer* and *Reign of Greed,* were devastating attacks upon the evils of the Spanish system, and they fired the rebels in the Philippines as *Uncle Tom's Cabin* inspired reformers in the United States. Rizal organized the Liga Filipina, a mild aristocratic effort to obtain improvement within the framework of the law. But the Spaniards arrested Rizal, tried him, and made the mistake of shooting him. The night before he died he composed his poem "My Last Farewell," and his sister smuggled it out of his prison cell in Fort Santiago. It is one of the great poems in the literature of nationalism, and its sentiments have done much to make Rizal the foremost martyred hero of the Philippines.

Rizal's compatriots were less given to peaceful methods for the achievement of independence. Andres Bonifacio and Emilio Aguinaldo led in the organization of a "Supreme Worshipful Association of the Sons of the People"—the Katipunan. They wished to oust the friars and break up the large estates. They wanted equality before the law and a bill of rights. They were anti-Spanish, even if it meant insurrection. Hostilities broke out on August 26, 1896 with the "Cry of Balintawak," the trade-mark of rebel insurgency. Spanish reinforcements came and some insurgents were defeated, but the insurrection spread throughout Luzon. The Spanish finally bought off Aguinaldo with the Pact of Biac-na-Bato. The insurgent leaders left for temporary exile, and the Spanish governors settled back for a brief calm before a greater storm. Revolution was in the air, and was well under way long before actual war broke out between Spain and the United States.

The *Maine* was blown up on February 15, 1898. When the Americans decided to extend hostilities to the Philippines, it was natural and logical for them to find any possible ally against Spain. Aguinaldo and his revolutionaries were in exile, some in Hong Kong and others in Singapore. American authorities arranged to expedite their return to the Philippines. Aguinaldo said that Admiral Dewey promised him independence, but the admiral denied this allegation. Whatever bargains were struck, Aguinaldo returned to the Philippines on May 19, 1898 and announced renewal of the struggle against Spain. From June 1898 to the following January the revolutionaries set up a constitutional republic at Malolos, the capital of Bulacan, some forty miles north of Manila, with Aguinaldo as president. But their dreams of independence were short-lived. When Spain collapsed and the United States took over, the *insurrectos* found themselves no longer in opposition to a distant, decadent, and helpless power, but face-to-face with an ambitious young nation whose leaders had some rather positive views on American destiny in the western Pacific.

The Philippines under the United States: A Handy Chronology of Important Events

1898. MAY 1. Dewey wins naval victory at Manila Bay.
AUGUST 13. Occupation Day. American forces occupy the city of Manila.

1899. JANUARY. President McKinley appoints first Philippines Commission under Dr. J. G. Schurman to investigate conditions in the Philippines.

FEBRUARY 6. Senate ratifies the Treaty of Paris, making peace with Spain.

1900. APRIL 6. President McKinley appoints second commission under William H. Taft to provide for civil government which would replace military government. The government was to be designed for the "happiness, peace, and prosperity of the people of the Philippine Islands."

1901. APRIL 19. Filipino insurrection ends when General Aguinaldo takes oath of allegiance to the United States.
JULY 4. Taft becomes the first American civil governor.

1902. JULY 1. The United States congress passes the First Organic Act of the Philippine government.

1907. Nacionalista party begins its active campaign for independence. Bicameral legislature is established, with the Assembly as the lower house and the Philippines Commission as the upper house.

1909. The United States grants virtual free trade with the Philippines.

1913. Governor-General Harrison initiates policy of Filipinization of the Philippines Commission and the civil service.

1916. Congress passes the Second Organic Act, the Jones Law. The United States goes on record with a qualified promise of eventual independence.

1920. Republican President Harding appoints the Wood-Forbes Commission to report on conditions in the Islands.

1932. DECEMBER. Congress enacts the Hare-Hawes-Cutting Bill, which is vetoed by President Hoover.

1934. MARCH 24. President Roosevelt approves the Tydings-McDuffie Bill, providing for the establishment of the Philippines Commonwealth.

1935. Manuel Quezon becomes the first president of the Commonwealth, and Sergio Osmena is elected vice-president.

1939. Philippines Economic Adjustment Act puts into effect some recommendations of the Joint Preparatory Committee on Philippines Affairs, intended to ease the economic shocks of independence.

1940. Amendments adopted which restore bicameral legislature and make it possible for the president to serve two consecutive four-year terms instead of one six-year term.

1941. DECEMBER 8 (Manila time). Japanese invade the Philippines and launch air attacks on Manila, Davao, and other American positions.

1944. President Quezon dies. Osmena succeeds to the presidency and is installed at Leyte on October 10.

1945. Manuel Roxas is elected as first president of the Philippines Republic.

1946. The United States withdraws its sovereignty and the Philippines become independent.

The history of the Philippines after 1898 is also the story of the United States in the Pacific. The American government—the congress, the army, the navy, and the state department—had already expanded American territorial interests far out into the Pacific, to Alaska and the Aleutians, to Midway and Samoa, and finally to Pearl Harbor, when the occasion came to strike at Spain in the Philippines. Assistant Secretary of the Navy Theodore Roosevelt was the foremost of the expansionists who saw in the Philippines a heaven-sent opportunity to establish a strategic position that would carry forward our continental westward movement, and would strengthen our commercial bargaining position in China and Japan. The Philippines would compensate for many diplomatic defeats which we had suffered during the pre-Open Door days in the breakup of China.

The government was far in advance of public opinion. The vast majority of Americans had no interest in transpacific affairs, no understanding of the international issues involved, and no appreciation of the values or perplexities of taking on the Philippines as a colony. Practically no American could have located the Philippines on a map without a long and haphazard search. Mass meetings, yellow journals, and blistering sermons whipped up the popular anger against Spain and its policies. "Remember the *Maine*," as a slogan, carried enough punch to guarantee general acquiescence in the plan to crush the Spanish fleet in Manila Bay. No one had a very clear idea what to do after the victory, but everyone celebrated when the news of Dewey's triumph reached American shores. "The country went wild with excitement. Dewey Days were celebrated in the principal cities. Streets were renamed for Dewey. Young women wore Dewey sailor hats, sipped Dewey cocktails, chewed Dewey Chewies—a new brand of gum—and wrote letters on 'Dewey blue' stationery."[1] Meanwhile Admiral Dewey sat in his flagship within sight of Manila, wondering whether to advance on the beleaguered city and debating what attitude he should take toward Aguinaldo and the insurrectionists, who were eager to take the leading role in driving out the helpless Spaniards.

On August 13, 1898 American troops entered Manila—in a matter of hours *after* a protocol of peace had been signed at Washington. The United States decided to hold the city, bay, and harbor of Manila pending the conclusion of a definitive treaty which would determine the control, disposition, and gov-

[1] Quoted in Clyde, *The Far East*, p. 282. The original reference is a manuscript by H. R. Lynn, "The Genesis of America's Philippine Policy," Lexington, 1935.

ernment of the Philippines. American opinion, although wildly excited by military victory, became apathetic in the main as soon as the intoxication wore off. The Anti-Imperialist League said, "Let us by all means keep our precious isolation and have no part in imperialism." Clergymen spoke of our Christian duty and our cultural obligations. The armed forces spoke of the wonderful bases in the Islands, and the American commercial interests lobbied, printed, and spoke about the opportunities for trade and prosperity. Many congressional orators boomed their thanks to God that the American flag had been planted on the distant horizons beyond the seas. The state department received friendly counsel from Great Britain and Japan to go ahead and annex the whole archipelago. In their view that was the surest way to keep it out of the hands of the upstart Germans.

President McKinley was in a very serious dilemma—to annex or not to annex. A delayed decision was impossible because the *insurrectos* defied the power of the United States and launched open rebellion. In their view they had been cheated and had merely exchanged one master for another. They foresaw a hopeless future in trying to shed the yoke of the United States. President McKinley's decision was for annexation. The *Christian Advocate*, January 22, 1903 tells why:

"The President explained to a group of Methodists: 'The truth is I didn't want the Philippines and when they came to us as a gift from the gods, I did not know what to do about them. . . . I walked the floor of the White House night after night until midnight; and I am not ashamed to tell you, gentlemen, that I went down on my knees and prayed Almighty God for light and guidance more than one night.

" 'And one night it came to me this way—I don't know how it was but it came: (1) that we could not give them back to Spain —that would be cowardly, and dishonorable; (2) that we could not turn them over to France and Germany—our commercial rivals in the Orient—that would be bad business and discreditable; (3) that we could not leave them to themselves—they were unfit for self-government—and they would soon have anarchy and misrule over there worse than Spain's was; and (4) that there was nothing left for us to do but to take them all, and to educate the

Filipinos, and uplift and civilize and Christianize them, and by God's grace do the very best we could by them, as our fellow men for whom Christ also died.' "

While the American army set about the business of putting down the guerrillas and administering the country, President McKinley appointed a commission under Dr. J. G. Schurman of Cornell to investigate conditions in the Islands. The commission's four-volume report recommended a territorial form of government, since "the Filipinos are wholly unprepared for independence and if independence were given them they could not maintain it."

On April 6, 1900 President McKinley acted on this report and appointed a second commission, under William Howard Taft, to provide a government in which civilian would replace military authority. Secretary of War Elihu Root and Mr. Taft himself were responsible for drafting the instructions to the commission. These instructions formed the basis of subsequent American policy and administration. The sovereignty of the United States was supreme. No promise of independence was to be given. With the exception of trial by jury and the right to bear arms, the Filipino was to enjoy all the guarantees of the American Bill of Rights. The Filipino was to be given the greatest possible influence and participation in government for which his education and increasing experience would fit him. The system of government should be designed "not for our satisfaction, or for the expression of our theoretical views, but for the happiness, peace, and prosperity of the people of the Philippine Islands, and the measures adopted should be made to conform to their customs, their habits, and even to their prejudices, to the fullest extent consistent with the accomplishment of the indispensable requisites of just and effective government."

When a civil commission has to operate in a military atmosphere, and has to make recommendations for the termination of the *status quo*, it is faced with red tape and a kind of obstructionism that always seems to accompany a military operation. Mr. Taft's job was true to type. He demonstrated in this difficult assignment the qualities that were eventually to place him in the White House.

When his report was presented, he was given the responsibility of carrying out the recommendations he himself had made. He became civil governor of the Philippines on July 4, 1901. He was firm in his conviction that independence was not to be thought of, but he was determined to enlist the cooperation of the Filipinos in his administration. He added three Filipinos to the commission and he maintained a paternal, in no wise democratic, attitude toward "our little brown brothers."

From 1901 to 1913 the ideas of Taft dominated American policy. Taft, as civil governor, as secretary of war, and as president of the United States, followed the slogan "The Philippines for the Filipinos," but he interpreted it with conservative, Republican caution. The fact that the Philippines were administered as a responsibility of the war department was in itself a revelation of American attitudes and ideas. Filipino aspirations were so insistent that they could not be ignored, but every step in the direction of political liberalism was taken in spite of American opposition or skepticism.

Early American government in the Philippines was a benevolent paternalism. Americans concerned themselves with cleaning up the plague-ridden Islands, promoting economic development, and providing a public education system. Dr. Heiser describes Manila at that time as a crowded slum, where "the wretched dwellers crept through human excrement under one another's houses to reach their own. Throughout the Islands, save for the antiquated and polluted Spanish water system, there was not a reservoir, not a pipeline, and not an artesian well. Plague was in every alley, the morgue was filled with victims of cholera, smallpox, or tuberculosis, and the Philippines had the highest infant mortality rate anywhere in the world."

Schoolteachers came in substantial numbers to work side-by-side with the public health officials. Businessmen emigrated from the United States, and many old-timers resigned from the army to stay in the Islands and make their fame and fortune in real estate or some other private venture for legitimate profit.

The succession of American administrators was high-minded and devoted to the public welfare. But no amount of paternal perfection could be accepted by the Filipinos as a substitute for independence. As Manuel Quezon said, he would prefer a government run like hell by the Filipinos to one run like heaven by the Americans. After an initial political timidity, when a Federal party declared itself for cooperation with the United States and eventual autonomy within the American union, a Nacionalista party began the long battle for independence.

From the date of the establishment of the legislative assembly in 1907, the Nacionalistas were in control. The party agitated for independence continuously, although it never talked much of what it would do after the goal was attained. The illiterate masses were interested in bread and circuses, and the Nacionalistas promised both. "After independence you will have no taxes, you will have to do less work to feed yourselves, and you will have plenty of time for fiestas." With that program, the Nacionalistas were certain to be victorious. And no people has ever had a more skillful or fighting leader than the Filipinos had in Manuel Quezon. After an original term in the Assembly, he became resident commissioner in Washington. He carried on his independence campaign in the halls of congress, and extrovert that he was, he never missed an opportunity to buttonhole a prospective friend and sell him completely on the justice of his cause.

When the Democrat Woodrow Wilson was elected to the presidency, the Nacionalistas instinctively felt that they were in for better times. Governor Francis Burton Harrison, reflecting the philosophy of his chief, dedicated himself to preparation for independence. This would be approached as rapidly as the safety and permanent interests of the Islands would permit. A native majority was established on the Philippines Commission, and Filipinos were appointed to many posts throughout the government which had been held previously by Americans. Republicans lamented that the administration "was going to the dogs," and that the civil service, which had been built up with expense and care, would now lose its standards of efficiency and be honeycombed with native graft and corruption. Most of the American population on the spot was, of course, solidly Republican.

In 1916 President Wilson approved the Jones Bill, which provided for widening autonomy in the Philippines and pledged the United States "to recognize their independence as soon as a stable government can be established therein." The Nacionalistas and the American Democrats insisted that stable government was already there. The Republicans demurred, and set up their own standards for assessing a "stable government."

During World War I independence became an academic issue. It was shelved in favor of the urgent business of fighting Germany. After the American return to Republicanism—to normalcy—Philippine independence received an inhospitable reception in the United States. President Harding sent the Wood-Forbes Commission to investigate the results of the Wilson-Harrison policies. As expected, their report condemned the Democrats for moving too fast. The policy of the Harrison regime had led to confusion and maladministration; the Filipino people lacked adequate education in political matters; there was irreconcilable diversity of opinion on the conditions of independence; the Islands were not ready economically or militarily for freedom; the Filipinos needed more time.

General Wood remained in the Islands to reimpose the executive authority of the United States. The Nacionalistas were furious, and Quezon girded for the battle, which he later said sent General Wood to his grave and himself to the sanitarium. President Coolidge opposed independence. His special investigator, Colonel Carmi Thompson, in his report in 1926, advised against it because of the political confusion and the economic crisis which would result if the umbilical cord to the United States were severed. The Americans endeavored to persuade the Filipinos to take their minds off independence and settle down to the serious work of self-improvement. Filipino tempers seethed while the Americans lectured. The American government carried on its obligations as "an imperial republic," while the American masses had long since lost their interest in the Philippines. Before the great depression, precious few Americans cared whether the Philippines were independent or not.

After the economic crisis of 1931, however, and the election of the Roosevelt administration, the nature of the problem of the Philippines changed. It was no longer solely a question of principle, but became a matter of economic interest.

For ten years after the signing of the treaty of peace with Spain, the United States was estopped from any discriminatory tariff legislation. It could not impose on the Spaniards any higher tariff fees than were charged against the Americans. Other nations had the protection of the most-favored-nation clause, so until 1909 the tariff in the Philippines was the same for everybody.

In that year the Americans adopted a policy of virtual free trade with the Philippines, together with substantial duties against competing foreign goods. The United States acquired almost a monopoly of both the import and export trade of the Islands. Primarily as a result of tying the Philippines to the American market, a number of agricultural industries boomed and acquired an overwhelming importance in the export trade and financial structure of the Islands. The sugar barons prospered; the tobacco-growers, cigar-makers, lumber kings, coconut plantation-owners and coconut processors garnered fortunes. Profits came easily and money flowed freely. Dollars poured into the Philippines, American investments reached $250,000,000, and American exports crossed the Pacific in tremendous quantities to complete the cycle of trade.

The Filipino clamored for independence on a political basis, but he dreaded it on an economic basis. While the United States held out the hope of independence, it made its foundation precarious by tying the economy of the Philippines to the American economic machine. There was no such thing as an Open Door in the Philippines; as a matter of fact, the average share of the United States in the foreign trade of its ward approached 80 per cent.

Then came the depression. Farm groups, patriotic societies, and labor organizations looked upon the Philippines as an economic menace. They switched to advocating independence. Everyone who had an ax to grind adopted an independence policy in accordance with his personal interests. If he belonged to the Dairymen's League, he would argue for independence. Butter would have a better domestic market if coconut oil, used in the manufacture of margarine, had to pay a tariff. It stood to reason that once the Philippines were on their own, they would be cast outside our tariff wall and would have to pay duties the same as any other foreign nation. A sugar-grower from Louisiana, Colorado, or California would also vote for independence for the

Philippines. The Islands' competing cane sugar would then be
denied free entry, and in normal times there is an embarrassment
of plenty in the sugar market. The Filipino growers have always
pointed out that they could not possibly hold their own against
domestic production or Cuban imports into the United States
unless they were allowed substantial tariff consideration. The
large American financial interests with holdings in Cuba naturally
exercised their influence for the Philippines' independence too.
An unsuspecting reader might receive through the mails a most
impassioned plea for human dignity, for the recognition of the
right to freedom, a most eloquent appeal for the United States to
relinquish the role it had so adequately played during the past
quarter-century—and then discover that it was only the surface
approach of someone who had a substantial investment in Cuban
sugar.

Conversely, if a person were an investor in the Philippines,
or if he made his living in commerce with the Islands, the chances
were that he would advise his congressman to vote against independence. He would feel safer if his contracts enjoyed the
protection of American law. Clergymen and high-minded intellectuals manifested genuine concern for the completion of the
American cultural mission in the Philippines. They feared that
the relaxation of American interest, or the withdrawal of American financial support, would plunge the Islands deeper into reaction and darkness. It was not uncommon to discover a pamphlet
or a sermon printed and circulated at the expense of an unmen-
tioned sympathizer who had his money invested in the Philippines.

These were the forces which operated upon American policy
after 1931. To all intents and purposes Philippine problems were
questions of domestic politics. Even before the election of Mr.
Roosevelt, the Filipinos were quick to translate into action their
new hopes of independence. Their attitude was "independence
regardless of economic consequences." A commission headed by
Sergio Osmena and Manuel Roxas helped the American congress
to make up its mind to pass the Hare-Hawes-Cutting Bill (December 1932). This bill provided for independence after a transition period of ten years, a quota limitation on Philippine imports

into the United States, a gradual application of the American tariff, and an annual immigration quota of fifty Filipinos into the United States.

President Hoover vetoed the bill. He challenged every major feature of its provisions, denounced it as a repudiation of America's moral responsibilities, and expressed his doubts that the Filipinos could maintain their independence. Since the Democrats had already been elected in November, the lameduck congress overrode the veto. The Filipinos were not happy over the restrictions in the bill and they refused its offer of independence.

Manuel Quezon diagnosed correctly American sentiment for independence, and he appreciated the opportunity to achieve his cherished goal with the help of the newly elected American president and congress. He engineered the Filipino rejection mentioned above. He sensed that the economic restrictions imposed by the Hare-Hawes-Cutting Bill would ruin the economy of the Islands, and he knew that political chaos would follow economic bankruptcy. He reasoned that the new independent government would be blamed for failure, and that his whole Nacionalista movement would be discredited. He also objected to clauses which would permit the Americans to maintain bases in the Islands. What kind of sovereignty would it be with foreign bases on your own sacred soil? Furthermore, Quezon did not relish the thought that the OS-ROX (Osmena and Roxas) combination would live in history as the commission which had pushed independence through the American congress.

Quezon determined to come to the United States himself and champion a new and improved bill. This bill became the Tydings-McDuffie Act, which was approved by President Roosevelt on March 24, 1934. It provided for a ten-year transitional period, at the end of which time the Philippines were to be given outright independence. During this period, Filipinos were to recognize the supreme authority of the United States and maintain true faith and allegiance to it. (This clause was later the basis of American complaints against Philippine collaborators with the Japanese.) Acts of the Philippines legislature affecting currency, coinage, imports and exports, and immigration could not become law until approved by the president of the United States. Foreign affairs

were under the direct supervision and control of the United
States, which was responsible for the defense of the Islands. The
United States reserved the right to review court decisions, limit
the public debt and foreign loans, maintain military and other
reservations, keep armed forces in the Philippines, and intervene
for the preservation of the government of the Commonwealth or
for the protection of life, property, and individual liberty. Looking toward economic independence, the act established a system
of quotas and graduated tariffs to cushion the shocks of readjustment. Specified quotas on sugar, coconut oil, and abaca, for example, were to continue on the free list for five years; but after
that time the products of the Philippines would have to accom-
modate themselves to the necessities of unfavored and unsubsi-
dized competition.

Quezon returned in triumph from Washington after the passage of this act, bringing with him an admiration for President
Roosevelt which, as he later said, gave him the strength to carry
his burdens through the bitter days of the government-in-exile.
He was welcomed as the acknowledged giver of independence,
the unchallenged leader of his own party.

The Filipinos met in a constitutional convention to draw up
a fundamental law for the eventual Republic and the interim
Commonwealth. The constitution of 1935 follows closely the
American model. It breathes the spirit of Roosevelt democratic
philosophy and provides a structure for self-government. According to its provisions, the president of the Philippines took over
the duties of the governor-general, and the American interests
were entrusted to the safekeeping of the high commissioner, who
was the direct representative of the president of the United States
in the Islands.

In 1935 the Filipinos elected Quezon as their first president,
for a single six-year term, choosing Sergio Osmena as the first
vice-president. President Quezon moved into Malacanan, the
palace of the former governor-general, and Mr. Murphy went
into temporary quarters where he established the office of the
high commissioner.

During the Commonwealth period, political power was centralized in the national government, which carried the labels of

democracy, but bore the earmarks of democracy as practiced in Latin America. President Quezon was the great *jefe*. He, and a chosen few of his colleagues in Manila, could give the word and change overnight an entire national attitude on a specific issue. Independent thinkers were all too few. Candidates for mayor, or for a seat in the Assembly, would eliminate themselves at the president's behest. He adjusted jobs and personnel all over the country like a child fitting together the pieces of a jigsaw puzzle. Rivals for a particular plum were obliged to fight it out against each other, and the winner would receive the presidential benediction. A veto from headquarters would end the campaign of an ambitious newcomer, but judicious allotment of spoils prevented widespread revolts.

Quezon was uncanny in his ability to win friends and influence people. He was uncompromising on the independence issue, but his political opponents (Americans) were often his closest companions. His poker and bridge parties were legendary. When driven into a tight spot, he had a most disarming way of turning apparent defeat to his own advantage. He often chided the meticulous Osmena for being so careful "that he would not let his own mind know how his heart felt." Quezon said he never felt that he needed to apologize for inconsistency, for changing his mind, or for acknowledging his mistakes. His political flexibility was an inevitable reflection of his mercurial disposition. He was very proud of his program for "social justice" and insisted that he was the champion of the little man. And just about every little man in the Philippines warmed instinctively to the colorful, dynamic *presidente*, who could make them laugh or make them cry, and make them believe that he was fighting for them in the cause of nationalism and independence. The devotion of the masses was such that in the election of 1941, Quezon, without lifting a finger in an effort to win the campaign, polled 90 per cent of the votes cast.

The Nacionalistas had a monopoly on the independence issue, and there was no other issue sufficiently important to inflame fighting tempers. By mere virtue of being in office, the Commonwealth government enjoyed a certain prestige and patronage, and benefited from the cooperation and support of the United

States. Tax refunds from the United States and American expenditures in the Islands during the period before the war provided an ample economic foundation for the maintenance of the power of the Nacionalistas. Whenever factional quarrels threatened the unanimity of the party they always ended in reconciliation. Quintin Paredes and José Yulo, Claro Recto and Manuel Roxas at different times formed combinations challenging Quezon and Osmena. But they bowed in humiliation and remained within the party fold.

Only three minority leaders ever achieved a measure of distinction outside the Nacionalista hierarchy. Pedro Abad Santos, although damned as a Communist menace, refused to compromise his position as the spokesman for the peasants of Pampanga, a province in Luzon north of Manila. He never hedged in his accusations against the fascism of the central government and never ceased his agitation for the improvement of the lot of the peasants. Wenceslao Vinsons, later killed by the Japanese, championed the miners of Camarines Norte and got himself elected to the Assembly in direct opposition to the Nacionalistas. Tomas Confesor repeatedly demonstrated his determination to think and act independently. He defied the machine exactly as he chose, and he won his spurs later as a leader of the guerrillas.

During the Commonwealth period there was little doubt about the attitude of the Filipinos toward the United States. Self-respecting people must prize independence and freedom above everything else. Opportunists used the freedom issue for domestic political maneuvering, and shouted that thousands of their compatriots under the United States "were writhing in the throes of hell." Others made political capital of the annoying evidences of racial discrimination, and they labeled the *Manila Daily Bulletin*, the American chamber of commerce, and the Army and Navy Club as anti-Filipino. But sensible and restrained leaders advocated independence in spite of their "boundless gratitude for the measureless benefits derived from the United States." On one occasion President Quezon said: "When that starry flag finally comes down from Santiago in 1946, it will find somewhere in its folds the grateful hearts of a people—a new and vibrant republic facing with optimistic hope its rising dawn."

Under the Commonwealth, the civil service suffered but still maintained high standards in most governmental operations. Nepotism and spoils played havoc with the traditional merit system inherited from the American regime. The legislature too often played the ignominious role of the rubber stamp and served the causes of political expediency and corruption. Despite the spirit of the constitution and meticulous devotion to democratic processes, legislatures were hand-picked and all too ready to do the bidding of the *presidente,* his kitchen cabinet, or some of his influential cronies who wielded a tremendous amount of power and influence even though they never held political office. The courts departed even further from the precedents of Spain, and assumed the characteristics of the American judicial system. The courts in the Philippines are subject to the same criticisms, and the same praise, as the courts in the United States.

The chief economic feature of the Commonwealth period was the perplexing exposure of the economic dependence of the Philippines upon the United States. More than eight thousand Americans made their homes in the Philippines before the war. These included businessmen, veterans who had married Filipina wives, missionaries, teachers, and civil servants. Their investments made possible the development of mines, lumber, shipping, utilities, bus and transportation companies, and merchandising establishments, which helped to make the Philippines progressive and modern.

Annual trade between the Philippines and the United States approached a half-billion dollars in 1940. Americans sold automobiles, food products, petroleum products, machinery, electrical equipment, and other items, and bought sugar, coconut products, Manila hemp, lumber, tobacco, buttons, and embroidery. Banks, shipping companies, insurance agents, and a host of commercial employees derived a profitable income from this trade. But few Filipinos were involved in it. The Filipino man in the street was little concerned about it and knew nothing of its potentialities or its implications.

American investments and American trade gave only negligible consideration to production that would increase and broaden the internal wealth of the country. The old Spanish land grants were respected by the American authorities, and new American investors often adopted the traditional practices of landlordism. While benevolent America was building schools and roads (largely with local taxes), introducing modern sanitation, and cutting down disease, imperial America was perpetuating a medieval economic system incompatible with the development of a healthy internal economy.

Free trade with the United States, which encouraged the money-crop system, brought profits to the landlords and the compradors, but lesser benefits to the masses of the peasants. Rice was imported although it could have been produced locally. Industries for the production of consumption goods were not established. The economic situation deteriorated more and more as the date for independence drew near. A Joint Preparatory Committee on Philippines Affairs made recommendations which resulted in the Economic Adjustment Act (the Tydings-Kocialkowski Act), approved by President Roosevelt on August 7, 1939. It lengthened the period for free entry or favored treatment of Philippines' exports in the American market, even beyond the proposed date of independence.

By the end of 1941, the Philippines were faced with a first-class economic crisis. Domestic economy faced complete disruption, and foreign trade lost every semblance of normalcy because of the gathering war clouds. An economic conference scheduled for 1944 promised slight hope of relief, but Filipinos began to pay more attention to Paul McNutt's proposals for re-examination. Influential persons on both sides of the Pacific began to think and talk about dominion status as a means of satisfying both the needs of the Filipinos and the long-term interests of the United States. The enthusiasm for independence was temporarily dampened by the realities of economics—and diplomacy—on the eve of the Japanese invasion.

Government finance during the Commonwealth period was comparatively sound but severely restricted. The general budget for 1942 proposed an approximate income of $40,000,000 and expenditures of $60,000,000. The deficit was to be made up by the use of the remaining surplus from previous years, and by the sale of bonds. In this budget 33 per cent of income was devoted to education, 15 per cent to national defense, 6 per cent was earmarked for executive control, 5.8 per cent for public health and sanitation, 4.8 per cent for interest on the public debt, and smaller amounts for the other government services. Sugar alone accounted for 43 per cent of the nation's taxes. A special budget based on refunds of the American excise tax on coconut oil provided the money for continued large public works and government loans to agriculture and industry.

As expenditures raced ahead of revenues, the Commonwealth depended more and more on the United States. President Quezon did not show the least inclination to cut down expenditures, with the result that prices and production costs skyrocketed. The peso was unassailable as long as it was linked with the American dollar; but it would have been faced with serious difficulties had the Americans not poured sudden and substantial amounts into the Philippines economy as part of the war effort.

The economic structure of the Philippines determined its social organization. At the top of the pyramid was a small group of land-owners and businessmen—mainly American, Chinese, Spanish, and part-Spanish. Immediately below them were the compradors, the bureaucracy of government employees, and a negligible middle class. These groups, forming a tiny fraction of the total population, received the major benefits that came from American rule. They lived in modern cities, sent their children to modern schools, built up their fortunes, and entered and controlled Philippine politics. At the base of the pyramid was the vast majority of peasants, who did not own their land or homes.

The fifth annual report of the high commissioner, covering the fiscal year ending June 30, 1941, points out the American benefits to schools, public health, self-government, and the national in-come; but it admits that "neither a sizable independent middle class nor an influential public opinion has developed. The bulk of the newly-created income has gone to the government, the landlords, and to urban areas, and has served but little to amelio-rate living conditions among the almost feudal peasantry and tenantry. The relative numbers of these have not been materially reduced. Maldistribution of population, of land, and of wealth in many forms continues. The gap between the mass population and the small governing class has broadened, and social unrest has reached serious proportions."

As the landless rural class increased, the government undertook measures of relief. It opened one large area in Mindanao, the Koronadel Valley, for settlement, and it bought, for resale to tenants, homesites in rural villages and large estates where tenancy troubles were evident. President Quezon secured the passage of laws to ameliorate the condition of the underprivileged and to forestall disorders. His "social justice program" established a court of industrial relations, extended to all municipalities measures for the welfare of tenants on rice lands, curbed the arbitrariness of sheriffs in ejectment proceedings, legitimized labor organizations, provided for improvement of labor standards and conditions (including an eight-hour law), authorized the president of the Philippines to acquire private lands for resale in small parcels, and imposed a tax on sugar, regulated in such a manner that the centrals (refineries) were obliged to give the planters a larger participation, the object being to enable the latter to pay better wages to their laborers.

In spite of this legislation, social unrest continued. Labor demonstrated a certain uneasiness and farm tenants resorted to riots. The Socialist-Communist leaders in central Luzon brought to the fore the question of totalitarianism. They protested against the philosophy of Franco-ism that permeated Manila, and they challenged the Emergency Powers Act of August 10, 1940, which granted emergency powers to the president. They criticized particularly the provision permitting him to require all able-bodied citizens not employed in any useful occupation to engage in farming or perform such duties as might be necessary in the public interest. President Quezon's emergency powers in the Philippines were comparable to those granted to President Roosevelt in the United States. Pedro Abad Santos, the peasant leader who looked like Gandhi, said, "Our country is dominated economically and politically by Spanish and Japanese fascists, through Filipino dummies, saboteurs, and traitorous public officials."

The Filipino craze for centralization brought about serious changes in the education system immediately before the outbreak of the war. American policy had aimed at the abolition of illiteracy, achievement of universal elementary education, opportunity for instruction in the English language for all, and the separation of church and state. Finances were provided by the local governments. The literacy rate had risen from 18 per cent to 48 per cent, and in 1939 nearly two million students (a little less than half the school population between the ages seven and seventeen) were in attendance at the public schools.

The Education Act of August 8, 1940 reduced the elementary school course, revised the curriculum, provided for half-day sessions only, made it compulsory to complete four grades, and transferred the financial support for the schools from the local to the central government. A further act contemplated a reduction of standards in the secondary schools because of an alleged shortage of funds. Opponents of these measures feared the proposed reduction of standards, and they were worried lest under the guise of reform a new and reactionary philosophy would be inserted into the curriculum. They shuddered at the prospect of losing the democratic basis for public education and making the school system a plaything of the bureaucrats. The principal Filipino educators in nonsectarian schools pointed out that a curtailment in public education would tend to force students into private and sectarian institutions. However, all education and other social problems were pushed into the background abruptly by the invasion of the Japanese.

The Philippines under Japanese Occupation: A Chronology for Handy Reference

1941. DECEMBER 8 (Manila time). The Japanese bomb Manila and other points in the Philippines. Invasion begins.
DECEMBER 30. President Quezon is inaugurated for his second term on Corregidor.
1942. JANUARY 2. Manila falls, after having been declared an open city.
JANUARY 23. The Japanese commander-in-chief sets up a cabinet, called the executive commission, consisting of six departments, under the chairmanship of the former secretary to President Quezon. The Japanese commander-in-chief also creates an advisory council, called the council of state, consisting of prominent political leaders.
JUNE 14. The Philippines adhere formally to United Nations declaration.
DECEMBER 30. Kalibapi, or Association for Service to the New Philippines, replaces the old political parties.

1943. MAY. Tojo visits the Philippines. He repeats his promise of independence and offers amnesty to guerrillas.

SEPTEMBER 7. The constituent assembly approves a new constitution, which in most important respects is similar to the bona fide constitution then in existence.

SEPTEMBER 25. Filipinos elect Jose P. Laurel president.

OCTOBER 14. The Japanese military administration "withdraws" as an independent republic is proclaimed. In Tokyo, Laurel, Vargas, and Aquino sign a pact of alliance but avoid the necessity of an open declaration of war.

NOVEMBER 13. President Roosevelt signs S. J. 95 continuing Quezon's term of office until the Japanese are driven out of the Philippines.

1944. SEPTEMBER. After American bombings begin, the Philippines proclaim a state of war against Great Britain and the United States. They avoid military conscription and avoid ordering the Filipino armies into the field against the Americans.

OCTOBER 19 AND 20. With the landings on Leyte, the campaign for liberation begins.

DECEMBER 8. Dissatisfied with the "Republic," Japan sets up a "Makapili," or League of Patriotic Filipinos, under the leadership of the most outspoken pro-Japanese Filipino leaders.

1945. JANUARY AND FEBRUARY. Liberation of Manila. During the months which follow, the American forces drive out the last remnants of the Japanese.

Prior to the outbreak of the war, there were approximately thirty thousand Japanese in the Philippines, and eighteen thousand of these were in Davao, a province in Mindanao. The men brought their families with them, and they took little interest in things Filipino, except land titles. The Japanese sought unoccupied areas in Davao and developed the Manila hemp (abaca) industry on a lease and contract system. Under this system a Filipino (maybe a government official) or an American would obtain a lease on land near a central Japanese establishment, like the Ohta or the Furukawa plantation companies. He would then execute a contract with the Japanese company whereby the latter guaranteed to clear the land, plant and manage the crop, pay all taxes, and return to the original lessee 15 per cent of the gross revenue. On occasion Japanese would marry Filipinas and the wives would lease the land, or Japanese would be able to operate through dummies. The Japanese companies would put in the necessary roads and other public improvements and assign small lots to Japanese farmers, usually of Okinawa blood. As emigration to the Philippines was closely controlled by the Japanese government, the companies, with the aid of the consul at Davao (who was also president of the local Japanese association), experienced no difficulty in controlling the individual Japanese. At a minimum capital cost, the Japanese came into control of almost half of the agricultural land in Davao. As American interest in Davao waned and that of the Filipinos remained apathetic, the Japanese increased their investments, looking forward to greater influence and prosperity after independence.

Japanese commercial penetration strengthened and broadened between the two world wars. By 1940 practically all Japanese commercial houses and shipping companies had agencies in the Philippines. Retail stores were concentrated in the larger cities, but they spread into the interior when the Chinese organized boycotts against them. The Japanese did business on a cash basis, unlike the Chinese, who advanced credit to the Filipino small farmers.

Through devious means, the Japanese had also obtained a limited interest in mineral production. Prior to 1941, Japan was the principal market for Philippine chrome, manganese, and copper, and the only market for their iron ore. They had a practical monopoly of offshore commercial fishing, and they had obtained tremendous logging and lumber concessions. They had established a fish cannery, a brewery, a bicycle factory, and several rubber footwear factories. In several instances they set up dummy corporations, in which the apparent principal stockholders were distinguished Filipinos.

The coming of war was not a matter between Japan and the Philippines. The United States was responsible for Philippine foreign affairs and the defense of the Islands. When war came, it was the result of conflicts of policy between the United States and Japan, and the Philippines were caught in the middle.

When the Japanese moved into southern Indochina in the summer of 1941, the United States answered with economic reprisals and the creation of the United States Army Forces in the Far East (USAFFE) under General MacArthur. These steps seemed ominous in Manila because of anticipated Japanese retaliation. Very few believed that the Japanese would actually precipitate a hara-kiri war; but everyone was jittery because of the apparent inadequacy of American troops and equipment. War spirit was in the air. It was common knowledge that merchant shipping was being routed through the Torres Straits, north of Australia, and that commercial vessels were being escorted by American cruisers in battle paint.

The Commonwealth government and the United States high commissioner took measures to prepare the population for the possibility of war. Differences of opinion compounded with public apathy, however, prevented efficient preparation of civilian morale. Military leaders gave cautious but clear warnings that in the event of hostilities, the Philippines would be incapable of successful resistance.

When the bombs came, the fires started, and American troops moved out of the open city, the Filipinos were brave, without rancor, and fantastically hopeful. For forty years they had looked upon the Americans as supreme and invincible. It was unthinkable that an Oriental army could dislodge the United States from its citadel in East Asia. It was reported that the pilots of the airplanes must certainly be Germans, and that the shiny new machines must represent the total strength of the Japanese air force. When the inevitable occupation of Manila came, every grim line on the faces of the once gay Filipinos registered disbelief. Said Carlos Romulo: ". . . on the rim of Asia, it seemed to us that the tremendous tide rising in the Far East would wash us out along with our dreams of democracy for which we had fought from Balintawak to Bataan. The white man was whipped—disgraced."

Bataan and Corregidor brought heartaches and death to individuals, but they meant glory and defiance for the Philippine nation. The Filipinos' hatred of the Japanese grew with each harsh measure that gave the lie to their smooth propaganda. The first Japanese leaflet indicated the main lines of their ideological warfare:

"Dear friends! Folks at home.

"Do you realize what you are fighting for. You probably sincerely believe that you are defending democracy from the aggressor but nothing could be further from the truth. Open your eyes and see what America has done to you so far. In order to advance their imperialist cause, they seized your country forty years ago and since then you have been abused, exploited, neglected and what is worse, you have been treated as an inferior race.

"The best sections of Manila, as you all know, have been seized by Americans and they own the best clubs, the best stores, the best residences in utter disregard of your just rights. You are scorned in public and made fun of in their exclusive clubs where you are not allowed admission. This is true in camps as well as in civilian life. Americans are better paid although they are no good as soldiers. Most of them come from the farms of the mid-west and manners and courtesy are not their forte. How can you expect such crude creatures to respect the rights of womanhood and the ideals of Filipino civilization?

"Do you realize why you are in the front lines? True to American tradition, they again expect you to pick their chestnuts from the fire, just as you have done for them against Spain forty years ago.

"The present fighting has been caused by America's greed to place Asia under its control. They could not do this as long as Japan, the most powerful nation in the Orient remained; so America and England formed a conspiracy to blockade Japan economically. We knew of this long ago, but not desiring to start a war in the Orient, we have restrained ourselves but now the hour for us to act has arrived.

"The future of Asia is at stake and we can no longer ignore its consequences. After four years of American trickery, the Chinese too have come to realize this fact and are now actively cooperating with us."

Japanese propaganda endeavored to sell "Asia for the Asiatics" and the "Greater East Asia Co-Prosperity Sphere." It tried to turn the eyes of the Filipinos from America to Japan. Tojo said in his speech at Manila on May 6, 1943:

"It has long been an outstanding cause of indignation to me that the great soul and spirit of the true Filipinos have been maliciously perverted and debilitated by long years of hypocritical exploitation under the American regime. Cleverly camouflaging their real aims under sugar-coated labels of justice and democracy, the Americans effectively carried out a policy of exploitation, giving you in exchange for your birth right of independence and virile existence, the ephemeral benefits of cheap materialism and a false sense of economic stability which in essence was an economic set-up based entirely upon reliance on America."

Japanese acts were the greatest debunkers of their propaganda. The military were not disposed to coddle the Filipinos. As they entered the city of Manila they shouted "Banzai" and sang the "Pacific March," which, according to eyewitness AP correspondent Russell Brines, "every drunk in Tokyo had been singing for the past two years." For psychological effect the Japanese exhibited looters and petty thieves in cages, or tied them to telephone poles, drenched them, and exposed them to the tropical sun. The Japanese soldiers lorded it over the native population and used the slap, the bow, and the barked order as badges of superiority. The *kempeitai* followed their traditional methods of "persuasion," or torture, to wring confessions from suspected saboteurs and spies. The Japanese military administration decreed the death penalty for political crimes, and warned that hostages would be taken and shot in any area where offenses were committed against the imperial occupying forces.

On the political side, the Japanese set up a new political party, totalitarian model, and installed a puppet government. They dominated the president of the Republic and the entire administrative machine, including the provincial governors and the municipal mayors. They controlled legislation, forcing the removal of all legal disabilities against the Japanese (such as the restrictions on landholding and immigration). They took over the police and the courts and organized district and neighborhood associations for the absolute regimentation of every feature of daily life.

The radio and the press brought constant reminders of the sacrifices Japan had made to save the Philippines from serfdom under American tyranny. Civilians were learning the Japanese language and the children were being taught Japanese "culture" in the schools. Through the motion pictures, which are fantastically popular in the Philippines, the Japanese hammered home the weakness of America, the strengthening bonds of friendship between Japan and the Philippines, and the greatness of the Mikado's empire.

The Japanese tried to de-Americanize the Islands. Dewey Boulevard was given a Japanese name, and Taft Avenue became the Road of Greater East Asia. American flags were insulted or destroyed, textbooks were scissored, postage stamps were defaced or over-printed, American holidays were tabooed, American films were banned, and snappy music was condemned. American sovereignty was ended by decree and Americans were subjected to bitter verbal abuse. Internees were scorned or maltreated, and prisoners of war were beaten or incarcerated under inhumane conditions. After the horrors of the Death March of the prisoners of Bataan, the Japanese changed their attitude toward Filipino soldiers and tried to win their support by the tactics of the "velvet glove." After two years of intensive de-Americanization, the Japanese ambassador was obliged to admit that the program was a failure, because the Filipinos were too steeped in the American way of life.

The Japanese economic program led straight to inflation, poverty, discontent, and disaster. Officials could not balance the government budget, nor extract from the Philippines the riches they had counted upon. The Japanese sent waves of technicians along with the military: mining engineers, chemists, agricultural experts, bankers, and economists "with fat portfolios and a cocky manner." The Japanese pilfered, stole, and expropriated. They shipped off to Tokyo all the chairs, automobiles, pianos, and refrigerators they could not use on the spot. They chained the economy of the Philippines to the Japanese war machine. They mined copper for Japan, raised rice and vegetables for the Japanese army, conscripted labor for defense works, and utilized all local industries according to the needs of Japan. Food, clothes, and the barest essentials of life disappeared from the regular markets, and prices on the black market climbed out of reach. Unemployment increased, wages declined, and the value of enemy currency fluctuated with Japanese military fortunes. With the complete collapse of the "mickey mouse" money, the Filipinos faced hunger and despair. Sabotage and "disloyalty" increased, and guerrilla activity became more fervent. Puppet President Laurel set up a bureau of investigation, and in one day his hirelings discovered one hundred and seventeen "unfaithful" in the heart of his dummy dictatorship.

The Japanese were ruthless in their treatment of the Chinese.

They refused to respect the Chinese officials who represented the Chungking regime. The consul-general and his staff were tortured and shot. All Chinese were carefully and continuously checked on, and many were driven to join the guerrillas in the hills. The Japanese paid no attention at all to Chinese property rights.

The social program of the Japanese was negative and ineffectual. It appealed to the Filipinos to reorient themselves toward their Asian neighbors. It glorified Spartan virtues and clamped upon Manila the austere atmosphere of Tokyo. The Japanese military administration closed the doors of the night clubs, but showed itself friendly to jai alai, horse racing, licensed prostitution, and gambling. As a sop to the Catholic complexion of the Islands, the Japanese gave lip service to religious freedom. They permitted the missionaries an irregular and limited freedom within the city, but they utilized their own religious corps to spread Japanese political propaganda. The language barrier was too formidable for the Japanese to achieve outstanding success in their social program. It was impossible for them to persuade the Filipinos to give up their rumba hour on the radio in favor of the eternal one-two-three-four of the gymnastic exercises which were broadcast directly from Tokyo.

Juan de la Cruz, the Philippine man in the street, lost his home, his children, and his reason for living in the flames of Japanese bombs. He hated the Spartan way of life that the conqueror imposed upon him, and he lived only for the warmth of spirit that made him want the return of the big things—and the little things—that remained in his memory. He rebelled against the bowing and scraping; he detested the humorless soldier who would slap his cheek if he dared to drawl the good-natured salute he used to give the Americans, "Hello, Joe." Juan was born to fun and gaiety. He disliked having to look over his shoulder before he even whispered to an intimate friend. Juan wanted to see life come back to the boulevards, to the barracks, and to the fiesta grounds. And he wanted to look up into the evening sky, and see the flaming sun dipping into Manila Bay, without any fear of enemy planes or bombs.

The bloodletting which accompanied the liberation was the climactic legacy of the Japanese to the Philippines. The documented story of pillage, slaughter, inhumanity, torture, and cold-blooded murder will color the lives and thoughts of the Filipinos for generations. Thousands were massacred in one of the most cruel orgies of the war. Every incident, every feature of the Philippines under the Japanese is overshadowed by the horrors of the sack of Manila.

There were few Quislings at the time of the Japanese entry into Manila. The politicos who remained in the city, and those who left with the Commonwealth government, acted upon the fiat of the president. Those who stayed conducted themselves with courage during the brief month of resistance before surrender, and those who went to Corregidor believed that they could hold out in that shell-pocked fortress until help would arrive. After the fall of Manila, feeling ran high against the puppets. The underground was angrier with their own betrayers than with the enemy. The Voice of Freedom from Corregidor said, "We shall be stern and ruthless in judgment as you have been traitorous and disloyal." But as the months passed, more and more leaders slipped over into the camp of Japan.

The short-wave radio in America received statements like these from the best-known collaborators of the Philippines: "I shall do all in my power to cooperate with Japan"; "I am filled with remorse and regret when I think how I opposed Japan"; and "I sincerely pray that the time will come when the planes I saw today will someday be piloted by youths of the Philippines, that they may fight side by side in the air with Japan in crushing the Anglo-Americans."

Filipino officials forgot their oaths of allegiance to the United States, and excused their actions by saying that it was impossible to do otherwise. The Americans had failed to provide defense, so what right had they to demand continued loyalty? These Filipinos said that their prime obligations were to the Philippines and that they served their country better in collaboration than would be possible in resistance. A puppet regime was the only alternative to an out-and-out Japanese military government. Of the elected members of the house of representatives, 30 per cent accepted positions under the Japanese, while 75 per cent of the senate also collaborated, as did most of the supreme court. Many of the landowners, industrial tycoons, and compradors did a flourishing business in "buy and sell" with the Japanese.

Just as the main support for the Japanese occupation came from the feudal landowners, the political leaders, and the propertied classes, so the major opposition came from the poor. "It might be said ironically that those who had profited most from the American rule in the Philippines were the first to betray it, while those who had profited least took up arms in America's and their own behalf."[2] Organizations like the Hukbalahaps (Huks, or People's Anti-Japanese Army), the Free Panay Guerrillas, the Blue Eagle Guerrillas, the Cavite Guerrillas, the USAFFE Guerrillas, and others conducted genuine and effective resistance against the Japanese. They provided an endless stream of information for the American forces, and they made the way easier for the American liberation. They made possible the victories at Leyte, Lingayen, and Manila. They saved American lives in the costly, unpublicized mopping-up campaigns which cleared the Japanese out of their foxholes and mountain dugouts.

From Liberation to the Establishment of the Republic

On the day before Christmas, 1941, President Quezon, his family, and some of his highest officials left Manila for Corregidor, and eventually for the United States. It was the wish of President Roosevelt that the government of the Commonwealth and the person of President Quezon should not fall into the hands of the Japanese. The legal and symbolic importance of keeping Quezon in the American camp outweighed the psychological repugnance of running away. Quezon's health was precarious, and his every instinct impelled him to stay with his people. It needed more courage for him to obey the orders of the White House than it would have required to stick it out and face the Japanese.

Quezon and Osmena were the heads of the government-in-exile throughout the war. They represented the Philippines in international gatherings, such as the meetings of the Pacific War Council, and they exerted every effort to persuade the Americans not to overlook the Pacific in their concentration on Hitler in

[2] Seeman and Salisbury, *Cross Currents in the Philippines*, p. 32.

Europe. The office of the Commonwealth in Washington acted as a clearinghouse for information on conditions in the Philippines, and cooperated with the state department and the office of the high commissioner in the department of the interior in making plans for rehabilitation. Some member of the Commonwealth government was always available for speaking engagements in the United States, or for arranging or participating in broadcasts via short wave across the Pacific. The Philippines' problems had to be kept before the American people and congress, and plans had to be made for the government of the Philippines during and after the liberation. Quezon died in August 1944 and the scholarly but elderly Vice-President Osmena inherited the problems incidental to the restoration of the Philippines-American regime.

From the very beginning, the Americans had pledged the people of the Philippines that their freedom would be redeemed and their independence established and protected. On June 29, 1944 Senate Joint Resolution 93 was approved. It recognized the Filipinos' valiant resistance to invasion, and stated that because of their unbroken record of loyalty, their demonstrated will to independence, and because "they have abundantly proved their capacity to govern themselves in an enlightened, progressive, and democratic manner . . . it is hereby declared to be the policy of the Congress that the United States shall drive the treacherous invading Japanese from the Philippine Islands, restore as quickly as possible the orderly and free democratic processes of government to the Filipino people, and thereupon establish the complete independence of the Philippine Islands as a separate and self-governing nation." This resolution also provided for the retention or acquisition of bases necessary for the mutual protection of the Philippines and the United States, and made mandatory the proclamation of independence on or before July 4, 1946.

On the same day, June 29, 1944, congress approved Senate Joint Resolution 94, establishing a Filipino Rehabilitation Commission. It was empowered to investigate and make recommendations covering all matters affecting postwar economy, trade, finance, economic stability, and rehabilitation of the Philippines. The commission was too small in concept and too limited in power to cope with the vast economic problems which arose, but it was an earnest of the Americans' intention to discharge their responsibilities for the creation of a sound basis for new life in the Philippines.

The Commonwealth government returned to the Philippines with the American troops, and the Philippines congress met for the first time in four years in June 1945. President Osmena found an entirely new spirit and attitude toward America on the part of his people. Their loyalty was no longer to the United States, but to the common ideals and common objectives of the two countries. They became more conscious of discriminations against them, and they found a new pride in themselves as they experienced a disillusionment in the power of the United States. The Filipinos looked upon the Americans not merely as their protectors and liberators, but as the cause of their suffering. They felt that they had a right to expect relief and rehabilitation from the United States. They had contributed to American victory; it was now the United States' turn to remember them in their distress.

In President Osmena's words, the forces of freedom brought food, medical supplies, and clothing. Immediate attention was given to the hungry and the sick, to the factory workers and the farm hands, the helpless victims who were engulfed in the tide of war. Between the landings on Leyte and the end of the war, the American army was obliged to retain its controls in the Philippines and to give first priority to the job of making the Islands a staging area for the attack on Japan. The lot of the Commonwealth government was not always a happy one. The army guaranteed law and order, distribution of food and water, and the prevention of epidemic diseases. The Commonwealth cabinet could do little more than listen to personal complaints and tales of woe, apportion jobs, and try to re-create some semblance of a political machine. It assumed minor responsibilities in administering price control measures, food distribution, investigating public records, instituting taxes and commercial regulations, and setting up local governments in newly administered areas. It had no money and no freedom of political action apart from the good will of the American army on the spot and a friendly administration in Washington.

President Truman made no significant changes in the postwar policies that had been contemplated by President Roosevelt. He appointed a new high commissioner and drafted a series of directives to him and to the heads of various government departments and agencies on October 26, 1945, recommending specific steps to carry out the United States program of assistance to the Philippines. President Truman directed the high commissioner to investigate agrarian unrest; the alien property custodian to make lawful disposition of enemy property; the attorney-general to investigate, charge, and try the collaborators; the secretary of war to assist in reorganizing the constabulary on a nonmilitary basis; the secretaries of war and the treasury to redeem emergency currency; and the secretary of the treasury to draw up a schedule showing the relative trend of purchasing power and the exchange rates of the Japanese Philippine peso during the period of invasion. He also directed the surplus property administrator to make available without cost surplus supplies for the Commonwealth government; the administrator of veterans' affairs to recommend legislation for aid to veterans; the president of the Export-Import Bank to make suggestions on restoring normal economic conditions; the War Shipping Administration to take all possible steps to supply adequate shipping; and the chairman of the Reconstruction Finance Corporation to direct the United States Commercial Company to carry on its program of exports on credits for two more years. Note that these directives were issued after V-J day, after the army had been relieved of its heaviest responsibilities, and after all these civilian agencies had a reasonable opportunity to enter the war-ravaged Philippines in order to discharge their duties.

Although some Filipinos and Americans dreaded to see the fulfillment of independence, no one suggested any delay or change in the schedule culminating on July 4, 1946. In spite of the bitter differences of opinion on the puppets and on the collaboration issue, a general election was held on April 23, 1946. The electorate (2,500,000 voted, while 500,000 eligibles stayed away from the polls) chose the Liberal candidates, Roxas for president and Quirino for vice-president, over the Nacionalista Osmena ticket.

The collaboration issue dominated the campaign. The Osmena faction had the support of the guerrillas, while the Roxas faction personified the collaborators. The guerrillas assumed a monopoly in loyalty because of their role in the liberation, and they were not disposed to give influence or position to those who had remained in contact with the Japanese. The guerrillas recalled with vehemence President Roosevelt's dictum that those who had collaborated with the enemy must be removed from authority and influence over the political and economic life of the country.

As a matter of fact, President Osmena had endeavored to implement that policy. He had been reminded very sharply by Secretary Ickes that collaborators should be weeded out before the election, or else the American funds for relief and rehabilitation would be appropriated with a great deal of reluctance. Osmena was not able to carry out his endeavors on the spot. The Philippines legislature was controlled by the ex-puppets, their committee on appointments was able to block Osmena's choices for political jobs, and a people's court for the trial of collaborators was pushed aside and made impotent. The collaborators had too many of the old-line politicians in their ranks, enjoyed too much public sympathy, and, in the opinion of some, received too many favors from the American army.

The apologists for the collaborators resent the name and say they took greater risks than the guerrillas. According to them, the collaborators served as spies, informers, and go-betweens under the very noses of the Japanese, and were constantly under the shadow of the constitutional police and Fort Santiago. They contend that there are some "good collaborators" just as there are some "bad guerrillas." Many who were obliged to remain in the cities actually accuse some self-styled guerrillas of fleeing to the comparative safety of the hills, and deserting their compatriots in order to save their own hides. They say that some guerrillas were no better than bandits—killing, stealing, and victimizing their own countrymen in the sacred name of patriotism.

Roxas himself, although exonerated by the army and returned to his one-star rank, was bitterly attacked by Mr. Ickes. The latter accused him of supporting the Philippines' declaration of war against the United States, helping to write the puppet constitution, and serving as an adviser to President Laurel. Roxas' supporters claimed that he was actually a leader in the guerrilla movement, that he acted as a restraining influence on the Japanese, that he never took any steps except in the interest of his own people, and that he never lost the confidence of General MacArthur or President Quezon.

The election was hotly contested, but Osmena had neither the strength nor the will to fight as he had fought as a youth. His coalition consisted of his own wing of the Nacionalistas, the Democratic Alliance, and the United Front. Osmena himself was interested in unity; he thought of healing rather than aggravating the differences between factions of his people, and he retired gracefully in favor of his younger opponent. Roxas gained the support of the veterans, the press, the landlords, the compradors, the civil service, the remnants of the old Nacionalista machine, General MacArthur, High Commissioner McNutt, and many influential Americans.

In spite of accusations of terrorism, hooliganism, and force, Roxas won by a clear majority of the voters. They chose to applaud him for his motives rather than criticize him for his acts. A vote for Mr. Roxas was salve for the conscience of the individual Filipino. Most Filipinos were not able to live as guerrillas. They had to stay at home, face the enemy, and match wits against him for their lives and welfare. It was impossible to defy him and expect to exist. They would have preferred the heroics of the hills, but that was neither practical nor possible. In voting for Mr. Roxas they rationalized their own decisions, and in placing their stamp of approval upon him they placed it upon themselves. Besides, he convinced the populace that he could get more aid from the Americans than President Osmena could. He was a chip off the old block, his followers were better known and better skilled in the old ways, and Quezon himself could not outshine Roxas in brains, energy, or oratory. Roxas was looked upon as the man of the hour, one who could heal old schisms, and lead vigorously in the paths of prosperity and reconstruction. Roxas appealed in his inaugural for charity and understanding. "Among the people there must be no recriminations or malignancies. Errors of mind rather than of heart must be forgiven." But while he pleaded for "malice toward none, and charity for all," seven opposition congressmen and three opposition senators were being debarred from their seats, and minority leader Confesor was moved to declare: "Fascism is on the march in the Philippines . . . [The majority senators] have laid the foundation of a totalitarian regime."

The Philippines Republic

In all Southeast Asia, the war left its ugliest psychological and physical scars in the Philippines. For three years the Filipinos were forced to squeeze, to lie, to compromise, and to evade. Cynicism uprooted faith, chicanery replaced open dealing, reliance upon brute force overshadowed dependence upon the pledged word, and personal, ruthless ambition cheapened the goals of security.

No nation faced independent existence under greater handicaps. President Roxas, in his inaugural address, declared: "The tragic evidence of recent history stares at us from the broken ruins of our cities and the wasting acres of our soil. The toppled columns of the Legislative Building before which we stand are mute and weeping symbols of the land we have inherited from the war. . . .

"There is hunger among us. . . . Prices race with wages in the destructive elevators of inflation. The black market with all its attendant evils of disrespect for law and public morality thrives in the channels of commerce.

"Plagues of rats and locusts gnaw at our food supplies. Public health and sanitation have been set back a quarter of a century.

"Housing for most of our urban citizens is shocking in its inadequacy and squalor. . . .

"Our communications are destroyed, stolen, or disrupted and many of our countrymen are still today cut off from the main currents of national life. Schools have been burned and teachers have been killed; our educational system is in large measure a shambles."

The statistics of destruction are assembled in macabre array in Senator Tydings' Report Number 755, November 20, 1945, which accompanied the Philippines Rehabilitation Bill. Losses of public property, Catholic property, and other church and private properties approached a billion dollars in prewar prices. Replacement costs might reach four or five times that amount. Cities were burned out, crops put to the torch, vessels sunk, work animals slaughtered, privately owned furniture, merchandise, and equipment demolished, and industries, utilities, and mines put completely out of commission.

Reconstruction was the foremost problem of the Republic. The American congress passed the Rehabilitation Act in 1946. It created a War Damage Commission empowered to pay out $400,-000,000 in war damage claims to Filipino and American claimants; provided for turning over $100,000,000 worth of surplus property to the Philippines; and authorized spending by eight United States agencies in various rehabilitation and training projects in behalf of the Philippines. The government of the Philippines set up a Rehabilitation Finance Corporation for extending credits to small borrowers on easy terms for reconstruction purposes, and it invited an agricultural commission from the United States to make pertinent studies and recommendations.

The United States spent $1,250,000,000 for Philippine rehabilitation from 1945 through 1947, and committed itself to spend another billion through 1951. Subsequent annual payments to veterans would run from $50,000,000 to $75,000,000. The rehabilitation program covered private war claims, roads and schools, ports and harbors, public health, air navigation aids, fish and wild life, the coast and geodetic survey, surplus property, and special considerations for veterans.

The American government—or the American people, perhaps —deserves credit for its role in reconstruction. Filipinos are quick to point out, however, that the whole country of the Philippines was blackened and burned by Japanese and Americans in the battle to secure for the United States a staging area for the invasion of Japan. They point out that the total moneys granted by the United States amounted to less than 20 per cent of the damage done to private property, and less than 10 per cent of that done to public property, and that Filipino veterans do not get all the advantages of the GI Bill. Some Filipinos say, "We feel that every cent of this was earned by priceless blood and treasure in a war not exactly our own. In the total of American aid given to all countries, the share of the Filipinos is niggardly indeed."

After a slow start, reconstruction swung into high gear in 1948. Streets and buildings took on a new appearance, and new construction exceeded the prewar average by ten times, in spite of world shortages of steel, iron, hardware, and cement. Reconstruction of private business enterprises overcame almost insuperable handicaps. The coconut and abaca industries were favored by good markets and high prices. The sugar interests found their mills destroyed, their machinery wrecked, and their plantations devastated, but they promised to recover peak production by 1950. At the mines—gold, copper, iron, manganese, and chrome—the surface plants and mills were destroyed, the underground workings caved in, timbers rotted away, and most mines were flooded. Miners and supervisory personnel were dispersed. Gold made a slow recovery, reaching an output of $9,000,000 in 1948 as compared with $42,000,000 in 1941. Rehabilitation would have been impractical had it not been for the high prices paid for gold by the Chinese smugglers. The other metals anticipated prewar production by 1950, but in the case of iron everything depended upon the reopening of the prewar market in Japan.

The rehabilitation of the rice lands was as much a political as an economic problem. Rice production was restored to normalcy without too much difficulty, but the poor peasants were still plagued with landlordism. Their cup of woe was the more bitter because of the loss of their carabaos, horses, cattle, and chickens, which the Japanese found to their liking.

The restoration of trade was essential for the rebuilding of a sound economy. The Philippine Trade Act (the Bell Act), passed by the United States congress in 1946, made provision for close Philippine-American trade ties beyond the granting of independence. The act provided for duty-free trade until 1954, and thereafter for increasing partial duties on goods until 1974. The act established a system of quotas for some Philippine exports, including sugar, cigars, scrap and filler tobacco, cordage, coconut oil, and buttons. The Philippines and the United States signed an agreement to carry out the terms of the act, but it contained a parity provision which was extremely distasteful to some Filipinos. This proviso (section 341) reads as follows:

"The disposition, exploitation, development, and utilization of all agricultural, timber, and mineral lands of the public domain, waters, minerals, coal, petroleum, and other mineral oils, all forces and sources of potential energy, and other natural resources of the Philippines, and the operation of public utilities, shall, if open to any person, be open to citizens of the United States and to all forms of business enterprise owned or controlled, directly or indirectly, by United States citizens."

This section necessitated an amendment to the Philippines constitution. Roxas favored it, in spite of its irritating features. Why should Filipinos be obliged to amend their constitution so as to open their resources to American development? Filipinos had no such rights in the United States. The United States opposed British preferential arrangements, and quotas in general, yet it insisted upon these special arrangements with the Philippines. The Americans also insisted that no rehabilitation money would be forthcoming unless the Filipinos accepted the Bell Bill. It sounded to the Filipinos exactly like a shotgun proposition. However, the Tydings-Bell program offered some economic help; without it there would be continued inaction and prostration.

The economic opponents of the Philippine Trade Act argued that it would guarantee the reincarnation of the old order. Eight years' free trade would permit the sugar, tobacco, and coconut oil people to reinvest and reap their profits from the export trade. It would neglect consumers' welfare and would stifle any infant industries at home. The political opponents of the trade act accused Roxas of selling out to the Americans, who were, in the words of one Filipino writer, "laying the ground work for the conversion of the Philippines into a Pacific edition of Cuba. . . .

"With this legislation the United States crowns its crusade to rescue the peoples of Asia from Japanese enslavement and deliver them to the American business men. If we are not rendered speechless with gratitude at this monumental event, it is only because—unfortunately—we are not American business men. We are just Filipinos—a nation of goddam thieves—a race of beggars always trying to get something out of Uncle Sam."

Even before the politicians got together on the basis for trade, businessmen started their cargoes moving. There was a lot of GI money in the Philippines and a universal starvation for American luxury items. Nylons, cigarette lighters, lipsticks, compacts, and costume jewelry flooded the Philippine markets. Imports were ten times exports, and finally thoughtful persons, particularly government officials, decided that steps would have to be taken to even the balance.

Some figures are unavoidable in the analysis of the trade picture. Total foreign trade for the fiscal year July 1947 to July 1948 equaled $850,000,000, an increase of almost 40 per cent over the preceding year. Imports were still twice exports, but the adverse balance was met by American rehabilitation expenditures, accumulated reserves, and expenditures of the armed forces in the Philippines. In the following fiscal year imports remained fairly constant, but exports increased by half. The United States accounted for more than 76 per cent of the total trade, supplying 85 per cent of what the Philippines bought and buying 62 per cent of everything the Philippines had to sell. Of the total trade, about one-third was controlled by American businessmen, slightly less by Chinese, and only 22 per cent was in the hands of Filipinos.

The twelve leading Philippine imports and exports for 1947 and 1937 are shown in the table which follows (figures in millions of dollars):

Exports	1947	1937	Imports	1947	1937
Copra	177.2	16	Cotton and manufacturing	76.7	17.4
Abaca	27	21.6	Grains	49.4	4.1
Dessicated coconut	9.5	6.3	Rayon and synthetic fibers	45.3	3.1
Coconut oil	6.9	20.5	Autos and parts	25.7	6
Copra meal	2.2	2.9	Iron and steel	23	19.8
Tobacco	2.2	5	Tobacco	22	3.6
Sugar	2	57.7	Dairy products	21.3	5
Maguey	1.6	....	Paper and manufacturings	19.4	3.8
Rope	1.4	1.4	Mineral oils	18.4	6.5
Embroidery	1.1	3.7	Fish and products	15.9	1
Lumber	.5	3.9	Chemicals	15	3.4
Gold	.5	2.5	Electrical machinery	15.5	2.8

Allowances must be made for price differentials. Prices in 1947 were about two and one-half times what they were in 1937. On the export side, there was a large increase in copra, and a lag in coconut oil and lumber. On the import side, the increases are fairly regular right down the line. Four years of war led to heavy purchases of consumption goods. Imports of iron and steel would have been higher had the goods been obtainable. The substantial imports of fish resulted from the disappearance of the Japanese from the fishing industry in the Philippines.

The Philippine government decided to subject imports to control after 1949. In spite of the protests of American businessmen, it determined to protect the integrity of its national economy and reduce the gap between exports and imports. It ordered drastic reductions on imports of wines and liquors, cosmetics, watches and clocks, photographic equipment, high-priced textiles, radios, cigarettes, and automobiles in order to conserve its dollars. The government was estopped from clamping tariffs on American products, but it was not prevented from reducing quantities.

The government has also aimed at the nationalization of retail trade. It wants a larger share for the Filipinos. It created PRATRA (Philippines Relief and Trade Rehabilitation Administration), with authority as a government trading company to prevent monopolies, hoarding, and profiteering, and to encourage and assist Filipino retailers. PRATRA buys supplies in the open market and redistributes them to Filipino traders, thus challenging the exclusive position which American agents and manufacturers' representatives enjoyed.

The Philippines Republic gradually withdrew its head from the sand in order to do business with Japan. Filipinos hated the Japanese individually, and they disliked reopening trade connections. But it was profitable, and if the Filipinos did not, the Chinese and the Americans would. The Filipinos resent the apparent American policy of rebuilding Japan—the great delusion—and they dislike the implication that Japan will become the workshop of the Far East. The Filipinos wanted reparations, but failing to obtain these in large amounts they resorted to a quiet exchange of iron for steel. Normal trade relations meanwhile awaited a peace treaty.

When the Philippines are cut off from their privileges in the American market, they will have to seek alternatives in Asia. According to 1948 figures, the Philippines carried on 2.6 per cent of their trade with China (primarily textiles from Japan re-exported through China), 2 per cent with Japan, and less than 1 per cent with India, Korea, Siam, Malaya, and Burma.

In the future a new inter-Asian pattern is likely to emerge. Before the war, from 1931 to 1938, the Philippines sold to Japan goods to the value of $45,000,000. Exports included copra, abaca, metallic ores and concentrates, scrap iron, leaf tobacco, lumber, and hides and skins. During the same years the Philippines bought from Japan goods to the value of $88,000,000. These imports included cotton and rayon cloth, towels, coal, cement, tiles, kitchenware, glass, toys, cameras, industrial acids, paper boxes, bicycles, corrugated iron sheets, cables, stationary and marine engines, and textile machinery and parts. During 1939, 1940, and 1941 the balance shifted, as Japan increased her purchases for war purposes. Japan then paid her deficits by profits on shipping and fishing, on the hemp plantations on Davao, and in remittances from Japanese families engaged in business in the Philippines.

This pattern could be re-created. If emotional conflicts were avoided, it could bring mutual profits. New trade relations could also be established between the Philippines and their neighbors in Asia. The Philippines would welcome rice from Indochina, Burma, and Siam, coal from French Indochina, cotton and jute from India, rubber and tin from Malaya and the Indies, and textiles from China. Outbound shipments from the Philippines could well include sugar and bananas, copra and coconut oil, gold and iron, abaca and lumber. It is unrealistic to hope that Asians will welcome the services of other Asians in shipping, fishing, agriculture, banks, or stores, so trade will have to be the overwhelming factor in the balance of payments.

Soon after its establishment, the Philippine Republic embarked upon a program of industrialization, which was in effect a continuation and expansion of plans inaugurated during the Commonwealth period. Before the war, a National Development Company operated textile mills, food-canning plants, shoe factories, a cement plant, and engaged in an assortment of other activities. After the war it devised a four-year plan which called for foreign and domestic capital for the development of power; for steel, paper, copper, wallboard, textile, ferroalloy, plywood, salt, and chemical industries; for sugar, tobacco, coconut, abaca, livestock, rice, and corn improvement; for the Manila Railway and inter-island shipping companies; for water works, coal mining, lumber processing, and fish-canning; and for applied research. The government also operates the National Bank and the Rehabilitation Finance Corporation. In addition, there are government corporations in the major agricultural industries. The government has a surplus property commission, a port commission, and a government enterprises council.

With so many government economic activities, it is clear why private investors now shy away from the Philippines. In 1947 only $12,500,000 capital was paid up in new corporations and $11,000,-000 invested in new partnerships. Most of this money came from established Filipino interests, with lesser amounts coming from Chinese and Americans. Among the conditions favorable for new investments, however, is the fact that the Philippines possess a balanced budget and a stable currency. The national debt is negligible. The peso is pegged to the dollar, and its convertibility is guaranteed by treaty at a rate of two to one. The creation of the Central Bank—to provide a securities market, to accelerate rehabilitation and industrialization, and to maintain equilibrium in the balance of payments—causes some misgivings in financial circles. The fear is that the administrators will abuse their powers and let their economic judgments be warped by politics, and as a consequence damage the stability and prestige of the peso.

The Republic maintained a wise balance between its economic potential and its social welfare obligations. President Roxas charted a course that provided funds for service to the underprivileged but preserved private initiative. Taxes in the Philippines have been comparatively light, but recent sales taxes and luxury taxes dipped more heavily into well-filled pockets. Foreign investments face heavier profit taxes and ominous double taxes.

The labor movement in the Philippines is in its infancy, but it possesses many of the overtones and characteristics of labor relations in the United States. Organized labor has united into a Congress of Labor Organizations (CLO) for higher wages and better working conditions. In many instances its demands are reasonable; in others, its agitation has been most critical where working conditions are best. Firms with the most progressive reputations—like the Philippine Refining Company, the Manila Trading Company, Benguet Consolidated, Luzon Brokerage, and the Luzon Stevedoring Company—have had their share of strikes.

Many issues have gone to the department of labor or the court of industrial relations, which have pronounced judgment on such controversial subjects as the closed shop, time and a half pay for overtime and Sundays, extra pay for the night shift, high-cost-of-living allowances, maternity leaves, bonuses, back pay for the Japanese occupation, vacations with pay, thirty days discharge time, and the definition of a decent standard of living. Organization has scarcely touched the agricultural workers as yet.

Labor does not hesitate to resort to strikes. It is perhaps unkind to say that holidays are always welcome, but they are. Laborers can live on their *parientes* (relations) for a limited time, while capital is likely to feel the pinch of a production stoppage almost immediately, with reserves and debts as they are. Labor asserts that the single cause of its unrest is the high cost of living, while capital charges "politics" and "communism."

In October 1948 the cost-of-living index for wage earners was 375, on the basis of 100 in 1941. Food was four times as high as in 1941, rents four and one-half times, and clothing and fuel twice as high. On the same basis, retail prices had remained constant around 250 since July 1, 1947. The average wage of agricultural laborers was $1.00 per day, of commercial laborers $1.22 per day, and of industrial laborers $1.30 per day. But the purchasing power of a dollar was slightly more than the purchasing power of twenty-five cents in 1941. Contrasted with these figures, a survey by the American chamber of commerce in Manila in 1948 revealed that a single American in Manila spent, on the average, $675 per month. A man and wife spent $900 per month, and a family of four spent $1,087.50 per month. Average rentals for a family of four were $216 per month, and basic food costs were $260 per month. To afford these prices, a businessman had to make a good income.

The twin nightmares of the average industrialist concerning labor relations were strikes and nationalization. A nationalization of labor proposal demanded that 60 per cent of the permanent personnel of any business, occupation, trade, or profession would have to be Filipinos. If the congress should enact this proposal into law, it would drive aliens out of business. Nationalization laws have already been passed for civil, mining, and chemical engineers. The congress has shown a disposition to restrict and control capital, and to try to limit technical and managerial help to Filipinos.

Through the years, profits have been high in the Philippines. Economic conditions have been generally prosperous since the war. The national cash position has been strong, the banks in excellent condition, and the trends rising in corporate investments, electricity production, building construction, and gross sales. Indexes are high in production, finance, and distribution. The national income is half again the prewar figure of one billion dollars, and a reasonable proportion of it is going into economic and social development. About one-quarter of the national budget is spent on education. Before the war, there were two million students in the public schools; by 1950, the figure will be nearly doubled. Any reasonable person, however, must anticipate a future rainy day and admit that when the postwar era of prosperity wanes in the Philippines—when American largesse diminishes— the Islands will face the harsher realities of postwar readjustment which have characterized the other areas in Southeast Asia.

Philippine Politics under the Republic

It was difficult in the chaos and poverty at the end of the war to re-establish a government system which would guarantee law and order and preserve and foster democratic processes. The constitution provided for respect for individual freedoms and legal equality, and the habits and thought patterns of the public, re- sulting from fifty years' exposure to American ideas, promised political stability; but the primordial struggle for existence gave a degree of lawlessness and criminality to practically every province and section of the country. A person walking on the streets at night automatically chose the middle of the road. Taxi-drivers were very careful in choosing passengers after dark, and they refused to enter any but the best-guarded areas. Robberies, kid- napings, and daylight assaults on passenger or cargo buses and trucks, as well as trains, were practically daily occurrences.

Within two years complete peace and order were restored in most of the national territory, but roving bands of bandits and Communist-led groups defied the government in central Luzon. These terms, "bandits" and "Communist-led groups," are the

words of President Roxas. He referred, of course, to the Hukbalahaps and the P.K.M., or National Peasants' Union. They, however,
defined the situation as agrarian unrest, or social reform, and
explained their defiance of the government as resistance to the
terrorism of the "fascist" administration and its hated agents, the
MP's, or military police.

Facts and arguments are hard to separate in the case of the
Huks. Their situation has many elements in common with the
situation in China and with left-wing, agrarian agitation in other
countries faced with the complications of returning to prewar
normalcy. Democratic normalcy has its embarrassments when it is
analyzed in the light of its economic inequities and social mal-
adjustments.

The Huks were organized in March 1942 in an area in Luzon
where the gap between the landlord and the tenant was widest.
They were the fighting guerrilla arm of "a United Front of the
Socialist and Communist Parties, the Civil Liberties Union, labor
unions, peasant groups, some intellectuals and middle class elements, religious organizations, groups representing the large
Chinese colony, and others."[3] The Huks fought continuously and
successfully against the Japanese in five provinces throughout
three years of the occupation. They captured a large number of
guns and kept the rice of central Luzon out of the hands of the
Japanese. The Huks took over the estates of collaborators and
abolished the abuses of landlord-tenant relationships on all lands
in their area of administration. They organized democratic local
self-government and did away with the feudal political system
in which the *cacique* was dictator in his own bailiwick.

Some landlords looked to the Japanese for protection, others
expected the Americans to restore the *status quo ante,* and still
others met the Huk challenge by voluntary adoption of the Huk
reforms. But the Huks killed many landlords in the social melee.
The Huks said it was because the landlords were collaborators;
the government said it was because the Huks were bandits. It
made little difference to the landlords, but it made all the difference in the world to the government, which had to restore law

---

[3] Seeman and Salisbury, *Cross Currents in the Philippines,* p. 33.

and order, implement social justice, and keep its eye on the possibilities of the spread of communism.

Land reforms were long overdue. Rents were intolerable, and
the peasant standard of living was pathetic. The guerrilla years
brought tiny glimpses of freedom to the peasants, and they liked
what they saw. They set more liberal rental terms for their land
and demanded better treatment for themselves and their families.
Politically, they continued their civil administration after the war.
They chose their own representatives to congress, governors,
mayors, and minor officials. In each *barrio* organization, they
named a chairman, judges, a defense chief, secretary, treasurer,
and police corps.

Some Communists belong to the Huks, but there is no ostensible
proof of Russian direction or Russian sympathy. The leader,
Luis Taruc, admits that he is a Communist, devoted to the party
line; "but in case Russia should invade the Philippines," he has
said, "that would be a violation of the Communism I believe in
and would leave me free to make new decisions for myself." The
Huks sought friendship with the Americans while the latter were
responsible for peace maintenance in their locality. But the Huks
were suspected of desiring to overthrow the government by force,
and they were outlawed by United States military officials. The
Huks protested against the fraternization between American officers and the *haciendaros* (landlords). When Filipino military police
replaced the Americans, the Huks alleged that the new MP's were
former constabulary men who had worked with the Japanese.
The Huks warned the secretary of the interior that there would be
no peace in Luzon until the MP's were withdrawn. The Huks
promised cooperation with civil police, and repeated their willingness to become a peaceful, loyal opposition if the government
would cease its acts of "persecution."

President Roxas assumed that the Huks were hooligans and
ordered the constabulary to give them neither rest nor quarter.
He said that any efforts at appeasement would encourage the
Huks to continue their criminal activities. He accused them of
seeking power through force and of victimizing the peasants in
order to put themselves in office. "Their methods are to create
social disorder, confusion, and chaos, to foster widespread discon-

tent, and to drive the people to desperation." Roxas alleged that they did not seek reform, because the government had already legislated the reforms which they advocated (a new tenancy law giving 60 per cent of the crop to the tenant; anti-usury measures; division of the large estates; opening new areas to settlement; and government aid to farmers). Finally, Roxas took the position that if the Huks were sincere, they would give themselves up to the courts and face a fair trial; but "as long as they continue to defy the government, we must deal with them as public enemies."

President Quirino, who succeeded Roxas on his death, tried a different line. Quirino entered into an agreement with the Huks and sent his own brother into their territory to negotiate with them. They were given an amnesty, and their elected representatives were permitted to take their seats in the congress. Luis Taruc came to Manila and promised to have his men surrender their arms. During the fifty days accorded for turning in arms, only one hundred Huks registered and only fifty turned in their guns. Taruc accused Quirino of breaking promises, and Quirino accused Taruc of violating his pledged agreement. Disorders continued in the territories "occupied" or "ravaged" by the Huks, and the adamant attitude of the Huks brought neither rice nor reform to their followers, nor law and order to their country.

Resistance to the Japanese invader deepened the sense of national solidarity, which was born in the revolutionary struggle against Spain and nurtured by the agitation for independence against the United States. Philippine nationalism accounts for the government's interest in the welfare of the Filipino traders and for the genesis of anti-Chinese policies. A supreme court decision in 1948 prohibited the ownership of any land, even a residential lot, by a foreigner. Through a special property-rights agreement between the Philippines and the United States, Americans are exempted from the effects of this decision. But Spaniards have $35,000,000 in property in the Philippines, the Chinese have $28,000,000, and the English $5,000,000; and they must be concerned over their titles.

The Chinese own less than one-half of 1 per cent of all the arable land in the Philippines, but Filipinos are hostile to their "privileged position." Chinese investments are increasing, their share of commerce is growing, and until recently they had a strangle hold on the rice trade. They had entirely too many Filipinos in their debt, and their willingness to work hard and long and to operate on a slender margin of profit, made it impossible for the Filipinos to compete against them. The Chinese store was usually tumble-down or modest; the Filipino demanded a flamboyant front. The Chinese had their buying organizations, their guilds, and their organized social pressures. Of 10,000 booths in the public markets, 1,535 were operated by Chinese, who were scarcely able to keep body and soul together on their meager profits. By law, these Chinese have been deprived of their livelihood. The Chinese retailers also faced disaster in House Bill Number 652, September 18, 1946, which provided for the gradual nationalization of the retail trade, limiting the right to carry on such trade to Filipinos and to corporations and associations at least 75 per cent of the capital of which was owned by persons owing allegiance to the Philippines.

The Chinese protest their treatment, but failing a strong government to support them, they must rely upon reason and their own chamber of commerce. They point out that they are virtually Filipino, with no desire to go elsewhere. They say, "We meet our obligations to the government and society; we help develop the country and its resources; we extend the nation's commerce and industry. That is so, because we are a part of the population, despite the difference in the pigmentation of our skin. We appeal to the Filipino people for justice, equality, and fraternity."

The Republic has had its problems in perfecting its democratic processes. The people must be better informed, instructed, and led along the right paths. Democracy is only partially developed. The people are too easily persuaded to surrender their prerogatives to the politicians in power. Among those politicians there are many who are public-minded and public-spirited, but there are others who, in the words of their opponents, are "power-drunk and in search of wealth through unholy alliance with the economic tycoons." So far as they are concerned, "the country can crash to pieces while the machine can do as it pleases, undeterred by prudence, love of country, or respect for the opinion of mankind."

Quezon and Roxas are hard men for today's leaders to follow.

Quezon was courageous and dynamic, Roxas was brilliant and tireless. Quirino's administration is marred by nasty scandals. Quirino inherited a tainted situation, and he has not succeeded in eradicating the sources of alleged graft and corruption. Regular and respected government services have been honeycombed with bribery, and the unusual opportunities for personal enrichment were not overlooked by some who were charged with the disposal of surplus property. Scandals have also arisen in connection with the cashing of government checks for veterans' payments and war damage claims.

The worst scandal involved many senators and representatives in the Chinese immigration racket. It is freely reported that the congress raised the quota of Chinese immigrants from fifty to two thousand per year. The law provided that immigrants could be brought into the country on presentation of a certificate of good moral character. It is further reported that these certificates could be obtained from obliging congressmen on payment of a fee ranging from five to ten thousand pesos per person. Quirino has a difficult job to clean up his own machine and to put an end to the ugly rumors that undermine faith in his administration.

Many basic political problems remain to be solved. Domination over the rest of the country by the island of Luzon must be relaxed. Whenever a local politician reaches a dead end, he comes to Manila to discuss his problem. Whenever a party boss in the capital has a political fence to be mended, he goes to the provinces on an inspection trip. Paternalistic and dictatorial tendencies must be cleared away, and the common man must be given the same practical opportunities before the law as prosperous lawyers, Spanish and American entrepreneurs, and professional politicians. It is unwise to expect Utopia. Many nations have had centuries of experience in self-government, yet they, too, have their problems in the reconciliation of law and liberty.

Elections in the Philippines take on the character of a national pageant. A year before elections for the presidency and the congress are scheduled, the potential candidates begin to weigh their chances with the machine and the electorate. Before the war, endorsement by the Nacionalista party was tantamount to election, particularly if the candidacy bore the blessing of President

Quezon. Now there are two machines: the Nacionalista and the Liberal. Technically, the Liberal party advertises itself as the Liberal wing of the Nacionalista party, because it is not willing to give up the advantages of its ancestry. The present Nacionalista party is the direct heir of President Osmena. Its chief support comes from the wartime government-in-exile, the self-styled guerrillas, and the local machines which were in areas immune from the Japanese military party. The Liberal machine is basically the old Roxas machine. It has absorbed the Nacionalistas who were members of the last prewar congress and the majority of the collaborators who were cleared at the time of the elections in 1946. This curious development occurred during the Roxas-Quirino administration. The best-known collaborators, like the Japanese puppet President Laurel, were still not cleared at the time of the 1946 election. This meant that they were not eligible for the best post-election plums. Therefore, after the general amnesty, they joined with the "outs," the Osmena Nacionalistas, in opposing the administration. When this paradoxical situation came to pass—with the most rabid guerrilla champions and the most notorious puppets in the same camp—there was a general shift in the rank and file of both parties. Some guerrillas could not tolerate the association with the puppets, so they deserted to Quirino; some collaborators who were cleared in time to join Roxas returned to the Nacionalista fold in the wake of their former chief.

The parties have differences in their platforms, but they are only paper differences. The determining factor in a man's politics is his personal devotion. The sharp issue of collaboration has become a dead letter. Party alignments will again depend upon the personal cleavages and reconciliations of the individuals concerned. Party labels are convenient and necessary for election, but they are not vital or even true indexes of party action.

The party machine has always endeavored to control the government jobs. Even the president is beholden to the party. The big three in the Liberal party in 1949—Quirino, Avelino in the senate, and Speaker Perez in the house—nominally controlled the machine. It was reported that Avelino wanted to make sure that Quirino did not become too popular and appeal directly to the people over the party's head. But Quirino did just that. While on a speaking tour in Mindanao, he announced his candidacy for the presidency on the Liberal ticket. His opponents called attention to the fact that he was speaking in an outdoor setting, and said that it was entirely fitting that he should announce his candidacy to the trees, for all the trees in Mindanao had cast their votes for the Liberals in 1946. The Filipinos know all the tricks of padding the election rolls.

Quirino's strategy was to force his own nomination by his party, in spite of any ideas that Avelino might have. If some Liberals were to protest Quirino's precipitate announcement, the party might split and come in second best in 1950. Party men often bury their "irreconcilable differences," however, and end up in warm embrace.

The Nacionalista party may choose to nominate Tomas Confesor, or some other symbol of the resistance; on the other hand, it may pick José Laurel, Camilo Osias, or some other outstanding collaborationist who would campaign vigorously without making any apologies for his patriotism or loyalty. For an American it seems hard to believe that the leading official under the Japanese could offer himself for the presidency in a free election so soon after the liberation. Nevertheless, Laurel's apologists say that at heart he is a true Filipino. He held out against conscription, he never sent the constabulary to the front, and he never performed a single act of collaboration except under *force majeure* or for the best interests of the Filipinos. His friends insist that Laurel is scrupulously honest and completely courageous. His greatest support would come from those who are disgusted with the Quirino administration.

Those who dislike Laurel point to his early career as an anti-white. They say that he precipitated the cabinet crisis of 1923 and that he opposed the Americans consistently and unreasonably. They say that he takes pleasure in holding office, that he had a good time in Japan, that he liked being president, that he meant every word he ever wrote and spoke in favor of a Japanese victory and an American defeat, and that he is a plain opportunist. Those who dislike him intensely say that he is completely selfish, that he had vast sums of money hidden in his home when the Americans entered it, and that he can never be excused for his treachery. One Filipino reporter expressed his opinions in these words:

"That a goddam traitor like Laurel should loom as a presidential possibility in the Philippines—that is our national tragedy, a tragedy made possible by Roxas and those who aided him. People would not turn to Laurel if the administration were not so corrupt, if it had not instituted a regime of one law for the landlords and another for the peasants. The greatest enemies of democracy in the Philippines were those gangsters who stole the last election from the opposition after enriching themselves with the people's money, whose army shot down the peasants like dogs, or shall we say like peasants."

It would be unprecedented for a non-party man to achieve the presidency, but Carlos Romulo is a possibility. He is the Philippines delegate to the United Nations, and has been doing his work with devotion and distinction. He has been out of the country, and therefore has no association in the public mind with the scandals of the Quirino administration. He has no machine to back him up, and it is unlikely that he will receive a nomination on a party ticket unless one of the parties wants a dark horse, or sees in Romulo the makings of a winner. He has intellectual and influential friends. He has a following running into the thousands dating from his days as editor of the *Philippines Herald*. He has the support of veterans, who think of him as General Romulo. He has an appeal to honest young businessmen who are not bound by the memories and traditions of Quezon's lieutenants, and who are not satisfied with either party as it stands.

As a new nation, the Philippines are conducting their diplomacy and international relations with a great deal of credit. The Philippines can never hope to establish a defense system that would be impregnable, so they have turned to the United States and the United Nations for support and strength. The Philippines concluded a treaty with the United States for the establishment of American military and naval bases for the common protection of the two countries. The Philippines do not look upon themselves as the Achilles heel in the American defense armor, but think that they are a defensible outpost for the United States. They have a small military force, and they maintain a well-trained and equipped constabulary. Their military program includes a citizen army, planned with the advice of a United States military advisory group.

The Philippines have concluded treaties of amity with the United States, China, France, Italy, and Spain, and have signed many other miscellaneous agreements. They have participated actively in the United Nations and its affiliated organs. The Philippines are members of the Trusteeship Council, UNESCO, the Food and Agricultural Organization, the International Civil Aviation Organization, the Committee on Non-Self-Governing Territories, the Commission on Human Rights, the Sub-commission on Freedom of Information and the Press, the Economic Commission for East Asia and the Far East, the International Trade Organization, the International Labor Organization, and the Korean and Palestine Commissions. Romulo has made his voice heard in the Indonesian affair, both at Lake Success and at the Asian Conference in New Delhi. The Philippines have established a foreign office and a foreign service, and they participate in the administration and control of Japan. They have a place of equality with other nations in any international gathering or diplomatic conference.

The Philippines now have a more realistic attitude toward the United States. Filipinos have seen and experienced contacts with millions of Americans. They have learned to take the bad with the good, the poor with the rich, and the uneducated with the cultured. They are aware of America's preoccupation with other than Filipino affairs, and they are more inclined to look inward for strength and inspiration. They are acting independently, and even when Americans disapprove of their decisions, they must applaud their independence. They are increasingly aware of their opportunities and their obligations to their immediate neighbors, and they are taking advantage of their Latin heritage to cement closer relations with Spain, Italy, France, and Latin America. Their representatives in the United Nations have drawn favorable attention to the capabilities of the Philippines in rising above their own perplexities to contribute to the solution of the greater problems of world peace and human well-being.

Suggested Reading

Abaya, Hernando J. *Betrayal in the Philippines.* New York. 1946.
Barrows, David P. *History of the Philippines.* Yonkers on Hudson. 1925. (Rev. ed.)

Benitez, Conrado, and Austin Craig. *Philippine Progress Prior to 1898.* Manila. 1916.

Blair, Emma, and James A. Robertson. *The Philippine Islands, 1493–1898.* 55 volumes. Cleveland. 1903–1909.

Brines, Russel. *Until They Eat Stones.* Philadelphia. 1944.

Clyde, Paul H. *The Far East.* New York. 1948.

Dennett, Tyler. *Americans in Eastern Asia.* New York. 1922.

Eckel, Paul E. *The Far East Since 1500.* New York. 1947.

Elliott, C. B. *The Philippines: To the End of the Military Regime.* Indianapolis. 1916.

———. *The Philippines: To the End of the Commission Government.* Indianapolis. 1917.

Emerson, Rupert, Lennox A. Mills, and Virginia Thompson. *Government and Nationalism in Southeast Asia.* New York. 1942.

Forbes, W. C. *The Philippine Islands.* 2 volumes. New York. 1928. (Rev. ed., Cambridge, Mass. 1945.)

Griswold, A. W. *The Far Eastern Policy of the United States.* New York. 1938.

Hall, Monroe. "Collaborators' Candidate," *Far Eastern Survey.* Vol. XV, No. 5. March 13, 1946.

Hayden, J. R. *The Philippines.* New York. 1942.

Heiser, Victor. *An American Doctor's Odyssey.* New York. 1936.

Institute of Pacific Relations. Books, pamphlets, and papers relating to the Philippines.

Jacoby, Erich N. *Agrarian Unrest in South East Asia.* New York. 1949.

Kalaw, M. M. *The Development of Philippine Politics, 1872–1920.* Manila. 1926.

Kirk, Grayson. *Philippine Independence.* New York. 1936.

Krieger, H. W. *Peoples of the Philippines.* Smithsonian Institution. Washington, D.C. 1942.

Malcomb, George A. *The Commonwealth of the Philippines.* New York. 1936.

Mill, Edward W. *One Year of the Republic.* Department of State Publication 2877, Far Eastern Series 23. Washington, D.C. 1947.

Pelzer, Karl. *Pioneer Settlement in the Asiatic Tropics.* New York. 1945.

Porter, Catherine. *Filipinos and Their Country.* New York. 1944.

Quezon, Manuel. *The Good Fight.* New York. 1946.

Rizal, José. *Noli Me Tangere.* Manila. 1912. (Translated by Charles Derbyshire as *Social Cancer.*)

———. *El Filibusterismo.* Manila. 1912. (Translated by Charles Derbyshire as *Reign of Greed.*)

Seeman, Bernard, and Laurence Salisbury. *Cross Currents in the Philippines.* New York. 1946.

Worcester, Dean C. *The Philippines, Past and Present.* New York. 1930. (Rev. ed.)

Annual Report of the United States Philippine Commission. Washington, D.C. 1901.

Annual Reports of the United States High Commissioner to the Philippines.

Report of the Joint Preparatory Commission.

Reports of the Governor-General.

INDONESIA

✤

THE Netherlands Indies was the official name of the Dutch dependency in the tropical East. It was, however, more generally known as the Dutch East Indies. Since World War II it has become better known as Indonesia, though its official title, if the Linggadjati Agreement between the Republic of Indonesia and the Netherlands is finally implemented, will be the United States of Indonesia. It lies directly under the equator, between southeastern Asia and Australia. With the Malayan Peninsula it forms what is often called the Malay Barrier between the Indian and Pacific oceans, dominating the gateways between the two. As an area in which great ocean highways converge it is comparable to the Caribbean and the Mediterranean seas.

Composed of half a dozen large and countless small islands, Indonesia covers an area four times as great as its actual land area of 733,000 square miles, or an area equal to that of continental United States. At the time of the last official census, taken in 1930, it had a population of 60,731,025; by 1949 its population was probably about 75,000,000. Taking into consideration its population as well as its area, it is the largest insular country in the world.

The East Indian Company, 1602–1800

The Dutch were not the first European rulers of Indonesia. When the first Dutch ships arrived in the Indies in 1596, the Portuguese had already been there for nearly a century, but they had established only a precarious hold. The Dutch drove them out of the archipelago, but this did not mean that the Dutch immediately came to control all of the East Indies. The East Indian Company, through which the Dutch operated in the East, was not

interested in governing, but in trading. The company soon discovered, however, that it could not trade successfully unless it also
governed. From Cape Town to Japan, including India, it set up
a number of trading centers and forts, and by entering into agreements and alliances with native rulers it also acquired an indirect
control or dominance over large areas in the Malay Archipelago.
By 1750 the company had largely shifted from a commercial to a
territorial and political basis. Its steadily dwindling profits, however, caused the company to collapse toward the end of the
eighteenth century, and in 1800 the Dutch government took it
over.

Net Profit Policy

During the latter part of the Napoleonic Wars the British occupied the Dutch colonial territories in the East; but with the
return of peace they restored the colonies to the Netherlands, with
the exception of Ceylon and Cape Colony, the halfway station on
the route from the Netherlands to the Indies.

In the early years after the Napoleonic Wars, the budget of the
government of the East Indies ran steadily mounting deficits, and
the Dutch government itself was experiencing grave financial
difficulties. To stop this drain and, if possible, to change it into a
surplus for the Dutch treasury, a policy known as the Culture
System was adopted. Heretofore, the Indonesians had been required to pay a proportion of their crops as land rent, or taxes, to
the government. Now, instead, they were to place at the disposal
of the Indies government a part of their land and a certain number
of days of work, and under the direction of government officials
cultivate crops for export. Fiscally the plan was very successful;
over a period of some fifty years, it poured millions of guilders into
the Netherlands treasury. However, serious abuses crept into the
administration of the system, frequently causing dire distress
among the Javanese peasants. Furthermore, by keeping out Western private enterprise, it retarded the economic development of
the country.

The Reform Movement

It was to arouse Dutch public opinion against the evils of the
Culture System that Edward Douwes Dekker, under the

pseudonym of "Multatuli," published in 1860 his famous novel, *Max Havelaar*. Dekker, a former East Indies official, was intimately acquainted with the operation of the system. Though he was not interested in a fundamental change of policy, desiring only the removal of abuses, his novel nevertheless gave tremendous impetus to the reform movement which was already in progress. The rise of the middle class to political power at about this time insured a change of policy, as the bourgeoisie wished to see the Indies opened to private enterprise and capital. The Culture System virtually came to an end with the passage of the Agrarian Law in 1870. Private enterprise began to replace state exploitation, with the government increasingly coming forward as the protector of the indigenous population.

The spirit of Dutch policy with respect to the Indies was gradually changing; but it was not until 1901, when a coalition ministry composed of the representatives of three Christian parties came to power under Abraham Kuyper as prime minister, that the change was signalized in an important government statement. In the "Speech from the Throne" of that year, the government declared, "as a Christian power, the Netherlands is obligated in the East Indian Archipelago to imbue the whole conduct of the Government with the Consciousness that the Netherlands has a moral duty to fulfill with respect to the people of these regions." The policy thus announced became known as the "Ethical Policy." A measure reflecting the new spirit was the cancellation in 1905 of a forty million guilder loan which had been advanced by the Netherlands treasury to the East Indian government. This was done in order that funds might be released in the Indies for the improvement of economic conditions on Java and Madura.

The Dutch had deliberately refrained from penetrating with their administration all of the vast territories of the islands outside of Java; but in the nineties, fear of foreign intervention and other factors convinced them that they could no longer delay establishing effective authority throughout the whole archipelago. This task was virtually completed by Governor-General van Heutsz (1904–1909), who as commander-in-chief of the Dutch army had a few years earlier successfully brought to an end the long and bitter war with the Achehnese, a tribe of fanatic fighters who inhabit the northern tip of Sumatra. It was also during the administration of General van Heutsz that the difficult task of laying the basis for a popular educational system was first seriously undertaken.

The Rise of Indonesian Nationalism

In so far as there is an Indonesian nation, it is the result of the three and a half centuries of Dutch rule. This is not to suggest that nationalism would not have developed among the peoples of the archipelago if there had been no Dutch or other foreign dominion; but in all probability it would have developed more slowly and taken different forms. It is true that there was in the fourteenth and fifteenth centuries the Javanese Empire of Madjapahit, whose domains at its zenith were almost coextensive with what later became the Netherlands Indies; but its life was of short duration. It soon fell apart and gave way to political chaos. By the time the Portuguese arrived there were many sultanates, some fairly large and some small, and many tribal chiefs. This division of the archipelago into innumerable petty states made conquest by the Portuguese, and later by the Dutch, possible. There prevailed a feudalism not unlike that of Europe in the Middle Ages. But the long period of Dutch rule brought about an integration in many spheres, so that there finally developed among the Indonesian peoples that feeling of unity which is at the heart of all nationalism.

Indonesian nationalism first expressed itself in an organized way with the founding in 1908 of *Budi Utomo,* Javanese for "Beautiful (or High) Endeavor." This society organized by Javanese intellectuals had at first only a social, economic, and cultural program, but later it also entered the political field. Soon afterward there was organized another society, called *Sarekat Islam,* which appealed to far more people, since it was based upon the common religious bond of Mohammedanism. The promotion of economic welfare and the advancement of the interests of Islam were the two main objects of the party. At its first congress, held in 1913, resolutions were passed calling for an evolutionary development of self-government for the Indies within the Dutch empire; but by 1918 the party had fallen under the control of radical leadership. At the 1921 congress the more radical elements were forced out; but it was a Pyrrhic victory that the moderates won, for the party, which had enjoyed a tremendous growth, now began to decline. The doctrinaire radicals went into the labor union movement, causing a series of bitter strikes. When in 1926 and 1927 the nationalist agitation culminated in armed outbreaks in Java and Sumatra, the Dutch became convinced that the radical trend of the nationalist movement was Communist inspired and had to be repressed.

An interesting phase of the nationalist movement was the establishment of a large number of so-called "wild schools," that is, schools not established or maintained by the government but by nationalist groups. The sponsors refused government subsidies for their schools, since they wished to be free from official regulation. The object of the schools was to give the children a strongly Indonesian, nationalistic training, as well as to bring the masses to a higher level of development. In this movement students played a leading role.

In the middle of the 1920's, Indonesian intellectuals organized "study clubs" for the discussion of social and political questions. From these clubs emerged new political parties, some of which soon acquired a large membership. From the Bandung Study Club there developed in 1927 *Partai Nasional Indonesia*, under the leadership of Sukarno, who two decades later was to become the president of the Republic of Indonesia. This party, which embraced the principle of non-cooperation with the Dutch, adopted nationalistic, revolutionary mass action as the method of achieving its ends. In 1929 the Netherlands Indies government officially dissolved *Partai Nasional Indonesia*, arrested Sukarno, and then interned him, first on the island of Flores and later in Benkoelen on Sumatra.

After 1930 the nationalist movement slowed down, probably because of two factors. First, the great depression, which was especially severe in the East Indies, made nationalist activity very difficult because of lack of funds. Secondly, the vigorous repressive measures of the East Indies government against the revolutionary tendencies of the nationalist movement kept many would-be adherents from joining. When the movement revived in the middle of the 1930's, it returned to a cooperative basis. The rise of fascism and national socialism abroad, and especially the threat from Japan, sobered its leaders and caused them to see the advantages of cooperating with the Dutch.

The Indonesian nationalist movement was still young and immature at the time of the Japanese invasion. It was strongest on Java and in parts of Sumatra, like the Minangkabau region. Borneo and the eastern half of the archipelago, with the exception of a few centers such as the Minahassa in northeastern Celebes, Ambon, and Timor, were untouched by it. Membership in Indonesian political organizations probably did not exceed 125,000. The party organizations were numerous and unstable; they waxed and waned over brief periods, confederated and fell apart again in rapid succession.

Dutch Policy with Respect to Indonesian Nationalism

The rise of the nationalist movement in the Indies took most Netherlanders by surprise; its rapid growth astonished them and filled a few with dismay. They had no idea that this disturbing force would so soon penetrate their dependency, so peacefully situated in an out-of-the-way corner of the world. The Netherlands government adopted toward it a policy of cautious, unhurried adjustment.

The East Indies government remained highly centralized and bureaucratic until after the rise of nationalism. Only a feeble beginning had been made to decentralize and democratize it. By the Decentralization Act of 1903 a number of local councils were created, but they enjoyed little power and they were undemocratic in character. Many of the members of the councils held office ex officio. A representative body for the entire country was not established until 1918, and its powers remained advisory until 1927. Intermediate representative bodies were created by legislation of 1922 and 1925, under which Java and Madura were divided into three provinces and a representative body set up in each. It was planned, as soon as conditions warranted, to attach representative bodies to the intermediate units of government which under this legislation had been created in the other islands.

Before World War II most Netherlanders had come to accept

the inevitability of Indonesian self-government, but they could not reconcile themselves to the thought of an independent Indonesia. Their ties with the Indies were too old and too numerous. There was also the feeling that without the Indies the position of the Netherlands in world affairs would be much reduced. They hoped to keep Indonesia a partner in a confederation. For a decade or more before the Japanese invasion, plans for a constitutional reorganization to that end had been widely discussed in both Dutch and Indonesian circles. While sympathetic with evolutionary nationalism, the Indies government repressed all revolutionary activities with determination. Most of the Indonesians convicted of revolutionary activity were either exiled to a remote prison camp on the Digul River in the wilds of New Guinea or interned in some district in one of the other islands. Thus Sutan Sjahrir, who later became minister of foreign affairs and then prime minister of the Republic of Indonesia, was in 1934 exiled to Camp Boven-Digul, but after a year was transferred to the small island of Banda, where he was interned. Mohammed Hatta, vice-president and, later, also prime minister of the Republic, shared the same fate. Until the Japanese invasion, they lived on Banda in a private house but under surveillance and confined to the island.

Extent of Self-Government in 1941

The term "colonies and possessions in other parts of the world" was removed from the constitution in 1922, and the East Indies government was granted greater autonomy. In 1925 the Indies Government Act was revised to conform to the revised colonial articles in the constitution. While the Indies government was granted a larger measure of autonomy, it was still a long way from having complete self-government. The governor-general was charged with the general administration, but he was to exercise his function in observance of the directives of the Crown. He thus remained responsible for general policy to the minister of colonies, and the latter responsible to the States General, the Netherlands parliament.

The Crown retained the right to suspend all ordinances passed by the Indies government when it deemed them to be in conflict with the constitution, the law, or the general interest, while the right of vetoing the Indies ordinances on the same grounds was left to the States General. Moreover, the States General retained the right to pass laws on all Indies matters, though it was required to consult the Volksraad—the central legislative body of the East Indies—before legislating on any matter affecting the Indies. The annual budget of the Indies government had to be approved by the States General, which also resolved budgetary deadlocks between the governor-general and the Volksraad.

The Crown enjoyed a wide power of appointment and removal. In addition to the governor-general and lieutenant governor-general, the Crown appointed the chairman of the Volksraad, the vice-president and members of the council of the Indies, the president of the high court, the commander-in-chief of the Indies army, the commander-in-chief of the navy in the Indies waters, and members of the auditing office.

The governor-general was invested with very large powers. The administrative system, even after the reorganization, was highly centralized, and there was little constitutional check on the governor-general. After 1927 he shared the legislative power with the Volksraad. Deadlocks between the two were solved in different ways. In case a bill sent to the Volksraad by the governor-general did not receive the concurrence of that body, the bill could be returned to the Volksraad for reconsideration, but such resubmission had to take place within six months of the rejection either by the governor-general or the Volksraad. If still no agreement was reached, the regulation could be promulgated by a general administrative order of the Crown. If the Volksraad failed to give its concurrence to a bill sent in by the governor-general within a specified period, and circumstances demanded immediate action, the governor-general possessed the power of issuing an ordinance upon his own authority.

Attached to the governor-general was the Council of the Indies, which was composed of five experienced administrators. While it still enjoyed much prestige, its actual influence had waned. The governor-general was free to consult it on a number of specific subjects and needed the concurrence of the council in only a small number of matters. In latter years the directors of the administrative departments had come in large measure to replace members of the council as the governor-general's advisers.

Exclusive of the chairman, the Volksraad had a membership of sixty. Under the provisions of the Indies Government Act, thirty seats were reserved for Indonesians, twenty-five for Netherlanders, and five for non-indigenous Asiatics (Chinese and Arabs). Ten of the Indonesian, ten of the Dutch, and two of the non-indigenous Asiatic seats were filled by appointment of the governor-general. The remaining seats were elective under a system of separate racial electorates, indirect voting, and proportional representation. The members of the local, regency, and municipal councils formed the electorates.

Constitutional provisions do not always give an accurate picture of how the government actually operates. Rarely did the governor-general resort to the certification of measures. Between 1927 and 1930 he asked the Volksraad to reconsider rejected proposals only thirteen times, and only four times did the Crown intervene in his support. During these years the governor-general accepted amendments by the Volksraad to over five hundred of his bills. In view of the fact that the Dutch and non-indigenous Asiatics had far greater representation in the Volksraad than their proportion of the population justified, and that a number of the members were appointed by him, it may be argued that there was no reason why the governor-general should have had any difficulty with the Volksraad. The facts above do not, of course, constitute an answer to criticism of the way the seats in the Volksraad were distributed among the racial groups; but it should not be assumed that the Dutch members of the Volksraad were always passive. This was by no means the case.

Before leaving this subject it should be noted that Indonesians were Netherlands subjects, and just as Netherlanders were eligible for membership in the Volksraad, so Indonesians were eligible for election to the States General. And, indeed, an Indonesian, elected on the Communist ticket, served as a member of the second chamber of the States General from 1933 until 1940, when the Germans invaded and occupied the Netherlands.

Before the creation of the provinces the Indies government was extremely centralized, but in the decade and a half after 1925 considerable progress was made in the creation of intermediate governments. Java was divided into three provinces: West Java (1926), East Java, including Madura (1929), and Central Java (1930). After years of discussion and preparation, the Outer Islands were finally in 1938 organized into three "governments"— Sumatra, Borneo, and the Great East (consisting of the islands to the east of Borneo). The chief difference between a province and a "government" was that the latter did not yet have a representative body. At the head of both provinces and governments were governors, who were appointed by and were responsible to the provincial council. The members of the provincial councils were chosen in the same manner as members of the Volksraad, and the seats were distributed among the racial groups in the same ratio.

The Dutch used indirect rule wherever possible. In Java and Madura it was the regency, with the semihereditary regent and the four native states of central Java with Javanese princes with high-sounding titles at their head, upon which the Dutch administration's superstructure was built. In the Outer Islands the native states had many forms, but for the most part they were petty sultanates. Sixty-two per cent of the area of the Outer Islands was under indirect rule, and a little less than half of the population. There were 278 native states in all of the Indies, of which 223 had a population of less than 50,000 and only two, both in Java, had a population of more than a million. The native states had jurisdiction over their own indigenous population only.

There are fashions in colonial policy as in other things. Two decades ago indirect rule was fairly popular, especially among liberals. It was provided because it preserved the old native culture while gradually integrating it with the requirements of modern life. However, it had its weaknesses as well as its virtues. The native rulers frequently could not keep abreast of the social and economic development of their people. Often the lavish expenditures on their courts weighed heavily on the welfare of their people. Many of the native states were too small for the demands of modern administration and it was difficult to build them into larger and more effective units. It was also argued that native institutions and customs were disintegrating and that nothing could be done to prevent it. Native societies could not be insulated from the disintegrating forces of the modern world. Another serious objection to indirect rule was the difficulty, if not the impossibility, of fitting the new educated class into the traditional framework of government.

In spite of these objections, the Dutch policy of indirect rule and the preservation of the best features of native institutions and customs had its merits. Mr. J. S. Furnivall, for many years a member of the Indian and Burmese civil service and now an adviser to the government of independent Burma, in his recent book, *Colonial Policy and Practice,* makes a comparative study of Dutch policy in the East Indies and British policy in Burma, and reaches some conclusions very favorable to the former. In Burma, where the British policy was almost the direct opposite of that followed by the Dutch in the Indies, there were, according to Furnivall, five grave evils: "The failure of western self-governing institutions; the growth of debt and agrarian distress; the multiplication of litigation and crime; the rise of disaffection and unrest among the Buddhist clergy; and widespread corruption in the judicial and administrative services. I suggested that these can all be traced to a common cause: the disintegration of social life through the inadequacy of law to control the working of anti-social economic forces. Although in other respects Dutch rule is open to criticism which does not apply to Burma, yet in all these matters Netherlands India presents a notable contrast."

The provinces of Java were divided into regencies, of which there were about seventy in all, with the semihereditary Javanese regent at their head. Normally the regent was succeeded by his eldest son, but only if he were qualified. If he were not, the office passed to a younger brother, or it might even go to a collateral branch of the family. The population of the regencies varied from 500,000 to 1,000,000. Attached to each regency was a council in which the Indonesians had an overwhelming majority. In the Outer Islands, the Indies government was attempting to develop group communities as units of democratic government. The Minangkabau tribe of Sumatra was thus organized, and its council was regarded as very successful. Since the cities contained a large European population, and because most of their problems had a technical character, the governments of urban municipalities were largely controlled by Europeans. The composition of the municipal council differed from the provincial and regency councils in that all of its members were elective. All members of the municipal councils and the European and non-indigenous Asiatic members of the other local councils were elected by direct vote of the qualified voters, while the Indonesian members of the regency councils were elected by indirect vote, each elector representing 500 voters.

All Indonesians who were Netherlands subjects, twenty-one years of age, residents of the regency, and who paid a tax to the regency, province, or central government were eligible to vote. The qualifications for electors were, in addition to the above: twenty-five years of age, male sex, and an ability to read or write. Qualifications for the right to vote for members of the municipal councils were the same for all races, and were as follows: Dutch subject, twenty-one years of age, ability to read and write Dutch, Malay, or the local language, residence within the city, and the payment of an income tax on an income of at least 300 florins ($175) per year. Because of these qualifications the number of voters was very small. Batavia, with a population of 533,000, had in 1938 only 12,749 voters, divided among the three population groups as follows: Netherlanders, 8,563; Indonesians, 3,468; and non-indigenous Asiatics, 718.

At the base of the governmental structure was the village, which had a strongly democratic character. Since Indonesia is almost wholly agrarian, the overwhelming majority of the people live in villages, or *dessas,* in which their lives are centered. The head, or chief, of the village was chosen by the people. He was assisted by a group of advisers, who were designated in accordance with local customs. While the head was alone responsible, he had to consult the village assembly before making important decisions.

Of importance in the training of a people for self-government is the opportunity offered to individuals to occupy responsible positions in the civil service. There were in the employment of the central government on October 1, 1938 a total of 73,354 persons, distributed among the various population groups as follows:

	Number	Per Cent
Europeans	14,395	19.6
Indonesians	58,041	79.1
Chinese	895	1.2
Other non-indigenous Asiatics	23	...
Total	73,354	100%

These figures do not include the employees of the local governments; in these positions the number of Indonesians was naturally much higher. Of the 14,395 Europeans in the government service, about half were recruited in the Netherlands; the others were predominantly Eurasian.

More significant even than the percentage of all the posts held is, of course, the type of positions held by each population group. The following table tells that story:

	Lower Personnel	Lower Intermediate	Purely Intermediate	Higher Personnel
Europeans ...	0.6	33.3	57.6	92.2
Indonesians ..	99.1	64.0	40.0	6.9
Chinese	0.3	2.7	2.3	0.8

This table indicates that the lower governmental positions were filled almost exclusively by Indonesians; that the intermediate positions were shared by the Indonesians and the Eurasians, with the lower intermediate positions filled predominantly by Indonesians, and the higher intermediate predominantly by Eurasians; and that the higher personnel was still overwhelmingly Dutch. As might be expected from the late development of higher education in the Indies, few Indonesians were found in positions requiring college or professional training. In the decade from 1928 to 1938 the Indonesians made considerable progress; but the significant fact is that aside from the important but semihereditary position of regent they had been entrusted with few highly responsible positions. Of the executive departments, only one had had an Indonesian as director, namely, the department of education. One large city in Java—Bandung—had an Indonesian mayor. It was not until the early 1930's that an Indonesian was elevated to membership in the Council of the Indies. However, in the last few years before the Japanese occupation two of the five members of the Dutch delegation to the meetings of the Assembly of the League of Nations and to the International Labor Conferences were Indonesians. One of the Netherlands representatives on the International Tin Committee was also Indonesian. After the Japanese occupation of the Indies, an Indonesian was made a member of the Netherlands cabinet in London as minister-without-portfolio.

Economic Life and Commercial Policy

After the adoption of a liberal policy in the third quarter of the nineteenth century and the opening of the Suez Canal in 1869, the economic life of the country began to take new form. Outside capital commenced to flow into the Indies. Railway and steamship lines began to spread a network of transportation facilities over the archipelago. Western enterprise in agriculture and mining began to thrive. Exports and imports increased steadily.

The amount of foreign capital invested in the Indies was estimated at about $2,000,000,000 in 1929. In 1939, after the considerable deflation of the depression years had taken place, the amount of foreign capital invested in business enterprises was estimated at about $1,150,000,000. Of this amount about 75 per cent was Dutch, 13.5 per cent British, and 2.5 per cent American. In addition, Indies government bonds of approximately $800,000,-000 were held abroad, practically all by the Dutch.

The share of the Netherlands Indies of the total world exports of a number of commodities in 1939 was as follows (in percentages): pepper, 86; kapok, 72; rubber, 37; agave, 33; copra products, 27; oil palm products, 19; sugar, 11; and coffee, 4. During this same year its share of the world's production of cinchona bark was 91 per cent, of tin 17 per cent, and of petroleum 17 per cent. The bulk of these products were also exported.

The East Indies foreign trade reached its peak value in 1920 when exports totaled $903,000,000 and imports $450,000,000 in value. In the following two years it declined by half, after which it again slowly increased, attaining the figures of $630,000,000 and $390,000,000 in 1928. With the great depression, the value of foreign trade declined precipitately, reaching the lowest point in 1935 when the value of exports and imports declined to about $220,000,000 and $120,000,000 respectively. The year 1937 saw considerable improvement, the value of exports for this year being over 100 per cent and imports about 70 per cent greater than two years before. For the year 1940, the value of exports amounted to $512,000,000 and of imports $244,000,000.

Until 1933 Dutch tariff policy with respect to the East Indies was very liberal. The tariffs of both Holland and the East Indies

were low, and there was no discrimination. It was the so-called
Open Door policy. Goods entering the Indies from the Netherlands paid the same tariff rate as those coming from other
countries. By contrast, goods entering the Philippines from the
United States, or Indochina from France, received 100 per cent
preference over goods coming in from other countries, since they
were exempt from all tariff duties. Goods moving from the dependencies to the metropolitan countries fell under the same regimes respectively. Only 18 per cent of the external trade of the
East Indies was with Holland (1939); while over half of the external trade of Indochina was with France, and about 80 per cent of
that of the Philippines was with the United States.

The world economic depression of the 1930's hit the East Indies
with great severity. As an important producer of raw materials and
foodstuffs for the world market it was caught in a very unfavorable
position. The price of the goods it exported fell much more rapidly
than that of its imports. The determination of the Netherlands'
government to remain on the gold standard as long as possible (it
did not devaluate its currency until September 1936, and then by
only 18 per cent) added to the Indies' difficulties as an exporting
country. By 1935 the value of exports had declined to less than a
fourth of what it was in 1928. To meet this crisis a policy of rigid
deflation was followed. Governmental expenditures were reduced
by nearly a half. With the decline of the Western export industries,
the native population was forced to return to the closed economy
of the native village. All of this involved much hardship and even
suffering.

Under these conditions the East Indies government felt itself
compelled to depart from the liberal trade policies that it had
hitherto practiced. The world depression had caused the development of an intense economic nationalism everywhere. Nearly all
countries adopted the policy of bilateral trade, which is best summarized by the slogan "We buy where we sell." The Netherlands
had to act to protect the export position of the Indies' articles
normally sold abroad.

The greatest difficulty was experienced in the trade with Japan.
Japanese goods flooded the Indies market during the depression.
From 1929 to 1935 the Dutch share of the East Indies imports

declined in value from 17.6 per cent to 13.4 per cent, but during this same period the Japanese share jumped from 10.2 per cent to 30.1 per cent. Japan was pushing not only Dutch but all other competitors from the Indies market. A comment on this situation frequently made was that the Open Door would soon mean the Japanese house. On the other side of the ledger, the story was quite different. During this period Japan's imports from the Indies remained practically the same. In 1929 Japan took 4.7 per cent of the exports of the Indies and in 1935, 5.4 per cent. In the meanwhile Europe and America were increasing their imports from the Indies. There was danger that this market for Indies products would be lost to competitors unless a reasonable share of the Indies market could be guaranteed these good customers. This was no easy matter, for the Japanese goods were cheap and within the purchasing power of the masses with their low incomes.

To remedy this trade unbalance a quota system was adopted and a number of reciprocal trade agreements concluded. At the same time, measures were taken to protect the native food supply and its prices. An import license system for rice and soya beans was encouraged in order to lessen dependence on foreign supplies. To bring production of a number of commodities in line with demand, control over production and exports was instituted for cinchona, kapok, tea, tin, rubber, and sugar. In the case of the four last-named commodities, the regulation was based upon international agreements. Taken as a whole, these measures represented a marked departure from former policy and involved extensive government regulation.

Effect of the German Occupation of the Netherlands on Dutch-Indonesian Relations

The effect of the German occupation of the metropolitan country was to make nearly every aspect of life in the Indies more autonomous. Cut off from the home country, Netherlanders in the Indies were thrust upon their own. Cultural, commercial, scientific, and religious groups and institutions could no longer look to the Netherlands for control, guidance, or renewal. As a result they became more self-reliant and assertive. Moreover, in the face of the threat from Japan, all population groups in the Indies drew closer together. The exiled Netherlands government in London, cut off from its parliamentary base, stood relatively weak over against the governor-general. During the war years leading figures from the Indies were drawn into the government at London, so that the latter became less a national and more an imperial government. Because of the very brisk demand for East Indies products, especially tin and rubber, the country's economic position was strong.

It was at this point that the Dutch government in London and the governor-general faced a dilemma. The ruthless invasion of the Netherlands by the Germans called forth among Indonesians of all classes an outburst of profound sympathy for the Dutch; and all but the extreme nationalists were prepared to cooperate actively with the Dutch, but on the basis of equality, in the creation of a Netherlands-Indonesian Union. The eager advances of the moderate nationalists, however, were coldly received by the East Indian government on the ground that nothing definite could be proposed so long as the people of the Netherlands could not be consulted. It was asserted that no changes could be made in the imperial constitution without their consent, or that of their parliament.

One can only speculate on whether the course of events might not have been different if the Dutch authorities had followed another policy. A positive answer cannot be given. The example of the Philippines is not in every respect reassuring. The Philippines had not only been promised independence, but a definite date had been set for its consummation, and a large transfer of power to that end had already been made. Nevertheless, all but a few of the leading men about President Quezon actively collaborated with the Japanese. But one thing the United States did have, which the Dutch failed in a large measure to win, and that was loyalty among the masses.

There were other factors in the situation which must be taken into account, such as the greater generosity with which a wealthy country of 135,000,000 people could and did treat its dependency of about 16,000,000, as compared with what a small country of less than 9,000,000 people could do for its dependency with 65,000,000. One does not have to hold a low opinion of human

nature to recognize more than a grain of truth in the facetious
definition of gratitude as "a lively sense of favors to come." Moreover, in this titanic struggle of armed power the prestige of the
Netherlands was extremely low. Overrun at home, the Dutch had
practically nothing with which to carry on the struggle against the
enemy. Both the Dutch and the Indonesians had to look to others
for liberation.

Nevertheless, the Dutch authorities had everything to gain and
nothing to lose in following a more accommodating policy. Tardi-
ly and without enthusiasm, they made only general promises. It is
true that the Dutch government-in-exile could not, without violating democratic principles, commit the Dutch nation to a specific
policy, which it might in any case repudiate. But the times called
for imagination and boldness. By yielding generously to Indonesian aspirations, they could probably retain much; by refusing
to concede anything, they stood in danger of losing all. Under the
circumstances they faced a very grave responsibility.

In February of 1940 there was introduced into the Volksraad the
Wiwoho Resolution, so called after its Indonesian sponsor, which
requested that an imperial conference be called and that the government of the Indies be modified in the direction of a democratic,
parliamentary system, with full ministerial responsibility to the
Volksraad. In response to this resolution, which came up for consideration after the German invasion of the Netherlands, the government, with slighting reference to ideals, declared that it could
make no promises because political reforms required the sanction
of the Netherlands parliament. At about the same time a resolution introduced by Thamrin, the leader of the Indonesian nationalists in the Volksraad, came up for discussion. This resolution asked
for the official substitution of the term "Indonesian" for "In-
lander," and of "Indonesia" for "Netherlands Indie." This request,
too, was brusquely rejected. This led to deep disappointment and
even bitterness among Indonesians.

Realizing that it had made a mistake, the government shortly
thereafter reversed itself in part by promising to call an imperial
conference after the war. To prepare for this, the governor-general
appointed a commission to ascertain by means of hearings what
political reforms the various elements of the population desired.

No one took this commission very seriously because it had no power to make recommendations, save on minor matters. A leading nationalist group called the GAPI at first refused to appear before it, but when finally persuaded to do so presented the commission with a memorandum in which future Netherlands-Indonesian relations were envisaged as taking the form of a confederation. This commission, composed of three Netherlanders, three Indonesians, and one Chinese, with Mr. F. H. Visman, a member of the Council of the Indies, as chairman, was appointed on September 14, 1940. Its report appeared a few weeks before Java fell to the Japanese.

Indonesian leaders had long pleaded for the establishment of an Indonesian militia. As early as 1913 *Budi Utomo* had advocated this, requesting that the creation of a militia be accompanied by the institution of a popular representative body. To this deep-seated desire of the Indonesian people the Indies government made no concessions until suddenly, on July 4, 1941, it introduced in the Volksraad a measure to create an Indonesian militia, but of only a few thousand, and withholding from the Volksraad any participation in determining how this militia was to be recruited. A large number of the nationalist members voted against the proposal; a smaller number of the nationalists withdrew from the work of the Volksraad. When Indonesians as well as Netherlanders asked whether the adhesion by the Netherlands to the Atlantic Charter meant that there would be a change in the future of Netherlands-Indonesian relations, the government replied that the signing of the charter gave no reason for a reconsideration of the objectives of its policy. The effect of all these acts was to alienate moderate Indonesian nationalists.

Basic Social and Economic Problems

In common with all tropical and subtropical countries, the Netherlands Indies faced a number of difficult socio-economic problems which had to be solved if political autonomy were to have any real meaning. The things that made it relatively easy for a small country like the Netherlands to hold in subjection a large country like Indonesia also make it difficult to give the dependency effective freedom.

HETEROGENEITY OF POPULATION

The official census of 1930 gave the Netherlands Indies a total population of 60,727,000. Of this total about 97.5 per cent were Indonesians, about 2 per cent, or 1,250,000, Chinese, and a little less than one-half of 1 per cent, or 250,000, were Europeans. In addition there were 116,000 Arabs, Indians, and other Asiatics. Of those classified as Europeans, probably as many as three-fourths were Eurasians. Of the Chinese, at least a third were Indo-Chinese—persons of mixed Indonesian and Chinese blood. The indigenous population is broadly classified as Indonesian, but it is composed of peoples or tribes differing considerably in language, customs, and cultural development. On Java alone there are seven such ethnic groups, although all but a small percentage of its population is accounted for by three peoples—the Javanese, 28,000,-000; the Sundanese, 8,000,000; and the Madurese, 9,305,862. On Sumatra there are nineteen, on Borneo two, and in the Great East thirty-eight ethnic groups, counting only those with a numerical strength of 25,000 or more. The distribution of the population over numerous islands, many of them small and widely separated from each other, retarded unification. Religiously the country is fairly homogeneous, almost nine-tenths of the population being Moslem. Nearly all of the Indonesian inhabitants of Java adhere to that faith, as well as the majority of those on Sumatra. There are, however, important religious minorities. Pagans, found on Borneo and the eastern part of the archipelago, number about three and a half millions. Over two million Christians, about a million and a half Buddhists (the Chinese), and a million and a half Hindus (the Balinese) constitute other significant minorities.

Social and cultural integration was also retarded by a notable feature of Dutch policy, namely, differentiation based upon race. It was most marked in the legal, educational, political, and administrative systems. Racial discrimination was not the object, for the Dutch in the Indies have been remarkably free from racial feeling. The policy was never consciously adopted; it just developed. In the last decades it was increasingly subjected to criticism. The justification most frequently advanced was that the social needs of the various racial groups differed greatly and could not be met by legislation applying to all alike. The Dutch saw no justification for compelling Indonesians to live under European law or Europeans under the customary law of the Indonesians, nor for compelling the children of all races to attend the same type of school.

In the Indies Government Act and in Indies legislation the population was classified into three groups—Europeans, Indonesians, and non-indigenous Asiatics. In education there was differentiation at the base and unification at the top. There were separate elementary schools for Europeans, Chinese, and Indonesians; but the intermediate and higher professional schools were open to all races. The Indonesians remained under the customary law of their own ethnic group, unless they chose to assume the status of a European. For the other two main population groups a great deal of unification had been achieved. With the exception of criminal procedural law and some rules of family law, the Chinese had been assimilated to the Europeans. However, there was a provision of the Organic Act that land could not be alienated to non-indigenous persons, a provision that has had profound consequences for the social and economic life of the country. Administrative positions were generally open to all Dutch subjects, regardless of race. An exception, however, was the highly important department of interior administration, which was divided into a European and an Indonesian corps, the two being kept quite distinct. In Java the European corps was gradually being withdrawn from the lower branches of the service. As has already been noted, the population was likewise divided into the three main groups for electoral purposes. Each group formed a separate electoral corps, and to each group a fixed number of seats in the representative bodies was assigned.

Some amalgamation of peoples is, however, slowly taking place. The difficulties created by the diversity of languages is to some extent overcome by the use of "market Malay," which is understood by all people living along the coasts. With Malay as a base but with a borrowing of words and terms from other indigenous and foreign languages, the nationalists have developed a new "Indonesian" language, which has become the official language of the movement and of the Republic. There has also developed some mobility among the peoples. In 1930 over a million Javanese were living outside of Java, and about 75,000 persons belonging to tribes in the Outer Islands were living in Java.

While there has been some cultural and social integration, differences in development are still very great among the Indonesians. There are the Javanese, Balinese, and other peoples with an old, highly developed culture, and there are the nomadic tribes in Borneo and the interior of New Guinea, who are barely out of the Stone Age. Among people differing so widely there could be no strong sense of unity. "There was no sentiment of Indonesian nationality," concludes Raymond Kennedy, the foremost American authority on the peoples of Indonesia in his book, *The Ageless Indies.* "The Javanese had a rudimentary sense of unity among themselves, and so did the Sumatran Malays; but between the two groups there was hardly a trace of a common bond. Even within Java itself, the Sundanese of the western districts considered themselves quite separate from the true Javanese of the center and east. The Indonesian population was split up by a great number of these divisions, with a wide variety of mutually unintelligible languages and an extensive range of cultural differences."

Similar views were expressed by Mr. G. H. C. Hart, an outstanding Dutch official in the Indies; but he added a significant conclusion. Writing in 1942, Mr. Hart stated, "The national consciousness is as yet by no means formed and mature, but while for forty years it was chiefly the Government who had been endeavoring to forge the entity, there are now at last mighty and active forces, which will in the future be the decisive power in shaping the destiny of the archipelago."

Before leaving this subject something should be said about the problem of the Chinese, who constitute a very important economic group in Indonesia. They have their own cultural life and wish to retain it. Relations between the Indonesians and the Chinese were not always of the most friendly character, chiefly for the reason that Indonesian laborers, small businessmen, and intellectuals met severe competition from the numerous Chinese. In 1945 hundreds of Chinese were slain and their villages set on fire by Indonesian extremists. The political loyalties of the Chinese were divided.

A third of them were not born in the Indies, and among them were many coolies, who were politically indifferent. The politically conscious Chinese were divided into three groups. There was first of all a group whose political interests were largely centered on China. Since their economic interests were in the Indies, however, it was frequently said of them that "They wish to eat from two plates." The other two groups had turned their minds wholly toward the Indies. One of these groups identified Chinese interests with the Dutch, and sought to maintain and promote its welfare and position in cooperation with the Europeans. But a small group had assimilated itself to the Indonesian population and made common cause with the Indonesian nationalists. The Arabs were divided in much the same way, save that there were no Arab coolies.

The position of the Eurasians was very difficult. Legally assimilated to the Europeans but frequently engaged in a desperate struggle for a livelihood, the Eurasians often found themselves in an unhappy role. Most of them were members of the Indo-European Union, which was nominally a party for all who considered the Indies as their home, but which was in fact the party of the Eurasians. Very loyal to the Netherlands, it nevertheless sharply opposed the government on several issues. In the last decade it had become more critical of governmental policy, and it had joined the Indonesian nationalists in demanding more autonomy for the Indies' government.

In the earlier days of the Volksraad, "associationist parties" —that is, parties seeking membership among all racial groups— were fairly strong; but with the rise of the nationalist movement they declined. Where held together by religious principles, as for example in the Christian Political party and the Catholic party, they demonstrated some permanence.

POPULATION PRESSURE ON JAVA

The population was distributed very unevenly among the islands. In 1930, 41,718,000 people lived on Java and the small dependent island of Madura. These two islands, comprising 7 per cent of the area, supported two-thirds of the total population of the Indies. The population of the other larger islands was as follows: Sumatra, 8,254,000; Borneo, 2,194,000; Celebes, 4,226,-000; Timor and adjoining islands, 1,656,000; Bali, 1,101,000; and the Moluccas and New Guinea, 893,000.

The contrasts in population density are striking. The population of Java and Madura was estimated at 49,000,000 in 1941. This is an average of 960 persons per square mile, and the population is increasing annually by about 700,000, or about 14 per square mile. The density of some districts runs as high as 2,200 per square mile, and one district near Cheribon had 4,100 per square mile! Bali, too, has a population density approaching that of many districts of Java. When it is noted that the population of Java is about 95 per cent rural, it becomes apparent how appalling this problem is. By contrast, Borneo in 1930 had a population density of only 10 per square mile, and the Moluccas and New Guinea only 6 per square mile. Sumatra in 1930 had an average of about 50 per square mile, but this varied greatly from district to district. In the West Coast district it reached about 100 per square mile.

The ability of the islands to support human life varies considerably. The two most important factors, naturally, are rainfall and the fertility of the soil. New Guinea and the islands near or on the equator have a heavy rainfall throughout the year. The islands south of the equator—Java and the chain of islands to the east of it—have less rainfall and also have a dry season. While Java has an abundance of rain, the precipitation decreases eastward along this string of islands. The islands in the southeast part of the archipelago and directly north of Australia are semiarid. Dutch Borneo and Dutch New Guinea, though they constitute about half of the total area of the Indies, support less than one-twentieth of its population. This is due in large part to the lack of fertility of their soil. The islands with the most recent volcanic activities have the richest soil. Since there has been no recent volcanic activity on Borneo and New Guinea, their soils have been formed long ago, and the soluble elements have been thoroughly leached by the heavy precipitation.

To this desperate problem of the overpopulation of Java there seem to be only two main solutions, and the Dutch were pushing both. One was the emigration of large numbers of young people from Java to the less densely populated islands where there was still fertile but unused land. This could be done on a large scale only through government encouragement, planning, and aid. It required a great deal of official propaganda to induce the Javanese peasants to leave their ancestral home for new and distant settlements. The pressure of poverty, however, and the vision of better conditions led many to make the venture. The costs per family to the government were at first so high as to seem to bar resettlement schemes on any scale; but after many years of experience most of the problems of administration were successfully overcome. The number of colonists leaving Java was steadily increased: 20,000 in 1937; 32,000 in 1938; 45,000 in 1939; 53,000 in 1940; 53,000 in 1941; and the figure set for 1942 was 65,000.

It is obvious that the removal of even 65,000 young people a year cannot ease the population pressure of an island where the average annual increase is over 650,000. If continued indefinitely, the end result might merely be the spread of the problem throughout all of the islands. The other chief measure relied upon was the rapid industrialization of Java. It was hoped that the effect of these two measures would be a speedy rise in the standards of living and a consequent drop in the birth rate. In the last few years before the Japanese invasion great strides were made under the leadership of such able, devoted, and progressive officials as Van Mook, Sitsen, and Hart; but no responsible person was under the illusion that the pressing problem caused by Java's teeming millions had been solved. As a result of the Japanese occupation and the events since the end of the war, the problem is now undoubtedly more acute than ever.

LOW STANDARD OF LIVING

Closely allied to the problem of the population pressure on Java is the low standard of living that prevails throughout the country. These standards are not low in comparison with those of neighboring Asiatic countries, but compared with those of the West they are extremely inadequate. The average area of tillable land farmed per family on Java was less than two acres, and the average annual income of the peasant family was under $30. In the Outer Islands the peasant family enjoyed an income twice as large. The total national income was both low and very unequally distributed among the three main racial groups. The average annual national income for the years 1937 to 1939 was estimated at about one and one-tenth billion dollars. Of this total, the share that went to the Indonesians was about three-quarters of a billion dollars, or not over twelve or thirteen dollars per person. Statistics indicate that in the years just preceding the war 32,000 Indonesians, 44,000 Chinese and Arabs, and 66,000 Europeans had an annual income of $475 or more; while 2,644 Europeans, some 600 Chinese, and 122 Indonesians enjoyed incomes of $6,400 or more.

These few figures reveal the main outlines of the social and economic structure of the Indies' society before the war. The Europeans formed the top and the Indonesians the base of the social pyramid, with the Chinese and Arabs in the center. This, of course, was the picture only in general outline. Eurasians, who were assimilated to the Europeans, had in many cases been practically absorbed by the Indonesian villages, whereas Chinese were found among the wealthiest people of the Indies as well as among the poorest. At least a third of the Chinese were coolies.

How to raise the standard of living—which means how to raise the per capita production—is the first problem of Indonesia as well as of the neighboring countries. A more equitable division of the existing income would be no solution to this basic problem, for even if the whole of the prewar national income had been distributed among the Indonesians alone, the per capita income would have been only seventeen dollars. The Europeans, by their managerial skill and knowledge of technology, probably contributed more to the national income than they received. Many Indonesians have come to desire most of the services which governments in the West now provide, but there is lacking the national income to maintain them. Traditional native economy, because of its low productivity, cannot produce sufficient revenue to meet the costs of these services. It was estimated that before the great depression 40 per cent of the government revenue came from the Indonesians, 40 per cent from Western industries, and 20 per cent from government industries. The East Coast of Sumatra, the prosperous center of Western agricultural enterprises, annually yielded a very large surplus of public revenue after the deduction of local costs of administration. According to the Visman Commission, the

Indonesian section of the population in 1913 contributed more in taxes than did the non-indigenous part, but in the years after that date the share of the Europeans and Chinese was greater. The rapid expansion of Western enterprises dates from about that time.

In this connection it should be noted that the East Indian government was itself deeply involved in economic activities. Aside from the usual government enterprises, such as the postal service and savings, the government owned and operated pawnshops, opium factories, telegraph lines, coal, gold, silver, and tin mines, and teak forests, as well as cinchona, rubber, tea, and gutta-percha plantations. A considerable share of the government's income came from the profits of these industries. Moreover, the revenue from the government enterprises remained within the country, and all of it went to the maintenance of government services. In these services and industries the government employed the most recent advances in science and technology.

The Indies government was thus highly dependent upon Western industries for necessary revenue to maintain and expand its social services. Indeed, the favorable position of the Indies in the world market was in no small measure due to the work of experimental stations and research laboratories, which enabled the Dutch to produce more effectively than many of their competitors. Unfortunately, the widespread introduction of Western capital and methods of production made it difficult for the Indonesians to advance economically. They often found competition against Western enterprises difficult, and they were not readily given positions of responsibility in them.

In this penetration of the Indies' economy by Western capital, organization, and technology, the Indonesians furnished the land and labor. Did the native population get much benefit from this unequal partnership? Was the trend in the direction of control over capital and technology by the Indonesians, or were the Westerners steadily obtaining greater mastery over the land and labor of the Indonesians? The best opinion seems to be that up to 1930 native production suffered from the introduction of Western capital and technology, and that its share in the total output had declined; but that after 1930 the trend was favorable to the Indonesians. To combat the depression, the government adopted a

new economic policy called a "crisis policy," but which was basic
and gave every evidence of becoming permanent. By means of this
policy, which involved extensive and thoroughgoing intervention
in the economic life of the country, the government made a tremendous effort to develop the economic life of the Indies and to
draw the Indonesians fully into this development. The Japanese
invasion put an end to this great effort to transform a colonial
economy in the interest of improving the welfare of the native
population.

LAND POLICY

Western enterprises, in order to operate, need access to resources—land, in the case of agricultural industries—and to an
adequate and dependable labor supply. In the early years Western
capital operating in the Outer Islands believed that such a labor
supply could be obtained only by importing "contract" coolies
from China and Java. The labor contract, with its penal sanction,
was for many years the subject of bitter controversy. Under the
terms of the contract, both employer and employee could be fined
or imprisoned for failure to live up to the agreement, but in addition, the contract laborer could be compelled to return to the
plantation from which he deserted to complete the period of his
contract, which was usually two or three years. The opponents
of this system won, and it had been completely discarded before
the war.

The Dutch policy with respect to land was one of the most enlightened ever adopted by a colonial power. In competition with
outside capital and entrepreneurs, the economically weak native
soon loses his land. This has been the practically universal experience in so-called "backward" areas. In Puerto Rico the United
States government has had to engage in a long struggle to overcome the evil of large-scale landholding by non-indigenous individuals and corporations. Under the East Indian Government Act
only indigenous persons were permitted to own land; they were
prohibited from alienating their land to other than Indonesians.

This law excluded from the right of landownership even
Eurasians, who are certainly as much Indonesian as they are
Dutch, and Indo-Chinese, some of whom are members of families

which have lived in the Indies for centuries. Non-natives could acquire ownership only of small tracts in urban areas. Non-indigenous persons and corporations could acquire the use of public land under leases or concessions for periods not exceeding seventy-five years, or they could rent land from the native owners. In the latter case, the contracts were carefully regulated by the government. As for minerals, the legal assumption was that all rights vested in the government concessions to exploit subsoil resources were granted for seventy-five years at most, and for a maximum area of one thousand hectares (one hectare equaling two and one-half acres). The government received rentals as well as a fixed percentage of the value of the production. The government also engaged directly in the export of some minerals, especially coal and tin, and indirectly through large stock owner-ship in tin mining and oil companies.

EDUCATION

Only slightly more than 6 per cent of the total population were literate in 1930, and, according to estimates, about 11 per cent in 1940. The percentage of literacy varied greatly among the various population groups. Of the Europeans (including the Eurasians), 75 per cent were literate; of the Chinese, 29 per cent; and of the Indonesians, 6.4 per cent. Literacy among the Indonesians varied greatly from island to island and even among districts within the same island. There was a higher percentage of literacy in the Outer Islands than in Java and Madura. In Sumatra, 10 per cent of the population was literate; in the Moluccas, 15 per cent; and in the residency of Menado (the Minahassa), 20 per cent. The last two, it should be noted, were the most Dutchified districts in the Indies. Relatively few people could read and write Dutch, probably not over 650,000 persons in 1941. The Dutch did not force their culture or language on the Indonesians. Those who could read and write Dutch were distributed among the chief racial groups as follows: Europeans, 200,000; Indonesians, 400,000; and Chinese, 50,000.

As compared with the Philippines, educational development in the Indies was backward, especially on the intermediate and higher levels. In 1939 there were 2,324,000 pupils attending elementary schools and 53,000 in intermediate schools. The number of persons who attended secondary schools was still small, and the Indonesians constituted only a small percentage of the graduates. In the school year 1938–39 the secondary schools graduated 777 students, of whom 457 were Europeans, 204 Indonesians, and 116 Chinese and Arabs.

Facilities for higher education were rather limited and the number of students small. In the academic year 1938–39 there were only 1,100 students enrolled in the university. The professional schools produced only 81 graduates, of whom 20 were Europeans, 40 Indonesians, and 21 Chinese and Arabs. Of the 81 graduates, 12 were in engineering, 30 in law, and 39 in medicine. Indonesian students were most numerous in medicine and law; the number in technology was extremely small. Many Europeans and some Indonesians and Chinese completed their higher education in the Netherlands. Not long before the Japanese invasion, plans were completed for uniting all of the professional schools in a university, and for adding two new colleges—of agriculture, and of philosophy, literature, and sociology. In contrast with some countries in the region, the secondary schools and colleges in the Indies maintained European standards.

There was much criticism of the educational system by both Dutch and Indonesians, and there were plans under way for basic reforms. It was attacked for its failure effectively to combat illiteracy, and because the education provided was not sufficiently related to the Indonesian environment, was too bookish, and did not place enough emphasis upon training for citizenship. Many Indonesians resented the separate schools for the different racial groups as savoring of racial discrimination.

A chief difficulty in the solution of the educational problem in Indonesia, as in other countries of the region and, alas, in many parts of the world, is financial. How can an adequate school system be paid for? Real progress in the campaign against illiteracy would require an immense expansion of existing educational facilities, which would involve enormous costs. Indonesia's national income is not large enough to defray the expense; yet economic conditions cannot be greatly improved until educational opportunities are more generally available. The two will rise together, but it will necessarily be a slow process.

The Japanese Occupation

"Japan is quite popular among us." So wrote Sutan Sjahrir in his diary on November 16, 1936. He continued: "Although most do not dare to say so openly, Japan has the sympathy of our people and the Japanese are the most popular foreigners in our country; our people have until now learned to know them from their best behavior." Later he wrote that sympathy for Japan was a way of expressing antipathy toward Dutch dominion, and that it had its roots in the Asiatic feeling of inferiority, which sought compensation in glorification of the Japanese. He added, however, that the Indonesians did not go so far as to wish to exchange Dutch for Japanese rule.

Japanese propaganda during the occupation was aimed at rooting out of the Indies everything that was Dutch or lent prestige to the Netherlands. Practically the whole Dutch population was interned, as well as a large number of Indo-European men and a few Chinese, Ambonese, Menadonese, and Timorese—ethnic groups most loyal to the Dutch. This wholesale internment of the Dutch was probably more for political than for military reasons. The rapid conquest of Indonesia had irreparably damaged Dutch prestige; the Japanese undermined it further by spreading rumors that Queen Wilhelmina had died, and by killing the Dutch government in London with silence. Whenever references were made to the Allies, Great Britain and the United States were mentioned, but never the Netherlands.

Shortly after the conquest of the Indies the Japanese launched their Three A Movement as the beginning of a campaign of political propaganda against the Allies and the West, carried on under the general theme of "Asia for the Asiatics," but, of course, under the leadership of Japan. It was called the Three A Movement after the first letter of the word "Asia," which appeared in each of the following slogans: "Japan, the Leader of Asia," "Japan, the Protector of Asia," and "Japan, the Light of Asia." An Indonesian was given the leadership of the movement, which sought to stimulate contributions with which to carry on the campaign by means of pamphlets and placards. This movement had some influence on the masses but very little on the intellectuals, and was soon abandoned.

The Japanese, however, continued their anti-Western propaganda. The youth, especially, received much attention. School children were trained in gymnastics and sports, and thereafter were given military drill and taught Japanese ideology. The Japanese organized military and semimilitary corps, chief among them being *Heiho* and the *Peta*. They were designed chiefly for guerrilla warfare in case of Allied landings, but to be useful in the Japanese service their members were subjected to large amounts of Japanese propaganda.

Indonesian officials who failed to fall in line with Japanese ideas were removed and replaced by more pliable Indonesians. Nearly all of the existing political parties were brought together in a Peoples' Strength Concentration, or *Poetera,* under the leadership of Sukarno and Hatta, later president and vice-president respectively of the Republic of Indonesia, and two other Indonesians, one a prominent Moslem leader. Further organization of political parties was prohibited. The cooperation of a leading Moslem political figure in the Concentration was a great gain for the Japanese, since hitherto the Moslem parties had adhered strictly to their policy of independent political action. Frequent attempts before the war to unite all Indonesian political parties had failed, chiefly because of this Moslem exclusiveness. *Poetera* and its leaders supported the Japanese in the war. Sukarno also used his influence to induce Indonesians to join Japanese labor battalions. Those who joined suffered severe hardships and many never returned.

At the time of the Japanese invasion, the Indonesian nationalist leaders, apparently after consultation, divided into two groups. One group, of whom Sukarno and Hatta were the leading figures, decided upon a course of collaboration with the Japanese to see what could be won for the nationalist movement by this policy. A second group, chief among whom were Sjahrir and Sjarifoeddin, both later to become prime ministers of the Republic of Indonesia, went underground to organize and carry on resistance against the

Japanese. Sukarno and Hatta continued collaboration long after it had become clear that they could gain nothing for Indonesian nationalism by doing so. Some Indonesian leaders, and Sjahrir especially, were very critical of their conduct. The latter attacked them in his brochure, "My Struggle."

When the Japanese began to lose their confidence of victory, they resorted to setting up puppet regimes and granting them independence. By this means they hoped to win these peoples and enlist them in resisting Allied landings. Such regimes were set up in Burma and in the Philippines in 1943. In Indonesia the Japanese moved leisurely, since the country did not seem to be threatened by early Allied attack. In June 1943, the Japanese prime minister, General Tojo, who visited Java the following month, promised the Indonesians participation in the government of their country. In September there was established a Central Advisory Council, along with advisory councils for municipalities and residencies. Sukarno became the president of the Central Advisory Council. Sumatra, which was under the jurisdiction of the Japanese military commander at Singapore, did not receive such a council until June 1945.

In November 1943, Sukarno, Hatta, and a third member of the Central Advisory Council traveled to Japan to extend to the Japanese government the "gratitude" of fifty million Indonesians on Java for the right to participate in the administration of the island. In September 1944, the new Japanese cabinet under General Koiso as prime minister promised that Indonesia would be granted independence. In March 1945, there was instituted on Java a Committee of Investigation for the Preparation for Independence. This committee announced in July that it had completed its work. It also adopted a "declaration of determination" proposed by Sukarno, according to which the Indonesian people were resolved to fight by the side of their comrade, great Nippon, against the Allied enemy, and to establish an independent state. In July 1945, when the military situation had become desperate for the Japanese, there was organized a New Peoples' Movement for the purpose of intensifying Indonesian support of the Japanese war effort. Sukarno was likewise the leader of this movement.

Proclamation of the Republic of Indonesia

On August 8, 1945, Sukarno, Hatta, and a third Indonesian, Wediodiningrat by name, left Batavia by plane for Saigon. They had been summoned by Marshal Terauchi, the commander-in-chief of the Japanese armies in the southern regions, to confer with him about the proclamation of Indonesian independence. At the conference with Terauchi on the eleventh, Sukarno and Hatta received Japanese decorations, and the three Indonesians were informed of Japan's decision to grant their country independence. On the fourteenth, the day before the Japanese capitulation, the delegation returned to Batavia. The Japanese surrender apparently occurred sooner than Terauchi had expected, for a Commission for the Preparation of the Independence of Indonesia was to meet on the nineteenth. In view of the reports of Japanese capitulation on the fifteenth, the commission met earlier, and after an all-night session decided to issue a proclamation of independence in the name of the Indonesian people. This was done on the seventeenth of August at eleven o'clock. It was not until the twenty-second that the capitulation was officially announced by the Japanese commander on Java.

Most Dutchmen are convinced that the Japanese government, seeing its rapidly impending doom, deliberately planted this political time bomb in Indonesia, and that various Japanese authorities on Java provided a second time bomb by turning over their weapons to Javanese extremists.

British Occupation (September 1945–November 30, 1946)

It had been expected that the American forces would occupy Indonesia, but not long before the Japanese capitulation this task was assigned to the British. The sudden end of the war found the British unprepared for this additional assignment, and as a result it was not until September 29 that the first British forces arrived. Moreover, they came in small numbers for the sizable task of disarming and repatriating 283,000 Japanese troops scattered over so large an area as Indonesia, and of liberating and protecting over 200,000 Dutch and other Allied prisoners of war and internees. With so few troops at his disposal and with a government of a "Republic of Indonesia" claiming jurisdiction over the country, General Christison, the commander of the British forces, found himself in an awkward position. The leaders of the Republic had worked feverishly to fill the governmental vacuum produced by the sudden collapse of Japan and the inability of the Dutch to reoccupy the country, but had not yet received the recognition of any country. Under the circumstances General Christison could hardly do otherwise than give some sort of de facto recognition to the Republic and request its cooperation in the fulfillment of his task. The Dutch, however, regarded this as an act of intervention and were bitter about it. Many Indonesians, especially the prewar administrative and police officials, who had been wavering, now began to line up with the Republic. As an acute Dutch observer put it, "The Republican house of cards has now received a firm foundation."

Early Dutch-Indonesian Negotiations

With the liberation of the Netherlands, the Dutch government returned to Dutch soil, the old ministry resigned, and in its place came a liberal cabinet composed largely of representatives of the Labor party. This government was desirous of moving forward rapidly and generously on the basis of Queen Wilhelmina's radio address of December 6, 1942, in which, on behalf of her government, the queen promised "to create the occasion for a joint consultation about the structure of the Kingdom and its parts in order to adapt it to the changed circumstances." She forecast "without anticipating the recommendations of the future conference, that they will be directed toward a commonwealth in which the Netherlands, Indonesia, Surinam, and Curaçao will participate, with complete self-reliance and freedom of conduct for each part regarding its internal affairs, but with readiness to render mutual assistance." The Dutch government, however, stated that it would not consult with Sukarno, who had collaborated with Japan and whose desire for freedom seemed to be without a sense of responsibility.

The Dutch objections to dealing with the representatives of the Republic lost much of their force when President Sukarno's collaborationist cabinet was replaced on November 14 by a new cabinet headed by Sjahrir, whose record was absolutely free from taint of collaboration with the Japanese. From that time on negotiations between the Dutch authorities and leaders of the Republic have gone on intermittently. Twice negotiations were interrupted by Dutch "police action" against the Republic, the first time in July 1947 and the second in December 1948. In the early months of 1946 Sjahrir and a small delegation went to the Netherlands for a conference with Minister-President Schermerhorn and his colleagues, but apart from this occasion the negotiations all took place on Java.

The Dutch government made an important declaration of policy on February 10, 1946. It proposed, in consultation with elected and authorized representatives of Indonesia, to agree upon a governmental structure for the kingdom and for Indonesia, based upon equalitarian, democratic principles. This structure would be for a limited period, during which the conditions would be created for a free decision as to whether the two countries should continue their relations on the basis of a complete and voluntary partnership. Any difference of opinion over the question whether that period should be further extended before a free choice was possible would be resolved either by conciliation or by arbitration. The structure of the government for the limited period would be determined by discussion and agreement on the basis of the following main principles:

(1) The establishment of a Commonwealth of Indonesia, partner in the kingdom, composed of territories with varying degrees of self-government.

(2) An Indonesian citizenship for all persons born in Indonesia; Dutch and Indonesian citizens to have all rights of citizenship in all parts of the kingdom.

(3) The regulation of the internal affairs of Indonesia by its own government, with a democratically elected representative body in which Indonesians would have a substantial majority; a ministry composed in political harmony with the representative body; and a representative of the Crown as head of the government.

(4) A few special powers for the representatives of the Crown, subject to responsibility to the government of the kingdom, for assuring fundamental rights, good administration, and sound

finances, these powers to be exercised only when these special rights and interests were violated.

(5) Guarantees in the constitution with respect to such fundamental rights as religious freedom, legal equality regardless of race or religion, protection of persons and property, independence of the judiciary, protection of the rights of minorities, freedom of education, and freedom of opinion and expression.

(6) Central organs functioning for the whole kingdom, composed of representatives of its various parts.

(7) The Netherlands' support for the application by Indonesia for admission to membership in the United Nations.

This proposal was unacceptable to the leaders of the Republic, who insisted that recognition by the Netherlands of the Republic as a sovereign state should be the starting point of the negotiations. On this basis of equality they were willing to accept close political relations with the Netherlands and cooperation in all fields. According to this view, the agreement would have to take the form of a treaty. Some Javanese nationalists disliked the idea of a federal structure for Indonesia. This dislike stemmed in part from a fear that it meant a Dutch move to divide and rule, but also from a desire to set up a unitary government which would give the concentrated population of Java a practically free hand to rule the whole of Indonesia.

This Republican counterproposal had attractive features for the Dutch government, which recognized that the Republic, regardless of its origin, was looked upon by the Javanese nationalists, and also to some extent by Indonesian nationalists outside of Java, as the translation into reality of their deep-seated longing for national self-expression and independence. However divided the groups within the government of the Republic might be, they found in it a common, unifying ideal, and Javanese nationalists could not be induced to give it up. The Dutch government also believed that once the Republic were given some form of recognition, it would abandon its revolutionary tactics and set its own house in order. It saw no insuperable difficulty in fitting recognition of the Republic into the framework of the declaration of February 10.

The Netherlands government therefore was willing to recognize the de facto jurisdiction of the Republic, but only over those parts of Java and Madura which did not belong to the areas under Allied occupation. The Indonesians, however, demanded that the Netherlands recognize the jurisdiction of the Republic as extending to all of Sumatra as well, and even made claims upon a large part of Celebes and other islands. The Dutch government freely admitted that Allied and Dutch authority was limited to a few key points in Sumatra, and that the Republic had set up a certain administrative apparatus there. It contended, however, that in many sections of the island there was no government at all, and that in other parts Republican authorities could barely maintain themselves and were in constant personal danger. The Dutch government likewise objected to putting the agreement into the form of a treaty. It contended that all of the demands of the nationalists could as well be guaranteed in a constitutional document.

Negotiations during the first year of liberation from Japan made little progress and seemed to have reached a deadlock. Meanwhile, a strange event had occurred in the Republic. During the night of June 27, 1946, Sjahrir and several other ministers were kidnaped. They were released after a couple of days, but President Sukarno declared a state of emergency and for several weeks assumed all power, military and civil. The kidnaping of the ministers was part of a plot to overthrow the government and was led by Tan Malakka, a Trotskyite Communist, and Soebardjo, a disaffected former minister.

Reorganization in Non-Republican Territory

In contrast with the situation on Java and Sumatra, in Borneo and the Great East the Dutch were able to establish law and order first and negotiate afterward. From July 15 to July 25, 1946, there met at Malino on Celebes a conference, called by Lieutenant Governor-General Van Mook, of representatives of Borneo and the islands to the east to consider governmental reorganization. This conference passed a number of resolutions the contents of which may be summarized as calling for the organization of the whole of Indonesia into a federation, the United States of Indonesia, composed of four parts—Java, Sumatra, Borneo, and the Great East. After consulting with representatives of minority groups—Dutch, Eurasian, Chinese, and Arab—in a conference held at Pangkal Pinang in early October, Van Mook proceeded to set up a government for the State of Indonesia in December. This was the first step in the direction of creating a federal state.

The Linggadjati Agreement

The Dutch ministry was reconstituted in July 1946, after the first postwar parliamentary elections had been held, but continued to be based upon a Labor-Catholic coalition. Negotiations during the first year had been retarded by the frequent necessity of hasty visits by Van Mook to the Hague for consultation, or by visits of Dutch cabinet members to Batavia. In August the Netherlands government decided to resort to an unusual expedient, namely, to send to Java a commission-general, composed of three members and clothed with extensive authority, to aid Van Mook in the discussions with representatives of the Republic. It was hoped that this would make possible speedier and broader progress. The commission would also assist Lieutenant Governor-General Van Mook in his governmental functions. The commission, headed by the former prime minister, Schermerhorn, arrived in Batavia in the middle of September. The new discussions with representatives of the Republic began on October 6, under the chairmanship of the British special commissioner, Lord Killearn. An agreement, called the Linggadjati Agreement after the hill station near Cheribon, Java, where the conference was held, was initialed on November 15, 1946.

This agreement, sometimes also called the Cheribon Agreement, contains eighteen articles, the chief provisions of which are as follows:

(1) Recognition by the Netherlands government of the government of the Republic of Indonesia as exercising de facto authority over Java, Madura, and Sumatra.

(2) Cooperation between the two governments in the rapid formation of a sovereign democratic state on a federal basis to

be called the United States of Indonesia, of which the Republic of Indonesia, Borneo, and the Great East would be the component parts.

(3) Drafting of the constitution of the United States of Indonesia by a constituent assembly composed of the democratically nominated representatives of the Republic and of the other future parts of the United States of Indonesia.

(4) Cooperation between the Dutch government and the government of the Republic in the establishment of a Netherlands-Indonesian Union, composed on the one hand of the Netherlands, Surinam, and Curaçao and on the other of the United States of Indonesia, in order to promote joint interests in foreign relations, defense, finance, and economic and cultural matters.

(5) Application by the United States of Indonesia for membership in the United Nations.

(6) Settlement by arbitration of any dispute arising from the agreement.

This important agreement still needed to be ratified and implemented. As the minister of overseas territories stated in his written comments on it, "This is no constitution, but rather a statement of principles. It is not a legal but a political document."

There was considerable opposition to the agreement in Holland, led by Gerbrandy, prime minister during the war, and Welter, who had been an official in Indonesia and a former minister of colonies; but it was approved by a substantial vote, 65 to 30, in the Second Chamber on December 20, 1946. The Central Indonesian National Committee, which served as the parliament of the Republic and whose members were appointed by the president, approved the agreement by a vote of 284 to 2; but two leading parties abstained from voting. It is also significant that at the same time another resolution was adopted, stating that one of the important tasks of the Republican government was to struggle for the independence of the non-Republican territories and to incorporate them as quickly as possible into the Republic. This resolution would hardly seem consistent with the terms of the Linggadjati Agreement.

The agreement was signed at Batavia on March 25, 1947. Throughout the period of negotiations there had been repeated outbreaks of violence, and the troubled atmosphere in which Linggadjati was finally made binding was indicated by Prime Minister Sjahrir's speech on this occasion. "Great is still the uncertainty, sharp the doubt and mistrust with respect to this important event. For most in our land the outlook upon the future is still vague and uncertain. . . . Bitter is still the hate, dark and clouded the skies of our beautiful country." He also spoke of relaxation and of refreshing air; but unfortunately these were to be of short duration.

Failure to Implement the Agreement

Hard as it was to reach the basic agreement, it proved even more difficult to implement it. The Dutch authorities finally concluded that the government of the Republic was either unwilling or unable to cooperate in carrying out the Linggadjati Agreement. Prime ministers of the Republic would accept Dutch proposals, only to be repudiated by their government. According to the Dutch, when agreements were made they were not kept. The Dutch made what it called "final" proposals on May 27, and when a satisfactory answer was not received it took "police action" against the Republic. At the request of Australia and India, the Security Council of the United Nations intervened. This body on August 1, 1947, requested the two parties to cease hostilities at once; but it did not order the Dutch troops to withdraw from the territory they had occupied. As a result, the Republic lost over half of its territory on Java and the economically important East Coast of Sumatra, as well as the Sumatran oil center of Palembang.

A Committee of Good Offices of the United Nations was set up to aid the Netherlands and Republican governments in arriving at a settlement of their difficulties. This committee, composed of representatives of Australia, Belgium, and the United States, was successful in inducing both parties to accept the Renville Agreement, so called because it was signed on the American naval vessel of that name. This agreement, signed on January 17, 1948, consists of three parts: a truce, twelve principles forming an agreed basis for a final political agreement, and six additional principles for the negotiations toward a political settlement. But the Dutch and Republican governments were no more successful in implementing this agreement than the earlier one. The Dutch again resorted to police action on December 19, 1948, this time occupying the remainder of the Republican territory.

Why did all efforts at implementation fail? To this question there is no single or simple answer. There have been charges and countercharges, incriminations and recriminations. Though the Linggadjati Agreement was approved by the necessary majority of the Dutch parliament by a substantial vote, this approval was granted because there seemed no other way out of the impasse and was therefore given reluctantly. Groups in the Republic of Indonesia were likewise opposed to the agreement, including the important *Masjoemi,* or Moslem party. Having signed the agreement, however, the Dutch were sincerely determined to carry it out.

It is difficult to escape the conclusion that there was never a real meeting of minds on either the Linggadjati Agreement or the Renville principles. The Dutch went on the assumption that until the United States of Indonesia and the Netherlands-Indonesian Union should be set up the Netherlands government was sovereign over the whole of Indonesia, and that in its relations with the Republic it was not dealing with a juridical equal but with a leading component of the future United States of Indonesia. In Linggadjati, Holland had only accepted certain basic principles for a program of far-reaching constitutional reform. The Republic, on the other hand, regarded itself as the sole and only authentic representative of Indonesian nationalism, and believed that it had achieved some sort of recognition as a sovereign state under the terms of Linggadjati and before the United Nations. The Republic's activities in continuing and seeking to extend its foreign relations, in its insistence upon retaining control of its army intact, and in its political infiltration in non-Republican territory all support this conclusion.

There is also much to indicate that the Republic believed that the heavy cost to the Dutch of maintaining armed forces in Indonesia would in time cause them to withdraw on almost any terms. Quite naturally, the Republic also relied rather heavily on foreign pressure in its favor. The leaders of the Republic apparently believed that because of fear of outside intervention,

the Dutch would not dare to resort to armed action, or if they did
so, that this would bring on foreign or United Nations intervention.
The Republican leaders were also mistaken in their view that
time was wholly on their side. The internal weakness of the
Republican government became increasingly manifest as time
went on. Its inability to control its army and terrorist bands,
especially the latter, finally drove even its best friends in the
Netherlands to desperation.

In Borneo and the Great East the Dutch were able to restore
their authority first and negotiate afterward. They first set up a
government for the State of East Indonesia and later proceeded
along the same lines for Borneo. After the military intervention of
July 1947, separatist movements developed in Madura and
Sundanese West Java. The Republic charged that these were inspired, instigated, and controlled by the Dutch. The Dutch, so it
was said, were playing the old colonial game of "divide and rule,"
and were whittling the Republic down so that it could be dominated in the proposed federation by non-Republican, Dutch-
controlled states. Even if one does not accept at its face value the
declaration of the Netherlands representative in the Security
Council that his government felt no obligation to repress spontaneous movements for autonomy by the various peoples of Indonesia, one must recognize the problem created by the peculiar
demographic and cultural conditions in this large, insular country.
The Republic naturally wished, and believed it had the moral
right, to play the predominant role in the future federation. A
unitary state structure was more in its interest than a federal one.
But this is not wanted, and is even feared, by most peoples of the
islands outside of Java.

By the last months of 1948 the struggle had developed into a
three-cornered affair. The leaders of the non-Republican territories, and especially of East Indonesia, began pressing the Dutch
to proceed with the establishment of the interim government for
the United States of Indonesia. They pointed to the provision in
Linggadjati which set January 1, 1949 as the date for the creation
of the sovereign federation, and became insistent that the Dutch
hold to it. This put the Dutch in a serious difficulty. They could
not afford to alienate the State of East Indonesia, yet they could

not reach a settlement with the Republic. The leaders of the Republic now also became alarmed, for they saw the development of a rival contender for the leadership of Indonesian nationalism, a leadership which though in a measure anti-Republican is not necessarily pro-Dutch. This fear may explain the reign of terrorism which was unleashed upon the Dutch announcement that they would proceed without the Republic.

The issue from the federationist point of view was summarized by Abdulkadir, Van Mook's Indonesian right-hand man: "Even if the Republic contends that a federation without its participation is an impossibility, the federalists are of exactly the opposite opinion. They consider a federation without the Republic in no way an impossibility. The Republic is no longer the most prominent part of Indonesia, neither as regards the strength of its population nor in economic respects. The federal union, on the other hand, can at present, financially and economically, lead its own existence and even if the current negotiations with the Republic end in deadlock—Allah forbid—a federation will yet be built up. One cannot wait for the Republic forever."

The Future

The Dutch did not regard their police action as a return to colonialism. In an official statement of December 18, 1948, announcing its impending action, the Netherlands government declared that it "will not go back or revoke any of the pledges which it has formally made with regard to the future of Indonesia; but it will not permit extremist or communist groups to prevent the realization of the aspirations of the vast majority of the Indonesian people." As Foreign Minister Stikker put it, "We have not crushed freedom, we will clear the road for its triumph." The Netherlands government has repeatedly declared that it is determined fully to carry out the terms of the Linggadjati Agreement. Important steps had already been made to that end. During 1948 the Netherlands constitution had been revised so as to make provision for the projected United States of Indonesia and the Netherlands-Indonesian Union, and the office of governor-general had been abolished and that of high commissioner of the Crown

created. In November former Prime Minister Beel was appointed
the first high commissioner to Indonesia.

The Dutch undoubtedly had reason to be apprehensive about
the leadership of the Republic and its internal condition. In
September 1948, there occurred a Communist insurrection, and
among its leaders was Sjarifoeddin, a former prime minister of the
Republic. The fact that the Republic was able to defeat the Communist forces greatly enhanced its declining prestige; but that
the movement has been really suppressed may be doubted. Nevertheless, the question still remains whether the Dutch police action
did not create as many problems as it solved. The Dutch authorities hoped by this act to repress terrorism, but instead they may
have created an irreconcilable nationalist group that will continue terrorism to the bitter end.

The proposed Netherlands-Indonesian Union represents a novel
idea in the political association of peoples living in quite different
environments and will require much good will on both sides for
its successful operation. Does enough good will remain after all
of the tragic events since Pearl Harbor? Waiving the question of
whether the United Nations Security Council properly exercised
jurisdiction in the case, it was a serious matter for a small state
like the Netherlands to defy its authority. The action also aroused
the hostility of Asiatic countries, and thus helped to increase the
tensions in a world already taut.

To prove the sincerity of its scores of declarations to Indonesia
and the world, the Dutch government will have to act quickly in
setting up the United States of Indonesia and withdrawing from
its administration. The new federal government, with inexperienced leaders at its head, will find itself faced with problems
which might prove too much even for an old, established government. Low living standards, the terrific pressure of population on
Java, illiteracy, the difficulty of maintaining adequate sanitation
and public health standards in a tropical country, the extensive
range of cultural development among peoples scattered over
widely separated islands, the presence of large, non-indigenous
minority groups like the Chinese—these are some of the more important and urgent problems with which the young state will have

to cope. All of the neighboring countries, whether independent or still in a dependent status, are experiencing grave social and political unrest. The situation in even the most favored is precarious. Will Indonesia fare better?

Four years after the surrender of Japan no settlement had yet been reached in the Indonesian problem. During this period the Netherlands twice resorted to "police action." In the last military action the Dutch forces took Jogjakarta, the capital of the Republic, occupied its remaining territory, and made prisoners of its leading officials, including President Sukarno and Vice-President Hatta. The United Nations Security Council again intervened and in March 1949 passed its thirteenth resolution on the Indonesian affair.

A third agreement between the Netherlands government and the Republic of Indonesia was signed on May 7, 1949 by Dr. Mohammed Rum for the Republic and Dr. J. H. van Royen for the Netherlands. The agreement conforms in general to the directives laid down in resolutions of the Security Council of January 28 and March 23—namely, the cessation of hostilities, the release of Republican political prisoners, the restoration of their authority in Jogjakarta, and discussions in Batavia and Jogjakarta on the time and conditions for a round table conference at the Hague, at which "discussions will take place as to the way in which to accelerate the unconditional transfer of real and complete sovereignty to the United States of Indonesia in accordance with the Renville principles." The preliminary conference has been fairly successful. If the round table at the Hague is equally successful the transfer of sovereignty to the new state of the United States of Indonesia will occur sometime before January 1, 1950.

The Dutch foreign minister, Mr. Dirk U. Stikker, on June 15, 1949 stated to a press conference at the Hague that the Indonesians want independence and the Dutch want them to have it, and that the Dutch believe that the majority of Indonesians want and need the support of Western democracies until a democratic government able to maintain law and order has had a chance to become firmly established, and until Indonesia's most pressing economic problems have been met. Because of the historical ties between the Netherlands and Indonesia the Dutch are prepared to offer the fullest cooperation to the United States of Indonesia, and have suggested as an instrument of such cooperation a Netherlands-Indonesian Union under which the relationships of the two countries would be defined by voluntary agreement between equal sovereign powers.

The foreign minister said that the Netherlands seeks no special economic privileges for its nationals in any economic relationship it may have with the future United States of Indonesia. Mr. Stikker stated further that the Dutch believe that the Western democracies should view all decisions with respect to the future of Indonesia in the light of advancing communism in Asia, and that the Western countries "should seek ways in which they can help Indonesia raise its standard of living, maintain and develop a democratic form of government, and stand as a bulwark of freedom in Southeast Asia."

EDITOR'S NOTE. Late in July agreement was reached between the leaders of the Indonesian Republic and of the other states of Indonesia on the establishment of a government for the whole of the East Indies. It will be a federation as demanded by the other states, and the representation of the Indonesian Republic in the federal House of Representatives will be limited to one third of the total number. The next stage will be a round table conference at The Hague between delegates of the Dutch and the various Indonesian governments.

Suggested Reading

Furnivall, J. S. *Netherlands India*. Cambridge (England) and New York. 1944.

———. *Colonial Policy and Practice: A Comparative Study of Burma and Netherlands India*. Cambridge (England). 1948.

Kennedy, Raymond. *The Ageless Indies*. New York. 1942.

Vandenbosch, Amry. *The Dutch East Indies, Its Government, Problems, and Politics*. Third Edition. Berkeley. 1942.

Vlekke, Bernard H. M. *Nusantara: A History of the East Indian Archipelago*. Cambridge, Mass. 1943.

Wehl, David. *The Birth of Indonesia*. London. 1948.

Wolf, Charles, Jr. *The Indonesian Story*. New York. 1948.

BURMA

❖

Pre-British Burma

ORIGINS OF PEOPLES AND CULTURE

THE ancestors of the various Mongoloid peoples who make up Burma's indigenous population apparently brought with them little by way of formal civilization from their original homes in eastern Tibet and western China. The principal Burman group, which migrated to the Irrawaddy valley as late as the eighth or ninth century A.D., had apparently experienced up to that time little or no contact with centers of Chinese civilization. They had developed no form of writing, no centralized political institutions, no formal legal system, and only primitive religious concepts. Intercourse with China continued to be impeded by the formidable mountain ridges of western Yunnan, separating the parallel Irrawaddy, Salween, Mekong, and Yangtse river valleys. This rugged plateau country, inhabited by non-Chinese hill tribes, has continued effectively to insulate Burma from Chinese cultural infiltration.

The first overt interference by China in Burma's affairs came in the thirteenth century when the Tartar forces of Kublai Khan invaded Burma, destroyed the Burman capital of Pagan (1287), and overthrew the first and in several respects the greatest of Burma's dynasties. But the Tartars found the country inhospitable and withdrew almost immediately. Brief military incursions from China during the seventeenth and eighteenth centuries obliged the Burmese rulers to acknowledge, as a kind of insurance arrangement, a tenuous vassal relationship to the Chinese court;

126

but political contacts between the two were normally unfriendly, and cultural exchange was very meager.

Predecessors of the Burmans proper included the kindred Arakanese population and a people known as the ancient Pyu, with both of whom the Burmans readily mingled. The more highly civilized Mons, who occupied the lower Sittang and Irrawaddy valleys and the Tenasserim coastal projection extending southward in the direction of Malaya, became enemies of the Burmans. Much less advanced than the Mons and probably among the earliest residents of Lower Burma were two major varieties of Karen peoples, the Sgaw and Pwo, who inhabited the less desirable jungle and mountainous portions of the area ruled by the Mons. The Karens were eventually enslaved by the Burmans and made little progress until freed by British rule and educated by Christian missionaries in the nineteenth century.

Several centuries after the main Burman group entered from the north, Shan tribesmen from South China, kinsmen of the Siamese, occupied the extensive plateau areas lying east of Burma's central valley system. More recent immigrants, known as the Chins and Jingpaw (or Kachins), occupied the mountains and hills to the west and north of the Irrawaddy-Chindwin valley. Important elements of the Kachins were actually moving into northern Burma at the time British troops reached the Chinese border in the 1880's. All of these latecomers, like the ninth-century Burmans, brought with them from China very little in the way of formal civilization.

Overland communication between Burma and India is even more difficult than between Burma and China. Formidable mountains separate Burma from India's Brahmaputra valley, while to the south a maze of parallel, jungle-clad ridges infested with wild animals and insect pests present an almost impenetrable barrier. Indian sea-borne contacts with Burma's coastal regions, on the other hand, date from ancient times. Indian merchant colonies in the Arakan, the Irrawaddy delta, and along the Tenasserim coast, although never established in force, became the principal entry points of Buddhist cultural infiltration, among the Mons and Pyu in particular. Buddhist groups in Lower Burma resisted resurgent Hindu influences after the tenth century, at which time Buddhism had largely been eliminated from India. At the same time Burmans maintained close relations with Ceylon, where Buddhism continued to flourish.

The ancient Pyu and the Mons of Lower Burma borrowed heavily from Indian culture. Sanscrit writing provided the pattern for the Pali script of the Mons, from which the modern Burmese writing was derived. The Buddhist scriptures transcribed in Pali, together with a residual mass of Indian history, legend, magical lore, and mythology, provided the literary basis for Burmese culture. Burmese architecture, painting, and wood carving also followed Indian patterns, which were particularly in evidence in the magnificent structures of the first great capital of the Burmans at Pagan.

Although Burmese culture eventually developed characteristics of its own, it was for the most part distinctly derivative, a kind of second-hand adaptation of Indian originals. The monosyllabic language of the Burmans, for example, fitted rather clumsily to the Pali script. Appropriation of new words from the Sanscrit likewise proved difficult. The Indian-style shrines of the Pagan period, which themselves were not structures with interior rooms, degenerated in time to the solid single-spired pagoda of the Burmans and the Shans. Difficulties of overland migration from India, and the Burman's disinclination to intermarry with Hindu Indians, combined with military aggressiveness, saved the country from the threat of being overrun by India's excess of population. The only significant intermixture between Indians and Burmans, and that in recent times, has resulted from intermarriage of immigrant Moslem elements from India with Burman women.

Thus it developed that whereas Burma's racial affinity was toward the Mongoloid peoples and its cultural background was borrowed largely from India, geographic factors enabled it to survive as a separate national entity resisting absorption by either India or China. The Burman state developed historically in the central rolling area some three to four hundred miles inland, where no natural barriers of mountains, forests, or delta swamps impeded transverse intercourse between the Chindwin, the Irrawaddy, and the upper Sittang valleys. Thus the kingdom of Burma was effectively insulated from direct outside contacts by land or sea, and generated in time not only a characteristic cultural pattern of its own but also a sense of national consciousness as well.

Burma's first great ruler and the founder of the Pagan dynasty, Anawratha (1033–77), unified a number of petty states in the central Irrawaddy valley and initiated a series of extensive irrigation works which transformed an arid region of considerable dimensions lying south of the present site of Mandalay into a granary for his kingdom. A portion of the Shan states first came under his control, and subsequently the coastal region nearest India inhabited by the Arakanese. Anawratha then allegedly became dissatisfied with the corrupted form of Buddhism which the Burmans had borrowed from the Pyu, and exploited the refusal of the Mon rulers of Thaton to share with him their copies of the uncorrupted Hinayana scriptures as the occasion for making war on the Mon state. In 1057 he captured the Mon capital in the lower Sittang valley, and ultimately he consolidated Burman control throughout Lower Burma, including the entire Tenasserim coast.

Once installed on the coast, the Burmans made fresh contact with Ceylon, the fountainhead of Hinayana Buddhism. Fired with enthusiasm for the new-found faith, Anawratha enshrined at Pagan a replica of the Buddha tooth at Kandy and constructed a magnificent capital which became a place of pilgrimage from distant lands. During the two and one-half centuries of the rule of the Pagan dynasty, architectural monuments were constructed at the capital which surpassed in both extent and magnificence anything achieved by the Burmans in subsequent history. The Burmans dedicated themselves to the idealized role of political champions of the pure Hinayana Buddhist faith.

For two and one-half centuries following the destruction of Pagan by the Tartar armies in 1287, the country was fought over by rival Burman factions. The Mons eventually re-established their control in the south, and migrating Shan tribesmen, some of them vassals of China's Mongol rulers, overran large sections of the upper Irrawaddy valley and the plateau to the east of it which now bears the Shan name. When in the middle of the sixteenth century

Burma was again united under the short-lived Toungoo dynasty, successive rulers exhausted the state's energies and wealth by repeated and largely futile efforts to conquer neighboring Siam. The weakened Burman kingdom was invaded at one time or another during the course of the seventeenth and early eighteenth centuries by the Ming Chinese, the Siamese, the Arakanese, and even by the Manipuris from India.

A major military effort by the Mons, from 1740 to 1752, succeeded in capturing the Burman capital at Ava and threatened to overrun the entire central region inhabited by the Burmans. The crisis brought to the fore a young Burman leader of ability, entitled Alaungpaya, who rallied the Burman forces and eventually expelled the Mons from the entire Irrawaddy valley. Alaungpaya's victory over the Mons was completed by the capture of their capital at Pegu in 1757. But the prolonged fighting in Lower Burma had by that time depopulated much of the area, reducing it to a jungle waste. Fishing and salt manufacture in the delta area during the latter half of the eighteenth century exceeded in importance the growing of rice. The development of the agricultural possibilities of the Irrawaddy delta was beyond the capabilities of a Burman state which centered in the interior and to which the coastal areas were only frontier marches.

Alaungpaya died in 1760 while returning from an abortive and costly invasion of Siam. His successors repelled one invasion from China, reconquered Arakan in 1785, and invaded Manipur and Assam during the second decade of the nineteenth century. By this latter move the Burmans developed a common frontier with the rising power of the English East India Company.

The Burman court at Ava, far removed from any apparent threat to its safety and confident of the military superiority of Burman feudal levies, entertained little respect for the European trading groups that had previously made numerous half-hearted attempts to establish footholds on Burman soil. On the occasion of Alaungpaya's capture of the Mon stronghold at the mouth of the Rangoon river in 1756, for example, he had beheaded several captured French artillerymen, adventurers who had aided in the defense of the place. The allegedly disloyal staff of an English

East India Company post located at the mouth of the Irrawaddy was similarly executed in 1759, without embarrassing results.

Burma's seaports acquired minor importance during the Napoleonic Wars as a haven for French privateers. The country's limited contacts with Roman Catholic and English and American Baptist missionaries after 1809 had afforded no basis for a realistic judgment of the outside world. The Ava government and the population of Burma generally were thus unprepared both politically and psychologically to be thrust into the current of the world's affairs. Prior to the arrival of the British in 1824, Burma had in fact been a backwater lying outside the main currents of the world's sea-borne trade to India, the Indies, and to China.

THE GOVERNMENT OF OLD BURMA

Burma's royal government was a despotism tempered by administrative inefficiency, by locally functioning feudal institutions, and by religious traditions of considerable influence. The court and the king's officials in the provinces were for the most part predatory rather than administratively constructive, while the more positive aspects of the government at the local levels were based on feudal principles. The king relied for military forces and police upon a system under which retainers owed personal fealty to chieftains who were their immediate political superiors. Local governmental functions were handled by circle headmen acting as hereditary squires for groups of villages numbering up to two score or more.

Burmese customary law was largely concerned with arbitral procedure; the objective was to reach agreement between disputants by means of a referee who received a fee for settling the difficulty. Recalcitrant members of any village could be expelled by community action and their land confiscated. The social gap between ordinary Burmans who owed their allegiance to the neighboring circle headman and the feudal retainers liable to military duty was not a wide one, for the two groups often lived in the same villages and worked together in the same rice fields.

Another force which tempered the king's despotism was the Buddhist monastic system, which afforded the entire male population a broad avenue to learning and social influence. The hierarchy of the monks extended from the court chaplain and the head ecclesiastical patriarch to the humblest mendicant serving as village teacher. The monastic orders themselves were loosely knit and exercised no coordinated political influence, but at all levels of society the wearers of the yellow robe were objects of veneration. The monks in old Burma were the custodians of learning and of conscience, the spiritual guides and teachers of the youth of the land, the embodiment of the very *raison d'être* of the Burman state. All Buddhist youths were expected to live as monks for a period of time. The system contributed an effective element of cohesion to Burman society, and the sanctions of the Buddhist faith operated as a disciplinary force.

British Burma
THE ANGLO-BURMESE WARS

Border difficulties between Burmese government forces and the East India Company's establishments in Chittagong and Assam came to a head in 1823, when one Burmese force attacked an English post at Shahpuri in Bengal while other contingents invaded Manipur and Assam. British Indian forces countered by attacking Rangoon by sea in May 1824, and although weakened by disease, they proceeded to advance on the Burman capital of Ava following the cessation of the ensuing rainy season. Meanwhile, other British Indian forces took possession of Manipur, Burman Assam, and the Arakan and Tenasserim coastal regions of Burma. In the treaty of peace signed in February 1826, the company acquired the Arakan and Tenasserim coastal strips but did not ask for the Irrawaddy delta, where a satisfactory northern boundary would have been difficult to establish.

The company placed Arakan under the administration of Bengal and succeeded within a short time in greatly expanding rice cultivation in the Akyab area. Tenasserim, on the other hand, proved to be so unprofitable that as late as 1840 the company was on the verge of retroceding it to Burma. Eventually the teak resources of the area were profitably utilized, and rice acreage was extended.

Although palace feuds at Ava prevented the government from

taking retaliatory measures against the British, apart from refusal to cooperate commercially with company-held areas, the atmosphere of Ava became so hostile in 1840 that the British residency there was abolished. Meanwhile the teak resources in Tenasserim became exhausted and timber firms began to look to Burman territory for new supplies.

A renewal of punitive British measures against the Burman kingdom followed hard upon the accession in 1852 of a new and aggressive governor-general, Dalhousie. An expeditionary force in 1852 occupied the lower Irrawaddy and Sittang valleys, and the company declared annexed an area extending northward beyond the Prome-Toungoo line, halfway to Mandalay. British forces were obliged to overcome spirited resistance, however, and they made no attempt to carry the war northward to the Burman capital. Eight years were required to pacify Lower Burma and to establish effective control. British administrators here made wide use of the traditional authority of the circle headman.

The third Anglo-Burmese war of 1885–86, which began as a quarrel between the British and the irresponsible King Thibaw over the latter's imposition of fines and his intrigue with the French, brought under British rule the surviving remnants of the Burman kingdom. The annexation precipitated a general state of rebellion throughout the country, which required the attention of a considerable force of British Indian troops for four years to bring under control.

ECONOMIC AND SOCIAL EFFECTS OF BRITISH RULE

From the material point of view, British rule accomplished marked improvements within Burma. Public funds were utilized for providing essential transportation facilities and other amenities; tax exactions, particularly those on internal trade, were greatly reduced; commerce increased; the area under rice cultivation expanded steadily, even before the opening of the Suez Canal in 1869 stimulated the expansion of commercial agriculture. The declaration of state ownership of all teak trees and the licensing of all cutting eliminated the wasteful exploitation of this valuable timber.

The social results of British rule were mostly negative. Throughout the latter half of the nineteenth century, village communities in Lower Burma became increasingly restive. Burmans neither liked nor understood the impersonal British Indian system of law, which was so vastly different from their own personal feudal obligations and from their customary law. This was particularly true with reference to the law of mortgage, for in old Burma a cultivator's ancestral lands were not subject to alienation to an outsider.[1] Factors responsible for social control were also weakened because of the declining influence of the Buddhist monks. Their authority enjoyed no governmental backing under British rule, and the disciplinary regulations within the hierarchy covering probationary status and the admission and expulsion of members fell into disuse. Many new villages lacked monastic schools, and even where these were available, well-to-do parents usually preferred to send their children to government and missionary schools where useful subjects, including English, were taught. It proved impossible to integrate Western-type schools with monastic systems of instruction. Although the tradition of popular reverence for the yellow robe of the monks persisted, the monasteries by the end of the century had lost their reputation for moral leadership and enlightenment and were tending to become a socially disruptive factor. Militant nationalist elements eventually took advantage of the relative immunity afforded by the yellow robe, and in some areas the monasteries actually became centers for the operation of lawless gangs.

The most important economic development during the last thirty years of the nineteenth century was the introduction of commercialized rice production in Lower Burma. With the opening of the Suez Canal, an overseas market was available for the first time for all of the surplus rice that Burma could produce,

[1] EDITOR'S NOTE. Under Burmese traditional law the judge was an arbitrator. His aim was if possible to satisfy both plaintiff and defendant, and the usual result in almost all cases was a compromise. In place of what all parties considered reasonable, the British substituted the Western idea that law was an exact command. The duty of the British judge was to ascertain disputed facts and pass sentence according to fixed legal principles. The British also replaced much of Burmese law with British Indian law, and this proved to be an important factor in the transfer of land from Burmese peasants to their Indian creditors. Burmese custom had protected the debtor against the loss of his land. British law, based on the sanctity of contract, upheld the creditor's right to foreclose when the peasant defaulted on his mortgage.

while the soil of the Irrawaddy delta and the abundant rains carried by the seasonal monsoon winds afforded physical conditions favorable for the indefinite expansion of paddy cultivation. By utilizing Indian coolie labor during periods of planting and harvest to supplement the efforts of the Burmese cultivators, and by permitting free scope to private moneylending operations, particularly those of the Chettyar community of South India, Burma achieved an annual expansion of the paddy acreage averaging 150,000 acres during successive decades down to 1930. Few cultivators once entangled in the toils of the moneylender were able to escape. The Chettyars developed a stake in Burma's economy estimated in 1930 at some fifty million pounds sterling, a sum slightly larger than all British investments in the country combined. Indigenous paddy farmers, who did most of the work of reducing the land to cultivation, emerged in the end holding virtually no equity in the land which they had developed.

Political changes were almost equally significant. Because the circle headmen and other feudal chieftains led the rebellion of 1886–89, Burma's pacificator, Crosthwaite, eliminated all traces of the traditional feudal allegiance, including even the administrative authority of the circle headmen. In its place he established the more or less artificial post of the village tract headman, who functioned officially as the government's local magistrate and police officer, as well as tax collector. The headman was usually the leading taxpayer of his village tract and as such was influential personally; but he was answerable not to the local residents but to the British deputy commissioner of his district, and consequently did not enjoy the respect which had been accorded his feudal predecessor. Because of the official status of the office of headman, incumbents were forbidden to participate in political activity, a ruling which contributed in the end to shifting political leadership into the hands of radical, irresponsible elements. The government became a highly centralized affair, remote from the villagers.

By the beginning of the twentieth century, the population of the paddy-growing areas of Lower Burma included a large number of landless farmers and laborers who wandered from village to village and were therefore in great measure immune from social control. The naturally volatile temperament of the Burman male lent itself to lawlessness and to nonrecognition of governmental authority, which the multiplication of police and courts proved powerless to curb. The virus of lawlessness struck Upper Burma during the course of World War I, when widespread displacement of the population within the area weakened social controls.

Meanwhile, British business enterprise had extended its operations far beyond the traditional bounds of the timber industry, rice milling, and the operation of river boats. The extraordinary demands of war accelerated the development of Burma's oil industry and encouraged the tapping of the lead and zinc resources of the northern Shan states and the wolfram and tin of Lower Burma. Other advances were made in cement and rubber production. British owners of industrial stocks realized immense profits from their investments. Even during the depression years, the annual dividends paid by many of Burma's industries averaged around 24 per cent. The increase in business activity was reflected in the expansion of Burma's export trade by two and one-half times from 1890 to 1914. Exports increased another 50 per cent between 1914 and 1926.

Except for the employment of a number of Burmans in the oil industry and a group of Karens in the wolfram mines, Burma's indigenous population shared very little in the profits of the industrial program. Indian labor manned the transportation services and the rice and timber mills; Moslem Chittagonians from Bengal operated the river boats; and Chinese were employed in the lead and zinc mines. Indian merchants controlled almost all of the rice exports to India, while the Chinese similarly controlled rice shipments to Malaya. So little of the business profits went into the hands of local consumers that Burma's annual imports were normally less than half the value of her exports, even though the imports included capital goods. Burma's villagers profited very little from the rising tide of business activity.

THE GENESIS OF MODERN NATIONALISM IN BURMA

Burman nationalism received its first important impetus during World War I, deriving encouragement from the activities of the

Indian National Congress party and from President Wilson's advocacy of self-determination for dependent peoples. The nationalist movement in Burma was associated with hostility to British rule, hatred of the Indian coolie and moneylender, and conservative Buddhist opposition to Western cultural influences generally. Constructive channels through which nationalist sentiment could find expression were generally lacking. A society which one observer aptly characterized as "anarchy boxed in" became surcharged with the potentialities of violent political explosion. When it became known in 1919 that the contemplated Montagu-Chelmsford reforms for India were not intended to apply to Burma, a representative General Council of Buddhist Associations (GCBA) demanded home rule and rejected out of hand any constitution falling short of that demand.

The dyarchy constitution which the British parliament granted to Burma in 1921 introduced the machinery of representative government, but also introduced elaborate precautionary measures that left unimpaired Britain's control of Burma's economic affairs. Under the dyarchy system, the governor exercised extensive powers including the appointment of half of the cabinet ministers, who were responsible to him rather than to the elected legislative council. Burmans who were elected to the council were not responsible to an alert and informed public opinion, and customarily formed a solid bloc of opposition to the ministry, refusing as a rule to accept office. On the local level, district councils chosen by indirect election were made responsible for administering such matters as sanitation, vernacular education, and public roads. The new system was so unpopular that the very name "dyarchy" became one of opprobrium. All but one faction of the General Council of Buddhist Associations boycotted the elections.

Successive dyarchy governments maintained themselves only by enlisting non-Burman support (British, Indian, Karen, and Chinese) and by following a cautious conservative policy. They stressed the maintenance of law and order, economy of expenditures, and the upholding of administrative standards. No important problems such as tenancy, rent control, or land alienation were attacked and nothing was done to limit Indian immigration. Such a program fell far short of satisfying the demands of Burman nationalists, who complained of the allegedly inordinate expenditures on police, courts, and civil services, and argued that more attention should be paid to so-called nation-building enterprises.

A considerable proportion of Burman nationalist sentiment operated within the boycotting elements of the GCBA, which were not represented in the elected councils and were even apart from the 12,000 village headmen. Hostility to foreign rule was aggravated after 1930 by economic distress, by distrust of British political intentions, and by the activity of politically minded Buddhist monks who controlled the rural votes and operated as political bosses.

When, in 1929, the Simon Commission undertook to assess the operation of the dyarchy system in Burma preparatory to the formulation of a new constitutional act for all of India, the commission expressed grave concern over the prevalence of crime and the negative effects of growing political agitation. But the commission saw no alternative to going forward in the direction of eventual self-government. As Burma could not possibly be fitted into the contemplated scheme for a federated India, the commission recommended Burma's separation from India under a new constitution.

Meanwhile the growing distress occasioned in Burma by the depression of 1929–32, which witnessed in three years a decline in the price of rice to one-third of the 1928 level, added greatly to popular unrest. Indian moneylenders, heavily involved, called in their loans and foreclosed mortgages on more than two and one-quarter million acres of paddy land in the Irrawaddy delta. Many Burman cultivators, unable to finance a new crop of their own without Chettyar aid, were compelled to seek employment in a depressed labor market in competition with Indian coolies who were also suffering from unemployment. The coalescence of political unrest, economic distress, and disrespect for governmental authority bred racial friction and rebellion.

Burma's first race riot in early 1930 was directed mainly at the Indians and to a lesser extent against the Chinese. At the end of 1930 a serious rebellion broke out in Lower Burma, sponsored by the leaders of several boycotting factions of the GCBA. Obscurantist rebel leaders invoked the assistance of both astrology and magic. The immediate grievances of the villagers were the government's continued collection of the hated capitation taxes (five rupees per household) and the pressure exerted by Chettyars for the repayment of loans. But the objective of the rebellion was to overthrow British rule. Resistance in certain parts of Lower Burma reached formidable proportions, and a major effort on the part of British Indian forces was required to restore order.

Increasing hostility to British rule carried over into the so-called Anti-Separationist political movement in connection with the elections of 1932. Suspicious villagers feared that parliament's proposal to separate Burma from India was designed as a means of isolating the country from the effects of the Indian nationalist struggle, thus retarding Burma's political advance. The Anti-Separationists rejected in advance any British-made constitution, and enlisted the support of elements of the Burmese electorate which had previously refused to vote. In spite of the overwhelming Anti-Separationist victory in 1932, the British parliament had virtually no alternative to proceeding with the separation of Burma from India as planned. Popular distrust of Britain's intentions proved to be groundless, for the Burma constitution of 1935 was fully as advanced as the one given to India.

BURMA UNDER THE 1935 CONSTITUTION, 1937–1941

The Character of the New Government. The Burma Act of 1935, which came into effect in 1937, provided for full ministerial responsibility to a majority of the lower house of parliament. It also accorded extensive emergency powers to the governor and established a property-holding senate, half of whose members were elected by the house of representatives and half appointed by the governor. The governor could veto acts of parliament and could certify any essential schedule of expenditures for which the parliament had refused to allocate funds. He exercised complete control over the so-called Excluded Areas—the Shan states, Karenni, and the Kachin and Chin tracts—which lay outside the jurisdiction of the parliament.[2]

[2] EDITOR'S NOTE. The Excluded Areas were the great horseshoe of mountains which surrounded the central valleys in which the Burmese lived. They comprised 43 per cent of the total area of Burma and 14 per cent of the population. Many

Although far from satisfactory from the Burman nationalist point of view, the new constitution did afford opportunity for a representative Burmese legislature to initiate corrective measures covering agricultural problems of long standing. Some of the reforms attempted, touching the regulation of rents and tenure and the redistribution of land through government purchase, were carelessly drawn. Insufficient time was afforded before the outbreak of war in 1941 to work out satisfactory adjustments in the laws. It was nevertheless clear that even a parliament which included a large number of Burman landlords was determined to inaugurate thoroughgoing agricultural reforms.

Orders in council which accompanied the 1935 act forbade alteration until 1940 of existing regulations covering the immigration of Indians into Burma. This reservation was a contributing factor to a recurrence in mid-1938 of widespread anti-Indian rioting. Defiance of police authority was general, and village headmen in many instances actually led the rioters. Verified casualties numbered more than one thousand, of which some two hundred were fatal. An investigation of the riot revealed not only virulent hostility to continued Indian immigration but also universal distrust of the police.

The successful operation of responsible government in Burma was handicapped by the absence of integrated political party organizations. Aspiring political leaders were all intent on expanding their respective coteries of personal followers in the parliament, because the political importance of any leader was directly proportionate to the votes he could command. As the lifetime of any cabinet depended on maintaining a working majority in the lower house, a minister's value to the government was measured not by his administrative capacity but in terms of the number of votes he could deliver when needed. Bribery and favoritism became the accepted means of acquiring a following and of paying

of the inhabitants were in a primitive, tribal stage of development, and needed a considerable advance in civilization before they would be capable of taking part in a democratic government. Often there was antipathy between the mountain peoples and the Burmese. In 1947 the Excluded Areas were included in the Burmese Republic, though with a substantial measure of local self-government. In 1948 the Karens set up their own state in Tenasserim and a considerable part of the Irrawaddy delta, and threatened to attack the hard-pressed government of Thakin Nu unless it recognized their autonomy.

off political debts. Civil service standards, which had previously been fairly high, declined alarmingly when it became apparent that support from Burman ministers was lacking.

Emergence of Leaders. The period of 1937–41 marked the rise of two important Burman political figures, Dr. Ba Maw, founder of the *Sinyetha* (Poor Man's) party, and U Saw, leader of the *Myochit* (Patriotic) party.

Dr. Ba Maw was a European-educated Burman, ambitious, astute, and colorful, who gained notoriety by volunteering as counsel for the defense in the trial of the Burman leader of the 1931 rebellion. He was elected to the legislative council in 1932 on the Anti-Separationist ticket, and served as minister of education until 1937. Ba Maw's *Sinyetha* party made a poor showing in the 1936 elections for the new parliament, but the majority Burman element in that body was so divided by factional rivalries that he was able, by clever manipulation in alliance with non-Burman elements in the house, to make himself Burma's first prime minister in 1937. Ba Maw was under constant harassment by political enemies, who eventually unseated him in late 1938.

U Saw, a politician of considerable force of personality, succeeded to the premiership in 1939. In contrast to his rival, he had received only a common-school education and attracted support from a stratum of the Burman population with whom the Europeanized Ba Maw had little in common. U Saw's newspaper, *The Sun,* was notoriously anti-British and also pro-Japanese. While in office, U Saw put through various agricultural reforms which Ba Maw had initiated, and he also negotiated an abortive immigration agreement with India. On his special mission to London in 1941 U Saw failed to obtain from Mr. Churchill an unqualified pledge of postwar dominion status for Burma. He was apprehended by British authorities in Palestine in the course of his return journey in early 1942 on charges of treasonable communication with Japanese officials in Portugal. He was imprisoned in Ethiopia throughout the war and was not permitted to return to Burma until early 1946. U Saw's efforts to recover political power were largely unavailing, and he eventually suffered execution following his conviction for engineering the assassination of Aung San in 1947.

Following Dr. Ba Maw's loss of the premiership, he organized in 1939 Burma's so-called "Freedom Bloc," dedicated to the achievement of immediate and unconditional independence. In 1940 Ba Maw resigned from the parliament and embarked upon a campaign of seditious political activities which led to his eventual imprisonment. He escaped from jail in the spring of 1942 during the course of the Japanese conquest and was subsequently selected by the Japanese to head the quasi-puppet regime that ruled Burma during the occupation. Ba Maw's personal vanity, his apparent support of oppressive Japanese requisitioning and policing measures, and his eventual flight to Japan in 1945 greatly damaged his political standing among Burman nationalists. He returned to Burma in mid-1946, but found himself without any significant popular following.

The Dobama Asiayone, or Thakin Party. A youthful Burman political group of great potential significance, known as the *Dobama Asiayone* ("We Burmans" Association), constituted the leftist fringe of the Burma Student Movement, which included both university and high school groups. Members addressed each other by the title "Thakin," the Burmese equivalent of the Indian "Sahib" (meaning master or lord), and implied in other ways that Burmans rather than the British should be masters in Burma. At the outset the *Dobama Asiayone* was active in the easy task of fomenting student strikes prior to examination time. Eventually they developed an organizational cadre which included youthful representatives in all Burman centers of education. The students had a primary grievance in the examination system, which was designed primarily to sift out the superior candidates for civil service posts and contributed little of value to the majority of the students who failed the examinations. Student groups eventually organized workers' strikes and initiated seditious attacks on British economic and political control generally.

A few of the Thakin leaders made contact in 1939 with members of the Communist party of India and began in a small way to propagate Marxist doctrines under cover of the *Dobama* banner. In a situation where foreign interests owned virtually all of the capital assets and constituted at the same time the most formidable barrier to the realization of nationalist objectives, it was easy to direct nationalist sentiment into opposition to capitalism generally.

The Thakins accepted Buddhism as an integral part of Burmese culture, but they did not take orders, as did U Saw and some other politicians, from politically minded monks. Nor did informed Thakin leaders repudiate Western learning and its technological achievements as some others did. The Thakins could not be bought off by governmental favors, for they condemned as strongly as did the British the corrupt practices of the old-line politicians. They also demanded economic as well as political independence. Some of them incurred prison sentences for their participation in Ba Maw's seditious "Freedom Bloc" campaign. By the end of the thirties, the *Dobama Asiayone,* although inexperienced and not numerically strong, was rapidly winning for itself a reputation for disinterested patriotism. This was probably more than could be said of any other party, for none of the political factions represented in the parliament enjoyed widespread popular support.

Approximately thirty of the Thakin leaders fled from Burma in 1941 at the invitation of the local Japanese consul and proceeded to Formosa, where they received training for the collaborationist role which the invading Japanese assigned to them in 1942. Various of these participated in Ba Maw's occupation cabinet.

SOCIAL AND ECONOMIC FACTORS

Burma's Agricultural Problem. Burma's prewar agricultural problem developed in aggravated form in the ten or a dozen districts of Lower Burma, where the steady expansion of commercialized rice cultivation had continued for many decades. Four-fifths of Burma's twelve and one-half million acres of paddy land were located in the Irrawaddy delta and in neighboring districts. Here an annual rainfall of eighty to two hundred inches falling between May and October made artificial irrigation unnecessary. Burman and Indian labor, Chettyar moneylender financing, and British governing and engineering skill made it possible for Burma by 1930 to produce annually for export some three to three and one-half million tons of surplus rice, an amount larger than the rice exports of Siam and French Indochina combined. Difficulty arose from the fact that this highly integrated undertaking found the Burman cultivator unable to realize any equitable share of the profits in competition with the moneylender, the store-keeper, the landlord, and the rice mill purchaser. The basic problems were the widespread alienation of land to non-cultivator ownership and rack renting of land to transient tenants.

Very rapid turnover in land titles, which characterized all Lower Burma, was a phenomenon entirely unknown in pre-British Burma and uncommon even in twentieth-century Upper Burma. In the latter area the vagaries of the rainfall and the consequent uncertainty of the crop did not attract commercial financing, nor was it greatly needed. In Lower Burma on the other hand, the Chettyars were liberal lenders where good land was the security, while Burman cultivators as a rule were careless borrowers. The latter were perennially in need of funds to repair bunds and plant the new crop, to tide over the family food supply until the next harvest, and to hire labor for harvesting. The Burman owner understood little about finance or court law, and as long as he got the requisite money for current needs he paid little heed to the terms of the mortgage he had to sign.

The Chettyar's policy was not to acquire landownership, but to obtain maximum cash income from owner occupants. Loans guaranteed the mortgage-holder from 18 to 48 per cent interest annually, depending on the risk; lenders sometimes deducted the interest in advance from the amount of the loan. Usually the residue of the harvested crop after all creditors' charges were paid provided insufficient food to last the cultivator's family through the ensuing year. Rarely were there any surplus earnings available to apply to the retirement of the mortgage obligation. Eventually the "owner" defaulted on his obligation and the mortgagee found a new occupant whom he installed as pseudo-owner under appropriate liabilities. No group could match the efficiency of the Chettyar community in the lending business, and other lenders frequently exacted even more exorbitant charges than did the Chettyars.

Landlord-tenant relations were particularly bad in Lower Burma, where during the thirties almost three-fourths of the paddy land was owned by non-cultivators. The bargaining position of the landlords was strengthened by the fact that some 40 per cent of the tenants changed their rented plots every year and 70 per cent within three years. Both Burman and Indian landlords could therefore force prospective tenants to bid against each other for the privilege of signing the one-year leases. Under such circumstances rents were often more exorbitant than the interest rates of the Chettyars. The evil social effects of land alienation and tenancy were recognized as early as 1900, but no corrective measures were attempted. From a commercial point of view the agricultural system worked satisfactorily as long as the annual surplus of paddy for export continued to increase and the price to the cultivator afforded adequate incentive.

The urge to do something to halt land alienation and rack renting and to encourage cultivator ownership was second in political importance only to the nationalist issue itself. The three major pieces of reform legislation enacted by the Burma parliament after 1937 attempted rather ineffectually to enforce fair rents and to regulate land alienation. The new regulations provided for increased cultivator ownership through government purchase and the acquisition of title under terms which forbade sale or mortgage of any agriculturalist's land to a non-agriculturalist. The laws did not impair existing titles, however.

The complete cessation of Burma's export of rice during the Japanese occupation plunged all Lower Burma into a degree of economic distress that dwarfed the hardships previously experienced in the depression of 1930–33. But the cultivators were conscious of one compensating factor. The Chettyars and the British law which guaranteed Chettyar mortgages and land titles had departed from the country, and Burmans generally were determined that neither should be allowed to return. The peasant demand in the postwar period for freedom from British rule was strongly influenced by such considerations. It was at this point primarily that national feeling coincided with the Communist party's demand for outright confiscation of foreign capital holdings. The adjudication of the legal titles, of Indian Chettyars in particular, to millions of acres of Burma's best paddy lands is a paramount issue in Burma's domestic politics, and it will doubtless constitute a matter of international controversy with the Indian Union in future years.

Labor. Prior to the war approximately two-thirds of Burma's workers were engaged in agriculture and animal husbandry. The indigenous population was predominantly agricultural, although many supplemented their incomes by cottage industries. In Lower Burma the livelihood of the population was dependent on the yield of the rice crop and the price that it brought. In Upper Burma crops included millet, maize, sesamum, cotton, groundnuts, tobacco, potatoes, sugar cane, and vegetables. Many unemployed cultivators in Lower Burma resorted to lawless means to supplement their incomes during the two off-seasons following the planting of paddy and following the harvest. Defiance of police authority was for many Burmans an exciting pastime as well.

Indian laborers prior to the war filled 85 per cent of the 90,000 jobs in factory industries and provided some 45 per cent of Burma's unskilled labor generally.[3] They helped harvest the rice crop and performed most of the work on the docks, the railways, and the river steamers. Others worked as house servants. Indian laborers were recruited as a rule by Indian *maistries* (labor contractors), who customarily took cuts from the pay checks of the members of their respective groups. Burma's political and business leaders demonstrated little interest in improving the lot of Indian industrial labor, with the result that the government's labor department languished from lack of funds. The department's efforts were confined for the most part to enforcing minimum standards of working conditions in some six hundred rice mills, one hundred or so sawmills, and more than a score of cotton ginning establishments.

There existed in Burma no generally accepted standard for wages and hours, and labor organization was rudimentary. In 1936 Burma's eight recognized trade-unions enrolled less than three thousand members, although some 700,000 persons were industrially employed, if mining, workshop, and transport workers are counted. Strikes and work stoppages among unrecognized labor groups were usually capable of being classified by the courts as riotous conduct.

One of the principal social changes introduced as a result of World War II was the organization of numerous Peasants' Unions

[3] With the exception of workers in the Bawdwin lead and zinc mines, virtually no Chinese worked in Burma as common laborers.

by both Communist and Socialist party agents. Both of these parties were organized in 1944, and their leaders were recruited for the most part from the ex-Thakins. Communist-sponsored groups encouraged their members to resist the payment of both rent and taxes, whereas the Socialists adopted a more moderate policy. The All Burma Trade-Union Congress sponsored by the Communists was much weaker than the Socialist-directed Trade-Union Congress, Burma, which included most of the rice mill and sawmill employees. Neither of the trade-union groups was as important politically as were the Peasant Union bodies. There were also the government employees' All Burma Ministerial Servants' Union and the United Trade Union Organization, composed of clerks working in Rangoon commercial firms.

Indian labor has occupied relatively a much less important role in postwar industry and transportation services than it did during the thirties. Comparatively few of the common laborers included in the four or five hundred thousand of Burma's Indian inhabitants who fled the country in 1942 have returned. The Indian government itself since 1946 has discouraged the immigration of Indian laborers not formerly resident in Burma until adequate safeguards for their welfare were assured. Burma's Indian population in 1948 probably did not exceed three-fifths of the 1941 figure of 1,100,000, and has apparently registered a net decline since the end of the war. The slow tempo of Burma's economic recovery program has prevented the development of any critical labor shortages in fields where Indians found employment in the prewar period.

Economic Capabilities and Trade Patterns. Burma's agricultural, mineral, and forest resources are capable of supporting a population much larger than the country's present seventeen million inhabitants. The population density in 1941 was approximately seventy-two per square mile. The total area under cultivation in any given year before the war, estimated at seventeen to eighteen million acres, might conceivably be doubled if all arable land were utilized as intensively as it is in some other parts of Asia. The yield per acre is also capable of being greatly increased. Large areas of potential rice lands in the delta of the Irrawaddy are awaiting development.

The steady expansion of Burma's rice acreage during the half-century prior to 1940, at an average annual rate of almost 150,000 acres, was accomplished with the cooperation of Burmese and Indian labor, Indian moneylender capital, and British technical, governmental, and transportation services. The total rice acreage fell during the course of the Japanese occupation to approximately 45 per cent of the 1940 level. If all of these abandoned acres are to be restored to cultivation, and if the expansion of cultivation is to be continued beyond the prewar maximum, the government of independent Burma will itself have to make good what the non-Burmans previously contributed to the agricultural program. Actions such as the expropriation of the Chettyars will not of themselves solve the production problem. Paddy cultivation by 1948 had recovered to around 65 per cent of the prewar level of twelve and one-half million acres. If adverse political and economic conditions should persist, it will require an indefinite period of time to accomplish full recovery. Approximately 1,200,000 tons of surplus rice will be available for export from the 1948 crop, whereas exports in peak years before the war reached 3,500,000 tons.

Burma's valuable mineral resources are badly balanced for purposes of industrial development. Before the war Burma's petroleum industry produced annually some 3,000,000 barrels of kerosene, 1,400,000 barrels of gasoline, and additional quantities of lubricating oil, paraffin, and candles.[4] Burma's oil contains such a high paraffin content that requisite fuel oils were normally imported in preference to consuming the more valuable domestic product. Virtually no petroleum products were produced during the Japanese occupation, and none since the end of the war. Burma's oil reserves are definitely limited, but the field is by no means exhausted and is capable of economic operation.

Burma's lead and zinc deposits are located in the northern Shan states. The Burma Corporation's Bawdwin mine and the neighboring smelting plant at Namtu produced annually before the war some 75,000 tons of lead, 70,000 tons of zinc concentrate, 8,000 tons of copper matte, 4,000 tons of nickel speiss, and around

---

[4] Annual production of lubricating oil was 150,000 barrels, and of mineral oils 300,000 barrels; 48,000 tons of paraffin and 4,600,000 pounds of candles were produced during a year.

6,000,000 ounces of silver. The Bawdwin mine operations are probably capable of 60 per cent restoration without incurring prohibitive initial expenditures, but impaired railway transportation to the area constitutes a serious impediment, aside from negative political considerations.

Tungsten and tin mines located in the Karenni and Tenasserim districts before the war produced 4,500 tons of tin concentrate, 3,500 tons of tungsten concentrate, and 5,000 additional tons of mixed tin and tungsten. The output of these metals recovered in 1947–48 to approximately 10 per cent of prewar production.

Burma's almost complete lack of commercially usable coal and her scanty supplies of iron ore veto the prospect of any large-scale industrial development within the country, even though hydroelectric power should eventually become available.[5] The most feasible lines of industrial development, except perhaps in the textile field where Burma's domestic cotton could be used, would appear to be the processing of Burma's raw materials—rice, oil, teak, and minerals—for export purposes.

Approximately one-third of Burma is covered with forests. The most valuable forested areas, containing teakwood (about one-fourth of the total), have long been controlled by the government. The government has claimed title to all teak trees since 1853. Burma's timber exports before the war included 230,000 tons of teak, three-fourths of which went to India. The forests themselves suffered little damage during the war, and under favorable conditions the timber industry could be expected to register continuous recovery and afford the government a dependable source of income. Burma's sawmill capacity had been restored by 1948 to half of prewar levels, but most of the postwar timber output has been utilized internally.

The war destroyed virtually all of Burma's railway passenger and baggage cars, around 85 per cent of the locomotives, plus important bridges, railway stations, warehouses, and shops. The tracks deteriorated from lack of maintenance care. By 1948 all of the main tracks had been restored, and locomotives and freight

[5] Before the war, Burma imported from India 350,000 tons of coal and some 50,000 tons of manufactured iron annually. Iron ore production was only 24,000 tons per year.

cars had been replaced to approximately 50 and 30 per cent, respectively, of prewar figures. But the volume of railway traffic continued low and the lines were operating at a heavy loss to the government. As Burma's railways normally ran at a loss before the war, there would appear to be no immediate prospect of restoring them to profitable operation.

Rangoon's port facilities, which handle the bulk of Burma's seaborne trade (prewar capacity 5,200,000 tons annually), were more than 50 per cent restored during the first three postwar years. This capacity for the time being was adequate to the demands. But Irrawaddy river transportation is woefully inadequate. The Irrawaddy Flotilla's prewar fleet of 600 river boats was more than 90 per cent destroyed during the war, and replacements have been meager. The problem is complicated by the fact that the Burma government took over the assets of the British Flotilla Company in June 1948, presumably with compensation although no figure was agreed upon. River boats are not available to transport all the delta-grown rice to the Rangoon mills, and the movements of such boats as were available were hampered by disorderly conditions. What had been before the war a highly profitable private transport operation functioned in 1948 at a heavy loss to the government.

Prewar British investments in Burma, which included nearly all of the large-scale industrial establishments, amounted to an estimated 50,000,000 pounds. Prewar income derived from this investment amounted to some 10,000,000 pounds annually, plus another 1,000,000 pounds from services rendered. Indian capital controlled a large number of Burma's smaller rice and sawmills, as well as equities in land. Burma's prewar invisible imports from India totaled perhaps 8,000,000 or 9,000,000 pounds annually, including £4,000,000 to the Chettyars, £2,000,000 in personal remittances, and £1,200,000 paid on account of Burma's debt to India.[6] Chinese businessmen operated general stores, inns, restau-

[6] EDITOR'S NOTE. Services rendered by foreigners may be called "invisible imports" to distinguish them from imported commodities. Included under this term are such things as payments arising from international indebtedness, postwar indemnities, banking and insurance charges, and charges on goods and passengers carried in vessels of another country. The economic history of Southeast Asia contains many instances of invisible imports in the form of continuing use of

rants, and licensed liquor and opium shops. Invisible imports from China consisting of remittances and interest probably amounted to less than 400,000 pounds sterling per year. All of these invisible import items were severely curtailed in the postwar period, except possibly the Chinese items. Burma's invisible exports in any direction have been negligible.

The prewar trade pattern was directed toward India and the United Kingdom, partly because of exchangeable currencies, imperial preference, and established business connections. On the other hand, accessibility and economic complementarity played a major part in directing more than half of Burma's trade toward India. The United Kingdom absorbed about 16 per cent. Japanese imports into Burma during the peak year of 1932–33 constituted only 12 per cent of the country's total imports; only 4 per cent of Burma's exports normally went to Japan. Except for the considerable rice exports to Malaya, Burma maintained little commercial contact with the neighboring peoples of Southeast Asia, whose products were much the same as her own. For a number of years Burma's postwar import requirements are likely far to exceed her purchasing capacity and the availability of such goods in world markets. Only Burma's limited access to Britain's dollar pool and the very high price received for her rice exports kept the country's balance of payments in a measure of order during 1946–48.

Health. The public health department of the prewar Burma government functioned effectively to check such epidemic diseases as smallpox, cholera, and plague, but this was accomplished in the face of popular hostility to compulsory inoculation and vaccination. The six general hospitals and the some three hundred smaller hospitals and dispensaries maintained by the government were inadequate to meet general health needs. The population suffered from the prevalence of malaria, dysentery, skin and eye infections, and venereal disease. Infant mortality was very high.

capital owned by foreigners, which requires the annual payment of interest or dividends to the foreign lenders. Examples are Burma's remittances to the Indian Chettyars, and the dividends on rubber and tin properties that are withdrawn by the foreign investors. In some countries, especially in Europe but also to a minor extent in Southeast Asia, invisible exports in the form of such things as tourist expenditures also have been important in the balance of trade. Apart from a small tourist trade, Burma has virtually no invisible exports since it has, for example, no Burmese merchant marine or capital invested abroad.

The public patronage necessary to support competent private medical practitioners was lacking in all but the more progressive urban centers. The American Baptist Mission maintained three hospitals, two of them well equipped, which trained a limited number of nurses. Preliminary medical training at the university had to be supplemented by professional training abroad. As a result, trained Burmese doctors were few, and a considerable proportion of Burma's medical officers were regularly recruited in India. Deterrent factors in maintaining public health were the vogue of traditional medical practices, which included a generous element of magic and astrology, and the rigid Buddhist taboo against the taking of life, even of rats and mosquitoes. Health problems were greatly aggravated during the war by lack of medicines and hospital care. Efforts to maintain health in independent Burma will be handicapped primarily by the dearth of trained doctors and by popular resistance to Western medical practices.

Education. Burma's prewar educational system operated at three levels. The oldest of these was the monastic school system, which every Buddhist youth was expected to attend for a longer or shorter period. Most of these schools have been notoriously inefficient in recent decades. Discipline within the Buddhist order was lax, and the monastic teachers were afforded as a rule no professional training for their tasks. The monks refused to accept governmental inspection designed to encourage the maintenance of reputable educational standards, with the result that their schools were denied assistance from public funds. Although monastic schools promoted male literacy in the Burmese language (sometimes reckoned as high as 56 per cent), they afforded students no outlet for useful employment and their instruction included much that a Westerner would class as misinformation.

The Buddhist order declined in morale and to some extent in popular regard during the Japanese occupation. In any case, outside observers agree that monastic schools lack both the capacity and the vitality to contribute materially to a constructive orientation of Burma's youth to the requirements of effective relations with the outside world. They might be capable of making a substantial contribution to social stability if the Buddhist order could generate sufficient vitality and moral vigor.

The system of government-sponsored vernacular schools was controlled after 1923 by locally appointed district school boards operating under the direction of elected district councils. The boards almost invariably overcommitted their allotted school funds, so that the rural vernacular schools were often poorly administered and frequently failed to come up to the government's minimum standards. Meager equipment, low salaries, inadequate teacher training, and low morale were the major factors responsible for their unsatisfactory performance. Furthermore, vernacular schools, like the monastic schools, offered to Burman youth little outlet for employment, so that most of the students dropped out after attending two or three years. Considerably more than half of Burma's prewar school population of children from five to eleven years were probably not attending school at any given time.

The Anglo-vernacular and English schools, which alone qualified students for university entrance and civil service examinations, were controlled directly by the education department of the central government and absorbed a large proportion of the available educational funds. Instruction in English was required under the Anglo-vernacular system from the fourth grade on, although much of the instructional subject matter available in English had little or no relevance to the background or experience of the students. Experimentation was discouraged by fixed curricula and uniform examinations. Approved non-government Anglo-vernacular schools, mostly missionary-sponsored, received grants-in-aid from public funds to meet half of their budgeted deficits. Mission schools before the war occupied a respected place in education and contributed a number of progressive innovations.

Centrally administered examinations covering all high school subjects determined pretty largely what the students were taught, and rote memorization of the answers to expected examination questions was the generally approved method of study. Educational standards were maintained, and elimination at the higher levels was particularly rigorous. Two-thirds of the Anglo-vernacular high school finalists regularly failed. One-half of the university students failed the comprehensive intermediate examinations required at the end of the second year, and more than one-third of the surviving candidates for the bachelor's degree regularly fell short of requirements. Only the honor graduates of the university could expect to enter the civil service Class I, while the 90 per cent majority who had fallen by the wayside at one point or another profited relatively little from their educational investment. The facts that the Burmese student memorized in school were normally irrelevant to any useful purpose aside from passing the examinations.

It is not surprising, therefore, that the system of rigorous examinations under the Anglo-vernacular system fomented student discontent. The university in particular and many of the high schools as well became hotbeds of nationalist agitation sponsored by the Burma Student Movement. Strikes were easily fomented just prior to examination time. Student activities in the 1930's began to take on an increasingly political character. Political activity was ordinarily shunned, however, by those students who were anxious to apply for a civil service appointment. For the nationalist-minded student leader, election to an office in the University Students' Union constituted a promising beginning for a political career. Both Thakin Aung San and Thakin Nu, who successively headed Burma's postwar governments, served in their student days as president of the University Student Union, and were active during the 1930's in fomenting student strikes.

Students who were subjected to the Anglo-vernacular school and university instruction developed some appreciation of Western learning and discounted somewhat the traditional Buddhist lore. It is significant that Burma's postwar leadership was drawn from these educated and semi-educated nationalists, who were hostile to imperialism but intent on keeping open Burma's windows to the outside world. The extent to which this point of view can command steadfast popular support once independence has been achieved is not clear.

Whatever the instructional content of Burma's future educational program, difficulties are sure to be encountered from student indiscipline, dislike of exacting standards of instruction, poor building facilities, the lack of necessary reference materials in the Burmese language, and the general inadequacy of government funds. New educational plans call for the eventual introduction of free compulsory primary education up to ten years in a single unified public school system. Initial instruction would be in the student's native tongue, but the study of English would be compulsory as a secondary language from the fifth grade on. The grant-in-aid system to mission schools has been abandoned, although provision is made for private schools to be eligible to be accredited and to receive government grants on a temporary basis pending the full operation of the public school system. It is not clear whether the paper plans will be even approximately realized in the foreseeable future, especially in view of other manifold problems that have developed during and since the war.

The Japanese Occupation of Burma
THE JAPANESE CONQUEST

The Japanese military victory in Burma in 1942 can be attributed in large measure to the surprising adeptness of the invaders in the art of jungle warfare. Burma's defenses were predicated on Britain's ability to hold Singapore and other sea approaches, coupled with the assumed impossibility of Japan's conducting sustained military operations across the trackless maze of mountainous jungle which separates Burma from Siam. No one anticipated the promptness with which the Japanese forces both overran Malaya and penetrated Burma's territory at a number of points.

Britain's defense of Burma might have been firmer if reinforcements sent belatedly to Malaya had been diverted to Rangoon instead; but there is no indication that this would have been sufficient to counterbalance Japanese superiority in jungle warfare. British tactics were based on the assumption that main arteries of transportation would of necessity have to be used by the invaders. The Japanese, on the other hand, avoided direct frontal attacks and continually outflanked British defenses by jungle marches to cut in the rear the lines of communication on which the British Indian forces were themselves dependent. Without having opportunity to oppose the main force of the invaders on grounds of British selection, the defending troops were obliged throughout the campaign to make a series of costly withdrawals that spelled defeat.

Rebellious Burman groups apparently assisted the Japanese by providing the guides and topographical intelligence required for these flanking maneuvers. Local incendiaries also harried the British and Chinese rear. Part of this assistance was afforded by Thakin-organized student nationalists, and part by politically minded monks who mistakenly believed that Japan, a Buddhist country, intended to install some kind of monastic hierarchy as the new government of Burma. The British forces nowhere enjoyed effective Burman assistance, but regardless of this factor the final outcome would probably have been the same. Whereas assisting Chinese troops staged vigorous resistance to the Japanese along the main Sittang valley approaches to Mandalay, it was the disintegration of Chinese defense operations in the Shan plateau that climaxed the final debacle. The invasion began in January 1942, and the campaign was completed before the onset of the rainy season in May.

CHARACTER OF THE JAPANESE OCCUPATION

The Japanese military regarded the conquest of Burma not primarily as an end in itself but as a step in the elimination of British control from all Southern Asia. India was therefore the principal objective. As a necessary condition for being afforded opportunity to draw upon Burma's resources and manpower in preparing for an attack against India, the Japanese, on August 1, 1943, granted to Burma the form of political independence and pledged assistance in developing the country's economy. Ba Maw's puppet government declared war on the United Kingdom and the United States. Burmans were used by the Japanese for police duty and home defense, but they were never sent to the front. The Japanese, in fact, spent far more effort in developing Subhas Chandra Bose's so-called Indian National Army as an instrumentality for suborning front-line Indian troops under British command than they did in drilling a Burman fighting force.

The initially favorable impression which many Burmans acquired of the Japanese, based on admiration for their disciplined efficiency, their demonstration of a considerable measure of Asiatic camaraderie, and their declared purpose of liberating Southern Asia from British control, began to disappear during the early months of the occupation. This revulsion of feeling developed long before the people were conscious of the ultimate cost in privation that the occupation would entail for them. A considerable portion of the Thakins became disgruntled and began to question Japan's alleged liberating intentions. By the end of 1943 a small but tightly integrated popular resistance movement had developed which was led by Thakins, several of whom had acquired Communist affiliations in India.

Popular hostility toward the Japanese was stimulated by the brutal cruelty of the Japanese military police (*kempeitai*), which acted as a law unto itself. The Japanese soldiery also displayed flagrant disrespect for village elders and Buddhist monks, and they infuriated Burmans by slapping the faces of all who failed to cooperate promptly. They offended the peasants by wantonly shooting valuable oxen whenever food requirements called for fresh meat. Many thousands of Burma's so-called "Sweat Army" were compelled to work on the Siam railway, on airfields, revetments, and other military installations. Meanwhile Japan made available no consumer goods to match the military currency which they paid out for supplies. The Japanese propaganda slogans concerning Burma's independence and the Greater East Asia Co-Prosperity Sphere carried mocking implications to all elements of the population before the end of the occupation.

Japan's initial plan to invade India in 1942 miscarried, partly because the first Indian National Army recruited in Malaya refused to participate in the planned movement by sea when explicit Japanese cabinet assurances regarding India's future independence were not forthcoming. The sea-borne invasion was eventually abandoned in favor of an overland attack from Burma. This undertaking ran into repeated delays because of logistic problems and the difficulties of the terrain. The final desperate effort of the Japanese in late 1944 to invade East Bengal and Manipur and to cut the supply line of General Stilwell's North Burma operation came perilously near succeeding. Only air power saved the beleaguered British Indian garrison at Imphal.

With the failure of this operation, Japan's military power in

Burma collapsed before the British counterthrust. During the final two months of the reconquest, the Burma National Army, led by Thakin Aung San, minister of defense, turned on the retreating Japanese in Lower Burma. This action assisted the early British recovery of Rangoon and made possible the trapping of a considerable portion of the Japanese army operating north and west of the city.

THE EFFECTS OF THE JAPANESE OCCUPATION

The physical destruction suffered by Burma during the Japanese occupation was enormous. It included the leveling of a large fraction of downtown Rangoon and all of Mandalay and of the important cities located on the railway and river routes connecting the two key cities. Transportation facilities by rail and river were heavily damaged. Buildings or residences which escaped military destruction or requisition suffered loss of all furnishings and movable fixtures during successive interregnums and the frequent forced evacuations. British-owned industrial facilities in minerals, oil, rice, timber, and cement were effectively sabotaged prior to withdrawal in order to deny their use to the Japanese.

Losses experienced in rural districts were equally heavy. Millions of acres of paddy land reverted to jungle growth; the clothing of the cultivators wore out; and a large fraction of the cattle population of important sections of the country disappeared due to military requisition and an epidemic of rinderpest. In Lower Burma, where surplus rice was unsalable and incentive goods were lacking, production dropped to a subsistence level and the right of the landlord to his rent and that of the government to its taxes were ignored. In Upper Burma, where the more varied form of agriculture proved advantageous just as it had in World War I, many debtors managed to pay off their obligations to creditors in cheap military currency, thereby accomplishing a mild revolution in land tenure.

Social losses arising from the Japanese occupation were especially serious. Amid the orgy of looting and scrounging, respect for property rights and police authority almost disappeared. Violent crime and dacoity (gang robbery) multiplied as firearms and ammunition became available to practically the entire population.

Serious fighting broke out in the delta in late 1942 between un-disciplined units of the Burma Independence Army and the Karens, who were suspected of Anglophile and anti-national lean-ings. The excesses suffered by the Karens apparently confirmed their worst fears as to what their lot would be under an inde-pendent Burman rule, and led eventually to their postwar demand for an independent Karen state comprising Tenasserim division and a part of the delta.

Educational activities were largely in abeyance throughout the occupation period. The population also suffered heavily from malaria. Epidemics of smallpox, cholera, and plague were checked only by drastic preventive measures on the part of the Japanese military.

The exodus of the British and Indian business and banking com-munities, from Rangoon in particular, in 1942 left the field open to the Chinese. The latter survived repeated squeezes applied by the Japanese and at the end of the war found themselves in a position to extend widely their economic operations.

The Japanese occupation greatly stimulated nationalism. The Burman population in particular emerged from the common ordeal of suffering unitedly determined to eliminate foreign control and impatient to run the country's affairs. The war ex-perience elevated to positions of political control the ultra-nationalist Thakin leaders, who in 1944 organized a clandestine resistance organization known as the Anti-Fascist People's Free-dom League (AFPFL), which was an amalgam of a number of anti-Japanese youth groups. The AFPFL constituted the only organized political group in the country at the end of the war. Its leadership, particularly General Aung San and the Communist leader Than Tun, Aung San's brother-in-law, was acknowledged to be far more honest and patriotic than the elder statesmen of prewar vintage had been. Unfortunately only a few of the AFPFL leaders had acquired any administrative experience, while a large proportion of Aung San's military following was undisciplined. The disorderly atmosphere of the war years tended to persist, and administrative efficiency continued at low ebb.

The task of restoring governmental authority was adversely affected by the agitation of Communist elements within the

AFPFL, who appealed to Peasant Union groups with their slogan of "no rent, no taxes." It was also the policy of the nationalist leaders generally to keep things in a state of unstable equilibrium as a means of maintaining pressure on British authorities to withdraw. The resulting situation clearly provided no solid economic or social foundations on which to build a stable political community.

One positive effect of the Japanese occupation was to impress upon Burma's leaders the importance of producing a larger proportion of the essential consumption needs of the population. But whereas all informed Burmans recognized the desirability of developing technological skills and manufacturing facilities, few had any training or experience in industrial or scientific fields.

Burma's Postwar Problems
REHABILITATION: THE BRITISH PLAN

Burma's legal government-in-exile, sitting out the war at Simla, India, devoted much effort to preparing detailed plans for the economic rehabilitation of the reoccupied country. These plans were based on three principal assumptions: (1) that an extended period of military rule, followed by strong civilian control based on the constitutional powers of the governor would be required to re-establish law and order and to restore essential economic activities; (2) that as the Burmans lacked both the capital resources and the technical training to effect the requisite economic rehabilitation, the postwar government would have to enlist for this purpose the services of teams of experienced personnel drawn from British firms active in Burma before the war; and (3) that under the circumstances nationalist objectives would have to be deferred for a period of perhaps five to seven years, until the essential requirements of economic recovery had been attained.

The Simla planners broke down the problem of rehabilitation into a score of so-called "project" units, such as railways, highways, river traffic, oil, timber, minerals, agriculture, rice exports, etc., and proposed that the various projects hire competent personnel to direct the recovery operations. Any profits realized beyond the cost of operations were to go to the government. Firms which had not operated in Burma prior to the war were precluded from participation in the recovery program. The British parliament authorized a non-interest-bearing credit of some eighty-seven million pounds to prime Burma's economic pump. Arrangements for the repayment of the British loan and for eventual ownership of the tangible assets of the several projects were to be made at a later date.

The project scheme was entirely unacceptable to the Burmans. They professed to see in it an indirect way of enabling British firms to recover their former monopoly control over Burma's industry and trade. They complained that neither the army's civil affairs officer, General Sir Hubert Rance, nor the succeeding civilian governor, Sir Reginald Dorman-Smith, was amenable to Burman political direction. As British funds and materials were being used and as British personnel was directing the effort, Burmans felt that their economic future was being decided without their own participation.

During the initial five months' period of military rule, General Rance realized substantial restoration of highway and railway transportation and put the Rangoon docks back into operation; but he managed to accomplish very little else in the way of recovery. When Governor Dorman-Smith took over control from the army's civil affairs section in October 1945, he was seriously handicapped at the outset by being denied the use of army trucks, jeeps, and other necessary facilities, due to the strict application of rules forbidding the transfer of any non-surplus lend-lease equipment to civilian agency use. The highway improvement program ran aground, and the collection of debris also came to an end. Civilian police services were for a time unable to obtain needed arms and transport facilities. Difficulties of procurement and distribution of relief supplies for Burma were also retarding factors. Agricultural activities and trade were hampered by disorderly conditions, while villagers in dire need of clothing and other supplies suffered from the breakdown of the administrative agencies responsible for the distribution of essential relief supplies. The government's cancellation of all Japanese-issued currency left most village cultivators without funds.

Political tension developed when the governor insisted on putting selected Anglophile Burmans into the key posts of his advisory executive council and rejected the sweeping demands of General Aung San, leader of the AFPFL, for a dominant position in the council. Relations became worse after the governor tried to encourage the development of rival parties to the AFPFL by repatriating U Saw and several of the old Thakin group who were opposed to Aung San.

By the summer of 1946 the British plan for the accomplishment of essential economic rehabilitation preliminary to the establishment of self-rule was obliged to give way before the Burman demand for early political independence and for full Burman control of economic recovery measures. Political issues thus usurped the center of the stage. Governor Dorman-Smith left Burma in June 1946, and the following August General Rance returned to become the new civilian governor.

INDEPENDENCE: THE BURMAN OBJECTIVE

By the time Governor Rance assumed his post in late August 1946, London had already installed Pandit Nehru as head of an interim Nationalist government in India. Governor Rance was prepared to pursue a similar policy of conciliation in Burma. The replacement of Dorman-Smith's executive council by a more representative one under Aung San's leadership in September 1946 was accomplished by friendly negotiations, even though the change was precipitated by a threatening strike situation in Rangoon. A basis for consultation was found in the fact that both the Burman leader and Governor Rance wanted to spare the country the disaster of renewed warfare. The governor's acceptance of an AFPFL-dominated council at this juncture not only prevented strife but also afforded an opportunity to salvage something of Britain's former political and economic stake in the country. Negotiations were made easier by the fact that the AFPFL during the previous summer had excluded Communists from high office within the League, and had openly challenged the inveterate practice of the Communists of using the AFPFL in devious ways for promoting party ends. As head of the new executive council, Aung San quickly ended the general strike threat. When the Communists renewed their strike agitation in mid-

October, they were promptly excluded from the ranks of the League.

Virulent denunciation of Aung San's policy of negotiation by the Communists and various elements of Aung San's own veterans' group, the Patriotic Volunteer Organization (PVO), influenced the Burman leader in November to demand of London the early negotiation of a definitive settlement. Terms were satisfactorily arranged in London in January 1947, amid mounting threats of revolutionary violence throughout Burma. Britain promised to grant self-government to Burma within a calendar year, under a constitution of the latter's own devising. During the interim period agreements would be negotiated governing defense relations and financial matters. The British concessions fell somewhat short of meeting the full demands of the nationalists, but Aung San's personal prestige and his unqualified affirmation of confidence in the sincerity of the British government's commitments enabled him, upon his return to Rangoon, to obtain AFPFL approval of his partial victory. In the April 1947 elections for the constituent assembly, the AFPFL candidates for the most part ran unopposed, and 190 of the League's candidates were returned in a total of 220 seats.

Despite Aung San's achievements as a negotiator and political leader, he was unable promptly to curb the revolutionary ferment that had developed during the several months preceding the London agreement. Widespread disorder prevailed in various sections of Burma, some of it Communist-inspired, some of it particularist, some of it simply anarchic and lawless. The League itself showed some signs of dissolving into its component parts now that basic objectives were about to be achieved. Further conferences at London in June 1947 clarified subsidiary questions relating to the future status of minority population areas within the new state. The negotiation covering defense arrangements was concluded in August 1947, but the terms were not published until October.

THE PROBLEM OF GOVERNMENT

Anarchic Tendencies. The assassination of Aung San and six of his cabinet associates by hired agents of the wily U Saw on July

19, 1947 dealt a staggering blow to Burma's government, for it eliminated a number of experienced and trustworthy leaders who could not be replaced. It also carried ominous portents for the future. If one so universally respected as Aung San could be slain in cold blood, then what authority could be devised which would command respect? Prompt action by Governor Rance in naming Thakin Nu, vice-president of the AFPFL, as Aung San's successor saved the state from falling into confusion. But Thakin Nu's government was obliged thereafter to wrestle with tasks of increasing difficulty without enjoying requisite support. Whereas all Burmans wanted liberation from foreign political and economic control, most of them rallied only to a leader and did not appreciate the political concept of a sovereign people making its will effective through representatives of its own choosing. Aung San's death removed the figure who had commanded the allegiance of virtually all Burman nationalists; his absence therefore opened the way for defections from the AFPFL.

The immediate political effect was to influence various leftist political groups, including the most important element of the Communist party (led by Aung San's brother-in-law, Thakin Than Tun), to rally to the support of Thakin Nu in the face of the revolutionary threat from reactionary elements. Cordial relations between the government and the Than Tun Communists continued for approximately three months. They came to an abrupt end with the signing of the final Nu-Attlee Agreement on October 17, 1947.

The Nu-Attlee Agreement. The Nu-Attlee Agreement of October 1947 recognized the Republic of the Union of Burma as a fully independent sovereign state as of January 4, 1948. Britain retained a claim on the allegiance only of those citizens resident within the new state who were also British citizens by virtue of connections outside of Burma, or who should subsequently elect British citizenship in accordance with a law to be passed by the Burma Union. In the financial section of the agreement, Britain canceled Burma's indebtedness arising from expenditures during the civil affairs period of the reoccupation and also approximately three-fourths of the sums already advanced by the United Kingdom treasury in meeting current budgetary deficits. Burma was apparently also assured limited access to dollar credits under Britain's control.

In return, Nu acknowledged the continuing validity of unexpired contracts conferring rights or benefits in Burma upon British subjects, or upon companies mainly owned or managed by British subjects domiciled in the United Kingdom. He also explicitly acknowledged the obligation to compensate owners of such foreign-held contracts or properties as might be taken over by the government. In an exchange of notes appended to the treaty, Nu agreed that except in emergency situations and within the limits of Socialist objectives as set forth in Burma's constitution, the Burma government would seek through prior consultation a mutually satisfactory settlement covering any action which was prejudicial to British interests.

Under the three-year Defense Agreement of August 29, which was made a part of the October settlement, the United Kingdom agreed to evacuate British military forces; to provide a naval, military, and air mission for training the new Burma army; to furnish gratis the initial equipment and supplies for such a force, plus priority for future purchase of needed munitions; to hand over a naval contingent of some two score small vessels; and to contribute substantially for a limited period to the cost of maintaining Burma's important coastal airfields. Burma agreed to invite no similar military mission from any country outside the British Commonwealth, and to accord to British forces the right of access to Burma's ports and airfields for the purpose of bringing help and support to Burma in case of need. The defense agreement would be subject after three years to cancellation by either party on twelve months' notice. Thakin Nu's decision to place Burma, temporarily at least, within the sphere of British security operations in Southeast Asia reflected the hesitancy of many Burmans to run the risk of cutting adrift from outside assistance until Burma had time to develop an army of its own. The possibility of future differences with India over property claims and of trouble with China over Burma's undemarcated Yunnan boundary were undoubtedly factors influencing the Burman negotiators.

The Drift toward Confusion. Restive political elements, including the Communists, strongly opposed the Attlee agreement. To the extent that this agreement opened the way to final consumma-tion of Burma's independence, an event which was duly celebrated on January 4, 1948, centrifugal forces were released which Thakin Nu had heretofore held in check only with difficulty. The Commu-nists and the PVO attacked Nu for having accorded to the British a special position militarily and a promise covering the protection of Britain's economic interests. Than Tun, now following the strict Communist line, declared Burma's independence reduced to a sham and demanded that Burma sever completely all British connections and expropriate all foreign properties within the country. His viewpoint was shared by disgruntled elements of the PVO, who also resented efforts on the part of the government to eliminate the military aspects of their organization. Communist plans for embarking on rebellion, inspired by contacts made in India, were disclosed prematurely in February, so that the entire party was outlawed in March 1948. Disorder throughout the countryside gradually degenerated into open rebellion.

By midsummer of 1948 Thakin Nu's government had lost con-trol over important areas of central Burma. Transportation and communication services from Rangoon to Mandalay were thoroughly disrupted. A powerful ally of disorder was the in-grained propensity of Burma's villagers to refuse to support governmental authority, by whomsoever wielded. In July parts of two Burman battalions of the army went over to the rebels, and the government's principal dependence for the defense of Ran-goon thereafter became the Karen, Chin, and Kachin contingents of the army. The army itself was commanded by a Karen. This situation emphasized the importance to the government of the continued loyalty of the minority groups, all of whom were bitterly hostile to the Communists.

The gloomy outlook was intensified in September by the assassination of U Tin Tut, the ablest conservative figure within the narrowing circle of AFPFL leaders. Meanwhile the economy of the country suffered a creeping paralysis, and the government's financial problems became increasingly more embarrassing. The government's hope of re-establishing its authority appeared to depend on the effective application of force, combined with popular revulsion against the severe sacrifices arising from Communist and other forms of rebellion.

Agriculture. The immediate requirement for restoring Lower Burma's rice production was to provide loans to cultivators and adequate incentive goods to encourage the resumption of cultivation. Loans of state funds, plus bonus grants to cover the cost of restoring additional acreage to cultivation, and the availability of consumer goods were successful by 1948 in increasing rice production, so that 1,200,000 tons were available for export. The government recouped its investment by realizing a huge profit from its monopoly of rice exports. The basic problem of recovering government loans, collecting land taxes, and enforcing payment of agreed rentals to landlords was closely associated with the re-establishment of governmental authority as such. Performance in such matters left much to be desired, for tax collections were very incomplete and only one-quarter of the loans were repaid. Communist-sponsored Peasants' Unions enlisted adherents on the basis of "no rent, no taxes" slogans, and wherever such unions gained a large following the government's authority was virtually superseded. Rangoon authorities made a counterbid for peasant support by decreeing that no landlord should collect in rentals more than twice the taxes paid. The move miscarried badly, for it alienated the conservative landlord group while failing to compete with the more sweeping offer of the Communists. Governmental control of the export of rice surpluses afforded the government no leverage to control local situations not dependent on such exports.

A final step in agricultural rehabilitation related to the enormous task of adjusting landownership claims for practically all of Burma. The entire prewar system of land settlements will eventually have to be reviewed. In 1948 the government undertook to redistribute the land in various free areas, but so much political favoritism was shown by the officials in charge of the operation that the action aroused intense dissatisfaction. Chettyar land titles and mortgages awaiting adjudication in Lower Burma constitute the major problem. Most cultivators of Lower Burma would probably applaud the proposal to confiscate Chettyar properties without compensation of any kind, but the government is aware that any such action would carry with it strained relations with the Indian government. At the same time it is clear that Burma is neither financially nor politically in a position to grant anything more than partial compensation in government bonds to meet Chettyar claims. Burman landlords foresee the prospect of an attack on all private holdings, but they are too few in number and too weak politically to raise any effective protest. More than any other single issue, the determination of a definite land tenure policy constitutes the crux of the contest between the government and the Communists for the allegiance of the Burman villagers. Confusion is certain to persist until Burma's hitherto propertyless paddy farmers recover an unquestioned stake in the land.

Industry. The Burma government's proposed scheme for socializing industry was confined in 1948 to taking over the Irrawaddy Flotilla Company and to extensive inroads in the timber industry, where existing law already gave to the state ownership of all teak trees. The government commandeered a number of sawmills and assumed responsibility for timber procurement in about one-third of the teak-bearing areas, including the most accessible ones. Private timber operations continue in other regions, however. Most of the sawmills and rice mills remained under private control. Other types of foreign establishments are functioning only on a marking-time basis. A bare beginning has been made in reviving the mining and oil industries, and nothing more could be expected until the government's policy is clearly defined and implemented.

BURMA'S NEW CONSTITUTION

Burma's new constitution, approved in 1947 before Aung San's death, called for the establishment of a Federal Union including Burma proper, a Shan state, and a Kachin state. The Karens and Chins were accorded considerable autonomy and explicit guarantees of the inviolability of their rights as minorities. The indigenous non-Burman elements were represented specifically in a chamber of nationalities, where they comprised 72 of the 125 members. The delegations of the various minority peoples within this chamber were designated to act also in the capacity of a representative assembly for their respective national groups. The AFPFL architects of the new constitution gave the minority groups virtually what they asked for in the way of self-rule, as a means of forestalling any demand for continued British control over non-Burman peoples. The Karen peoples were so intermingled with the Burmans and Mons throughout Lower Burma that the full Karen demands for a separate state were considered at the time not to be feasible.

The prime minister and his cabinet under the new constitution were to be responsible to a chamber of deputies numbering about 250 members elected from single-member constituencies on an adult-suffrage, non-communal basis. Legislative enactment was by concurrent action of the two chambers, and, in case of disagreement, by a majority vote of the chambers sitting jointly. The combined chambers elected the Union president for a five-year term, but the prime minister was the real executive. The chamber of deputies was accorded wide legislative powers covering money bills, definition of citizenship, regulation or expropriation of private property and determination of compensation therefor, imposition of compulsory labor service in emergencies, control of land tenures, and power to redistribute land to cultivators severally and to cooperative farming organizations. Development of Burma's resources in lands, forests, minerals, fisheries, and all potential sources of electric energy was to be carried out by companies in which citizens of Burma owned at least 60 per cent of the stock, barring specially voted exceptions to cover periods of not longer than twenty-five years.[7]

The final interpretation of the constitution and the laws was entrusted to a supreme court of the Union appointed by the president and the prime minister. The judges of the court were not subject to legislative interference and were removable only on grounds of misconduct or incapacity. The bill of rights included all the usual guarantees and freedoms characteristic of liberal

[7] EDITOR's NOTE. The result of this restriction was that no new capital was invested in Burma. In June 1949 Thakin Nu's government decided to waive this requirement, since it had come to realize that foreign capital must be attracted if the plans for Burma's economic development were to be carried out.

governments, save only in the area of individual ownership of productive property, where the rights of the state were paramount.

CONCLUSION

The task of developing an effective government for Burma is made difficult by the lack of any genuine experience with representative institutions on the part of most of the population. Public opinion enters little into the partisanship of the immediate followers of rival leaders. The widespread dispersion of firearms is particularly serious in view of the long-established habit of regarding centralized governmental authority as something alien and hostile, and therefore not deserving of popular recognition or respect. This is doubly unfortunate because the central government under the new constitution must perforce bear the principal responsibility for foreign relations, for determining land policy, for maintaining health services and educational standards, and for promoting rehabilitation of essential communications, transport facilities, and industrial development generally. Political divisions are broadly based on differing attitudes toward the acceptance or rejection of Western economic and cultural influences, and on economic considerations associated with landownership and utilization. The economic potential is present in Burma if political difficulties can be overcome.

The chances of success would appear to turn on the emergence of vigorous and trustworthy leadership capable of re-establishing effective controls and at the same time of satisfying essential popular demands; but no leadership can function satisfactorily apart from popular realization of the country's vital stake in developing an orderly as well as a progressive society. There is in the background the possibility that anti-foreign elements may eventually take over control and attempt to return to eighteenth-century feudal standards.

EDITOR'S NOTE. During the months that this book was in the press there was a marked deterioration in the situation. Thakin Nu's government was tardy in carrying out the settlement made with the Karens, and an attempt to disarm them apparently confirmed their distrust of its good faith. The result was a more dangerous revolt than any of its predecessors, and signs of unrest appeared among the other non-Burman peoples. No firm alliances were formed between the various factions that were fighting the government, though there seems to have been cooperation on a few occasions between the Karens and the Communists. The People's Volunteer Organization (PVO) achieved the unique distinction of fighting on opposite sides. In some districts it joined Thakin Nu's troops in attacking the Karens, while in others it cooperated with the Communists against the government.

Thakin Nu's only hope was to maintain his government's *de jure* status and obtain revenues from rice exports while negotiating with both the Karens and the PVO. The latter demanded that they receive their back pay for all the months during which they had been in revolt, and that they and the Communists be taken into the government. The Karens, the most powerful and the least radical of the rebel forces, agreed to a tentative settlement in April. They were to have an autonomous state inside the Burmese Union and their own Karen army. A few days later Thakin Nu rejected the terms, apparently under pressure from extreme Burmese nationalists in his government and army, and the war was resumed.

By July 1949 Thakin Nu maintained effective control only in Rangoon and the other seaports and in widely scattered districts in the interior. The rest of the country was in the hands of dacoits and rebel factions, each fighting for its own hand, though it was reported that the Communists and the PVO were negotiating an alliance. The government continued to lose popular support and was further weakened by the withdrawal of some of its Socialist supporters from the cabinet. Expenditure far outstripped revenue, foreign trade declined, and national bankruptcy was in sight. Rice, the staple export, could be brought to the ports only by means of naval convoys, since the rebels had cut almost every line of communication by road, rail, and river. The rice export in 1948 was less than half what it was before the war, and the prospects for 1949 were worse owing to confusion throughout the delta area. This caused grave anxiety in India and Malaya, which depend upon imports of Burmese rice to feed their people. Both were alarmed at the prospect that the Communists might gain control of Burma, possibly with assistance from Red China, and so aggravate their own domestic Communist problems. India was also concerned because the rice lands owned by the Chettyars in Burma would be expropriated without any compensation whatever if Communists obtained control.

The whole of Burma is in a state of semi-anarchy, confusion, and threatened territorial fragmentation. There is talk of an appeal to the people, but a free election is impossible and even if held would be futile. Thakin Nu does not have the power to re-establish his control, and has three choices open to him. He can come to terms with the Karens, which will anger some of his Burmese supporters, or with the PVO and the Communists, which would mean his political extinction. Secondly, he can set up a military dictatorship, and there have been signs that increasing power is being placed in the hands of General Ne Win, who is commander of the army and is also vice-premier, minister of defense, and judge of the high court. There are too few trained Burman troops, however, to establish strong military rule. The third choice is to accept the mediation which was offered by Great Britain, India, Pakistan, and Ceylon.

When this mediation was first suggested it was denounced by most Burmese nationalists as a sinister maneuver of British imperialism, and was apparently cold-shouldered by Thakin Nu himself. By early summer, however, an additional threat had developed on Burma's Chinese border, and it is possible that he might accept some kind of mediation in order to obtain financial and other assistance from abroad. He indicated that he would like military equipment and a gift of $100,000,000—euphemistically described as a loan—from the government of Great Britain. Burma's leaders have shown so much political ineptitude and irresponsibility that effective utilization of any loan would appear to require outside supervision of its expenditure, an unpopular course which the government would be loath to take. If Thakin Nu asked for mediation he would be attacked as a tool of the foreigner. Even assuming that mediation were accepted by the warring factions, it would be far from easy to reconcile the rival leaders' ambitions for power and their ideologies. The four British governments have agreed to do all they can to support Thakin Nu, but have not yet decided what form their help will take. There are few grounds for expecting any immediate improvement in the situation.

Suggested Reading

Andrus, J. Russell. *Burmese Economic Life*. Stanford. 1947.

Burchett, Wilfred G. *Bombs Over Burma*. Melbourne. 1944.

Cady, John F., Patricia Barnett, and Shirley Jenkins. *Development of Self Rule and Independence in Burma, Malaya, and the Philippines*. New York. 1948.

Christian, John Leroy. *Modern Burma, A Survey of Political and Economic Development*. Institute of Pacific Relations. Berkeley. 1942.

———. *Burma and the Japanese Invader*. Bombay. 1945. (Revision of *Modern Burma*.)

Collis, Maurice Stewart. *The Burmese Scene: Political, Historical, Pictorial*. London. 1943.

———. *Trials In Burma*. London. 1945.

Dodwell, H. H., ed. *The Cambridge History of India*. Vols. V and VI. Cambridge (England). 1929.

Furnivall, John Sydenham. *An Introduction to the Political Economy of Burma*. Edited by J. R. Andrus. Rangoon. 1938. (2nd rev. ed.)

———. *The Fashioning of Leviathan: The Beginnings of British Rule in Burma*. Rangoon. 1939. Also *Journal of the Burma Research Society*, Vol. XXIX. 1939.

———. *Progress and Welfare in Southeast Asia: A Comparison of Colonial Policy and Practice*. New York. 1941.

———. *Educational Progress in Southeast Asia*. New York. 1943.

Geren, Paul. *Burma Diary*. New York. 1943.

Hall, Daniel George Edward. *The Future of Burma*. Rangoon. 1936.

———. *Europe and Burma—A Study of European Relations With Burma from the Earliest Times Up to the Annexation of Thibaw's Kingdom in 1886*. London. 1945.

Hall, Harold Fielding. *The Soul of a People*. London. 1926.

Harvey, G. E. *History of Burma from the Earliest Times to the Beginning of the English Conquest*. London. 1925.

Marshall, Harry Ignatius. *The Karen People of Burma: A Study in Anthropology and Ethnology*. Columbus, Ohio. 1922.

Seagrave, Gordon Stifler. *Tales of a Waste-Basket Surgeon*. Philadelphia. 1938.

Shwey, Yo [Sir George Scott]. *The Burman, His Life and Notions*. (3rd ed.) London. 1910.

Stamp, Laurence Dudley. *A New Geography of India, Burma, and Ceylon*. London. 1939. (Burma section, pp. 356–414.)

Warburton, Stacy Reuben. *Eastward! The Story of Adoniram Judson*. New York. 1937.

MALAYA

❖

British Rule, 1786–1939

THE English East India Company was looking for a careening station in the Bay of Bengal where warships could refit when disabled in sea battles with the French, and so avoid the long voyage to Bombay. It also wanted a trading post from which to extend its commerce with the East Indies, which the Dutch were still trying to monopolize. In 1786 the company's agent, Captain Francis Light, bought from the Malay Sultan of Kedah the uninhabited island of Penang. A few years later the sultan also sold a tract of land on the mainland opposite the island, now known as Province Wellesley, so that the company controlled both sides of the harbor. The terms of sale were that the British were to pay the sultan $10,000 a year as long as they held the two ceded territories; and this amount has been paid ever since. Penang turned out to be a heavy liability and a great disappointment as a trading center. It lay far to the west of the trade routes in the East Indies. Few Asiatic merchants were willing to make the long voyage through the Straits of Malacca, especially since they swarmed with Malay pirates.

Sir Stamford Raffles was a most uncomfortable servant for the East India Company. His employers acknowledged his zeal, his ability, his intense patriotism, and his great knowledge of the East Indies. The trouble was that he was that contradiction in terms, a government official with an adventurous streak. Raffles lacked proper respect for the little tin gods and their orders; and the company never knew what he would be up to next. He was determined to break the monopoly of commerce that the Dutch were trying to re-establish. In 1819 he persuaded Lord Hastings, the governor-general of India, to give him permission to establish a settlement in a more strategic position than Penang. Knowing the vacillation of his superiors, Raffles then moved so quickly that he had secured Singapore before they had time to countermand his instructions.

Singapore Island had a population of 150 Malay pirates and belonged to the Sultan of Johore, who was glad to cede it in return for an annual pension of $5,000. As Raffles had expected, the Dutch protested vehemently. But as Raffles likewise had foreseen, they had not a legal leg to stand on, since Johore was an independent kingdom which owed them no allegiance. So the company refused to give up Singapore, particularly since its trade grew remarkably from the very beginning. From 1819 to the present there has been a continuous growth in wealth and population.

The island has an excellent natural harbor, and it lies at the focal point of the trade routes. The great ocean route from the Baltic and Murmansk to China and Japan passes within sight of Singapore. It is also the geographic trade center for Malaya and the western islands of the East Indies. To these natural advantages Raffles added low taxes and free trade. There were no import or export duties and a minimum of regulations, while Dutch seaports were burdened with heavy dues and red tape. Raffles made Singapore a port where it was cheap and easy to carry on business, and he foresaw that this oasis of free trade would break the Dutch monopoly. Apart from minor deviations his policy has been followed ever since, and it has made Singapore one of the principal seaports of the world. With the exception of its tin smelter the city has no important industry, but it has grown rich on the transit trade. Ocean-going vessels unload the manufactures of Europe, America, and the Far East. Small local steamers distribute them to Malaya, Sumatra, Western Borneo, and countries as far away as Burma, Siam, and French Indochina. On the return voyage these ships pick up cargoes of Straits produce, such as rubber, tin, oil, pepper, palm and coconut oil, and salt fish. They are sorted, graded, and sometimes processed, and reshipped to their destinations overseas.

The decayed Dutch seaport of Malacca was exchanged in 1824 for the equally valueless British possession of Benkoelen in Sumatra. Penang, Malacca, and Singapore became the Straits Settlements, with an area of 1,542 square miles. They are the only part of Malaya which is British territory and where the government of Great Britain has sovereign powers. All persons born there are British subjects. The rest of Malaya is composed of nine protected Malay States. In each of them the legal sovereign is the sultan, and the authority exercised by the British is derived from treaties made with the different states.

This extension of power lay almost sixty years in the future when Raffles founded Singapore. The British in Malaya were isolationists and intervened as little as possible in the affairs of the Malay States. The latter were decaying into a condition bordering on anarchy. There was constant warfare among the sultans, and civil war between rivals to a throne was frequent. The power of the sultans declined, so that there was nothing to check the feuds of the rajas or Malay nobles who were nominally subject to them. The only constant factor was misrule. Piracy flourished and trade fell off. On top of this came trouble in the tin fields of Larut in Perak. The 40,000 Chinese miners who worked them were divided into rival secret societies which fought one another, and their feuds, together with Malay piracy, began to injure the trade of the Straits Settlements. These events coincided with the beginning of the period of modern imperialism, and the British government decided to intervene in Malaya.

Between 1874 and 1909 the nine Malay States were brought under British control. Each sultan signed a treaty by which he agreed to accept a British resident or adviser, and to follow his advice in all matters except those that concerned Malay custom and the Moslem religion. This made the British the real rulers of the Peninsula, even though legally every act of government was done in the name of the sultan. In return he was guaranteed succession to the throne, and an assured income that was probably more than he had been able to count on for two hundred years. His prestige was carefully preserved, and he received all the outward marks of ceremonial respect that often seem to be more important to an Asiatic ruler than the realities of power.

Originally the British did not intend to reduce the sultans to the position of figureheads. The resident was to act through persuasion and not give orders. During the first years of British rule this practice was followed. Before taking action the resident secured the convinced cooperation of the sultan and his Malay rajas, and carried them with him in his reforms. This policy was feasible as long as change took place slowly, but it broke down when an economic revolution began that transformed Malaya within about twenty years. Chinese and Indian immigrants poured in in such numbers that eventually they outnumbered the Malays and altered the whole racial character of the Peninsula. Simultaneously there was a heavy investment of British, and to a much lesser extent Chinese, capital in tin and rubber. It has been estimated that by 1914 the value of foreign, chiefly British, capital invested was $194,000,000.

In the 1880's Malaya was still a picturesque backwater, a museum piece of Asiatic feudalism. By the 1900's it had become inextricably involved in the economic life of the modern world. The government was no longer concerned with civil wars and piracy but with malaria control, educational policy, and the world price of tin and rubber. The Malays were a minority in the developed areas, and the Peninsula was dominated by the British and Chinese. In less than a generation the Malays had been catapulted from the Middle Ages into the twentieth century. They were unable to adapt themselves to the precipitate change, and their point of view continued to be feudal and conservative. This is not surprising, since Europeans took five or six centuries to carry out a similar mental development.

The result was that the British residents no longer had time to act through persuasion. Urgent problems kept crowding on them thick and fast, and settlement could not be deferred until medieval-minded sultans were convinced of the necessity of twentieth-century solutions. So, especially in the economically developed Federated Malay States, the residents took a short cut, issuing orders which the sultans were bound by treaty to accept. Politically the Malays were pushed out of their own house onto the doorstep. Economically they suffered the same fate at the hands of the Chinese. It is difficult to see how this could have been avoided, given the totally unexpected development of tin and rubber, but it left the British government with an uneasy conscience.

The Malays were conservative rice farmers and fishermen with a strong aristocratic tradition. They believed that it was for the sultan to govern, while the duty of the common man was to be loyal to his ruler and obey orders. Even as late as 1939 there was no desire for democratic government, apart from a tiny minority of English-educated Malays. During the interwar period a few sultans who had received an English education and understood twentieth-century problems began to take a real part in the government of their states. The majority, however, were as feudal-minded as their people, so that the blind led the blind.

A few years before the war the Chinese laborers on the Selangor rubber estates went on strike for higher wages. The Chinese Communists took over control and perverted a legitimate strike into a race and class war. Their object was to create hatred of the British and Chinese estate owners. The British resident of Selangor believed that the strikers were justified in their original demands and was determined that wages must be raised. He was equally resolved to break the strike quickly, before the violence fomented by the Communists had injured the racial harmony that was typical of prewar Malaya. The Sultan of Selangor was a survival from the pre-British period, when war and piracy were the only professions worthy of a gentleman. His suggestion was to execute a dozen strike leaders and order the rest back to work. If they refused, he proposed to liquidate another batch and keep on until the survivors obeyed orders. To carry the sultan with him, the resident would have had to give him about six months of intensive lectures on trade-unionism, the equitable division of profits between capital and labor, and twentieth-century humanitarianism. The old man would not have believed a word of it, and meanwhile the Communists would have succeeded in their purpose. So the resident overruled the sultan and went ahead with his own policy.

The British government felt that it had a special responsibility to the Malays since they alone were the genuine "people of the country," and because Britain had taken over control at the request of the Malays themselves and not by conquest. For this reason only British and Malays were eligible for the Malay civil service, which carried on the administration. Chinese and Indians were excluded, since the Malays disliked and looked down upon them and would have bitterly resented being placed under their rule. The British government also felt that democracy could not be established in Malaya until the Malays had acquired a twentieth-century mentality and were able to hold their own. Until that took place, democratic government would merely mean that the Chinese, who are far more astute and mentally mature than the Malays, would run the country politically as they already did to a large extent economically.

The prewar government was very complicated: a country of 52,528 square miles, somewhat smaller than Florida, had no less than ten separate governments. Penang, Malacca, and Singapore made up the Straits Settlements, a crown colony whose governor was also high commissioner or general supervisor of the nine Malay States. Four of them, Perak, Selangor, Negri Sembilan, and Pahang, had joined in 1896 to form the Federated Malay States. They contained the greater part of the tin mines and rubber plantations, and in 1931 the Malays were only 26 per cent of the population. Each of the five unfederated Malay States had its own separate government, and their sultans refused to join the federation because they had greater independence and more authority than the sultans of the Federated Malay States.

Theoretically, His Excellency the governor and high commissioner sat upright upon his throne, laying down the law to the peoples committed to his charge and accountable to no one save the colonial office and the parliament in London. In practice His Excellency's posture was less dignified but more useful, since he made a habit of keeping his ear very close to the ground. Legally he controlled every organ of government in Malaya except the courts of justice and the auditor. He laid down executive policies and recommended officials for promotion or dismissal. The governor was assisted by three advisory bodies, the executive and legislative councils in the Straits Settlements and the federal council in the Federated Malay States. All three had a majority of officials, and a minority of unofficial members nominated by the governor from among the leading British, Malays, Chinese, Indians, and Eurasians. There was complete freedom of debate, and an unofficial member of the legislative and federal councils could introduce a bill on any subject. The official majority however was required to support the governor's policy, so no bill could become law without his approval. The councils were really advisory, and the governor controlled legislation and finance as well as the executive.

The governor was a benevolent despot who rarely used his legal powers, but ruled by compromise and persuasion. The most important exception was when the colonial office ordered him to pass a particular measure. The governor was entitled to object; but if he was overruled he had to obey and pass the bill through the council by means of the official majority. Apart from this the governor never persisted in any policy to which the unofficial members of council seriously objected, unless he considered it a matter of vital importance. Normally he tried to arrange in advance a compromise which satisfied at least the majority of the unofficial members; and if he failed, the proposed measure was dropped.

The conciliatory attitude of the governor explains why before the war the very large majority of the peoples of Malaya had no desire to change the form of government. There was a good deal of grumbling at this action or that, and the freedom of the press gave an untrammeled opportunity to blow off steam. The Malayan newspapers cherished a robust tradition of "apostolic blows and knocks" that was characteristic of United Kingdom journalism a century ago; and it was always open season on governors. When a new one arrived he was praised to the skies, but that meant nothing. "Unconscious of their doom the pretty creatures play." The moment the governor offended public opinion in the slightest he was lambasted with as much exuberant ferocity as if he had set up a Soviet police state in Malaya. Yet whenever the Straits Settlements Association—a tiny handful of Europeans and Straits Chinese—suggested some modest approach toward democracy, the newspapers unreservedly condemned "the crass folly of a few misguided idealists."

Results of British Rule

The bulk of the Malayans were satisfied with the government because they felt that it had protected their interests. It had "fairly well maintained the chief virtues of bureaucracy—efficiency, integrity, and impartiality." The Malay attitude was, "We like government to consult our interests; but when it gives an order, we like to obey it." Most of the Europeans, Chinese, and Indians were far too engrossed in their business interests to trouble themselves with constitutional changes. Despite all the criticism there was a general feeling that the administration had been just and reasonably enlightened, and that any change would probably be for the worse.

The benevolent despotism had a good many achievements to its credit. Three totally dissimilar Asiatic races lived together in outward harmony, an almost unique achievement in a nationalistic world. One of the most unhealthy regions in the tropics had been made one of the healthiest by lavish government expenditure and unremitting effort. In 1937, 8.5 per cent of the expenditure of the Straits Settlements and 7.1 per cent of that of the Federated Malay States was for public health. The staff was made up of 362 European and 2,056 Asiatic medical and health officers, nurses, and health inspectors. The hospitals were very good, and the public health work was of a high order, especially in the towns. Because of lack of funds and the insanitary habits of the people, rural sanitation was more backward, as it was everywhere in the tropics. Perhaps the outstanding achievement was the control of malaria. The Institute for Medical Research had won an international reputation for its investigation of tropical diseases. The King Edward VII College of Medicine at Singapore trained Asiatics as doctors, dentists, and druggists. Infant welfare, maternity, and school medical work were developed on a considerable scale after World War I. In Singapore the death rate from all causes fell from 51 per 1,000 in 1911 to 24 in 1936.

The government felt that it had a special duty to educate the Malays, and its Malay vernacular schools were its outstanding achievement in the field of education. Attendance was free and compulsory for boys if a school were within reasonable distance, and most of the boys and a growing minority of the girls were receiving an education. Parents could not see the sense of wasting an education on a girl, but this attitude was rapidly changing. Free vernacular Tamil schools were opened for the children of Indian immigrants, partly by the government but chiefly by the rubber estates on which many of the Tamils were employed. The Chinese insisted that their children must learn Chinese for cultural and English for bread-and-butter reasons. They set up private Chinese vernacular schools which charged fees. The government gave grants to the better schools, about a third of the total number, which satisfied the standards of the department of education.

Every bright boy wanted an English education in the belief that this would lead to a white-collar job, and save him from the socially degrading necessity of manual labor. As in other Asiatic countries, supply exceeded demand, and by the thirties there was a small intellectual proletariat of would-be office workers for whom positions did not exist. English education was given in government and missionary schools, the latter receiving a grant-in-aid when they conformed to the requirements of the department of education. Small fees were charged, but a liberal provision of scholarships enabled gifted students from the vernacular schools to receive a free education in English. Technical education was given in a farm school, commercial schools, and several trade schools which trained skilled mechanics. Raffles College in Singapore gave three years of arts college education leading to a diploma.

The bulk of the Malays are small rice farmers, and in addition many of them have rubber and coconuts as cash crops. Before the war about 40 per cent of the rubber was grown on their small holdings. The principal work of the department of agriculture has been to raise the Malay standard of living by making their farming more efficient, through research and by persuading the Malays to adopt the results of the investigations. Rice needs an assured supply of water at certain stages of growth, while it is equally important to drain it off at other times. This was the task of the drainage and irrigation department, which considerably increased the rice acreage.

A high though uncertain percentage of the Malays are heavily

in debt to Chinese or sometimes Indian moneylenders. Many
have lost their holdings to their creditors and have become their
tenants. In other cases the Malay debtor is compelled to sell his
crop to the moneylender at less than the market price. The government tried to help the Malays by fostering the creation of cooperative credit and marketing societies, but with very limited
success. The Malay has no business sense, and much of his
borrowing is for unproductive purposes such as marriage ceremonies. He lacks foresight and plunges cheerfully into a morass
of debt from which he can never extricate himself. He is God's
own gift to such an astute businessman as the Chinese.

Labor in Malaya was predominantly Indian and Chinese, since
the Malays usually refused to work for regular hours at fixed
wages. The tin mines have depended chiefly on Chinese and the
estates on Indians, and both races supplied the labor in the towns,
on the railways, and in the public works department. There was
very little manufacturing in Malaya apart from the tin smelters.
Trade-unions were just beginning to make their appearance in the
thirties. The government tried to regulate conditions of labor and
prevent abuses, but the attitude of the two races was very different. The Chinese are strong individualists who prefer to run their
own affairs, and they resented and largely evaded the official
attempts to protect them. The Indians (most of them Tamils from
southern India) were never so happy as when the government
was holding their hands. An elaborate labor code was evolved for
their protection and was enforced by government inspectors with
wide powers.

The Malayan and Indian governments together strictly
scrutinized the methods of recruiting laborers in India and the
conditions on the ships which brought them to Malaya. The
Malay government fixed wages and hours of work and prescribed
minutely the exact type of free housing the employer must provide. It had rigid requirements for the provision of pure drinking
water, sewage disposal, and antimalarial work. The estate owner
must also furnish free medical and hospital attendance for the
laborer and his dependents, pay maternity benefits, and maintain
a crèche for young children as well as a school for the older
ones.

Trade and Investment

The British imposed no restrictions on the investment of foreign capital in Malaya, and this explains why the Japanese controlled all the iron mines, which supplied a third of their annual imports of iron ore. The total foreign investments in Malaya before the war were estimated at $454,500,000. Of this total $372,000,000 was invested in various business enterprises, the British share being about $260,000,000. Most of the remaining $82,500,000 was made up of government loans, which were floated sometimes in Great Britain and at other times in Malaya. American investments were $24,000,000, and the French, Dutch, and Japanese were also represented. In addition to the above there was about $200,000,000 of Chinese capital. The principal investments were tin mines, rubber and palm oil plantations, banks, shipping, and large companies which were both importers of foreign manufactures and exporters of Straits produce.

Malaya produced 41 per cent of the world's rubber and 29 per cent of its tin in 1938, the last normal year. Of the 3,302,000 acres under rubber 46 per cent was owned by European, chiefly British, companies; 15 per cent by Chinese and other foreign Asiatics; and 39 per cent by Asiatic small farmers, the majority being Malays. The production of rubber in 1938 was approximately 361,000 long tons, but the total export was 527,000 tons, with a value of $153,000,000. (In these figures, Straits dollars have been converted into American dollars. The Straits dollar was worth 56 American cents before World War II, and 47 cents after it.) The explanation of the discrepancy between production and exports was that much of the rubber grown in Sumatra, Borneo, and Siam was sent to Singapore, where it was graded and shipped overseas.

Tin production in 1938 was 43,200 long tons, two-thirds of the output coming from British-owned and the rest from Chinese mines. The quantity exported was 61,200 tons, valued at approximately $54,000,000. Exports included not only the tin smelted from Malayan ore but also the tin from large quantities of ore sent from Siam, Burma, French Indochina, Africa, and Australia. The attraction was the cheapness and efficiency of the Malayan smelters, which were the largest and most modern in the world.

The production of palm oil and pineapples was on a small scale but increasing. Rice, the staple food, was grown only by the Malays, and the crop supplied 36 per cent of the requirements of the population. From the point of view of production, the weakness of Malaya was that its prosperity was overwhelmingly dependent upon the world price of tin and rubber.

Apart from them, the mainstay of the dependency was the entrepôt trade of Singapore. One phase of this was the import and transshipment overseas of rubber, tin, and other tropical produce from the countries of Southeast Asia. In return Singapore sent to them a wide range of manufactured articles from Europe, the Far East, and India. The trade was essentially one of exchange, and the two sides were complementary: the produce paid for the manufactures, and the machinery of collection was closely inter-locked with that of distribution. One important item in the re-export trade was petroleum oils from the fields in Sumatra and Borneo. They were sent to Singapore as the most convenient center for transshipment to Japan, the Dutch East Indies, and Australia.

In 1932 moderate preferential duties were established for im-ports from the British Empire, but they did not greatly increase the sale of goods from the United Kingdom. In 1938 it supplied 18.6 per cent of the imports into Malaya, the British Empire (largely India) 18 per cent, and the United States 3 per cent. Another 27 per cent came from the Dutch East Indies (rubber and petroleum), and 16 per cent from Siam (rubber, tin, and rice). The principal markets in 1938 were the United States, which took 30 per cent, and Great Britain, 14 per cent of the exports. The United States was by far the largest market because of its heavy purchases of tin and rubber. In 1938 it bought 55 per cent of the tin and 41 per cent of the rubber. Europe and the British Empire each took about 17 per cent of the exports.

Malays, Chinese, and Indians

On the eve of World War II Malaya had a high degree of prosperity, and outwardly there was a notable harmony between the three divergent races which made up the bulk of the popula-tion. There were indications that this racial amity was drawing to a close; but to appreciate the situation a more detailed study is necessary of the racial composition of the country. The statistics are taken from the latest census, that of 1947; but the ratio between the three Asiatic races is almost the same as in 1941. In 1947 the population of Malaya was 5,808,000. Of this total the Malays numbered 2,512,000 or 43.3 per cent, the Chinese 2,608,000 or 44.9 per cent, the Indians 605,000 or 10.4 per cent, and the Europeans (principally British) 17,940 or three-tenths of 1 per cent. The Malays, who had been in an overwhelming majority in the pre-British period, were outnumbered by the Chinese. They were still the largest single race in the Malay States, where they numbered 2,395,000, and were 49.2 per cent of the population, as against the 1,880,000 Chinese who were 38.6 per cent. In Singapore, however, 728,000 or 77.4 per cent of the population of 938,000 were Chinese, and only 12.1 per cent were Malays. Moreover, the number of Malays who were indigenous to the Malay Peninsula was less than the above figures indicate, for about 14 per cent of their number were Malaysian immigrants from the Dutch East Indies.

The Malays regarded themselves as the only "people of the country," and looked upon the Chinese and Indians as unwanted immigrants who came in after the British had established law and order and made it safe for them to do so. Only the Malays regarded Malaya as their native country and gave undivided loyalty to it. With the majority this attitude was not patriotism in the Western sense. It is true that a minority of English-educated Malays were beginning to develop a feeling of patriotic attachment toward the whole of Malaya. The peasants, however, had a sentiment of personal loyalty toward the sultan of their state, and regarded Malays from other parts of the Peninsula as foreigners.

The actual numbers of Chinese and Indians in Malaya had little relation to the number permanently living there, since the majority were transients who eventually returned to their native countries. They looked upon Malaya as a place of temporary exile to which they had emigrated because they could make more money there than at home, and they had no intention of remaining all their lives. About a third of the Chinese, the Straits Chinese, had been born in Malaya, and the percentage was increasing. Birth in Malaya, however, did not necessarily imply permanent settlement there, for even some of the Straits Chinese went home to China. The average Indian immigrant stayed about three years, though there was a growing tendency to settle permanently and about 40 per cent had made Malaya their home.

The Chinese immigrants naturally felt no loyalty toward Malaya, since their only motive for coming there was to make enough money to get out and go home. They regarded themselves as citizens of China temporarily living abroad. Some but by no means all of the Straits Chinese had accepted Malaya as their permanent home, and had developed a feeling of loyalty toward it and the British Empire. They combined this feeling with a strong affection for China. For many of the Straits Chinese their first loyalty was to China, though the strength of their feeling varied with the length of the family's residence in Malaya. Many of them strongly supported Chiang Kai-shek's Kuomintang party, and their loyalty to China was heightened by the growth of nationalism there. This attitude did not mean that the Chinese were disaffected toward Great Britain, apart from the small but powerful Chinese Communist party. The non-Communist Chinese approved of the British as just and honest rulers who had enabled them to make money. The British held the Malayan cow while the Chinese milked it.

Chiang Kai-shek's National government did its best to prevent the growth of Malayan patriotism among the Chinese. It insisted that all Chinese living abroad were Chinese citizens, even though they and their ancestors for several generations might have been British subjects by birth. This dual nationality of the Chinese was one principal reason why the Malays after the war objected to giving them full rights of citizenship. The Chinese government used various methods to carry out its policy. There was a branch of the Kuomintang party in Malaya, and intimidation as well as persuasion was used to compel the Straits Chinese to join it. Many of the Chinese private vernacular schools were really propaganda centers for teaching little Chinese that they were patriotic Chinese citizens and that they must on no account develop loyalty toward

Malaya, which was only their temporary place of exile. The British government was only partially successful in checking this propaganda.

In our nationalistic world two races or religions in the same country spell trouble—as witness Palestine, Ireland, India, or Czechoslovakia. Prewar Malaya, however, had three antagonistic elements, and the growing Malay, Chinese, and Indian nationalisms were beginning to sharpen the clash. The war heightened nationalism in Malaya as everywhere else, and the risk of a triangular nationalist conflict is greater today than in 1941. The Malays and Chinese disliked each other, and both looked down on the Indian Tamils. The causes of conflict were and are religious, racial, economic, and political. The Malay is a Moslem, and he considers the Chinese and Indians unbelievers of the lowest kind. He has one God, while they have many. His mosque is bare of images, while their temples contain (to him) blasphemous statues carved in human form. On a point of ritual the Moslem regards the pig as the unclean animal, while to the Chinese it is his dream of a perfect dinner. The result is a latent hostility which can be brought to the surface by religious zealots or agitators. The same thing has happened in Palestine during the past quarter-century.

To do the Chinese justice, they feel an equal contempt for the Malay. They say that he has no business sense, and the Chinese can run rings around him every time. The Chinese assert that they would not condescend to marry a Malay. The progeny would absolutely wreck the family business. The Malay for his part will not allow his women to marry pig-eating infidels. So the solution of racial assimilation through intermarriage is ruled out. The Chinese and Indians will continue to remain undigested lumps in the body politic.

Culturally the Malays and the Chinese are poles apart, and the latter have certain racial characteristics that prevent any narrowing of the gulf. They are very clannish and have a genius for cooperation, along with an equally marked capacity for helping one another at the expense of the outsider. Witness the difficulty which trained Malays find in obtaining positions as office clerks

or skilled mechanics, because the Chinese have entrenched themselves and combine to exclude the people of the country.

Economically the Chinese have a strangle hold on Malaya. In
the whole dependency there appear to be only seven Malays who
own small businesses, and this leaves a vacuum filled by the
Chinese. They have a triple monopoly of retail trade, produce
buying, and moneylending at extortionate rates of interest.
Usually all three roles are filled by the same individual, and a large
part of the Malays are head over heels in debt to him. Competition among the Chinese is eliminated by price rings, and the
Malay is overcharged for what he buys and paid too little for his
rubber or rice. He realizes he is being exploited and resents it.
Politically the Malays fear that under a democratic form of government they will be ruled by these same unpopular foreigners. This
seems very probable, since most of the Malays are naive and unso-
phisticated, while the Chinese are aggressive, shrewd, and have
a gift for working together.

Before the war and to a lesser extent after it the tension remained below the surface. The Malay is reserved and scrupulously
polite, and he is too proud to condescend to show his feelings. He
is also an easygoing soul, very unlike the hard and fanatical Arab.
As a good Moslem the Malay comforts himself with the conviction
that the heathen Chinese and Indian will burn in very literal
hell-fire, so why not leave it to Allah to right the balance hereafter?
Moreover, the prewar Malay was quite content to entrust all
affairs of government to his sultan and the British. This is less
true since the war.

There was and is one small but influential group of Malays
that is consciously and actively anti-Chinese. This is the English-
educated minority, which under self-government will provide
the leaders. Before the war they appreciated the Chinese threat;
they also had a special motive for hostility because the Straits
Chinese were beginning to demand admission to the government
services on equal terms with the British and Malays. The Malays
insisted that no Chinese should be placed in authority over them.
They said that when their sultans agreed to govern in accordance
with British advice, they never bargained that the British official

would be a Chinese British subject. It seems inevitable that the educated Malays will gradually arouse the peasant 90 per cent against the immigrant races, as has happened in Palestine. Twenty-five years ago only the educated Arabs were actively opposed to Zionism. The peasant majority were merely potentially hostile, for religious and other reasons. The educated Arabs fanned this smoldering dislike into a flame. Malaya may go the same way, except that it will have three and not two nationalisms.

Japanese Conquest

When the war broke out in 1939 the British government decided that Malaya's most valuable contribution was to produce as much tin and rubber as possible, in order to provide American dollars for the purchase of munitions. European men in Malaya were prevented from joining the British army in Europe by refusing them exit permits except in special circumstances. After the fall of France compulsory service in the Malayan Volunteers was introduced for all Europeans between the ages of eighteen and forty-one. Since practically all were key men in business, banking, plantations, or government service some exemptions had to be allowed, but 89 per cent were conscripted.

The Volunteers were maintained at a high level of efficiency and fought throughout the campaign alongside the regular troops. Only Europeans were conscripted, but Asiatics were encouraged to join. There were 10,500 Volunteers, of whom 2,400 were Europeans. The government formed civilian defense services in all the towns. They comprised air raid wardens, firemen, and transport and medical services. There was no lack of volunteers, chiefly the Chinese, most of the European women, and the men who were too old to join the Volunteers. There were few Malays, since most of them lived in the villages. These units served with conspicuous courage and devotion to duty up to the end, in spite of heavy losses during the Japanese bombing attacks.

At the time of the fall of Singapore it was said that the British were defeated because their exploitation had so alienated the Malayans that they refused to fight and organized a fifth column to help the Japanese. As in every country, a few individuals did serve the invader, either for pay or because they had a grievance.

But there was no fifth column, and the overwhelming majority were loyal to British rule. There is no authenticated case of any Malay ever having fired on British troops. The stories that were told of such incidents had their origin in the fact that the troops had little knowledge of the Malayans and could not distinguish between a Japanese, a Malay, and a Chinese. Moreover, the Japanese in their infiltration tactics habitually disguised themselves as Malays.

On innumerable occasions Malayans of all races brought military information, gave food and shelter to British stragglers who had lost their way, guided them back to the army, and after the fall of Singapore helped them to escape from the country. More than this the Malayans could not do, because they had no arms or military training. After the invasion began there was no time to train them or indeed equipment with which to arm them. Over a thousand Chinese volunteers who took part in the defense of Singapore had to be given clubs. The only unit that was properly equipped and trained was one battalion of the Malay Regiment. It began the campaign with 846 Malays, and less than one hundred were left alive when the battalion surrendered with the rest of the army at Singapore.

The reason for the defenseless state of Malaya was the strong pacifism of the public of Great Britain during the interwar period. Any attempt to raise Malayan troops would have provoked an outcry that the government was militarizing a peaceful people in the pursuit of its own imperialistic ambitions. After the fall of Singapore a British cabinet minister admitted that it had not been practical politics to train the Malayans to fight. The theory was that in case of need the British army would defend the country. The British public, however, had insisted on disarming below the level of safety. All-out rearmament did not begin until May 1940; and between then and Pearl Harbor the time was too short to make up for the years that pacifism had wasted. The fall of Malaya was the inevitable result of Britain's general unpreparedness for war in 1939, and for this the British people and governments were responsible.

The original plan for the defense of Malaya was based on the fact that a Japanese attack would have to be launched from Japan itself, which was 3,000 miles away. The invaders were to be defeated at sea before they reached Malaya. The defense of the Peninsula was to be based on sea and air power. For this reason a naval base was built at Singapore, and airfields were constructed in various parts of the Peninsula. The disasters of the war in Europe decided the British government that neither warships nor airplanes could be spared for Malaya. The navy was strained to the uttermost in the Battle of the Atlantic and in holding the Mediterranean after the fall of France. Airplanes were urgently needed to defend Great Britain, to reinforce the army in Egypt, and, when Stalin made his urgent appeal for help in 1941, to prevent Russia from being knocked out. As yet Malaya had not been attacked, and Churchill decided not to lock up airplanes which were not immediately required, when they were desperately needed in actual theaters of war.

Three events that the British had never anticipated took place in 1941 and greatly increased the threat to Malaya. They had always counted on France's assurance that she would defend Indochina; but by July 1941 the whole of the French dependency had given in to Japan virtually without a fight. This brought the Japanese to within 647 miles of Singapore and gave them a base in southern Indochina where they accumulated troops and stores for the invasion of Siam and Malaya. Siam surrendered after a war that lasted only a few hours. This enabled Japan to land troops and supplies at Singgora, a Siamese seaport on the road and railway systems that led to Singapore, and only fifty miles north of the Malayan frontier. The crippling of the American fleet at Pearl Harbor freed the Japanese from any fear that an attack would be made on their sea line of communications.

The revised plan was that Malaya would be defended by ground troops against a probable attack from the north; but they too were so urgently needed elsewhere that they were not sent to Malaya in sufficient numbers. When the war began on December 7, 1941, there were 86,900 troops in Malaya. Of these approximately 76,300 were British, Australian, and Indian regulars, and the remainder Malayan volunteer battalions. Later reinforcements brought up the grand total to 125,000, although the strength in Malaya at any one time was considerably less than this. There were armored cars but no tanks, and the antiaircraft guns for the defense of towns and airfields were about 40 per cent of the number required. The British government had agreed that 336 modern aircraft would be sent to Malaya by December 1941. The number actually there was 152, including 60 fighter planes. None of them were modern and the majority were obsolete or obsolescent. Reserves of aircraft were about a third of what they should have been.

Some of the troops had been in Malaya long enough to complete their training, but the majority had arrived so short a time before the outbreak of the war they had been unable to do this. Officers and men were good material but young and inexperienced, and they had been sent out to Malaya half-trained. The reinforcements that arrived in 1942 were of the same caliber, with the additional disadvantage that they had been trained for the wrong kind of war. A British division and an Indian brigade that had been preparing for desert warfare in Africa were diverted to Malaya while at sea. Casualties had been so heavy that these reinforcements were thrown into action within a few hours of landing, without having time for any training in jungle warfare or acclimatizing themselves to fighting in the temperature of a Turkish bath. Instead of a range of vision that extended to the horizon they found themselves in a country where visibility was often only a few feet. Reinforcements of aircraft arrived at intervals, but they were never more than enough to make up for the wastage of planes destroyed by the Japanese. A great part of the pilots were fresh from flying school and had had no combat experience.

The Japanese are estimated to have used about 150,000 veteran troops and 300 tanks in Malaya. The divisions employed were among the best in the army and had been thoroughly trained in jungle fighting. Probably they were the highest quality in the world at that time for the type of warfare in which they were engaged. Enemy aircraft are believed to have been between 300 and 400, with first-class pilots. The performance of the Japanese Zero fighter was far superior to that of the British Brewster Buffalo.

The paramount military necessity was to prevent the Singapore naval and air base from being captured, so that it would be

available when at last a British fleet and air force arrived. The
defense of Malaya beyond the area necessary for the protection of
the base was a secondary object. There were, however, about
eighteen airfields scattered throughout the Peninsula, prepared
for the air force that never came. It was vital to deny their use
to the Japanese, since otherwise they would serve as bases for
attacks on Singapore. Since air defense was lacking they had to
be protected by the army. This compelled General Percival, the
British commander, to spread out his troops thinly throughout
the whole of Malaya as far north as the Siamese frontier, 450
miles from Singapore.

An attack from French Indochina or southern Siam was expected, but there was an additional complication. From the beginning the Japanese had almost complete command of the sea,
and this became absolute on December 10, 1941, when torpedo
bombers sank the only two battleships, *Prince of Wales* and *Re-
pulse*. The Japanese also had an overwhelming air superiority,
which rapidly became increasingly complete as the few British
machines were shot down. To oppose the enemy's control of the
sea and air the British had only three light cruisers, eight destroy-
ers, and a totally inadequate air force. It was impossible to prevent
the Japanese from landing troops wherever they liked along the
coast. A further factor in their favor was that along the 450-mile
stretch of both the east and west sides of the Peninsula the coastal
plain slopes gently to the sea, so that a landing is easy to make
and hard to prevent. General Percival was afraid that if he sent
most of his troops north to meet the invaders, the Japanese might
suddenly land another army in the southern part of the Peninsula
and capture the Singapore base. The general therefore kept about
a division and a half of his best troops at Singapore and the
adjacent Malay State of Johore. This left only two weak divisions
to oppose the Japanese in northern Malaya. One division was
stationed at Kota Bahru in Kelantan, to protect the airfields of
the east coast, and the second was in Kedah near the Siamese
border to guard those near the west coast.

The Japanese attacked on December 8, both at Kota Bahru and
across the Kedah-Siam frontier. The British and Indian troops
on the east coast were gradually forced back, but by far the

heaviest fighting was in western Malaya. Here the single British Indian division was opposed by three or four Japanese divisions and two tank regiments (300 tanks). The Japanese were able to relieve a tired division with fresh troops, but this was not possible for the defenders. After six weeks of incessant fighting and marching in an enervating climate the men were exhausted, and their losses were severe. Brigades were reduced to weak battalions, and battalions to companies. The morale of the half-trained troops, particularly the Indians, suffered from uninterrupted retreats, heavy losses, tank attacks, and air bombings.

Within a week of December 8 the Japanese had almost complete command of the air. So many of the obsolescent British aircraft had been destroyed that the remainder were withdrawn to Singapore. From then on the army fought blind without air reconnaissance, and it had no air cover against the constant Japanese air attacks that accompanied the assaults of their ground troops. As the half-trained reinforcements arrived piecemeal from India and Britain, they were thrown into the battle of the west coast. In spite of heavily adverse circumstances the British and Indian troops kept on fighting to the last and often inflicted very severe losses on the Japanese. Toward the end of the campaign they began to learn the enemy's jungle tactics, and sometimes turned the tables on them very successfully.

The British policy was to play for time, delaying the Japanese advance down the Peninsula until adequate reinforcements arrived. The Japanese object was to force the pace, and in the opinion of Field Marshal Lord Wavell they won the campaign by six weeks. Two quotations from British dispatches make it clear that the Japanese gained the victory by a combination of superior forces and better tactics. "The progress of the Japanese army was quicker than had been anticipated, chiefly as the result of its possession of an armoured component, its superiority in jungle warfare, its superiority in the air, and its ability to pass parties in boats down the West coast round the left flank of our army. [Again and again a sea-borne landing behind the defenders led to a further retreat.] Infiltrating Japanese frequently got behind our forward troops and formed road blocks on their lines of communication which proved difficult and sometimes impossible to clear." "The Japanese troops undoubtedly outmanoeuvred ours by their superior mobility, training and preparation."

The final scene was the battle for Singapore. The Japanese had 100,000 seasoned troops, at least 175 tanks, and complete control of the air. The British troops numbered 85,000, of whom 70,000 had arms; but many were very inadequately trained. Some of the most recent reinforcements had never fired a rifle, and the remnants of the air force had been withdrawn to Sumatra. After several days' fighting the Japanese had captured most of the depots of army supplies and almost all the reservoirs. Only twenty-four hours' water supply remained for the 1,000,000 population of Singapore. The Japanese "had established a moral ascendancy which made the resistance of the Singapore garrison half-hearted and disappointing." On February 15, 1942, General Percival surrendered to General Yamashita.

The Japanese tried hard to gain the support of the Malayans; but they failed because they have an absolute genius for alienating any people over whom they establish control. The Greater East Asia Co-Prosperity Sphere blatantly meant power and wealth for the Japanese and sweat and obedience for the "liberated" races. Nevertheless the conquest had some permanent effects. The Malayans had had complete trust in Britain's power to defend them, and her defeat gave a blow to her prestige from which it cannot recover. This effect was heightened by the failure of the British government to investigate the causes of the disaster, or even to publish the dispatches on military and air operations until 1948, when they finally appeared in the London Gazette. No attempt was made to make known the facts, so that the British case went by default. The result in Malaya was that at public meetings Communists could assure their audiences, without fear of contradiction, that the troops ran away. In the East more than in the West, if the prestige of the ruling government is affected its authority is undermined.

The tyranny and oppression of Japanese rule stimulated Malayan nationalisms. All three races were led to feel that they would be happier if they could manage their own affairs without foreign control. The Japanese followed the policy of "divide and rule," and stirred up the latent Malay hostility toward the Chinese.

But they completely failed in their effort to arouse hatred against the British.

An underground movement was organized soon after the fall of Singapore. The moving spirits were the Chinese Communists, though a minor role was played by the Malays and the Kuomintang Chinese. The Communists raised a force of some 6,000 to 7,000 men, and about 300 British were parachuted into Malaya to organize them. Arms and food were dropped, and by 1945 the guerrillas had disrupted rail traffic in Malaya. Plans had been made by which they were to paralyze the whole of the enemy's communications when the British army attacked; but the Japanese surrender made these arrangements unnecessary, and the British landed without resistance on September 5, 1945.

Reconstruction

Malaya was the only colonial dependency in Southeast Asia where the prewar rulers were welcomed back with triumphal arches instead of hand grenades. The streets of the towns were filled with rejoicing crowds, and the British troops received a tumultuous welcome. The only jarring note was that in various places the Malays began to kill any Chinese they could lay their hands on. These incidents were partly due to the success with which the Japanese had increased Malay hostility toward the Chinese. Moreover, Chinese guerrillas had extorted money and food from the Malay peasants, and in some cases the latter were paying off old scores. Patrols of troops suppressed the outbreaks by early in 1946.

A correspondent who traveled from Singapore to Siam in September 1945 wrote of "the deliriously happy people; the gaunt, rusting tin dredges; the silent, untended avenues of rubber trees; the disease-ridden human wrecks staggering back to their homeland after their nightmare experiences on the Burma-Siam railway." The Japanese had stripped the hospitals of their equipment and neglected health work. The result was a great increase in malaria and other diseases and a sharp rise in the death rate. Sanitation in the towns was extremely bad, and drinking water was unsafe. Roads and railways needed extensive repairs, and the bridges blown up during the British retreat had to be rebuilt.

The police had declined sharply in numbers, efficiency, and morale, and were very short of equipment. The Japanese occupation had given the Malayans less respect for human life, and after the surrender it was easy to obtain firearms. The result was an outbreak of violent crime unparalleled in Malaya's history. The criminals were mostly young men of eighteen to twenty-four, and the chief offenses were armed robbery, murder, extortion, and kidnaping. The Chinese secret societies, the murderers' and criminals' trade-unions, were very much in evidence.

Prewar Malaya imported two-thirds of its staple food, rice. In 1945, semistarvation was widespread in the towns; the Japanese failed to ship in enough food, and Malayan production declined. The British bought what rice was obtainable abroad but could get only limited quantities, since production had fallen sharply in Burma and the other rice-exporting countries. Cultivation in Malaya was stimulated by means of subsidies, guaranteed prices, and extensions of the irrigated areas; and by 1948 production was somewhat larger than before the war. The government introduced rationing and sold rice at far below cost, but the ration was much less than the prewar consumption.

Cotton clothing and all other necessities were equally scarce. There was a flourishing black market where the workmen bought everything that they could not obtain at the official fixed prices. They demanded higher wages in order to pay the fantastic prices of the black market. This played into the hands of the Chinese Communists, whose aim was to prevent the economic recovery of Malaya by an epidemic of strikes. Wages and costs of living were two to three times as high as before the war, but prices gradually began to fall as larger stocks of consumer goods reached Malaya. There was still a serious shortage of rice, however, and the prospect of increasing imports was poor, owing to the spreading civil war in Burma.

The work of rebuilding the social services began at once, but prewar standards have not yet been restored. The hospitals were re-equipped as far as possible, sanitation in the towns was improved, and antimalarial measures were reintroduced. In 1947 the infant mortality rate in Singapore was 87.3 per 1,000, the lowest ever recorded. Substantial progress was made in restoring roads and railways. By 1948 the seaports were rapidly regaining their prewar capacity through the rebuilding of docks and warehouses. However, in 1946 the crime wave was so serious that troops had to be used against the armed gangs that had imposed a reign of terror on towns and villages in the Peninsula. Gradually the police were somewhat strengthened in numbers, training, and equipment, and were able to tackle armed criminals on equal terms. Crimes of violence continued to be much more frequent than before the war, and the government was sharply criticized for not taking more energetic measures. Apparently the police were not brought up to proper strength until after the outbreak of the Communist revolt in 1948.

Most of the schools were pretty thoroughly looted during the Japanese occupation, and some of the teachers were executed. The British reopened the schools as quickly as possible in 1945, and all the students flocked to them who had been unable to get an education during the period of Japanese control. There was an acute shortage of teachers and school equipment. The subjects taught are much the same as before the war, but some important changes are being made in educational policy. Before the war most of the Chinese private vernacular schools were not given financial help, and a free primary education was provided only for Malays and Tamils. The postwar policy is that a free primary education lasting six years shall be given to all Malay, Chinese, Tamil, and English-speaking children.

Another change is that English is to be taught as a second language in the vernacular schools and is no longer to be confined to the English-language schools. It is intended to use the schools to create a common Malayan citizenship. The total number of children at school in 1946 was 487,688, or about twice what it was before the war. Plans are now in hand for creating a University of Malaya, with faculties of arts, science, and medicine. The prewar Raffles College and the King Edward VII College of Medicine are to be combined, and the staff and curriculum expanded by the addition of, for example, departments of engineering, law, and Asiatic studies.

The cost of reconstruction played havoc with government finances, since it took more than half of the annual budgets.

Taxes (largely derived from tin and rubber) were increased and an income tax imposed; but the revenue fell far short of expenditure, and each year there was a heavy deficit. Fortunately prewar financial orthodoxy had accumulated a revenue surplus of about $216,000,000; but the budget estimates anticipated that by the end of 1948 this would have shrunk to $11,000,000. This calculation made no allowance for the Communist revolt of 1948. In January 1949 the high commissioner stated that its suppression was costing about $125,000 a day, and this heavy expense may force a curtailment of reconstruction. A few weeks later the government of Great Britain agreed to pay part of this cost. Malaya also floated local loans for $58,000,000. In 1948 American officials described the dependency as on the verge of insolvency. Malayan businessmen are not worried by this; they point to the recovery of production and trade, upon which the revenue depends. They are confident that Malaya will weather this storm as it did the great depression and all the other slumps of its checkered history.

The financing of the social services, the native standard of living, and the general prosperity of Malaya depend chiefly on the exports of tin and rubber. Before the liberation careful plans had been made for their restoration, and these were put into operation as soon as the British troops arrived. It was discovered that the Chinese tin mines, which use a minimum of machinery and depend mainly on hand labor, could begin mining as soon as electric power was restored. This condition was soon fulfilled, and a large part of the postwar tin has come from Chinese mines. The British, however, owned two-thirds of the mines, and their restoration was a different matter. They had used a minimum of labor and relied upon machinery, particularly the bucket dredge. "Like Noah's Arks of corrugated iron they float in their mud holes with a chain of buckets running through their metal intestines and scooping out ore and mud from the alluvial deposits" (Purcell).

Before the war a dredge cost $450,000, but afterward the price was anything up to $1,600,000, and it took two years to build. Of the 103 dredges in use in 1941, 22 had been destroyed, and all the rest damaged in varying degrees during the British retreat in 1941–42. Few British tin-mining companies could afford to rebuild their dredges until the government carried out its promise to pay compensation, estimated at $75,000,000, for wartime damage. There was also a long delay in obtaining materials for repairs, and by the end of 1947 only 56 dredges were in operation. As a result, tin production in 1947 was only 36,079 tons, though this was a great improvement over the 8,432 tons of 1946. It was, however, a sad falling off from the 80,651 tons of 1940. The damage to the smelters was in process of being repaired, and Siam and other countries once more began to ship their ore to Singapore for smelting. In 1947 the export of smelted tin from Malaya was 29,889 tons, and of this 54 per cent was bought by the United States.

Rubber was in a better position: the Japanese had cut down the trees on only 2.5 per cent of the 3,302,000 acres which were planted before the war. There had, however, been widespread destruction of buildings and machinery on estates, and great deterioration in workmen's housing, sanitation, and the control of malaria. The direct loss was estimated at $200,000,000.[1] The Japanese had sent many of the Tamil coolies to build the Burma-Siam Railway, and only about a third of the prewar labor was available. Costs of production on estates were 74 per cent higher than before the war, and the industry suffered from strikes and lawlessness. The Malays owned 40 per cent of the rubber acreage, and with their inexpensive methods of manufacture they were able to begin production at once.

Hanging over Asiatic and European rubber alike was uncertainty as to how large a share of the American market would be pre-empted by synthetic rubber. By 1948 rubber had regained its prewar status, and plans had been made for replanting with high-yielding trees which gave about three times as much as ordinary trees. In 1947, 645,000 long tons of rubber were produced, the largest amount since the war. The entrepôt trade revived, although imports of rubber were lessened by the disturbances in the Dutch East Indies. The total exports of rubber

[1] In 1949 the British government agreed to grant $80,000,000 toward the cost of the Malayan war damage compensation scheme. It also offered an interest-free loan of $74,000,000 if required.

from Malaya in 1947 were 954,000 tons, of which 48 per cent went to the United States, 17 per cent to Great Britain, and roughly 4 per cent each to Canada and Russia. Most of the palm oil estates had resumed production, and the quantity exported in 1947 was 68 per cent of what it had been before the war. The coconut and pineapple industries were also beginning to recover.

The imports into Malaya in 1947 were $643,000,000 and the exports $620,000,000. A comparison with prewar statistics is misleading for two reasons. The value is higher because of the rise in prices since the war, but the volume of commodities involved is less. There are also restrictions on imports and exports, such as those imposed by the Malayan governments to limit purchases that have to be paid for in hard currencies. This is one reason for the small amount of trade with Japan. The Dutch government has limited trade with the Indonesian Republic to prevent the export to Singapore of rubber and other produce that belong to Dutch nationals. It is clear, however, that the sources of supply and markets are essentially the same as before the war, and that the entrepôt trade of Singapore has recovered much of its importance. The United States continues to be the principal market: in 1947 it took 33.3 per cent of the exports, chiefly tin and rubber, and supplied 10 per cent of the imports. Great Britain is still the leading supplier of manufactures, providing 19 per cent of the imports and taking 16 per cent of the exports. Australia supplied 6.2 per cent of the imports and bought 3 per cent of the exports. The East Indies accounted for 19 per cent of the imports and 9.4 per cent of the exports, while Siam's share was 8.4 per cent of the former and 1 per cent of the latter.

Self-Government and Rival Nationalisms

During the war the British government decided to introduce constitutional reforms in Malaya. It was cumbersome and inefficient that so small a country should have ten separate administrations. During the Japanese invasion the necessity of corresponding with so many authorities had often caused delay in carrying out military requirements. Since 1917, moreover, it had been the British policy progressively to grant self-government to the tropical dependencies. India and Ceylon were just about to reach the final goal, and other colonies were on the way toward it. No progress had been made in Malaya, owing to the three antagonistic races, the policy of giving special rights to the Malays as the people of the country, and because legal sovereignty in the Malay States lay with the sultans and not with Great Britain. There was no demand in Malaya for a change, but the British government decided to force the pace toward democracy. As sometimes happens to reformers in a hurry, it stirred up a hornet's nest.

British authority in the nine Malay States was derived from treaties with the sultans, and fresh arrangements would have to be made before the new policy could be carried out. In October 1945 Sir Harold MacMichael was sent to Malaya and negotiated treaties whereby Great Britain obtained "full power and jurisdiction." In other words, the sultans transferred their complete rights of legal sovereignty to the British government, which thereafter could take any steps it chose without further consultation with them. At the same time MacMichael investigated the conduct of each sultan during the Japanese occupation and decided whether he should be deposed or retain his throne. MacMichael did not speak Malay and had no knowledge of the customs of the people. He spent a few days in each state and returned to London with his treaties in January 1946.

The British government announced that the nine Malay States, together with Penang and Malacca, were to be combined in a Malayan Union, while Singapore remained a separate crown colony. Practically all power would be concentrated in the central government of the Malayan Union, though each state would have a council with such powers as the Union government delegated to it. The sultan would retain his throne and salary, but his chief function would be to preside over a Malay advisory council. Its main duty would be to pass laws on matters affecting the Moslem religion, subject to the approval of the governor. During the prewar period the sultans had been politely and inevitably removed upstairs to the attic. Under the postwar arrangements they were to be pushed out on the roof.

Malayan Union citizenship was to be given to all without discrimination of race or creed. It would carry with it complete

equality of rights, including admission to the administrative service of the Union, which the Straits Chinese had demanded and
the Malays stubbornly resisted. Citizenship would be granted
to all who were born in the territory of the Union or in Singapore,
and to immigrants who had been living there for ten out of the
preceding fifteen years. Future immigrants could obtain Malayan
citizenship after only five years' residence in the Union or Singapore.

Soon afterward the storm broke, for the new constitution
wrought the miracle of making the Malays politically conscious.
Another striking development was that the leadership was not
taken by the sultans; on the whole, they were a moderating influence and were pushed forward by their followers. The real
leaders were the English-educated Malays. The majority of these
belonged to the aristocracy, the traditional governing class, and
the principal leader was Dato Onn Bin Jafaar, prime minister of
Johore. The peasants were aroused to intense hostility against
the MacMichael treaties, and branches of the political movement,
known as UMNO (United Malay National Organization), arose
in every town and village. There were threats of a mass non-
cooperation movement. The sultans protested that Sir Harold
MacMichael had rushed them into signing the treaties. He had
sworn them to secrecy and given them no time to consult their
European friends or one another. The dual nature of MacMichael's
mission had inevitably implied to the Malays, "No signature, no
confirmation as sultan." Another reason the sultans signed was that
seventy years' experience had led them to believe that Britain's
actions had always been for the good of the Malays. They had
"the implicit faith in England that a child has for its father," and
at first they accepted MacMichael's assurances that the treaties
would "strengthen the Malays and their country."

The Malays were willing to agree to the two basic principles
of the new constitution. These were federation of the nine states,
and the granting of equal political rights to non-Malays who
had really made Malaya their home and were prepared to swear
allegiance to it. The Malays refused, however, to accept virtual
annexation; they insisted that the sultans must be restored to
their prewar position as the legal sovereigns, and they required

guarantees that the grant of equal citizenship would not lead to the Malays being ruled by the immigrant Chinese. They also demanded that the MacMichael treaties be scrapped and new ones negotiated. In April 1946 the British government gave way and appointed a working committee of representatives of the administration and the UMNO to draft more acceptable terms. Later a committee mainly composed of Chinese and Indians was set up to make its recommendations; and in 1947 the British government drew up a revised constitution on the basis of these various proposals.

The MacMichael treaties and the scheme for a Malayan Union were dropped. The sultans regained their prewar position as the legal sovereigns, and a Malayan Federation was set up by the joint action of King George VI and the nine sultans. This was far more than a mere matter of form: it emphasized that the sultans were the legal source of authority and that the new constitution was not imposed upon them, but was drawn up with their consent. The king would have complete control of the defense and foreign affairs of Malaya, and the sultans would govern in accordance with British advice as formerly. The central government of the Federation was to be composed of a high commissioner and executive and federal councils. One of the special responsibilities of the high commissioner was to safeguard the position of the Malays. This was one of the points upon which the UMNO was most insistent. Federal executive authority would be exercised by the high commissioner assisted by an executive council composed of official and unofficial members chosen from the various races in Malaya. The high commissioner must assent to all laws.

The legislative council, which passed all laws and financial measures, was composed of fifteen officials and sixty-one unofficial members. At first the latter were to be nominated by the high commissioner; but as soon as practicable election would be substituted. It was calculated that thirty-one of the unofficial members would be Malays, and the rest Europeans, Chinese, Indians, and Eurasians. This was only just, since the Malays were an absolute majority of those who regarded Malaya as the object of their loyalty. It did not please the Chinese, who wanted to reduce the Malay membership to twenty. By special arrangements, the Malay members of the council had something approaching a veto on immigration policy. This was important, since the fear of the Malays was that they would be swamped by new arrivals from China. The executive authority in each state would be the sultan and his executive council. The council of state, or legislature, would have legislative and financial powers. The powers of the states were limited and those of the federal government very extensive in legislation, finance, and the executive. This was inevitable, since most problems of government transcended state boundaries and required uniform treatment.

The qualifications for automatic Malayan citizenship were complicated and less sweeping than in the original Union proposals. The Malays insisted on excluding persons born in Singapore and the large number of Indians and Chinese born in the territory of the Federation who eventually returned to India or China. Roughly speaking, citizenship was given automatically to Malays, and to Indians and Chinese British subjects of the second generation born in federal territory. Immigrants (mainly Chinese) could become naturalized citizens if they had lived in the Federation for at least fifteen years and intended to remain there permanently. The Malays rejected the original Union proposals which required only five years' residence anywhere in Malaya.

A naturalized citizen had to take a citizenship oath, but he was not required to forswear allegiance to his former country. This is the unique feature of Malayan citizenship—many citizens will have a dual nationality. Indians will be Malayan citizens and British Indian subjects. Chinese will be at the same time Malayan citizens and citizens of China. Some of them will also be British subjects by birth. China insists that no Chinese can divest himself of his Chinese nationality, even if he has been born in a foreign country. The Malays forcibly pointed out that Chinese and Indian immigrants, and an unknown number of those born in Malaya, did not regard it as their adopted country. Instead, their loyalty remained with China or India. The British government, however, insisted on this form of citizenship, in the hope that it would weld the three races together in a common Malayan patriotism.

Most of the Malays were satisfied with the new federal constitution, but hostility toward it soon appeared among the immigrant races and a small Malay minority. Conservative and well-to-do Chinese opposed it because the exclusion of Singapore, with its predominantly Chinese population, and the restrictions on naturalization favored the Malays. The Chinese feared too that their economic interests would suffer, owing to the slight Malay majority in the federal legislature. The Chinese Communists opposed it on principle, since their object was to create disunion and strife. The Indians objected that insufficient attention was paid to their rights.

Malay opposition came from Putera, which was made up of several small parties. One important element was the left-wing, English-educated Malay intelligentsia. Putera was equally hostile to British rule and to the sultans, and hoped eventually to unite Malaya with the Indonesian Republic of Java and Sumatra. It demanded a united Malaya, including Singapore; immediate and complete democratic government through an elected central legislature; and equal citizenship rights for all who made Malaya their permanent home. Some of the elements in Putera tried to foment Malay racial hatred of the British by accusing them of responsibility for the failure of the Malays to engage in retail trade and tin mining. Putera was unable to win the backing of the large majority of the Malays, who supported the UMNO. The British government declined to give way to the protests, and the Malay Federation was established in February 1948. There are signs that the moderate Chinese and some of the Indians will cooperate in working the new constitution.

Federation is merely the first step in setting up a Malayan democracy. The establishment of the UMNO is a good sign, as it shows that the Malays of the different states are beginning to work together. It is encouraging that they agreed in principle to grant rights of citizenship to immigrants who were genuinely loyal to Malaya.[2] A weakness is that the number of competent Malay

[2] By midsummer of 1949 the UMNO was apparently insisting that only Malays could be government officials. The Chinese and Indians were demanding equal rights of citizenship in all respects, and the gulf between them and the Malays seemed to be widening.

leaders who understand the problems of the twentieth century is very small.

On the debit side, democracy will fail unless friendly relations can be established between the three Malayan races, and unless Chinese and Indian citizens abandon their foreign loyalties. The Malays, and particularly their leaders, are hostile to Chinese economic exploitation and fearful of political domination. Malay nationalism has been strengthened by the war and the political agitation that followed it. The Kuomintang party has renewed its activity, and the indications are that many of the Chinese will not give undivided loyalty to Malaya. They apparently want to have Malayan citizenship and the privileges that go with it, yet still remain Chinese citizens. Recently one of them wrote the following letter to the *Straits Times*: "I was born in Penang, but I claim to be a Chinese and I am proud of being one. If the British choose to bestow upon me all the privileges and freedom extended to their subjects and if the Federation likewise offers me citizenship, I am not too proud to accept these favours from both; but I shall still remain a staunch son of my motherland, China. If the British were at war with China, I shall fight for China."

Similarly, Nehru told the Indians that they would have to choose between loyalty to India and to Malaya. It appears that the majority have chosen India. Serious trouble may arise if the Malay majority in the federal legislature bans further immigration, or if Chinese and Indian officials and judges are given authority over Malays. Three discordant nationalisms may make Malaya another Palestine.

Harmony would be easier to establish now if the problem had been attacked earlier. Before the war nothing was done to weld the people into a Malayan unity because the British, following their usual policy of toleration, allowed each race to develop freely as it chose. The British dislike intensely any attempt to mold their own thinking, and they felt that they had no right to impose their own political ideas upon peoples who showed no desire for them. About the only exception was the not overly successful attempt to check Chinese patriotic propaganda. The result is that Chinese nationalism has been growing for thirty years, and Indian for a shorter period. These trends are harder to counteract now than if the attempt had been begun earlier.

The difficulty is increased by the effects of World War II. It intensified nationalism and also created a demand for the rapid attainment of self-government. Undue delay in granting this demand will create suspicion and hostility. Yet self-government cannot succeed if the future voters of Malaya are going to pull in three separate directions. The Hindu-Moslem conflict in India is a parallel; but in Malaya the three races are so intermingled that it would be impossible to partition the country. It is essential to replace racial antagonism by cooperation, but events are moving so rapidly that time is running out.

A far more determined effort than formerly will have to be made to prevent the Chinese vernacular schools from working against the growth of Malayan national unity. Most of these schools are short of funds, since they are largely dependent upon the fees paid by their pupils. Before the war government grants were paid to those that complied with the standards set by the department of education. The result was that they were very unwilling to jeopardize their assured income by teaching the children that they were Chinese citizens exiled in Malaya. The majority of the prewar schools, however, received no grant, either owing to their refusal to apply, or because their standards of instruction were too inferior to qualify for it. The government would now be wise to subsidize all the Chinese schools. This would not only make them much more hesitant about teaching Chinese nationalism, but would also give them the money that they need to raise their standards.

Prewar facilities for training Chinese teachers were inadequate, and the majority were immigrants from China. They were often ardent Nationalists and members of the Kuomintang party, and they used their classes as a vehicle for Chinese patriotic propaganda. A large number of other Chinese teachers were Communists, and there is good reason to believe that many of the terrorists engaged in the present Communist revolt are the products of the prewar Chinese private schools. The remedy is that the government must train Straits-born Chinese who are Malayan citizens and substitute them for those who have come from China.

The Kuomintang party and the Chinese consuls have also worked to keep the Chinese loyal to China. It will be necessary to restrict the latter to their proper consular duties and prevent them from interfering in the domestic affairs of a foreign country. As regards the Kuomintang, the large majority of the Malayan Chinese have supported Chiang Kai-shek and contributed handsomely to his party funds. The British government has raised no objections, though it has tried to prevent the intimidation that was sometimes used to persuade unwilling Chinese to join. Toleration can be carried too far, however, when a foreign political party works against the unity of the country where it has been allowed to establish itself. The Chinese Communist party has few members, but through its organization and its control of many of the trade-unions its power is out of all proportion to its numbers. Its foreign loyalties and its deliberate efforts to gain control over Malaya make it the enemy of the British policy of establishing democratic self-government.

Singapore, excluded from the Federation, has its own government and special problems. Singapore is strongly opposed to tariffs because its prosperity depends on the transit trade, while the Federation derives much of its revenue from import and export duties. The two parts of Malaya were kept separate for this reason and because the Malays opposed Singapore's inclusion, owing to its overwhelming Chinese majority. Singapore is a separate crown colony with a governor, an executive, and a legislative council. The latter has nine official and thirteen unofficial members. Three of the unofficials are elected, one each by the European, Chinese, and Indian chambers of commerce; six are elected by the general body of voters; and four are nominated by the governor to represent any important group that fails to win a seat in the election. The vote is given to all British subjects over twenty-one. There are no property or literacy qualifications, and to aid illiterate voters each candidate uses a symbol such as a telephone, a football player, or a bottle of beer.

The Communist Revolt

The Communists came out of the war with increased prestige as the leaders of most of the guerrillas who had fought against the

Japanese. It was clear from the beginning that they were making a determined effort to gain power. The British policy was to accept their offers of cooperation at face value. The Communists for their part did not as yet feel strong enough to risk a revolt, so they decided to use the same economic weapon—control of the trade-unions—that has proved so effective in France and other countries. Two factors favored them—the complete freedom of the press, public meeting, and association allowed by the British government; and the discontent of the workmen due to high prices and the scarcity of food and other necessities.

The Communists were very active in organizing unions among Chinese and to some extent Indian laborers. The separate unions were combined in a general labor union for each state, and these in turn were joined in the Pan-Malayan General Labor Union. The formation of the unions was not spontaneous; they were organized from the top downward by the Communists, who sometimes used intimidation to persuade the workmen to organize. The Communist press told its readers that "the British fascists were worse than the Japanese," and that Britain's aim was to enslave and starve the people.

Strikes for higher wages were easily brought about. The real aim of the Communists was not to help the workmen, but to paralyze economic recovery and discredit the British government. The ultimate object was to overthrow British rule and set up a republic under their own control. Many strikes were called without prior negotiations, and sometimes men who wanted to work were compelled by threats to strike because their "leaders," whom they had never elected, had made demands about which the men had never been consulted. In 1946 two abortive attempts were made to paralyze the government by a general strike. The Communists maintained contact with the Communist parties in China, India, and Australia.

The British Labor government strongly favored the formation of trade-unions and was anxious to improve wages and living conditions. A British trade-union official was appointed labor adviser in Malaya to help the workmen organize effective trade-unions, and to assist in setting up industrial courts with representatives of employers, workmen, and the general public for the arbitration of labor disputes. The government disapproved of strikes where the real purpose was political, but it was scrupulously careful not to interfere with the rights of labor.

The Communists took full advantage of this forbearance and laid plans for an armed revolt. Several months after hostilities began in 1948 the British government announced that it had captured ample documentary evidence to prove that the intention was to set up a Communist republic in Malaya, and that "the stage manager who dictates their every move sits in the Kremlin." Mr. Bevin, the foreign minister, linked the outbreak with the Communist revolts in other countries of Southeast Asia, as part of a concerted Cominform plan to drive out all Western influences. The revolt appears to have taken the British government by surprise, despite warnings of the impending trouble several months before it occurred.

The uprising began with an epidemic of strikes and murders, which soon developed into a guerrilla war. The Communist forces were estimated at between 4,000 and 5,000, almost all of them Chinese and the very large majority immigrants from China. Part of them were guerrillas who had fought against the Japanese. Most of these were boys and girls in their teens; they had found the underground "a veritable Communist forcing-house." [3] Some of the terrorists were professional Chinese criminals, who naturally welcomed so unrivaled an opportunity to practice their profession.

The victims were several hundred European rubber planters and tin miners or Chinese members of the Kuomintang party.[4] The latter were killed because the Chinese civil war had spread to Malaya. The Europeans were murdered because one purpose of the revolt was to paralyze tin and rubber production, and so prevent the return of prosperity to Malaya. The economic recovery

[3] In 1948 two British trade-unionists were sent by the Labor government to investigate the Malayan trade-unions. They reported that volunteers who joined the guerrillas to fight the Japanese were for three years given an intensive Communist education, with the avowed object of preparing for a Communist republic of Malaya. After the war the former guerrillas were organized in societies under Communist influence, and were called out to join the revolt in 1948.

[4] Between May and November 1948, 264 civilians were murdered, of whom 190 were Chinese and 21 Europeans. Of the 280 terrorists killed, 273 were Chinese.

of Great Britain would also be hampered, because the tin and rubber sold to the United States provided more dollars than the exports of Britain herself. The police and troops in Malaya were too few to give protection, and the isolated Europeans had no arms with which to defend themselves.

After the trouble started the government hastily added 3,000 men to the police, enlisted 35,000 special constables, and brought in about a division of regular troops. Large quantities of arms were distributed to the European planters and mine managers. They turned their scattered bungalows into small fortresses, enlisted Malay guards, and moved about their properties with an armed escort. R.A.F. planes patrolled the east coast of the Peninsula to stop gunrunning, and arrangements were made with the Siamese authorities to prevent the guerrillas' receiving help from the Chinese Communists in Siam. The Communist party was banned, and the Pan-Malayan General Labor Union, by which it controlled the individual unions, was suppressed. Convicted Communists in some cases were deported to China, but the trials had to be held in secret to prevent terrorization of witnesses.

The very large majority of the Asiatic population was on the side of the government, for this was in no sense a popular nationalist movement. It was an attempt by a handful of well-organized gangsters to impose their will on the country. Especially at first they terrorized whole districts, and individual Asiatics who supported the British were murdered. The government could not expect widespread active support from the Malayans until it showed it was able to protect them.

The Communists began with all the advantages. Their plans were fully laid, and they had the element of surprise. They had hidden large quantities of arms at the end of the war, and they had an excellent intelligence service, for many of them were seemingly peaceful laborers by day and guerrillas only at night. The Communists split up into small bands and had their headquarters in the jungle which covers a large part of Malaya. From there they made hit-and-run attacks which were difficult to foresee or prevent. Hunting for a handful of guerrillas in a jungle is very much like looking for a needle in a haystack. Moreover, many of the government troops were inexperienced, and the majority were new to jungle warfare and did not speak the vernaculars.

These difficulties were overcome by the enlistment of over 26,000 Malay armed police who knew the jungle better than the enemy. At the same time the troops were trained in jungle warfare. By the autumn of 1948 they were beginning to operate in self-contained units of about ninety men apiece. The government believed that about a year would be needed to hunt down the Communist guerrillas. Meanwhile, the planters and miners in their barricaded bungalows continued the production of tin and rubber.

By the summer of 1949 constant harrying was beginning to force the guerrillas to abandon the more settled areas and retreat deeper into the jungle. Slightly over one thousand had been killed or taken, and captured documents complained of lack of popular support, especially from the Malays. "We were deluded into thinking that a single stroke would vanquish the enemy. Our reports of the enemy's strength were inaccurate. We have been forced into a defensive position." The anti-Communist Chinese were beginning to lose their fear of the terrorists and to refuse to pay protection money. To an increasing extent they were giving the government information about the plans of the guerrillas. This is of great importance since experience in other countries has shown that regular troops cannot crush guerrillas unless they receive information about their movements from the local population. This can be provided only by the anti-Communist Chinese. The Malays have cooperated whole-heartedly with the British throughout the campaign, but their usefulness as intelligence agents is limited owing to the hostility between them and the Chinese.

There were indications that the next stage in Communist strategy would be to leave small bands to continue terrorism near the towns, while withdrawing the bulk of the Communists into the sparsely inhabited jungle near or perhaps across the Siamese frontier. The difficulty of ferreting them out there can be measured by the fact that it sometimes takes twenty-four hours to cover two miles. There will have to be joint action by the British and Siamese forces. Too great hopes should not be placed upon the latter, since the Siamese army is small, only moderately well equipped, and without battle experience.

Ultimate success would be assured if the outcome depended solely on the campaign inside Malaya. But whether enduring security can be established depends on what happens in the adjacent countries of Southeast Asia and in China. Once the Communists have conquered southern China, there is the danger that they will infiltrate reinforcements into Malaya. Hitherto the strategy of the leaders in Malaya has been amateurish, and a few hundred fully trained experts in guerrilla fighting, prepared to take great risks, could do far more damage than the present terrorists have achieved. In the struggle against the Communists the whole of Southeast Asia is a single unit.

Suggested Reading

Clifford, Sir Hugh. *Malayan Monochromes*. London. 1913.
———. *Bushwhacking and Other Asiatic Tales and Memories*. New York. 1929.
Coupland, Sir Reginald. *Raffles, 1781–1826*. Oxford. 1926.
Emerson, Rupert. *Malaysia, A Study in Direct and Indirect Rule*. New York. 1937.
Emerson, R., L. A. Mills, and V. Thompson. *Government and Nationalism in Southeast Asia*. New York. 1942.
Maxwell, Sir George. *The Civil Defence of Malaya*. London. 1944.
Mills, Lennox A. *British Malaya, 1824–1867*. Singapore. 1925.
———. *British Rule in Eastern Asia*. London. 1942.
Purcell, Victor. *Malaya: Outline of a Colony*. London. 1946.
———. *The Chinese in Malaya*. London. 1948.
Swettenham, Sir Frank. *Malay Sketches*. London. 1895.
———. *The Real Malay*. London. 1900.
———. *British Malaya*. (4th ed.) London. 1920.
———. *Footprints in Malaya*. London. 1942.
Winstedt, Sir Richard. *A History of Malaya*. Singapore. 1935.
———. *Britain and Malaya, 1786–1941*. London. 1944.
———. *Malaya and Its History*. London. 1949.

FRENCH INDOCHINA

❖

THE strategic importance of French Indochina was suddenly revealed to the American public when the peninsula was used by the Japanese as a springboard for their lightning offensive in the Southwest Pacific. Besides its strategic location, it furnished the Japanese war machine with a large supply of vital raw materials such as rice, coal, and rubber. Today the prospect of a Communist victory in China brings again to the forefront the importance of Indochina, where French troops are now fighting the Nationalist government of Viet Nam led by the Moscow-educated Ho Chi Minh.

French Indochina comprised the colony of Cochin China at the southern tip of the peninsula, and the four protectorates of Tongking, Annam, Cambodia, and Laos. Despite its name, which is justified by geographical position and the cultural impact of China and India, Indochina is more a barrier than a highway between the two giant countries of the East. The life lines of the peninsula are above all maritime: land communications with Thailand, the western neighbor, are tenuous; and chains of mountains separate China from the northern provinces of Tongking and Laos, forming a wall that is pierced only by the Haiphong-Yunnan railroad, an engineering feat, but of limited commercial and military value.

Indochina is often pictured in the guise of an Annamite coolie balancing on his shoulder a long pole with two racks of rice hanging at each end; they represent the rice-growing deltas of the Red River in the northern province of Tongking and of the Mekong River in Cochin China, the two centers of wealth and population. In between them, elongated Annam has a few densely populated coastal plains separated by long stretches of jungle and forest.

Mountains and high plateaus, sparsely populated, occupy most of the interior. The kingdoms of Cambodia and Laos, which separate Thailand from the coastal provinces, are inhabited by some three million Cambodians, descendants of the ancient Khmers who built the magnificent temple of Angkor Wat, as well as by the more primitive Thais of Laos. Some tribes of Indonesian origin form scattered groups throughout the country, totaling less than 5 per cent of the population of Indochina.

Some seventeen million Annamites, who now call themselves Vietnamese, occupy the deltas and coastal plains of the three eastern provinces of Tongking, Annam, and Cochin China. They make up three-fourths of the total population, its more energetic and industrious element, and live crowded on less than 8 per cent of the total area of the country. From overcrowded Tongking they have spread south into Annam, where they clashed with the Hindu civilization of the Cham and the Khmer, and finally into Cochin China, from which the Cambodians were ousted in the eighteenth century. They even penetrated into Cambodia, where some two hundred thousand Annamites have settled. The unhealthy climate of the interior, where malaria prevails, has prevented mass emigration and increased the dangers of overpopulation.

In bad years the peasants of the northern provinces go hungry; if it were not for the surplus of rice from the less populated and richer Cochin China, famine would decimate a population that under French rule has increased faster than the production of rice. From fifteen million in 1910, the Indochinese peoples came to number more than twenty-three million in 1940. The density of population in the Mekong is one of the highest in the world, while production of rice per acre is far below that of less thickly populated Japan.

Whether he owns his tiny parcel of land, as in northern Annam and Tongking, or whether he is a tenant farmer as in Cochin China, the Vietnamese peasant has an extremely low living standard. Usury adds to his misery; Vietnamese, Hindus, and especially the Chinese, who have been the traditional middlemen and moneylenders, obtain usurious interest rates in spite of French efforts to establish agricultural credit banks and cooperatives.

The basic unit of society in Tongking and Annam is still the village, an autonomous community bound together by strong religious and social obligations. Villages are economic units as well; they often have their cooperative system of irrigation, their communal granaries, even their communally owned land, which may comprise as much as 26 per cent of the cultivated land in Annam and 20 per cent in Tongking. As in China, family ties are all-important; the father is the priest of the ancestral cult and has complete authority over his children.

The predominance of Chinese culture is also evident in the literature and religion of the Vietnamese people and until recently in the elaborate imperial structure and mandarin system. Annam was under Chinese rule from 181 B.C. to 939 A.D.; after its liberation, the strong imprint of Chinese civilization remained.

In 1673 the partition of Annam into the two states of Tongking and Cochin China brought about a long series of dynastic quarrels which permitted the intervention of the French. Thus in July 1789, the very month the Bastille was stormed, a Catholic bishop was leading a party of French soldiers on behalf of one of the warring factions. With the unification of all Annamite lands under the new emperor, Nguyen Anh, at Hue, French influence declined. However, persecutions of missionaries led to diplomatic protests and furnished the pretext for opening up trade by force.

Cochin China was the first conquest. After the capture of Saigon, its principal city, in February 1859, the Emperor of Annam sued for peace and by the treaty of 1862 ceded to France the three eastern provinces of Cochin China. Two years later Cambodia, where Siamese influence had been strong, became a French protectorate. The conquest of Tongking and Annam was undertaken in 1867 and concluded, despite Chinese opposition, in 1893. By the turn of the century France had completed the conquest of Indochina and created under a governor-general a centralized administration grouping the colony of Cochin China and the protectorates of Tongking, Annam, Cambodia, and Laos.

Some 43,000 Europeans and *assimilés* lived in Indochina in 1937, mainly in Cochin China and Tongking. Of these, 36,000 were French and 2,700 naturalized Frenchmen. By contrast with the Dutch in the Indies, the larger part of the French remained

in the colony for less than ten years. The proportion of administrators, customs and police officials, and military men was also greater
than in the Dutch Indies. The danger of malaria in the hinterland,
especially in altitudes of less than 3,000 feet, partly explains the
French reluctance to follow the Dutch example.

The Chinese have traditionally played an important role in the
Indochinese economy. They numbered 419,000 in 1931 and
326,000 in 1936. Benefiting from a privileged status, they were
effectively organized in guilds and mutual aid societies. Their
knowledge of Annamite psychology and culture made them useful
intermediaries between the French and the native population,
while their foresight and perseverance gave them the advantage
over the Annamites in business matters. A comprehensive system
of rice purchasing gave them a quasi-monopoly of the rice market;
it also made them moneylenders, brokers and speculators, importers and exporters, peddlers and manufacturers. The main centers
of their activities were Cholon and Saigon in Cochin China. They
also played an important role in the fish, hide, and wood industries,
and monopolized the culture of pepper. They were often criticized
for their skillfulness at evading laws and regulations, for their
tendency to return to China once they made their fortunes, and
especially for their harsh treatment of the native peasants, often
kept in debt by their usurious loans.

Indochinese Economy

Rice is by far the most important culture in Indochina, which
is one of the three great rice-exporting countries in the world. It
forms 90 per cent of the diet of the people and some 50 per cent
of the total exports. The dangers of monoculture are evident: not
only do poor crops mean famine, but the elasticity of the demand
from rice-importing countries does not guarantee a steady income.
Thus the Dutch Indies imported 377,000 tons of Indochinese rice
in 1931, but only 43,000 tons on the average between 1933 and
1937. China, the main customer, received 900,000 tons in 1935,
and only 290,000 tons in 1936.

Moreover, the almost exclusive cultivation of rice is closely
linked to the evils of overpopulation. Pierre Gourou, in his study
of the Tongking peasants, estimates at 60 per cent the number of

farmers owning less than one acre of land, and at 63 per cent the number of taxpayers who had no land or less than half an acre. The fact that the population under French rule increased faster than the production of rice in the deltas is due not only to a lower death rate but also to the reluctance of rice-growing peasants, conditioned by their environment, to experiment with new crops, new methods, and new lands. Poverty adds to their inability to show foresight and initiative. It forces the peasant to cultivate with primitive methods a crop that furnishes immediate returns for his labor and is readily negotiable. The Chinese middleman can profit by the fatalistic outlook of the rice-growers and keep them in debt.

"Overpopulation," wrote Charles Robequain in his study of the economic development of Indochina, "is the fundamental problem, the one on whose solution depend all the others. The education of the native masses can succeed only when there is a minimum of material comfort. While people are hungry, no social change can be accomplished—no matter how desirable. Politics and economics are closely linked: the native must, of course, have a growing share in governing his own country; but also, in order to carry out these duties, he must have a larger daily ration of rice, supplemented with other foods, to build up his physical strength."

Perhaps the success of French colonization can be measured by its effectiveness in dealing with the central problem of overpopulation and subsequent undernourishment. Since birth control was out of the question, efforts in three directions were or could have been made to remedy the situation: the opening of new rice fields and the improvement of rice cultivation; the introduction of new crops, especially in the hinterland; and finally, the development of industry.

It was most difficult for the French to introduce radical transformations in the deltas of Tongking and northern Annam, where almost every inch of the soil was under cultivation, and where the deep-seated tradition of one of the densest populations in the world prevented rapid innovation. The dikes along the Red River were extended and improved, and within their framework a system of primary and secondary canals was built. It was in the

Mekong delta in Cochin China, however, that profound transformations took place. There the land was drained, and large
rectilinear canals, for both irrigation and transportation purposes,
were dug at great cost. They became the life arteries of Cochin
China; along them were built long rows of houses that contrast
with the village concentration in Tongking. The area under cultivation grew from half a million hectares in 1880 to 2,200,000
hectares in 1937 with a corresponding increase in population and
rice exports. The system of canals was not completed, however,
by the creation of enough secondary and tertiary canals.

As in Tongking, little was done to improve the quality of rice,
the methods of cultivation, and the marketing and credit facilities.
The Chinese monopoly on the purchase of rice, for instance, not
only kept the evil of usury, in spite of French attempts at creating
cooperatives and credit institutions, but made it impossible to
deliver to the mills a product of uniform quality and size able to
compete with Burmese or even Siamese grain. With the exception
of corn, which is largely reserved for exportation to France where
it is used as cattle feed, few other crops have been developed. It
is to be noticed also that Cochin China, despite the large increase
of its population (from 1,679,000 in 1880 to 4,484,000 in 1938),
has not been an adequate outlet for the surplus population in
Tongking. The increase was due more to the lowering of death
rates than to the emigration from the north.

The tremendous growth of rubber production in Cochin China
and Cambodia, from 300 tons in 1915 to 10,000 tons in 1929 and
70,000 tons in 1939, did not directly benefit the Vietnamese. No
more than 17,000 Tongkingese and Annamites were employed on
Cochin Chinese rubber plantations, where three-fourths of the
total production is to be found. Moreover, French monopoly contrasts with the situation in Java, where some 50 per cent of the
rubber was produced by the natives before the war. Large-scale
rubber plantations owned by Frenchmen are the rule, and the
monopolistic trend is illustrated by the role played by the important *Société Financière des Caoutchoucs*.

The difficulty of obtaining and keeping an adequate labor
supply on the plantations, where living conditions have become
generally far superior to those found in the deltas, illustrates the

reluctance of the Vietnamese to expatriate themselves. Improvements in the control of malaria have not changed their attitude toward the "bad water" country where evil spirits threaten the life of the new settlers. The cult of ancestors also militates against inland colonization: it is considered almost sacrilegious to abandon village and family. It is significant that, with the exception of Cambodia, no more than 150,000 Vietnamese live outside the coastal regions. Besides the Vietnamese reluctance to leave familiar surroundings, several factors explain the lack of success in the colonization in the hinterland. The principal ones are the prevalence of malaria, difficulties of transportation, the small number of French colonists with agricultural ambitions, and, until recently, the lack of a comprehensive program of agronomic research and development.

Attempts have been made to develop the production of tea and coffee; they have met with mediocre success. Efforts at cotton raising have failed. The traditional culture of silkworms as well as that of pepper is on the decline. Cattle and pig raising, largely in Cambodia and Laos, is a relatively unimportant source of wealth. The immense forests of the interior have been until recently wastefully exploited both by primitive natives, who burn large stretches of forest to obtain their temporary fields, and by Chinese and Vietnamese wood merchants. The most successful utilization of natural resources was still the traditional fishing industry, largely under Chinese control; fish forms an important part of the people's diet as well as of the country's exports.

Perhaps the most efficient remedy for overpopulation would have been found in the industrialization of the colony. Indochina is well endowed with three basic necessities for the development of modern industry: labor, raw materials, and power. Capital and technical knowledge could have been furnished by the French. Unfortunately the interests of the Indochinese peoples clashed with those of French industrialists. As a result, most of the mining products were exported and processing industries remained at an early stage of development.

Coal, mainly anthracite of good quality, is to be found in Tongking where two large companies, the *Société des Charbonages du Tongking* and the *Société des Charbonages du Dong Trieu* produce 92 per cent of the total output—nearly 2,500,000 tons in 1939. About two-thirds of this coal was exported, the rest being used to produce fuel for the railroads and electricity for the cities. Other minerals were tin and zinc, as well as small quantities of iron ore, chromium, manganese, and bauxite; 38,000 tons of phosphate were mined in 1938.

Some 50,000 workers, mainly Tongkingese, were employed in the mines and formed a temperamental labor force. Few of them stayed on the job more than a few months at a time, although living and working conditions were much improved during the twenties and the thirties.

The processing industries developed slowly, although faster than in the rest of the French Empire: 300,000 tons of cement were produced yearly, as well as some 10,000 tons of cotton yarn and fabric and 1,800 tons of tobacco. There were many rice mills and rice distilleries, and some sugar refineries.

The slow tempo of industrialization has been due largely to the effects of the tariff policy imposed by France to benefit her own industries, especially textiles, iron and steel, and machinery. Until the depression of the thirties Indochina's balance of trade in the Far Eastern countries, especially China and Japan, was highly favorable, while its trade with France showed a large excess of imports over exports. The depression, which restricted the demand of Indochina's neighbors, forced the metropolitan country to buy more goods from the colony. In 1935, for the first time, France bought more than she sold her colony. A publicity campaign made Indochinese rice popular with French housewives; from 1933 to 1937 France imported an average of 647,000 tons of rice, or 41 per cent of the total exports. Even 150,000 tons of anthracite found their way to France around the Cape of Good Hope!

The imperial character of the trade relations between France and her colony, although highly satisfactory to France, presented some dangers to Indochinese economy. The high tariffs set up by Far Eastern countries were partly in retaliation for French protectionist policy. Indochinese tariffs prevented the competition of cheaper foreign industrial goods, especially Japanese, and thus restricted the demand for manufactured articles. More important, French interest in keeping a quasi-monopoly of the Indochinese market prevented the development of an important textile and perhaps metallurgical industry, as well as the processing of such natural resources as wood, bamboo, rubber, copra, cattle, and fish. Large-scale electrification in the deltas could have given impetus to traditional handicrafts in the villages, where skilled artisans are numerous, forming as much as 7 per cent of the population in Tongking and 4 per cent elsewhere. Markets for manufactured goods answering Far Eastern needs would have been found both in Indochina and in China, Indonesia, Malaya, and Thailand.

Besides the obvious metropolitan interest in reserving a market for French goods, other factors explain the slow tempo of industrialization. Among them are the French monopoly of investments, the lack of facilities for technical training coupled with the lack of industrial and commercial aptitude among the Vietnamese, and the absence of a comprehensive plan for the utilization of natural resources. The latter is being remedied today, but perhaps too late.[1]

The impact of Japanese occupation on the economy of Indochina is difficult to ascertain. New roads and airfields were built; the production of phosphates, jute, ramie, and cotton was increased. On the other hand, shortages, especially of manufactured goods, inflation, monopolistic exploitation, the dislocation of transportation, and the lack of foreign markets weakened Indochinese economy and increased living costs.

Soon after liberation, the struggle between France and the Nationalist government of Viet Nam led to catastrophic consequences. Only 9,000 tons of rice were exported in 1947, as against 109,000 tons in 1946 and 1,500,000 tons in 1940. Burning and looting of plantations and the interruption of communications have cut down the production of rubber to one-half that of 1939. Only 48,000 tons of coal were exported in 1947, as against 1,500,000

---

[1] Between 1932 and 1936 the average of the major exports of Indochina was as follows: rice 49.2 per cent; corn 14.0 per cent; rubber 8.4 per cent; coal 5.6 per cent; and dried fish 4.7 per cent. France's share of Indochina's foreign trade showed the following marked increase:

	1911–1920	1921–1930	1931–1937	1938
Exports to France	19.6%	20.9%	48.1%	53.0%
Imports from France	29.6%	43.2%	57.1%	57.1%

tons in 1939. Sabotage and guerrilla attacks have forced many mines to stop production entirely.

In the long run the prospects for the economic development of Indochina, especially through industrialization, are good, providing several conditions are fulfilled: an early peace settlement, the availability of foreign capital and technical skill that France could perhaps furnish by herself, and the development of economic exchanges, especially between the Far Eastern countries. In addition, an all-out effort would have to be made to introduce new crops and scientific methods of cultivation, to colonize the interior, to reform the system of land tenancy and ownership, and to improve credit and marketing facilities. Education is a necessary condition of economic development, and in turn is linked to the problem of overpopulation and low living standards. The solution to Indochinese economic difficulties may be found in the moral resources of the new Nationalist movement rather than in the economic resources of the country.

The French Record

Measured in statistics of production and trade, of road and railroad mileage, even of sanitation and education, the progress under French rule is obvious. Indochina was exporting 700,000 tons of rice in 1900, almost 2,000,000 tons in 1937; about 200 tons each of rubber, corn, and coal in 1900, and in 1939, 78,000 tons of rubber, 1,500,000 tons of coal, and 546,000 tons of corn. If the foreign trade is measured per capita, Indochina compared favorably with India, but was still behind the Dutch East Indies and the Philippines. Thirty-six thousand kilometers of roads, of which 18,000 are paved, and 3,000 kilometers of railroads were built. A modern irrigation system was added to the ancient one to protect and enrich the deltas.

In 1939 half a million children attended grammar schools; 10 per cent of these went on to higher elementary schools and 1 per cent to secondary schools. The University of Hanoi had 631 students in 1937, most of them Vietnamese. Four hundred and fifty medical institutions were staffed with 110 European and 240 native doctors who made monthly tours of rural areas and attempted to prevent tropical diseases, especially malaria. Labor conditions were much improved following World War I; new labor codes and a body of labor inspectors were created to control the recruiting of coolies and to establish better living conditions and shorter hours of work.

This record, however, tells only one side of the story. Vietnamese Nationalists are objecting to the abnormally low wages of agricultural and industrial workers—about one-third the wage of the Moroccan laborer and one-thirteenth those of the French worker. They point out that the beginning of improvement in health and living conditions, especially in the rubber plantations, has not yet eliminated unscrupulous exploitation, and that very little has been done to improve the lot of the Vietnamese peasants, even in the fight against usury. Indirect taxes, which form 70 per cent of the federal budget, weigh heavily upon the people. What is the use of improving sanitation, they ask, if the main cause of mortality, undernourishment, is not corrected? They feel that Indochina has been exploited by a handful of French colonialists for the direct advantage of France and not for the good of the Vietnamese.

When we leave the domain of material accomplishments, the impact of French civilization is even more difficult to evaluate. A successful synthesis between Eastern and Western standards cannot easily be reached. Greater order and justice have often resulted in greater disorder and injustice. Transgressors are no longer delivered to the elephants and the abuses of mandarin rule have largely been suppressed, but the introduction of rules of law based on a philosophy of individualism has weakened the all-important family and communal ties. Inequalities without the compensation of the security that family and village had provided were less bearable away from home and under the anonymity of French rule and of capitalistic methods. The floating population of agricultural workers in Cochin China and industrial workers in Tongking have been deprived of the advantages of their own civilization while not yet enjoying those of Western civilization. Slow reforms and improvements could not always keep up with the accumulated if vague and inarticulate resentments of insecure workers and peasants. Both Nationalist and Communist propaganda could thus find receptive ears.

Even more dangerous was the frustration of the native élite, anxious to be educated in the thought and ideals of the West, yet denied the use and benefit of their new knowledge. The rights of equality and liberty could not be taught and denied at the same time. The discrepancy between the values professed by the French and their actual performance could only inflame many young intellectuals and lead them to revolt.

Their need for self-realization could have been partly fulfilled by the opening of responsible administrative posts to the educated natives and by the progressive introduction of self-government. But, in contrast to the practice of the British and Dutch colonial administrations, few responsible positions were open to the natives, and when subordinate posts were offered to them, the discrepancy between their salaries and those of their French colleagues was a source of dissatisfaction. On the other hand, the British aim of teaching self-government to the dependent peoples did not appeal to the national experience and psychology of the French, used as they were to a highly centralized government at home. The *République une et indivisible* was not to teach colonial peoples how to become independent. As Professor Mills remarked, "the development of colonial self-government has no place in French policy. The powers of the legislatures in Indochina are much more limited than in Malaya and Hong Kong; and the intention has been that the dependency should be drawn progressively closer to France, as an integral part of a closely knit empire dominated by the mother country."

The neat hierarchy of French colonial administration was modeled on the Napoleonic pattern and amounted in practice to rule by the permanent officials of the ministry in Paris and by the French administrators on the spot. It is only rarely that the personality of the governor-general, a politician rather than a colonial administrator, could assert itself against the centralizing tendency of the permanent officials. Thus Albert Sarraut's liberal policy on the eve of World War I could not undo the rigid structure built by Paul Doumer at the turn of the century. Associative principles of a few enlightened governors could not fully counteract the assimilative tendencies of the administration.

In principle the governor-general had quasi-absolute powers, including the right to dissolve and suspend advisory native councils. The only limitation to his rule came from Paris in the form of laws and decrees, as well as in the persons of the inspectors of colonies, sent periodically to investigate his administration. The governor of Cochin China and the chief residents of the four protectorates were responsible to the governor-general. In turn, they exercised control over the residents of the provinces, who supervised the local administrators. In Cochin China these were almost exclusively French, while in the protectorates the so-called indirect rule made the native administrators completely subservient to French officials. Consultative bodies had native members, but these were limited to an oligarchy of merchants, landowners, and local notables.

Such a system may have given the French a sense of security. The price to be paid for this overprudent paternalism was the discontent of a native intelligentsia that was ready to seize the first opportunity to reject French rule. A vigilant police could stop attempts at rebellion, but the imprisonment of thousands of political offenders could only feed the movement of liberation. The danger of shutting the native élite off from administrative posts was not recognized until the reforms of Georges Mandel in 1938; they came too late and were not made on a sufficient scale to affect the temper of the Vietnamese intellectuals. "France cannot educate élite groups," wrote Louis Jovelet in *Le Monde* in April 1947, "—and that is her real mission in the world—unless she really intends to use them. Does one heat a boiler if one does not intend to use its steam? It is because the French failed to understand the absolute truth of this maxim that their achievements in Indochina, Tunisia, and Algeria have been partially jeopardized. The French must put an end to the paradoxical situation created by the existence of huge countries organized and policed through French efforts, whose élite she has educated, but to which she has not yet granted local self-government although their largely illiterate masses send deputies to the National Assembly."

A just criticism of French policy and methods was made by one of the foremost American authorities on Indochina, Virginia Thompson: "Despite sporadic application of liberal and even socialistic theories to Indochina, the general administrative trend has been toward a divide-and-rule policy as the best means of hampering the growth of Annamite nationalism. . . . Eleventh-hour gestures of liberalism, inspired by the fear of a European war . . . were all too tardy and too inadequate to counteract the results of a half-century of cultivation of disunity and distrust among the native intellectuals and the failure to give the masses any real cause to rise to the defense of a government that had never awakened their loyalty by extensively improving their standard of living."

Japanese Occupation and Its Aftermath

From the beginning of the "China incident" France maintained an uneasy neutrality, while cautiously allowing trade with South China over the Tongking-Yunnan railroad. French caution was explained by the inadequacy of Indochinese defenses and by the lack of a coordinated policy with Great Britain and the United States. Japanese pressure on the French administration increased with the Soviet-German pact of 1939 and the outbreak of war in Europe. Threats soon led to aerial attacks on the Yunnan railroad, and on February 29, 1940, the strategic Chinese island of Hainan was seized, bringing Japanese planes one hour away from the coast of Indochina. The absence of the British fleet from Far Eastern waters and the hesitancy of American policy left the French without support; with France's defeat in Europe, Japanese pressure against Indochina became irresistible.

The colony was a major Japanese objective. Its occupation would shut off the traffic on the Yunnan railroad and make vital raw materials available; it would furnish a base of attack against Chungking and, more important still, against the rich British and Dutch possessions in the Southwest Pacific. On June 20 the French yielded to Japanese demands that all traffic with China be stopped and that a Japanese control mission be sent to key points on the railroad. General Catroux, who was suspected of Gaullist sympathies, was replaced as governor-general by Vice-Admiral Decoux. On September 22 the latter acceded to new Japanese demands: Japan would land troops immediately at Haiphong and establish three air bases in Tongking, garrisoned by 6,000 men. This capitulation, however, did not satisfy the Japanese commander of the Canton army, who attacked French outposts and seized the fortified town of Langson, further strengthening the Japanese hold on Indochina.

Synchronized with these Japanese moves was a Thai offensive to regain territory lost to the French long before. In January 1941, after a series of border incidents in Cambodia and Laos, Admiral Decoux accepted a Japanese "offer" to mediate the dispute. On March third, the French yielded again and ceded one-third of Cambodia and the Laotian territory west of the Mekong River to Thailand.

The whole of Indochina was occupied by Japanese troops on July 25, 1941. For reasons of expediency, the French administration was retained. It is difficult to appraise the behavior of the French colonialists during the four years of Japanese occupation. The prevailing attitude seems to have been *attentiste*—wait-and-see. Frequent tours of inspection kept the illusion of continued French rule, while Radio-Saigon played up the theme of Petain-Confucius, the wise man who kept Indochina "neutral" in a world conflict. While real collaborators with fascist sympathies were a minority, the fear of native nationalism hindered the growth of an organized underground resistance, especially any based on co-operation with the Vietnamese. Native uprisings were severely suppressed by French troops as Communist coups, and thousands of Nationalists were imprisoned. Resistance was largely limited to slowdown tactics by the provincial and local administration where it was difficult for the Japanese to exercise control.

Many officers were apparently ready to lead their troops against the Japanese in conjunction with an eventual Allied landing, but they were outwitted by the Japanese. On March 9, 1945, an ultimatum demanded closer cooperation for the "joint defense" of Indochina. It was refused by Admiral Decoux. The next day the Japanese troops moved in swiftly and effectively against the French garrisons, and French officials were arrested. On March 10 a Japanese broadcast declared that "the colonial status of Indochina has ended." The Emperor of Annam, Bao-Dai, issued a declaration of independence soon followed by similar declarations from the Kings of Cambodia and of Luang Prabang.

From then on resistance was almost the monopoly of the Viet

Minh League, or League for the Independence of Viet Nam (Tongking, Annam, and Cochin China) under the leadership of Ho Chi Minh, who had refused to recognize the "independent" government of Bao-Dai. His guerrillas received some American weapons and technical aid from OSS officers. They increased their activities, especially in Tongking where they freed seven provinces in the north from the Japanese. When Japan collapsed in August, they were ready to move in and occupy Hanoi and Saigon. The week of the Japanese surrender, a Viet Minh congress was held near the Chinese border which formed a provisional government under the presidency of Ho. The new government established itself at Hanoi and issued a Declaration of Independence of Viet Nam, or Land of the South. A national committee took power in Saigon after a huge demonstration had proved the popularity of the Viet Nam government. Order was maintained and relatively few Frenchmen were molested; most public services continued to function; political prisoners were liberated. It seemed that independence had been achieved. "We are convinced," states their Declaration of Independence, "that the Allies who recognized the principles of equality at the conferences of Teheran and San Francisco cannot fail to recognize the independence of Viet Nam."

The Potsdam Conference decided that French Indochina was to be occupied by British and Chinese troops with the sixteenth parallel as the line of demarcation. It soon became a line of political demarcation as well, for the British and Chinese interpreted their orders "to disarm the Japanese and restore law and order" in sharply contrasting manner. When General Gracey arrived in Saigon on September 13, 1945, he found the administration entirely in the hands of the Viet Nam leaders, but he refused to negotiate with them. He released and rearmed the French and helped them to seize power in Saigon; with French reinforcements pouring in, the occupying forces gained control of the cities, although the greater part of the countryside remained in the hands of Viet Nam guerrillas. Early in 1946 British troops were withdrawn and the French resumed complete military and administrative responsibility, with Admiral d'Argenlieu as high commissioner and General Leclerc in charge of military operations.

In the sector north of the sixteenth parallel the Chinese, while proclaiming a policy of non-interference in internal affairs, had left the Vietnamese in control of the administration. French troops were refused permission to enter the zone and repeated French assurances that they were ready to take over were ignored. It was not until February 28, 1946, that an agreement was reached between France and China concerning Indochina. In return for concessions on the Yunnan Railway and for recognition of the special status of their nationals in Indochina, the Chinese consented to withdraw their troops from Tongking and Laos. The Vietnamese having agreed to the landing of French troops in Haiphong, France found herself again the sole foreign power in Indochina, but now Tongking and Annam were controlled by a Nationalist government apparently enjoying wide popular support. Cambodia and Laos had anti-French governments, and in Cochin China the underground Vietnamese movement was continuing political activity and guerrilla warfare.

French control was easily re-established in Cambodia and Laos. On January 7, 1946, an agreement was reached with the King of Cambodia, followed by a similar agreement with the King of Luang Prabang, who became King of Laos on August 27. Their governments were granted a degree of autonomy, but always subject to the control of a French governor who was to have the dual role of "adviser" to the king and representative of the French Union and the Indochinese Federation.

Negotiations with Viet Nam led to the signing of an accord on March 6, 1946, that declared an end to hostilities and allowed French troops to occupy Tongking. By this agreement the French government recognized the "Republic of Viet Nam as a free state having its own government, parliament, army and finances, forming part of the Indochinese Federation and the French Union," and accepted a referendum as the means of deciding the vital question of whether Cochin China should join the Vietnamese state. The agreement also stated that negotiations concerning the diplomatic relations of Viet Nam, the future status of Indochina, and French cultural and economic interests in Viet Nam would soon be undertaken.

For that purpose a conference was held at Dalat, Cochin China, in April. The essential points of difference between France and her former colony at once became evident. On June 1 Admiral d'Argenlieu announced that in response to popular pressure for autonomy a provisional government had been set up in Cochin China. This action, while presented as a provisional measure by the French, was considered by the Vietnamese as a violation of the March 6 agreement. It created a most unfavorable atmosphere for the negotiations between Viet Nam and France that were undertaken at Fontainebleau in July. Another move by Admiral d'Argenlieu almost wrecked the conference: while discussions were in progress at Fontainebleau, he called a second Dalat Conference with representatives from Laos, Cambodia, Cochin China, and South Annam, but none from Viet Nam. The Vietnamese delegates walked out of the Fontainebleau Conference in protest and nothing was accomplished beyond the signing, on September 14, of a *modus vivendi* providing for the cessation of hostilities and settling certain cultural and economic questions.

The uneasy quiet that followed the September 14 agreement was broken by a series of clashes which soon led to open warfare. On November 23, Haiphong was bombed by the French and thousands of people were killed or wounded. On December 19 the Vietnamese made a surprise attack on the French garrisons in Tongking and Annam. The "formidable preparations which must have been started weeks ahead" were described by Monsieur Moutet, minister of France overseas, in a broadcast from Saigon on January 7. "I was sent here to deliver a message of peace but arrived to find a full-fledged war in progress. Now military operations must be allowed to proceed so that vital communications can be re-established." The situation was so serious that French reinforcements had to be rushed to Indochina. In spite of vigorous efforts—110,000 of France's best troops are fighting the Vietnamese—a stalemate has been reached (June 1949). French troops occupy the cities and have maintained some lines of communication, but most of the hinterland belongs to the Nationalists. The destruction brought about by the Annamese scorched-earth policy and the French bombings of villages has dislocated the economic life of the country and greatly increased the risk of famine. The war has also made a solution based on concessions by each side more problematical than ever.

Although Admiral d'Argenlieu, whose name had become synonomous with reactionary colonialism, was replaced as high commissioner in March 1947 by Emile Bollaert, a Socialist, France's basic position on the status of Indochina as a part of the French Union has remained unchanged. It is questionable whether serious efforts have been made in recent months to end the present impasse. The desire of Viet Nam for independence will be difficult to reconcile with France's interest in maintaining close ties with her overseas territories.

Vietnamese Nationalism

Vietnamese nationalism is a product of the West. Once the tools, techniques, and especially the ideas of the West were assimilated by a native minority, the myth of Western superiority was no longer acceptable. The early inferiority complex and passive acceptance were replaced by a vigorous assertion of claims that derived from a new consciousness of national identity.

Wherever the impact of the West was superficial, as in Laos and Cambodia, the Nationalist movement was also weak. Native leaders were inclined to maintain their privileged position under French rule. Nationalism was much more vigorous in the coastal provinces where there was a middle class of intellectuals and professional men. It had democratic and even socialistic overtones. The fact that Rousseau and Karl Marx impregnated the national aspirations of the discoverers of the West explains why so many well-to-do Vietnamese, identifying their interests with continued French rule, felt indifference and even hostility. This lack of social solidarity was a source of weakness for the early Nationalist movement, which was further handicapped by the apathy of the poverty-stricken peasants.

The first World War gave a new impetus to Vietnamese nationalism, which, until then, had been the monopoly of a few educated young men whose ill-coordinated efforts were easily suppressed by an efficient police. New conditions were created by the war that stimulated the desire for liberation. One hundred thousand Indochinese had been sent to France as soldiers and workers, often against their will; many came back with revolutionary ideas. Promises made during the hour of peril were not kept. Above all, the process of economic development, speeded up by the war, created a dissatisfied and insecure proletariat, receptive to Nationalist and revolutionary propaganda. Yet the Nationalist movement between the two wars lacked the necessary dynamism and discipline to challenge French domination. The only important revolt, the Yen Bay affair of 1930, was easily and ruthlessly crushed. The various Nationalist groups, in the words of Virginia Thompson, "ebbed, flowed, and subdivided, with the Communist elements showing the only signs of preserving vitality." The Revolutionary Party of Young Annam, created in 1915, was soon weakened by the jealousy of its leaders and by the opposition between its Nationalist and Communist wings. It died in 1929 when the Communists left the party. The Nationalist Annamite party, which was a replica of the Kuomintang, was a terrorist organization made up of young people, mainly students; it never had more than 1,500 members. Some of its leaders were arrested after the Yen Bay mutiny, and by 1933 the party had disintegrated. It had been unable to keep discipline among its members or to arouse the masses.

The Communist party, born in 1925, was more successful. By 1931 the party had some 1,500 members and perhaps 100,000 sympathizers. This was due partly to the able leadership of Nguyen-Ai-Quoc, alias Ho Chi Minh. Born in Annam some fifty-eight years ago, he went to France before the first World War and there joined the Communist party. After the armistice, he represented Indochina at the World Peasant Conference in Soviet Russia and remained in the USSR for some time, studying revolutionary techniques. He spent several years in underground activities in Indochina until arrested by the British in 1931 at Hong Kong where he was imprisoned for two years. In the meantime, most of his lieutenants had been suppressed by the French police. The party nevertheless continued its underground activities and became the backbone of the Viet Minh, or League for the Independence of Viet Nam, which was created in 1939.

Imprisonment and illness have not affected Ho's abilities as an organizer and statesman. His prestige as a symbol of the resistance to foreign rule was increased by his guerrilla war against the Japanese and by his easy assumption of power after their capitulation. He talks a language easily understood by the people of the cities and the country, whether intellectuals, workers, or peasants. His program is nationalistic and anti-colonialist rather than communistic. "The battle that we fight is not directed against honest Frenchmen, but against the cruel domination of French colonialism . . . *corvée, gabelle,* forced consumption of opium and alcohol, crushing taxes, absolute lack of liberty, permanent terror, moral and material misery, shameless exploitation."

In contrast to the weak, divided Nationalist movement before World War II, Vietnamese nationalism now appears widespread, militant, and self-confident. It has become a genuine mass movement. The enthusiasm of the crowds at Saigon and Hanoi after the liberation, and the elections of January 1946, the first general elections in the history of Indochina, in which more than 90 per cent of the people voted, testify to the appeal of the new nationalism, which has been further tested in the present war. Whether this Nationalist movement is also democratic in the Western sense is an open question. Have the tradition-bound peasants, interested only in the affairs of the village, suddenly broadened their horizon to encompass national affairs? Or is the satisfaction they derive from seeing men of their own race replace French administrators the measure of their present democratic ambition?

Circumstances were highly favorable to the rise of the Nationalist movement. The Viet Minh could fill the vacuum left by the Japanese surrender and the elimination of the French administration. Vietnamese guerrillas were ready to seize power and had the support of the Chinese. The new government had at its disposal effective means of indoctrination. Ho's prestige was unrivaled and made for a national unity unknown until then. He had his own shock troops to which were soon added youth organizations, recently liberated political prisoners, Vietnamese soldiers and noncommissioned officers of the French Indochinese army, and even some Japanese deserters.

The dislocation of Indochinese economy that resulted from the war was also an asset. Production as well as imports and exports had fallen to a fraction of the prewar level; overcrowded Tongking, no longer supplied by Cochin China, suffered from famine. People who had nothing to lose and everything to gain eagerly responded to the appeal of Ho, who promised not only liberation from the French but from the landlord, the tax collector, and the moneylender. The activity of his government was convincing enough. The new administration was relatively efficient. A double drive was conducted against illiteracy and famine; new crops were planted on a large scale to supplement rice.

A constitution was adopted that included a modern bill of rights and provided for universal suffrage of all men and women over eighteen, a single assembly, a president elected by the assembly, and a cabinet. Provincial and local councils, also elected by universal suffrage, were to appoint executive committees and to do away with the centralized administrative rule of the French as well as with the rule of the "notables" and mandarins. Local autonomy was to be balanced by enough centralization to bring about national unity, correct local abuses, and permit technical services—among them, propaganda—to operate efficiently.

The international situation was also highly favorable to the new Viet Nam. The two great victors and China were anticolonialist. At Chungking, Henry Wallace had made a semi-official speech condemning colonial imperialism; American officers in Indochina were sympathetic to the Viet Minh. The United Nations appeared willing and able to impose its principles. Great Britain was giving an example of timely withdrawal. Above all, France appeared helpless.

Quite suddenly the Vietnamese people were faced with the disintegration of an order that had seemed immutable. Native leaders now appeared, attesting to the reality of the liberation and giving the traditionally resigned masses the exhilarating sense of their new power. Oriental fatalism makes for the pragmatic acceptance of total change. If nothing can be done against the inevitable, everything must be done to facilitate the fulfillment of destiny, once its meaning is made obvious. Rather than hatred of the French, there was perhaps the conviction that French rule had definitely passed away and that a new cycle had begun which moved men to action and violence, but for the sake of a new harmony. Perhaps the Japanese occupation did less to bring about this conviction than the sudden elimination of French rule in March 1945, followed by the Japanese capitulation a few months

later. Even the vigorous French reaction in Saigon was interpreted
as the irresponsible and immoral gesture of a handful of adventurers soon to be punished for their criminal faux pas. Ho
did not fail to appeal to the sense of destiny of his compatriots
as he pointed out the imminence of their inevitable victory.

It was difficult for the French to reassert their lost prestige
and power. Had not Radio-Saigon glorified Vichy's defeatism
and proclaimed that an Allied victory would be the doom of the
French Empire? It was hard to present the Allied victory as a
victory for France when thousands of Vietnamese resisters had
been arrested by the French and when French resistance to
Japanese rule had been less evident than French collaboration.
The fight for liberation had not been a common experience leading to mutual understanding and common goals. The sudden
crumbling of French rule had only widened the gulf separating
the two groups that had lived apart and had little in common.
Being no longer inevitable, the French rulers were more foreign
than ever, and much less acceptable.

Under these conditions, the March 1946 agreement providing
for "the independence of Viet Nam within the framework of the
French Union" was probably interpreted by the Vietnamese
leaders not as an invitation for the return of even limited French
rule, but as a face-saving formula; the goal was the complete
sovereignty of Viet Nam with a status similar to that of Eire
within the British Commonwealth. However willing to compromise with the French over cultural and even economic matters,
the Viet Nam government has remained adamant over the two
crucial questions of the integration of Cochin China into Viet Nam
and recognition by France of complete Vietnamese sovereignty
with its attributes, a national army and an independent foreign
policy.

On March 24, 1947, Ho again stated the goal of his government. "If France is willing to recognize our unity, our independence, our economic, military, and diplomatic rights, as the
United States has done in the Philippines and Great Britain in
India, our people are disposed to bring to France their friendly
collaboration. If not, if France wants to restore the colonialist

regime in our country, we are determined to a long resistance, until we realize our unity and independence."

The French Position toward Viet Nam

Although Title VIII of the new French constitution does not directly apply to Indochina, whose relationship with France is to be established by treaty, it is not irrelevant to the problem of Franco-Vietnamese relations. It illustrates France's concern with maintaining the continuity of her sovereignty and thus explains her inability to meet the demands of Viet Nam. The newly de-fined status of the French Union may even be the main reason for the failure of negotiations at Fontainebleau in September 1946.

The conflict between Right and Left over the character of the new French Union became evident after the rejection of the first constitutional draft in June 1946. The Left—Communists and Socialists, helped by a group of deputies from overseas territories—asked for the administrative autonomy of these territories and for the creation of a federal structure to be gradually established by free negotiations between the representatives of the various territories and those of France. Equality of status and even the right to secede would be granted. This program was rejected by the parties of the Right and Center who feared that it would lead to the disintegration of the Union. Premier Georges Bidault threatened to resign. The Left finally gave in and, against the protest of the native deputies, accepted a compromise between the unitarian and federalist formulas in which, as a constitutional lawyer has put it, "the federalist element is at best a draft on the future, at the worst simple window-dressing."

The embryonic federation provided for federal bodies with purely advisory functions. The real authority over French Union affairs lies with the French national assembly in which only 12 per cent of the deputies are elected by the overseas territories. Legislative power over criminal matters, public liberties, and administrative organization is specifically reserved to the national assembly, which, by determining the methods of elections, can preserve the status of the French colonists both in the national assembly and in the local assemblies. As Pierre Cot told the constituent assembly: "You say that you are building a federation. Well—no. Let us not have the hypocrisy to say so, we are *not* building a federation. For a federation implies equal states. In a federation everyone has equal rights and equal duties."

To build the "reality of cooperation on the right to refuse cooperation" has always appeared to the cautious and legalistic French mind a most dangerous formula. In contrast to the British goal of forwarding self-government and ultimately giving independence to the colonial peoples, the French aim has been to assimilate and to centralize in order to build up a community of 110,000,000 Frenchmen. A deep sense of insecurity following World War II has increased this traditional concern with a greater France; it is widely believed that in an unsettled world the very independence of France rests on her ability to maintain close ties with her overseas territories. "It is a fact," said Premier Ramadier in February 1947, "that in the middle of the twentieth century, a nation of traditional size is condemned to be a satellite unless it becomes the center of its own constellation. . . . France alone would be an enslaved France and that is why the problem of the Union is the problem of the very liberty and existence of our country." Also indicative of this sense of insecurity are the frequent warnings in press and parliament that should France leave, another power would step in and become the trustee of the Indochinese peoples.

For the French, Indochina is the key to the preservation of the Union and of France's position in the world. The recognition of Vietnamese sovereignty would start a dangerous precedent for North Africa and Madagascar. The peoples of the Union must be content with limited autonomy, while entrusting the authority to coordinate Union defense and foreign policy to France. Constitutional provisions and treaties must be made that will prevent a fatal disintegration. "The members of the French Union held in common the totality of their resources to guarantee the defense of the whole Union," states Article Sixty-two of the French constitution. "The Government of the Republic assumes the coordination of these resources and the direction of the policy necessary to organize and implement this defense." To the Vietnamese demands for independence Monsieur Bollaert could answer: "We shall remain. The French political parties are unanimously resolved that France shall not be dispossessed. The Constitution . . . makes the French Union, of which Indochina is an integral part, an institution of the Republic. The French Union thus gains a constitutional basis which precludes any notion of abandonment."

The French insistence on directing the destinies of the Union from Paris implies that the delegate of the French government in Saigon—the former governor-general—will exercise wide powers of control over the federal assembly in order to make effective the policy decided upon in Paris. This is the substance of the official declaration of March 1945, which made the ministers of the federal council of Indochina responsible to the French delegate rather than to the elected assembly. Admiral d'Argenlieu made it clear that while the French would be content to play the role of adviser to the state governments, France was to be the "guide" of the federal government; his successor, Monsieur Bollaert, also stated that France intended to "maintain her position on the federal level," at least as far as the control of the foreign policy and armed forces of the Indochinese Federation were concerned.

Directly related to this problem is the status of Cochin China. The economic and strategic importance of this area is obvious. Should it become an integral part of the State of Viet Nam, as the Vietnamese insist that it must, the massive superiority of this state would jeopardize the autonomy of Cambodia and Laos and would endanger the authority of France over the federation. Most significant was the declaration by Monsieur Moutet in March 1947 that Tongking, Annam, and Cochin China would have to find a formula guaranteeing their respective autonomy since a fusion of the three Annamite provinces into a single state would force Laos and Cambodia to seek safety in another union—a declaration that is hardly compatible with the agreement of March 1946. On another occasion he emphasized France's responsibilities toward the minorities: "We have a duty toward the masses in all these countries. We cannot give up our role of protector, even to the new government; on the contrary. But it is understood that we shall not continue to govern directly."

Relatively less important than the problems of defense and foreign relations is the economic question. Ho has stressed the need for French economic aid and the desirability of exchanges between two complementary economies. The French government, for its part, has accepted the principle of economic autonomy for the Indochinese Federation. There remain, however, certain obvious difficulties. To what extent is this autonomy compatible with the existence of the closed economic unit that the French would like the Union to form? Will France accept the industrialization of Indochina that is necessary to raise the living standards? If so, will she be able to invest heavily, or will she accept the competition of foreign investments? How will French assets be protected against an eventual policy of nationalization by the Vietnamese government? Undoubtedly French colonialists are putting pressure on the government, through the parties of the Right and Center, to protect their positions. A French periodical even suggested that on the very eve of his peace trip to Indochina, pressure by the Popular Republican Movement caused Monsieur Moutet to receive orders from the government not to deal with Ho Chi Minh.

There is no doubt that mutual mistrust has been increased by the mistakes made by both sides. Ho alluded in January 1947 to the series of misunderstandings created by Admiral d'Argenlieu and other colonialist elements. Similarly the former Socialist minister, Eugene Thomas, returning from Indochina in April 1947, criticized the attitude of some French administrators and businessmen who had made an atmosphere of confidence impossible. The French are equally suspicious of the present Viet Nam leaders as the men who launched the attack of December 1946. The fact that Ho and his foreign minister, Giap, are Communists has become a major obstacle to an understanding in proportion as the French Communists have divorced themselves from the government and the majority of the French people. Not only the MRP but even many Socialists have come to oppose dealing with Ho, in spite of his authority and prestige. The Rightist leaders especially, including Monsieur de Gaulle, show a firm intention not to deal with leaders whose aim is to force the French out of Indochina in order to make their country a vassal to Moscow.

The issue of communism cannot be dismissed as a rationalization offered by the French for continuing their rule. Undoubtedly the influence of the Communists is immensely greater than is indicated by their numerical strength. Only ten of the 300 delegates in the national assembly of Viet Nam are said to be Communist, but it is likely that Communists have seized key positions in the administration. On the other hand, there is little doubt about Ho's prestige with non-Communist Nationalist elements. There is no leader in sight who can challenge his popularity.

The little information available concerning Communist strength and strategy is often contradictory. Thus Ho, who incidentally denied that he was still a Communist, appeared most anxious to reach an agreement with France. It was even said that the French authorities in Tongking did not look unfavorably upon the elimination of the other parties by the Viet Minh, since the former were even more anti-French. But there is some evidence that the Communists looked upon the March 1946 agreement as a mere tactical advantage. The London *Economist* published a circular sent by the central committee to the local branches of the party during the period of truce that called for expulsion of the French within two years by the use of sabotage and boycott.

The creation by the French in June 1948 of a puppet government for Viet Nam under the leadership of Bao-Dai, the ex-Emperor of Annam, and Nguyen Van Xuan, head of the French-sponsored Cochin Chinese state and the only Annamite general in the French army, can be viewed with some misgivings. This government has apparently agreed to guarantee French control of the military forces and diplomatic relations of Viet Nam and also granted tangible economic advantages. But it is doubtful that the Bao-Dai government will appeal to more than a fraction of the conservative elements. Its only hope of success would seem to lie in the growing despair of the Vietnamese people, who may soon again value peace more than independence.

The opposition of Ho's government to French pressure has not been weakened. The war continues and is leading the country closer to economic collapse. Although unpopular in France, hostilities are likely to continue in the absence of a genuine desire on the part of the French to deal with Ho. The establishment of the puppet government has made such a *rapprochement* most unlikely. Given the trend of French and world politics, a compromise between the French and Vietnamese claims to sovereignty is hardly conceivable. The division of East and West, by weakening the efficiency of the United Nations and the concern of the United States for dependent peoples, has made it impossible for the time being to bring about a settlement through international pressure.

The prospect of a Communist victory in China may, however, lead the United States to revise its policy toward Southeast Asia. It may be decided in Washington that the best strategy would be to encourage the formation of a league of the peoples of Southeast Asia under the leadership of non-Communist, nationalist elements, a solution that would meet with the approval of India and probably of Great Britain. In such case France might be persuaded to sign an agreement under which Viet Nam would, with United Nations supervision, be progressively granted complete independence and French troops would be gradually withdrawn. For it is possible that the stubborn resistance of Viet Nam has opened French eyes to the power and determination of the Nationalist movement, as well as to the real interests of France. Not only is France's power position weakened by the present conflict, but it is questionable whether she would obtain tangible strategic advantages by remaining in Indochina. The problem is above all one of prestige, involving the fear of weakening France's ties with the dependent peoples of Africa as a consequence of a sudden departure from Indochina.

Perhaps a face-saving formula may be found that will maintain for some years the appearance of France's "continuing presence" while granting Viet Nam the substance of its independence. This would require not only the services of a third party to guarantee the observance of the agreement and to reassure both signatories, but perhaps the withdrawal of Ho and Giap in favor of middle-of-the-road leaders acceptable to both the Vietnamese and the French.

Suggested Reading

Blanchet, André. *Au Pays des Balilas Jaunes.* Paris. 1946.
Emerson, R. E., L. A. Mills, and V. Thompson. *Government and Nationalism in Southeast Asia.* New York. 1942.

Ennis, Thomas E. *French Policy and Developments in Indo-China.* Chicago. 1936.

Furnivall, J. S. *Educational Progress in Southeast Asia.* New York. 1943.

Gourou, Pierre. *Land Utilization in Indo China.* New York. 1947.

Guynh, Pham. *L'Evolution intellectuelle et morale des Annamites.* Paris. 1922.

Hammer, Ellen. *The Emergence of Viet Nam.* (Mimeographed.) New York. 1947.

Handler, Joseph. *Indochina: Eighty Years of French Rule.* The Annals, Vol. 226. March 1943.

Lévy, Roger. *Extrème-Orient et Pacifique.* Paris. 1935.

Lévy, R., G. Lacam, and A. Roth. *French Interests and Policies in the Far East.* New York. 1941.

Mus, Paul. *Le Viet Nam Chez Lui.* Centre d'Etudes de Politique Etrangère. 1947.

Nguyen-Ai-Quoc. *Le procès de la colonisation française.* Paris. 1926.

Pillai, P. P., ed. *Labour in Southeast Asia.* New Delhi. 1947.

Pinto, Roger. *Aspects de l'évolution gouvernementale de l'Indo-Chine française.* Saigon. 1946.

Robequain, Charles. *The Economic Development of French Indo-China.* New York. 1944.

Roth, Andrew. *Japan Strikes South.* New York. 1941.

Roubaud, L. *Vietnam.* Paris. 1931.

Thompson, Virginia. *French Indo-China.* New York. 1937.

———. *Labor Problems in Southeast Asia.* New Haven. 1947.

Viollis, A. *Indochine S.O.S.* Paris. 1935.

SIAM

❖

Political History of Siam

BEFORE World War II Siam was going through a period of political transition from administration by the absolute monarchs of the Chakri dynasty to administration by the People's party, which came into power by a bloodless revolution in 1932. The Chakri kings had ruled without interruption from 1782. For the first three reigns the dynasty was handed down from father to son. The second of the three kings should have been followed by his son Mongkut. However, a younger half brother secured the throne and Mongkut went into the Buddhist priesthood until after his brother's death in 1851.

During the quarter of a century before he became king, Mongkut obtained a profound knowledge of Buddhist wisdom and became friendly with Westerners, from whom he learned English, Latin, and the scientific lore of Europe and America. When he came to the throne in 1851 he determined to alter the foreign policy of his predecessors and to encourage the flow of Western influence into Siam. As a consequence of this farsighted policy his successor and son, Chulalongkorn, was prepared to undertake the progressive steps necessary to adjust Siam to the Western world. The old feudal system was abandoned; a civil service was organized; slavery was abolished; the judicial system was revised; the farming out of taxes was abandoned and the system of taxation was improved; a postal system was organized; and a railroad was begun.

The next two Chakri kings, Vajiravudh and Prajadhipok, ruled for ten years each. Vajiravudh was a brilliant man with a great love for literature, art, and the theater. He paid little attention to matters of state. Prajadhipok, on the other hand, felt his responsibilities of state and, when he saw his country slipping into troubled financial waters because of the world depression, sought practical ways to deliver it from danger.

King Prajadhipok, in consultation with an American political adviser, Raymond Stevens, considered modifying the method of government and studied two draft constitutions with the idea that a constitutional regime might meet the needs of the times more adequately. Concurrently, a Siamese commoner, Luang Pradist Manudharm (personal name Pridi Banomyong), a law professor in Chulalongkorn University, drafted a constitution for Siam and planned and executed, with the aid of the military, a bloodless revolution on June 24, 1932. Pridi Banomyong called his political party the People's party. The general public did not participate in the revolution, which was essentially an expression of the discontent of the minority who had received a Westernized education.

In a flush of high-mindedness, Pridi Banomyong and his followers permitted the supreme position of prime minister to go to an experienced civil servant, Phya Manopakorn, who included in his cabinet many of his friends. The bureaucrats who formed that first government were emotionally tied to the monarchy and accordingly took steps to make the king absolute again. King Prajadhipok was still on the throne as constitutional monarch, but the officials were accustomed to regard him as absolute. Custom was hard to break.

The issues came to a climax over the economic policy of Pridi Banomyong, which Phya Manopakorn claimed was communistic in character. Phya Manopakorn forced Pridi to leave the country on April 12, 1933, and it seemed for a time that the cause of the People's party was lost. An "Act Concerning Communism" was passed to make sure that communism would not rise again. The king instructed Phya Manopakorn to form a new government, which he did on April 1, 1933. His first government had lasted 281 days, and his second one lived only 81 days, until June 20, when it was interrupted by a second revolution led by Pridi Banomyong's friend, Colonel Phya Bahol Balabayuha, who became premier. Colonel Bahol was second in command of the army before the 1932 revolution and was very popular with both the military and civilian population.

Pridi returned to Siam in September and in March 1934 was officially cleared of the charge of being a Communist. The commission of investigation excluded Pridi's economic policy as part of the evidence on the ground that it was irrelevant. King Prajadhipok felt too constrained by these events and abdicated in 1935 in favor of his nephew Ananda Mahidol, a schoolboy in Switzerland.

Phya Bahol continued in power until December 1938. During that period there was a continuing struggle for power between Pridi Banomyong and Luang Phibun Songgram, who came to prominence during 1933 when there was an abortive royalist rebellion led by H. H. Prince Bavoradej, former minister of defense. Luang Phibun took the lead in restoring order to the nation and during the process gained great influence. He was then a major and later became field marshal and leader of the militarist nationalist group within the revolutionary party, while Pridi was the leader of the civilian section. Phya Bahol was able to maintain a sort of balance between Phibun and Pridi until December 1938 when Phibun took over and became prime minister. He continued in the post until July 1944.

The pattern of the nationalism of the People's party began to become more evident after Phibun came to power. A symbol of the times was the change of name from Siam to Thailand on June 24, 1939. The Siamese had always called themselves Thai and their country Muang Thai, or the Land of the Thai. They desired that foreigners refer to their country as Thailand, even as they themselves did. The new name lasted until after World War II when, in order to avoid a minor point of irritation in peace negotiations with the British government, which had never accepted the new name, the change was made back to Siam on September 8, 1945. In August 1948 preparations were under way to change back to Thailand again.

The People's party sought to perpetuate itself by maintaining virtually a one-party system of government. The original People's party was dissolved at the request of King Prajadhipok in 1933 and became a social club. The king believed that the nation was not ready for political parties, and the nationalists saw an opportunity to please the king and assure their own control. No effort was made to develop a plural party system until March 26, 1937 when Nai Thong Indra, an elected member of the assembly, applied for permission to register a political party. Other groups began to organize and to ask permission to register. On May 20, 1937, the council of ministers announced that the time was not yet ripe.

In order to be sure of political control, the government began arresting individuals who showed active dislike or opposition to it. Political prisoners became numerous. Those suspected of plotting against the government were exiled on an island; a number of prominent persons were actually executed. This treatment of political prisoners was so unusual for Siam that several books and a play were written about it.

Political parties were again discussed in the assembly in 1940, and on September 11 a political parties bill was ready to be presented to the assembly for vote. The bill excluded Communist, royalist, and dictatorship parties. At this point, the Japanese began to move toward Indochina, and on December 20, 1940 the assembly agreed to defer decision. Concurrently with this development, the transitory provisions of the constitution were under discussion. Chapter VII of the constitution of December 10, 1932 was made to consist of "transitory provisions" which guaranteed the dominance of the revolutionary group for ten years from the date of accepting the provisional constitution of June 27, 1932. An alternative terminal date was set for any time less than ten years if half of the people who were entitled to vote for the candidates of the assembly should succeed in passing an examination in primary education. It was realized in debate in the assembly that if the transitory provisions lapsed the government could not succeed itself in a popular election. On September 17, 1940 it was accordingly voted to extend the transitory provisions an additional ten years beyond the original terminal date of June 1942. The one-party system seemed assured.

Although there have been nine governments since the overthrow of Phibun in 1944 by Pridi, political power has essentially continued to lie in either the Phibun or Pridi branch of the original People's party. The only exception has been the ephemeral government of Khuang Aphaiwong from March 6 to April 6, 1948, when he tried to establish himself independently of Phibun by organizing a royalist party.

Since World War II the newspapers have made Siamese political parties seem real by using party names in referring to the various groups struggling for power. These groups are not political parties as such, but are personalized followings of prominent individuals, around whom they cluster in the hope of securing political status. The various names of the so-called political parties are consequently without significance. The important thing to know is the name of the man leading any particular group. At this writing, in August 1948, major political strength apparently continues to lie in the People's party, with Phibun and Pridi competing for leadership. At the moment Pridi is in China with an indictment against him in connection with the murder of King Ananda Mahidol. His followers say it is a political move, and there are ominous rumblings of a possible coup d'état against Phibun, which is one of the favorite methods of holding an election in Siam. Khuang Aphaiwong, who is the only non-People's party political figure of any stature in the country, does not seem to be actively in the competition. So the original nationalist group perpetuates itself.

Social and Cultural Changes

Another manifestation of the new nationalism appeared in efforts to alter the cultural practices of the people. A government-sponsored campaign was begun in 1939 to make the people stop chewing betel, to clean up the streets, to inculcate Western social manners and practices, to require the adoption of a Westernized version of dress, to simplify the language into a basic style, and in general to refashion the social habits of the population. For instance, on March 15, 1941 the prime minister, Luang Phibun, issued an appeal to Siamese women to dress themselves in a manner worthy of a civilized nation and befitting the national honor and dignity. The women were to let their hair grow long and were to cease wearing the traditional *panung*, which is similar to the Indian *dhoti*. National dress contests were held. Men and women were required to wear shoes and hats when appearing in public places or on public vehicles.

The new ways were embodied in a series of government pamphlets which formed the "Emily Post" reference work for educated Siamese. Those who did not conform were fined or punished by not being given access to public vehicles or places. It was inconvenient not to conform. Although there was much resentment and the campaign was characterized scornfully as *smai sai muak* (hat-wearing period), a profound effect was made on the nation. After the fall of Phibun in 1944 there was no great swing back to old cultural practices. M. R. Seni Pramoj, while prime minister after the war for a few months, tried to revive some of the old customs, but without success. He himself wore the *panung* but won no following.

The educational system was also overhauled by the nationalists. The idea was to control the schools so as to develop the sort of citizens that would support the party. As there were important Chinese and Malay minorities whom the Siamese desired to assimilate, school controls were developed with an eye on them. The ministry of education rigidly prescribed subjects of study, textbooks, hours of study, and examinations. All teachers had to be registered with the government, and no teacher could change from one school to another without permission. Attendance reports were required, and separate registers were kept for children in the compulsory attendance age group, between the ages of seven and fourteen, and for children outside this group. The writers of school texts found a prolific source of income because an accepted text was immediately a best seller throughout the nation.

In the spirit of the times the government also attempted to control the religious life of the nation. The purpose was to equate patriotism with Buddhism. Patriots were Buddhists, and if persons attached themselves to other religious bodies, then they were not patriots. Pressure was put on all civil employees to be Buddhists. Those who were not Buddhists might lose their jobs or at least could not hope for advancement. The movement became quite evident in September 1940 when two Thai officers left the Roman Catholic church to become Buddhists. Then a woman asked for a divorce on the grounds that her husband had been beating her to convert her to Christianity. In January the trend became still clearer when a Siamese Christian worker appeared at a public gathering distributing scriptures. The police had difficulty rescuing him from the crowd.

In February two of the leading Buddhist societies prepared to accept large numbers of converts. In April a mass meeting of over four thousand, led by high officials in the government, inducted over seventy converts from Christianity. Leaders of the Protestant church were among them.

Relief from this sort of pressure was not found until the end of the Phibun government in 1944. Though the pressure has been less since World War II, the idea has been thoroughly planted that good Siamese are good Buddhists also. It is probable that there is little official pressure on non-Buddhists to become Buddhists, but there is no doubt that Siamese generally are self-conscious and reluctant about exchanging Buddhism for another religion. They have seen the disadvantages of such a course under the nationalist regime. There is an indication, also, that some pressure is still being applied. The *Kiatisak* of July 28, 1948 mentioned that the practice of making students declare themselves Buddhists at swearing ceremonies conducted at schools was reintroduced by the education authorities on July 20, the beginning of Buddhist Lent. The secretary to the minister of education said they were only reintroducing old practices which had been neglected.

Since one of the most important aims of a nationalist regime is to secure firm control of all aspects of national life, the Siamese were concerned with the problem of the Chinese and Malay minorities, particularly the Chinese. There were in Siam between two and three million Chinese or persons who acted like Chinese, and about half a million Malays. The Chinese were located in the commercial centers of the country, but chiefly in Bangkok and the peninsula. The Malays formed a solid mass in the four southern provinces. As the Siamese saw the problem, in order to assimilate these two important minority groups they had to restrict immigration and educate them in the Siamese language and culture, while preventing them from learning too much of the Chinese or Malay language and customs.

The Chinese offered the chief problem in immigration, as there was only a slight movement of Malays across the border. Various control methods were used against the Chinese, such as setting a high tax on residence, registering all Chinese in Siam, and requiring Chinese immigrants to carry a card showing their entry was legal. These methods did not work. The war came and brought a momentary pause in developments.

After World War II the Chinese and Siamese governments signed a Treaty of Amity on January 23, 1946 and established diplomatic relations for the first time in modern history. Embassies were established in each country. Then the Siamese set a quota of 10,000 Chinese immigrants per year, the Chinese government objected, and the struggle began again. The Siamese found that Chinese were sifting into the country like rice through a lattice floor. They tried counting the excess numbers against the following year's quota, but without success in stopping the flow. After the return of Phibun to power on November 8, 1947, the Siamese government began a tough program of control, deporting Chinese who entered Siam illegally; but there is no indication that the flow of Chinese has slackened.

The Siamese feel that control of this problem is vital to their national identity. They fear that if the proportion of Chinese continues to grow, and if China as a nation should settle its internal differences and take an active interest in expanding its influence among overseas Chinese communities, then Siam would virtually lose its sovereignty and independence as a nation.

Great importance has been put on the school program for educating Chinese and Malay children in the Siamese language and culture. The program was initiated actively in 1933 with the enforcement of the primary education laws as outlined above. The Chinese objected strenuously because they had made such extensive investments in schools in all parts of Siam. New schools were being erected constantly. The general procedure was to appoint local Chinese scholars as principal and head teacher, and to secure the rest of the Chinese faculty from either China or

Malaya. One or two Siamese teachers were engaged to teach the Siamese language. The Siamese government attempted to reverse this procedure by permitting Chinese to be taught only as a foreign language. Thus the faculty would have to be Siamese in character.

The Chinese tried to have two faculties, one of which functioned within the law when a school inspector was sighted, and a second which carried on at other times. Government pressure was irregular through the years, so that at times the Chinese were able to maintain the semblance of Chinese schools while at others they reluctantly conformed. In general Phibun's administrations have been tough in administering the educational laws. With Phibun's second advent the struggle was sharply renewed, and the government closed so many Chinese schools that the Chinese claimed they hadn't a single school operating. Such severe treatment apparently brought them into line, and the schools began opening again according to legal requirements. The years from 1933 to 1948 have been stormy ones in the relations between the Chinese schools and the Siamese government. By their ingenuity and vigorous tactics the Chinese have frustrated the efforts of the Siamese government to teach Chinese children the Siamese language and culture.

The Malays met the new school situation in stubborn silence and willful ignorance. Malay children, under the encouragement of their elders, attended Siamese schools for years without learning to read. They used Malay at home and continued in their traditional fashion as far as possible in the hours when not attending school. They particularly resented being required to make obeisance to an image of Buddha. This ceremony was explained to them as meaning respect for the sovereign power of the nation. Moslem leaders found this difficult to believe.

The Malays in Siam had had more tolerant treatment in previous years. Provision had been made in the Civil and Commercial Code of 1925 that Moslems should be governed in matters of family and inheritance by Moslem law. A five-member Islamic board of examiners was established which selected four Islamic judges, one for each of the provinces, who were to sit with Siamese judges and advise them on matters of family and inheritance. In

1940 this practice was discontinued while the Phibun government was stressing its program of education and indoctrination in things Siamese.

After World War II the Moslem leaders appealed and were granted again, on December 3, 1946, the usual privileges. Moved by a sense of victory, during 1947 the Moslems began to press for wider application of Islamic law and even to talk about political separation from Buddhist Siam. In the *Straits Times* of October 30, 1947, news correspondent Miss Barbara Whittingham-Jones reported, after a 250-mile trip through the four Malay states in South Siam, that school buildings were closed and deserted, and that Malay opposition was strengthening under the leadership of Che Mahmood Mahyiddeen, the youngest son of Raja Abdul Kadir, the last installed Raja Patani.

According to Miss Whittingham-Jones, a seven-point petition was sent to Bangkok demanding: (1) the appointment of a single individual with full powers to govern the four districts of Patani, Naradhivas, Yala, and Setul, and in particular having authority to dismiss, suspend, or replace all government servants, this individual to be locally born in one of the four districts and to be elected by the people; (2) 80 per cent of the government servants in the four districts to profess the Moslem religion; (3) Malay and Siamese to be the official languages; (4) Malay to be the medium of instruction in the primary schools; (5) Moslem law to be recognized and enforced in a separate Moslem court other than the civil court where the one-time *kathi* sits as an assessor; (6) all revenue and income derived from the four districts to be utilized within them; and (7) the formation of a Moslem board having full powers to direct all Moslem affairs, under the supreme authority of the head of state mentioned in (1).

The Malays formed a South Siam Representative Committee to represent their cause. Prominent Moslems called upon the prime minister, who promised to send the director-general of the department of the interior to investigate the situation. He said he would consider dividing the four provinces into seven administrative regions, as formerly, in order to give more attention to the needs of each region; and that he would consider appointing a Moslem as high commissioner for the provinces.

After the director-general returned from his inspection tour he stated in a press conference on February 18, 1948: (1) that he had instructed the civil officials of the four provinces to allow full freedom of worship, and that not only would Moslem schools be permitted to close on Friday but provincial offices would also close on that day; and (2) that certain Moslem leaders had been arrested and charged with sedition because of their promotion of a separatist movement aimed at making the four provinces part of the Malay Federation, and that there were actually only a few discontented persons in the provinces.

The situation in the four provinces was discussed in a debate on the policies of the Khuang government on March 8, 1948. The prime minister stated that new officials had been appointed to replace the ones against which there were grievances; that the people had been given full religious freedom; and that he was ready to discuss any further questions with prominent Moslems. The Moslems were not satisfied, and after Phibun became prime minister on April 8 they renewed their requests. During all the discussions, the leading advocate was Moslem Senator Hadji Banchong. At no time was it clear whether there was an actual separatist movement, or whether the Moslems were merely dissatisfied over their inability to have their children educated in the Malay language and culture.

A show of force was made by the Malays on April 26, resulting in many deaths. Subsequently many Malay villagers fled into Malaya. The government issued a proclamation on June 9 urging the people to return and expressed the sympathy of the administration. The ministry of education on July 14, 1948 authorized the establishment of a central Moslem college for the four provinces, and for primary schools granted that one hour a week be allowed for the teaching of the Islamic religion and eight hours a week for primary instruction in the Malay language. The Malays in South Siam were thus to receive the same sort of treatment that the Chinese had secured, as the major part of the curriculum was still in Siamese. It was evident that the Siamese government had no intention of modifying materially its program to control Chinese and Malay minorities in the hope of assimilating them.

Siamese Economy

The People's party began its career with six principles which it began to implement in 1932. The principle of economics was to have been embodied in a national economic policy drafted by Pridi Banomyong, but there was such violent opposition to it that it was never promulgated. However, parts of it were adopted after Pridi became minister of finance in December 1938. The purpose was to weaken the strong hold that alien Chinese and Europeans had on the economic life of the nation and to put Siamese into business, either as individuals or through governmental control and participation. Some aspects of the program were not new but were amplifications of current practices. The government already owned shares in the Siam Paper Company. It operated a sugar factory at Lampang, a silk factory at Nakhon Rachasima, a tobacco factory at Bangkok, an oil refinery at Klong Toi, and a cannery at Pak Chang. It then began to move into the business of making cement, wine, leather, cigarettes, and other consumer goods. It moved against alien control of such industries as birds' nest concessions, food vending, salt and tobacco production, driving of vehicles for public hire, butchering and retailing meat, domestic shipping, fisheries, sales of liquid fuel, rice milling, teak forestry, and tin mining. Obviously the government could not take over management or even participate in all of these lines of commercial activity as easily as it could pass the laws making it possible. But progress was made, and aliens moved out of some commercial lines entirely and became less important in others. For instance, the British and American oil companies withdrew rather than attempt to continue under impossible conditions.

In some commercial lines the Siamese took charge but continued to employ the same people who had done the work before. Many Siamese-controlled ventures did not do well because the Siamese lacked experience and did not have the energy of the Chinese. The program was interrupted by World War II. After the war, when Siam was trying to re-establish her international trade relations, many if not most of the controls were relaxed. For instance, the Fuel Oil Act was nullified, and the British and American oil companies returned to do business as usual. However, the government continued to control or participate in business. Alien firms seeking to establish themselves were asked to grant substantial control of stock, usually 51 per cent, to Siamese.

The government tried to give the impression to non-Siamese that it was relaxing controls and was getting out of business. A survey of government proposals and acts during the postwar years, however, reveals a continuing determination to control and participate in all sorts of commercial ventures. In June 1946 plans were formulated for the expansion of government-controlled air lines to operate within the country. In August the ministry of industry announced that it was sending men to study the canning industry in Australia and to purchase the necessary machinery. In September it was planned to purchase machinery and equipment for a cigarette factory and to quadruple current production. In the same month it was announced that the committee investigating government corporations had decided to give up certain unproductive factories, to continue to hold shares in cloth and rubber factories, to sell shares in a hides factory, a canning factory, and in a forestry products company, and to share control with municipalities in paper factories and abattoirs.

In November the cabinet authorized the Industrial Promotion Company to raise by internal loan *baht* ten million for business expansion. (Before World War II the *baht* was roughly valued at three to one dollar. Since the war the official rate has been set at ten to one, while the open market rate, which is used even by banks and the government itself, has varied from twenty-three to one to eighteen to one. Now that Siam is a member of the World Fund and Bank, it is expected that an official rate will be set that will approximate the open market rate.) In January 1947 a new cotton factory was approved for northeastern Siam. In February the Thai Ship Company, a semi-government firm, was amalgamated with the Transport Company, a governmental concern. The two companies would operate river transport and bus lines.

In the lives of the villagers, and in the raising of rice, the government also took an active role. In July 1946 the ministry of agriculture allotted *baht* eight million for the promotion of rice farming in areas not under cultivation. In September 1946 the government considered a *baht* fifty million rural development fund. According to the plan, 3,500 communes (*tambon*) would receive about *baht* 15,000 each for financing local projects. The plan included a chain of cooperative stores for the sale of general goods including paddy seeds, livestock, and farm equipment. Planning for each community would be done by local representatives including the *kamnan*, the *phuyaiban*, the inspector of education, and some leading citizens. (The *phuyaiban* was the village chief, or chief of the commune, while the *kamnan* was chief of the next larger administrative unit, known as a *tambon*, which included from eight to twenty or more villages.) The funds might be used in starting cottage industry, kitchen gardens, poultry and animal farming, and other projects that would tend to make the communities more independent of alien businessmen.

The foregoing plan to improve the economic situation of the farmers looked good on paper and was no doubt inspired by sincere good intentions. Perhaps, however, the farmers need less rather than more government participation in rice farming. Before World War II Siam exported about 1,500,000 tons of rice, and the farmers received about 60 per cent of the export price. In 1948, although the price of rice from Siam had increased about six times, the farmer received only about twice as much. In fact he received only about 27 per cent of the export price as compared to 60 per cent before the war, while the government took over 60 per cent for its services. The government was succeeding in one respect, however, and that was in squeezing the alien middleman. Before the war his take amounted to almost 40 per cent of the export price, while in 1948 it was less than 10 per cent.

When Prime Minister Phibun made his statement of policy on April 21, 1948, he said that in regard to building up a solid social structure his government would: (1) arrange for social insurance for the benefit of workers and employees; (2) establish and expand cooperative societies in various forms, especially those whose purpose was the acquirement of capital, the sale of paddy and other agricultural produce, and the purchase of land, and cooperatives for consumers; (3) foster trade associations; (4) promote various occupations on the principle that those engaged in each should be enabled to become owners of the business or factory in which they worked; and (5) undertake to operate any big business or industry that was beyond the capacity and capability of individuals or that affected public safety, while giving an opportunity to the public to hold shares; or alternatively, to allow individuals to operate such businesses or industries, while the government held an appropriate number of shares.

Phibun's statement of policy indicated that he intended to continue to bring the government into business to help the Siamese peasants and businessmen economically against the former business interests, which were largely alien. In the postwar years and at the time Phibun spoke, the government's policy was to require Siamese ownership, generally government ownership, of 51 per cent in foreign investment deals. A further development was reported in the *Bangkok Post* of August 19, 1948, to the effect that there would be created four new agencies: a government purchasing bureau, a central distribution company, a trade promotion bureau, and central cooperative stores. These agencies would compete directly with private trading concerns.

Under the absolute monarchy during the years before 1932, the policy of the government was to depend largely upon the Siamese state railways for passenger and freight transportation. The highway system was built not to compete with the railroad but to act as feeder lines. Accordingly, the railroad extended from Chiengmai in the north to the southern border at Malaya, where it connected with the railway system of that country. The lines were meter gauge, as were those in the other countries of Southeast Asia. The highways in Siam were generally metaled roads incapable of carrying fast traffic. They were in disconnected networks so that it was impossible to drive a car for any great distance. There was some air traffic, both internal and international, but not a great deal.

The constitutional regime put considerable emphasis on the development of communication systems. The railroad was regarded as adequate, so new programs of road construction were planned. By the time that World War II began it was possible to drive out of Bangkok south to Hua Hin, and north and east to the Korat plateau and to the Indochina border. In fact the Indochina road was completed within the week that the Japanese opened their attack, thus facilitating their advance. The airports within Siam were improved, particularly the Bangkok port of Don Muang. Major international air lines went through Bangkok en route to Indochina, Singapore, and Australia.

During the war the Japanese pushed road construction along certain routes they desired to travel, particularly between Burma and Siam. They used war prisoners and local labor to build a railroad from Kanburi to Thanbayuzayat in Burma. They also improved the road at Chaiya across the Kra Isthmus, as well as the roads leading out of central Siam to Burma.

Since the war the chief problem has been to restore the railroad, which was badly smashed by bombs. Much has been done in rebuilding bridges and repairing roadbeds, but there is still in 1948 great need for locomotives and rolling stock and for machine-shop facilities. Some stock has been purchased from India and the United States, but more is required before the railroad can approximate its prewar efficiency. Very little highway construction has been done since the war.

Considerable progress has been made in aviation. During the war new airfields were developed and old ones were improved. Don Muang airport at Bangkok was given heavy use during and immediately after the war. There are plans for its repair and enlargement, and *baht* thirty million have been allocated for this purpose. This airport handles the traffic of fourteen international air lines and is an air crossroads between Pacific Ocean countries and those to the west. Local air lines are also being developed in which the Siamese government has an interest.

The publicity department news bulletin informed the public on June 10, 1948 that the council of ministers had resolved to grant concessions to individuals, companies, or cooperatives for the construction and operation of highways where such projects could not be undertaken by the government due to lack of funds and manpower. It also stated that the ministry of communications was ready to grant a concession for the rebuilding of the Siam-Burma railway and for the operation of passenger and freight train services on that line between Kanburi and the terminus at the Burma frontier, as well as a concession for the running of train services on the Surat-Pangga line in South Siam. The government was also offering concessions for the construction of wharfs at four of the principal ports outside of Bangkok. The government's desire for improved communication facilities was leading it to the point of being willing to grant concessions to private industry.

World War II and Its Aftermath

The Siamese owe their national security to their awareness of international trends on a world-wide basis and to their ability to adjust themselves to fit the times. They were the only small nation in the Far East that survived the period of colonial expansion at the end of the nineteenth century. They were quick to sense the rise of Japan and its significance to them. In 1933 the Siamese delegate to the League of Nations refrained from voting on the Lytton Report, and so did not condemn Japanese aggression in Manchuria.

Commercial and social relations were deliberately strengthened between Siam and Japan during the years preceding World War II. Japanese techniques and methods were copied in administering Siam. The Siamese were seeking to arrive at a basis of understanding with the Japanese. In 1925 Siam bought goods from Japan worth $2,250,000. In 1935 the amount was $12,150,000, or about 29 per cent of Siam's import trade with all nations. In 1940 and 1941 Japanese economic missions swarmed in Siam, and Japan began buying large quantities of Siamese rice, tin, and rubber.

Japan and Siam drew closer together politically during the peace conference in Tokyo in 1941 when the Indochina border dispute was settled in Siam's favor. It was pressure from Japan that led the French government of Indochina to relinquish 27,000 square miles of Cambodia and Laos to Siam. A small group of highly placed Siamese officials, including the prime minister, Luang Phibun Songgram, took a pro-Japanese line. They went so far as to identify Siam with Japan after war began by declaring war on Great Britain and the United States on January 25, 1942.

This act has been a subject of dispute ever since. Many Siamese believed that Phibun was acting in the best interests of his nation. Others regarded him as a war criminal and so condemned him. Aside from such considerations it was a diplomatic blunder, for a declaration of war must be secured by victory in order to be successful. Such a wily diplomat of the past as Prince Devawongse would never have put his nation in such a difficult position. If Siam had made no declaration of war it would not have been necessary to arrange a peace agreement with Great Britain. There would then have been no question of free rice as required in the agreement of January 1, 1946. In fact, many thorny problems might have been avoided if Siam had come out of the war without qualification as a country invaded by the enemy. The United States government chose to ignore Siam's declaration of war, on the ground that it did not represent the intentions of the people. Consequently there was no need for a Siam-United States peace agreement. At any rate, there was a powerful minority in Siam that had prepared the way for the country to enter the war on Japan's side.

Before the war the Siamese laid plans for the removal of military and political strength from Bangkok to more defensible locations. Phibun planned to establish a military city at Lopburi and a political capital at Petchabun. Lopburi was an ancient Siamese capital city located less than a hundred miles above Bangkok on the Chao Phya River. Petchabun was farther northeast, about two hundred miles from Bangkok on the Pasak River, located in a cul-de-sac of hills approachable only from the south. The political capital would thus be well protected by the military headquarters at Lopburi. A highway system was to be developed from Lopburi to Petchabun. Construction was begun at Lopburi before the war and at Petchabun during 1943. The Petchabun project cost so heavily in money and lives that Phibun's political opponent, Pridi Banomyong, was able to cause his overthrow and establish the first of the Pridi governments with Khuang Aphaiwong as prime minister in July 1944.

The contest between Phibun and Pridi for political control, which had been going on for years before 1941, continued during the war. When Japanese troops entered Siam on December 8, 1941, Phibun offered only token resistance and then agreed to provide the Japanese with necessary facilities. Pridi on the other hand resigned his post as minister of finance and made an abortive attempt to establish an independent government in North Siam.

He was made regent and remained in that post until King Ananda visited Siam after the war in January 1946.

Pridi organized a Siamese underground movement to oppose the Japanese and provided secret facilities for Allied officers, both American and British, who worked with a Free Thai Movement organized in the United States and Great Britain. Allied forces working with the Siamese underground developed airfields and imported extensive amounts of arms in preparation for an attack against the Japanese. Pridi was ready to move before the end of the war came, but was requested not to take action by the supreme Allied commander of the Southeast Asia Command and by the American acting secretary of state. Although Pridi was ready to act, the Southeast Asia Command was not in a position to come to his support at that time, and it was feared that he and his underground might be destroyed uselessly. Pridi thus ended the war in good repute with the Allied powers and in political control of Siam, an authority which he exercised through Prime Minister Khuang Aphaiwong after Phibun was ousted in 1944.

Khuang Aphaiwong served as prime minister until August 1945. During his regime he began to get ideas that he could establish himself politically apart from Pridi. He attempted to take independent action on a number of occasions, with the result that he alienated himself from Pridi, who ousted him.

The leader of the Free Thai Movement in the United States during the war was the Siamese minister at Washington, Seni Pramoj. Pridi felt that Seni was the obvious man, therefore, to re-establish Siam's good relations with the Allied nations. He accordingly invited him to return to become prime minister. While waiting for Seni Pramoj to arrive, Pridi set up a government with his friend Thawi Bunyaket as prime minister. This government was in office until Seni took over in September 1945.

Seni's government lasted only until shortly after the signing of the British-Siamese Agreement of January 1, 1946. Pridi and Seni fell out almost as soon as they met. Each man had very positive ideas about the administration of Siam. Seni had been out of the country during the crucial war years, and was handicapped by his inexperience in high administration and by his ignorance of the actual political forces within the country. He found himself up against a tough and experienced legislative assembly, which had come through a rough and tumble experience under the Japanese and knew a great deal about the processes of legislation under adverse conditions. Seni was out of his depth from the beginning.

To salvage the situation, Pridi again tried Khuang Aphaiwong as prime minister, but let him go in March and took the job himself until August 1946. On June 9, 1946, the day before King Ananda was to leave by air in a special United States plane to go to Washington as a guest of the American government, he was found dead of a bullet wound in his forehead. A commission of inquiry was able to go no further than to decide that the king had died as a result of suicide, accident, or murder. King Ananda was succeeded by his brother, Phumiphon Adundet, who was eighteen years of age.

In August 1946 Pridi's old friend and former colleague in government, Thamrong Nawasawat, for many years minister of justice, accepted the post of premier and continued as long as Pridi held political control. Pridi's authority was challenged by Phibun in 1947. After the war Phibun was held for trial as a war criminal, along with other prominent persons who had been in his following. At the trials the court decided that it could not properly try persons for acts committed when there were no laws forbidding them, nor could it try them under laws which were passed subsequent to such acts. Phibun was released and began to organize his forces, both political and military.

Phibun was ready to act months before he did, but was restrained by his fear that he was unpopular with the Allied powers. He finally decided that these fears were groundless and staged a coup d'état on November 8, 1947. Phibun did not appear in a prominent role, but used younger officers to bear the brunt of public comment. He appointed Khuang Aphaiwong as an interim prime minister until elections could be held under a new constitution which he issued by fiat on the day of the revolution.

There was no loss of life and the country was quiet. Elections were held in January, and the Khuang government was confirmed as the regular government on March 6, 1948. Khuang selected for his cabinet some of the ablest men in the nation, who had excellent reputations and who had been active under King Prajadhipok. The obvious intention was to create a good impression and secure recognition from the Allied nations. This was promptly achieved. Phibun waited the decent interval of a bill collector, thirty days, and on April 6 had himself named prime minister by the supreme state council, which he had set up under his new constitution to replace the old regency. The king, Phumiphon Adundet, was still in Switzerland.

Postwar Economic and Political Problems

There was little opposition to Phibun among the Siamese. His foibles in changing cultural practices seemed less important than his known ability to maintain a strong government. Many people felt that the nation needed a strong man to cope with such problems as corruption and inflation, the two major troubles besetting the nation. During the war the Siamese had become accustomed to indulging in irregular practices to annoy the Japanese. They became skillful in creating hindrances to Japanese supply trains. They mastered the techniques of featherbedding every job. These were virtues during the war but became vices that hurt themselves after it was over. High officials indulged in scandalous graft and public dishonesty, and enriched themselves at the expense of the nation. There is no evidence to indicate that corruption lessened under Phibun in 1948. Several of his leading officials are regarded as the most flagrant offenders.

Inflation continued in 1948 without abatement. The open market rate of exchange between the *baht* and dollar was twenty to one, while before the war it was three to one. The country in 1948 was actually moving back to normal conditions in the economic field, in spite of inflation.

Perhaps the major problem in Siam is political instability, as shown by the nine regimes that have briefly held office since the war. Interestingly enough, however, all of the governments assumed the policies and responsibilities of the preceding administrations, so there has been a sense of continuity.

One problem faced by Siam after 1945 was to reach an agreement with the British settling the state of war. The British proposed to negotiate simultaneously with the Siamese at Kandy,

Ceylon, a political agreement of purely British interest and an agreement on military matters of Allied interest. The purely military agreement was not difficult and was signed September 8, 1945. The political agreement became a matter of discussion between the British and American governments, because of United States interest in any settlement that might have implications in regard to United States-Siam relations. American opposition to specific provisions was discussed at length, and on most points the United Kingdom agreed to ease up.

On January 1, 1946 the agreement was signed, containing a provision in connection with rice to which the United States objected. Under this provision the Siamese agreed to provide free of cost at Bangkok a quantity of rice equal to the accumulated surplus then existing in Siam, not to exceed a maximum of 1,500,000 tons. The United Kingdom then decided to modify its position; and in connection with a Tripartite Rice Agreement, in which the United States participated and which was signed May 6, 1946, the British made a side agreement with the Siamese that Siam would export a minimum of 1,200,000 tons during the succeeding twelve months, and that any shortage would be delivered at a later date free of cost to the United Kingdom. The idea was to give Siam an incentive to speed up exports of rice.

Under the Tripartite Agreement a Combined Siam Rice Commission was set up at Bangkok to expedite the export of rice, in accordance with International Emergency Food Commission allocations. Siam failed to deliver rice as expected, so a new rice commitment was set on December 24, 1946 which reduced the amount still to be delivered by August 31, 1947 to 600,000 tons. The full amount was not delivered, but the penalty was not administered because it was felt that Siam was doing the best it could under difficult circumstances.

Tin was another of Siam's major products that the world needed after the war. It was estimated that the tin left on British and Australian properties in Siam on December 8, 1941 and the tin mined from them after that date amounted to about one year's output, or roughly 15,000 tons. The owners sought compensation for this metal from the Siamese government, and it seemed for a time that no tin would be exported until a settlement was reached. Although almost all tin interests in Siam were

British and Australian, the United States was vitally interested. Consequently on December 7, 1946 a tin agreement was signed by Siam, the United States, the United Kingdom, and Australia which aimed to move the tin while providing for a settlement of British and Australian claims.

Siam agreed that the amount of tin involved was 15,992.7 tons; that it would deposit to United Kingdom and Australian account an amount representing the prewar operating profit per ton in sterling; that a tin commission would be set up to expedite tin shipments for a limited time, the actual life being until September 30, 1947; that the price of tin would be on a fair level with the price in Malaya; and that all tin concentrates were to be available in equal shares during the life of the tin commission to the United States and United Kingdom if they desired to purchase them. The United States actually bought most of the tin metal and its half of the concentrates. After the expiration date of the agreement, it expanded its buying of concentrates as far as possible. This was a new development in Siam-United States trade relations, and it was brought about by the desire of the United States to make full use of the Texas smelter. Tin mines were very slow in getting under way again, and by August 1948 it was estimated that the year's production for 1948 would not exceed 5,000 tons, or about a third of normal production.

Rubber regained its usual production figures more rapidly than other products. Under the British-Siamese Agreement of January 1, 1946 Siam agreed to participate in international arrangements in regard to rubber. The Combined Rubber Committee, set up to make international allocations, ceased on December 31, 1946, so that since that time Siam has been selling rubber on a free market. Production is about normal again, or about 50,000 tons a year.

Teak has been one of the slowest of Siam's products to recover because of the nature of the industry, which requires about seven years to bring lumber from tree to mill. The British had heavy investments in Siam's teak industry, so this product entered into the agreement of January 1, 1946 also. This agreement provided that teak from British concessions be returned to the owners; that British leases valid on December 8, 1941 be restored; and that payment be made for losses. There was no international board for allocation. In its efforts to recover teak logs for the British, the Siamese government virtually paralyzed the industry. There was little production during 1946 except by a Siamese company on agreement with the British companies. In late 1947 the British companies began to take over their properties and resume business. Teak exported at high prices during 1946 and at the present time was chiefly produced before the war. Production is now getting under way, however.

A problem with economic implications facing Siam after the war was the settlement of Allied claims for war damage loss. Article Three of the British-Siamese Agreement of January 1, 1946 provided that the Siamese assume responsibility for safeguarding, maintaining, and restoring unimpaired British property, rights, and interests of all kinds, and provided for payment of compensation for losses or damage sustained. The United States felt that its citizens should receive most-favored-nation treatment, and entered into negotiation with the Siamese and British governments with a view to agreeing on categories within which claims would be considered favorably.

Toward the end of 1946 a draft of the terms of reference for claims was delivered to Siam and the United Kingdom for consideration. It was not intended that other reasonable and equitable categories which might arise would be excluded, but these were offered to expedite settlement. Wherever possible, property should be returned; compensation should be paid for damage to such property; interest should be paid at 4 per cent on the value of the claim until its settlement; and some types of claims should be paid in dollars and others in *baht*, depending usually upon where the property was obtained and the kind of currency originally paid. There were many other details in the agreement, but in general the idea was to arrive at a fair value of the loss and a reasonable interest on it until the day of settlement. Such intangibles as good will and anticipated profits were not held as valid items to be subject to claim.

The British had much heavier interests in Siam than the United States, and consequently set up a British-Siamese Claims Committee in Bangkok. The United States did not feel this necessary, as American claims were few and generally small. Furthermore, the Siamese government expressed its intention to make rapid and fair settlement. Most American personal property losses were settled by the middle of 1948. There remained only several corporation claims, which in their very nature required more preparation and consideration both by the claimants and by the Siamese government. In general, personal claims were settled at about 70 per cent of the amount demanded. As such things go, this represented very fair treatment. In August 1948 the British and Siamese were still working out a settlement on the extensive British claims, which involved comparatively large investments.

French relations with Siam were cool after the war because of the loss of Indochinese areas to Siam on May 9, 1941. The French and Siamese governments made use of the good offices of the American government and negotiated a settlement of their differences at Washington. An agreement was signed on November 17, 1946 that nullified the Tokyo convention of May 9, 1941 and provided for the return of the disputed areas and for a conciliation commission to examine ethnic, geographic, and economic arguments for confirming or revising the pre-1941 boundary line.

The conciliation commission met in May 1947 and made its recommendations at the end of June. It did not support Siamese claims to the territory, but suggested that arrangements be made for ensuring adequate supplies of fish to Siam from the Tonlé Sap. It also suggested that the two governments should agree to establish at Bangkok an international consultative commission for the study of technical questions of common interest to the countries of the Indochinese peninsula. As the disputed areas had been peacefully returned to Indochina in December 1946 awaiting these findings, there seemed to be no further action called for. France accepted the decisions immediately, but Siam did not indicate her acquiescence until May 1948.

After settling its differences with the various Allied governments, the natural move for Siam was to seek membership in the United Nations. One spur to the Siamese to return the areas in dispute to Indochina was that France was prepared to veto Siam's application for United Nations membership unless the territories were returned. France sponsored Siam's application as soon as their agreement was signed. However, the Soviet government took the position that since Siam had a law forbidding communism, and since Russia and Siam had no diplomatic relations, it would veto Siam's application. It seemed for a time that Siam would fail to achieve membership at the General Assembly of 1947, because the time was short. However, Siam pointed out that it had begun negotiations for the establishment of diplomatic relations with Russia before the war and had renewed those negotiations after hostilities ended. It also stated that it would annul its law against communism. Russia then refrained from voting, and Siam became the fifty-fifth member of the United Nations.

It was not until May 4, 1948 that the Soviet minister presented his credentials at Bangkok. The Russians established a legation with a staff of about twenty. In addition to these, there were about another score who acted as guards, messengers, and performed lesser tasks. Such a staff attracted attention because of the few Russians in Siam. There were many non-Russian Communists in Siam, however, either Chinese or Viet Minh. The Siamese Communist party was very small and had little influence. After the opening of the Soviet legation there was considerable speculation as to its relations with the Chinese and Viet Minh Communists in Siam.

In August 1948, Siam seemed to be the only country in Southeast Asia not being actively troubled by Communists. In Indochina the Communist-dominated Viet Minh regime of Ho Chi Minh was succeeding in denying all but the major centers to French forces. In Burma the Socialist government of Thakin Nu was being shaken by Communists, who were acquiring control of most of the nation and arranging themselves into position to threaten Rangoon. The British in Singapore and the Federation of Malaya, with its capital at Kuala Lumpur, were troubled by Chinese guerrilla bands, which the British said were Communists attempting to set up a Communist state in Malaya. Both Chinese Kuomintang and British persons were being murdered, and their property was being damaged or destroyed.

Because of the foregoing situation in neighboring countries, Siam was nervous and appeared to be ready to take armed action when necessary. This nervousness was accented for the Phibun government by the knowledge that Pridi Banomyong was planning to return to political power if possible. It was feared that he might be willing and ready to use such alien armed forces as the Chinese Communists and the Viet Minh. An additional cause for nervousness lay in the impending trials of several Siamese for the murder of King Ananda. Pridi had been named as one who was involved in some way in the case, and an order for his arrest had been issued. In August 1948 his whereabouts were unknown, but his followers were believed to be ready to use the occasion of the trial for a coup d'état.

Phibun, however, seemed to be fairly secure in his control of the nation. Most of the military were supporting him, and the majority of the Siamese did not object to him. He was conducting his administration along lines that indicated his intention to continue his previous policies with some modification to fit the times. He seemed able to overcome the occasional efforts made by some military and civilian elements to unseat him. On October 2, 1948 he nipped a budding military revolt by arresting a number of high officers, including three generals and a colonel. The army general staff seemed to be seriously crippled by the arrests. On the civilian side, such notables as Thawi Bunyaket, once prime minister, Direk Chayanam, once foreign minister, and Thamrong Nawasawat, also prime minister at one time, were arrested, perhaps as a precautionary measure since they did not seem to be identified with the military revolters.

Phibun renewed his plans to build Lopburi into a military city. He felt that the military forces would be better cared for and more powerful if held outside of Bangkok. He revived his cultural program on a mild scale in an effort to urge the country on toward modern ways. He renewed his emphasis on controlled education and initiated a plan for establishing government secondary schools in every province. It was not clear whether the quality of the government was becoming increasingly military because Phibun was a militarist, or because the disturbed situation in other parts of Southeast Asia led him to take military precautions.

Suggested Reading

Graham, W. A. *Siam.* 2 vols. London. 1924.
Landon, Kenneth P. *Siam in Transition.* Chicago. 1939.
——. *The Chinese in Thailand.* New York. 1941.
Thompson, Virginia. *Thailand, the New Siam.* New York. 1941.

THE CHINESE
in Southeast Asia

THE Chinese in Southeast Asia (as is true of their race elsewhere in the world) are almost exclusively drawn from the southeastern Chinese provinces of Kwangtung, Fukien, and Kwangsi. The reasons for this are many, but foremost among them is the proximity of these provinces to the area, and the fact that the similarity of their climates made it easier for the immigrants to survive the conditions when they arrived.

This emigration, however, was frowned on both by the administration and by public opinion. The laws of the Ch'ing (Manchu) dynasty laid down that "all who clandestinely proceed to sea to trade or who remove to foreign islands for the purpose of inhabiting and cultivating the same, shall be punished according to the law of communicating with rebels and enemies, and consequently suffer death by being beheaded." Chinese religion, too, condemned those who deserted the graves of their ancestors as "unfilial." However the pressure of economic necessity and the hope for gain were too powerful to be overcome either by the fear of punishment or the demands of ancestor worship, and the Chinese went abroad in large numbers. The coming of the West to Asia greatly stimulated this emigration, for the Portuguese, the Spanish, the Dutch, the British, and the French in their turn created the conditions of order that were so necessary for successful trading.

Generally speaking, the Chinese immigrants into the countries of Southeast Asia were exclusively interested in gaining a livelihood, and, if possible, earning a competence that would enable them to return to their native land at an early date; and they took very little share or interest in local politics. They supplied labor for mines and to a lesser extent for estates; but although many of them were peasants in their native lands they were usually not well disposed toward agriculture when they immigrated, preferring more lucrative kinds of employment. Where they would have taken to rice cultivation, local laws prevented them from so doing. On the whole they were the middlemen and the retail traders, providing the medium of economic intercourse between the Europeans and the natives of the Southeast Asian countries. In Siam, too (which has never been under Western domination), they occupied a leading place in trade. Usually their commerce was organized on a family basis and up to recent years they have left the large joint-stock enterprises to the Europeans.

The Chinese Revolution of 1911 produced in the long run a great change in the attitude of the overseas Chinese. From being conscious only of their family, clan, or tribe they became aware that they belonged to the Chinese nation, divided politically though it was. The Chinese Nationalist party, the Kuomintang, received great support from the Chinese of Southeast Asia, and the new nationality law of China, claiming all Chinese as nationals of China according to the *jus sanguinis*, was the source of much friction between the Chinese immigrants and the local governments.[1] Communism too, after Chiang Kai-shek had, in 1927, purged the Kuomintang of its leftist elements, gained more and more adherents among the overseas Chinese, especially among schoolteachers and the laboring classes.

[1] EDITOR'S NOTE. Chinese nationality is obtained at birth, whether in China or abroad, by a child whose father was a Chinese national. There are some exceptions, as when a female Chinese marries an alien, but these rarely arise now in Southeast Asia, where increasingly both parents are Chinese. The general rule is that nationality is determined by racial descent or *jus sanguinis*. British law has elements of *jus sanguinis*—that is, a British father may transmit his nationality to a foreign-born child by registering the birth at a British consulate, providing that at the age of twenty-one the child formally accepts British nationality in preference to that of his country of birth. The primary emphasis of British law however is upon *jus soli*, or nationality according to the country of birth. Under these circumstances Chinese children born, for example, in the Straits Settlements have dual nationality. They are Chinese nationals *jure sanguinis* and British *jure soli*. No success has attended the various attempts to reconcile the conflict of laws.

Obstacles to obtaining exact information regarding the numbers of Chinese in Southeast Asia are first, the conflict between the Chinese definition of nationality and that of the local government, and second, the fact that the war of 1939–45 and the subsequent civil disturbances in several of the countries have prevented the taking of new censuses, and the existing censuses are mostly out of date. In Malaya, Burma, British Borneo, and the Philippines the censuses have referred to *ethnic* Chinese (i.e., Chinese by race) while in Siam and Indochina those enumerated are Chinese by national status according to the law of the country. Estimation of the numbers of Chinese is thus further complicated. However, the following table giving estimates of the Chinese in Southeast Asia is thought to be not very far from the truth.

PROPORTION OF ETHNIC CHINESE TO TOTAL POPULATION IN
SOUTHEAST ASIA, 1948

	Chinese	Total Population
Burma	300,000	17,000,000
Siam	2,500,000	16,000,000
Indochina	450,000	27,000,000
Malaya	2,600,000	5,800,000*
British Borneo	220,000	800,000
Indonesia	1,500,000	70,000,000
Philippines	100,000	19,500,000
Total	7,670,000	156,100,000

* EDITOR'S NOTE. Malaya is the only country where the Chinese actually outnumber the original inhabitants. This seriously increases the difficulty of establishing self-government.

Let us now consider the Chinese in the several countries in the order of the numerical strength of the communities.

Malaya

The first undoubted landfall in the history of the Chinese in Malaya is in 1349 when a Chinese trader speaks of the native people living "mixed up with the Chinese" in Tumasik, or Old Singapore. After Tumasik had been destroyed by the Madjapahits, Malacca was founded by Malay refugees from that settlement; and in 1403 (says the Ming History) the emperor sent an emissary there with presents. To the king of the country he gave a commission as a ruler, a seal, a suit of clothes of silk brocade, and a yellow umbrella. The next noteworthy event was the arrival in 1407 of the Chinese admiral, Cheng Ho. In 1511, the great Portuguese viceroy, Alfonso d'Albuquerque, conquered Malacca.

Under the Portuguese the Chinese traders, who had hitherto visited Malacca only during the monsoon season, made permanent settlements. These settlements, however, were never very large (about 400–500 persons all told) and they increased very little under the Dutch, who took Malacca from the Portuguese in 1641. The greatest number of Chinese in Malacca during the Dutch period was in 1750 when it reached 2,161.

The first British settlement in Malaya was at Penang, founded in 1786. Singapore was founded by Raffles in 1819, and the policy of free trade attracted the Chinese in large numbers to the Straits Settlements (Singapore, Penang, Malacca, and Labuan) in spite of the widespread piracy in these waters. Meanwhile the Malay States had fallen into a condition of political decay verging on anarchy. This was not improved by the arrival of Chinese miners in increasing numbers after 1850 to mine the newly discovered tin deposits in Perak, for with them they brought their secret societies with their methods of intrigue and intimidation.

After the British had intervened in the Malay States in 1874 and succeeding years and had established order, the way was clear for the opening up of the country. The tin industry expanded greatly toward the end of the century, and the rubber industry (an entirely British creation) became profitable about 1905. The Chinese flocked into Malaya in ever-increasing numbers to provide labor for the tin mines and rubber estates, to work as artisans and in a score of handicrafts, and as shopkeepers and traders in nearly all the towns and villages of the Peninsula. Malaya became very prosperous, and the Chinese holdings were estimated in 1937 at United States $200,000,000. The result, however, of this immigration of Chinese and others was that the whole racial pattern of Malaya was altered in a small space of years. In 1911 the Malays numbered 1,437,000 and the Chinese 917,000 in a total population of 2,673,000; by 1941 the total had more than doubled and the Chinese were for the first time the majority community; in 1947 the total population was 5,818,000, including 2,600,000 Chinese, 2,500,000 Malays, and 600,000 Indians.

In the early days the Chinese had married Malay women, but when the floodgates of immigration were opened in the later nineteenth century, there was no further intermarriage between the races. The Chinese, after the revolution in China in 1911, came much under the influence of Chinese nationalism and the Kuomintang, and the seeds of communism were also sown among them.

When the Japanese occupied Malaya in 1942 between three and four thousand Chinese Communists fled to the hills, where they formed guerrilla units to resist the Japanese. Later contact was made with them by British officers sent in by submarine, and an agreement was signed with the guerrillas (known as the Malayan Peoples' Anti-Japanese Army) whereby they were to assist the intended invasion of Malaya. After the Japanese surrender when the British returned to Malaya the Communists tried to make the British position untenable, using the weapons of the strike and intimidation of Chinese, Malays, and Indians. In June 1948 this action was converted into open terrorism, the object of which was to paralyze the economy of Malaya by murdering planters and miners (whether Europeans or Asiatics), and to prepare the way, if possible, for the declaration of a Malayan Communist republic. The plan miscarried in its major objectives, but the nature of the country is such that it would take many months before the terrorists were finally rounded up—nearly four-fifths of Malaya being still under jungle and swamp in spite of eighty years of intensive development.

After the liberation, the British government had introduced a new constitution, creating a Malayan Union of the Peninsula (Singapore remaining separate); but the innovation caused such vigorous protest on the part of the Malays that the Union was abandoned and a Federation was substituted, in whose legislature the Malays had the predominant voice. Malaya's main political problem today remains that of finding a method of reconciling the claims of the Malays, the Chinese, and the other races of Malaya to equal citizenship and a share in the government of the country.

Modern Malaya is the creation in the main of British leadership and Chinese enterprise. Without the Chinese, Malaya would still be as it was in 1874, a few settlements on the banks of the rivers and along the coasts, with a population of not more than 300,000 and with no roads, no railways, no public buildings, no hospitals, and no courts of law.

Siam

According to Chinese official sources the number of Chinese in Siam is about two and a half million; but according to Siamese official figures the number is only slightly over half a million. This discrepancy is due to the difference in the Siamese and Chinese definition of "Chinese," the Siamese considering all persons born in their country as Siamese unless their birth is registered with a foreign consulate. (There were no Chinese consuls in Siam until 1946.) In 1937 the census of Siam showed 524,000 Chinese in a total population of 14,424,000.

The Chinese had been visiting and residing in Siam for centuries, but their immigration in large numbers is a matter only of the last century. In the time of King Phra Narai (1656–88) there were only about 3,000 Chinese settled in the country. Between 1840 and 1850 their annual immigration averaged 15,000.

Before the rise of nationalism in China and Siam there was no problem of assimilation. In three generations the newcomers were completely absorbed into the Siamese people. During the process of assimilation these people performed a necessary function in Siamese society. They were a source of new energy to a people who suffered from the usual tropical lethargy, and since Siam was underpopulated throughout its history, there was no threat that the nation would be swamped in a flood of alien immigration.

A combination of factors was to change the situation within the few decades following 1910. The first was the growth of a feeling on the part of the two peoples that they had separate national entities that were being threatened by foreign encroachment. The other important factor was that with increasing immigration Chinese women were, after 1910, accompanying their men in large numbers and thus creating a wall against assimilation. The feeling of separation on the part of the Chinese was more and more fostered by the Chinese government. A sense of nationality was also growing among the Siamese. By 1920 the two communities were deeply conscious of their separateness.

This feeling of apartness was accentuated by the growing Siamese fear of Chinese economic encroachment. As in other countries in Southeast Asia, the Chinese had secured a dominating position in the trade of the country; and as in the Philippines and Indochina this included a virtual monopoly of the trade in the most vital of all commodities—rice. At the same time the Siamese felt that Chinese politics were creating in their midst an *imperium in imperio* that might eventually threaten Siam's own political existence.

Friction between the Chinese and their hosts turned upon the question of education more than upon any other single factor. After the Siamese revolution of 1932 the Siamese government became more and more determined that the Chinese children in their midst should be educated to be loyal Siamese citizens and not citizens of a foreign power. The Siamese felt that the Chinese private schools, teaching through the medium of the Chinese language, were alien in character and purpose to their own ideals. From the beginning they were founded to preserve the foreign culture of a minority population and to perpetuate the Chinese language and Chinese nationalism. Whenever the law conflicted with their purpose (the Siamese alleged) the Chinese got round it if they could—if not, they disobeyed it.

The fight in the field of education continued for many years and is still going on. Especially since the war with Japan, it has become complicated by the growth of communism in Chinese schools in Siam. The teachers, being underpaid and therefore discontented, were fertile ground for the growth of Communist ideas, and these they imparted to their pupils, whatever the wishes of the parents may have been. So it happened that in a large degree the Chinese merchants were fighting on Chinese Nationalist grounds for the promotion of a system of education strongly impregnated with Communist doctrine.

As in the Philippines, the loosening of the Chinese hold on trade has been a prominent plank in the government's platform, and many laws have been passed both to restrict Chinese participation in business, especially retail business, and to encourage the Siamese in commercial pursuits. The obstacle to the success of the policy has been (as elsewhere) the acumen of the Chinese and the reluctance of the indigenous people to take to trade.

The Siamese have endeavored since the end of the war to reduce Chinese immigration to a minimum. In January 1946 a long delayed Treaty of Amity was concluded between Siam and China, but it cannot be said that it produced any great change for the better in the prevailing atmosphere. In November 1947 occurred the coup d'état which brought Marshal Phibun Songgram back into power; and with this coup the apprehension of the Chinese was reinforced, since during the period of the Japanese ascendancy the marshal had been identified with a very definitely anti-Chinese policy.

Indonesia

The Chinese community in Indonesia differs from that in Malaya, Siam, and Indochina in being much smaller in relation to the total population (1,233,000 to 60,727,000 in 1930) and in being more widely distributed. Thus the community has never quite attained to the status of a "menace," though the fact that the Chinese have here, as elsewhere, been the middlemen between the natives and the Dutch has had the usual result of bringing them under suspicion.

When the Dutch first landed in Java they found a scattered population of Chinese working in every province of the island, but it was not until the Dutch established their rule that their numbers became considerable. Governor-General J. P. Coen, who founded Batavia in 1619, laid down what he considered should be the policy of the Dutch East India Company—that it should limit its trade to being "a mighty wholesale dealer," that the Dutch burghers should act as middlemen, and that retail trade should be left to the Chinese. In the long run, however, it was the Chinese who became practically the only middlemen in the community.

The Dutch attitude toward the Chinese was not altogether consistent—at one time they encouraged their entry into the Indies, but usually they tried to keep their numbers down and to subject them to strong control. In 1740 there occurred a massacre of the Chinese by the Dutch, assisted by the natives, in which about 10,000 were killed. But they soon recovered their numerical strength. By the nineteenth century they had an established position in Java. As Mr. Jan O. M. Broek says, "generally speaking, the natives form the agrarian base, the Chinese and the Arabs the commercial middle class, and the Westerners the small but ruling apex of the socio-economic pyramid."[2]

The awareness of nationality, as distinct from that of tribe, clan, and family, that followed on the revolution in 1911, was increasingly manifest among the Chinese of Indonesia. They began to agitate for an improvement in their civil status, especially after the Japanese had obtained an equal legal status with Europeans. Their nationalist activities, however, engendered the suspicion of the Dutch, who regarded the constant display of the Chinese flag as an impingement on their sovereignty. At the same time the people of Indonesia were more than ever sensitive to the dominant position of the Chinese in internal trade and to their control of moneylending; and it is significant that the first Javanese nationalist organization, the *Sarekat Islam,* founded before 1914, was intended mainly as a defense against the economic encroachment of the Chinese.

Of the 1,200,000 Chinese in Indonesia in 1930, roughly 750,000 were born in the islands and 450,000 were immigrants. The Indonesian-born were known as *Peranakans* and the immigrants as *Sinkhehs.* Traditionally the Chinese male immigrants had married native women, and it was only within a decade or so before 1930 that the immigration of Chinese women attained to dimen-

---

[2] EDITOR'S NOTE. An incident that took place during the thirties in Sumatra illustrated the economic power of the Chinese. A Dutch importer sold goods on ninety days' credit to a Chinese retail trader. The latter was unable to pay because he lost the proceeds of the sale of the merchandise in gambling. He asked his creditor for a further consignment of goods on credit, in return for his promise to repay the money when he could and to refrain from gambling. The Dutchman refused and said that he would bring suit for the recovery of the debt.

Immediately all the other Chinese traders of the district refused to pay what they owed, and threatened that they would buy nothing from the Dutch importer in future. He could have collected his debts by a series of court actions, but he was powerless against the boycott, which would have ruined him. He had no choice but to accept the terms of the original Chinese debtor. In addition he was forced to print a public apology and to contribute handsomely to the funds of the Kuomintang party.

sions worth mentioning. The distribution of women was very unequal, and while the over-all ratio was 642 women to every 1,000 men, in Sumatra there were only 450 women to every 1,000 men. Those Chinese who first came to Indonesia in large numbers were from Fukien (Hokkiens), and those of other tribes were not numerous until the late nineteenth century. Hakkas, however, had been settled in West Borneo since about 1740. They and the Teochius are numerous in Bangka and Billiton. Cantonese (about 135,000) were fairly well distributed over the archipelago.

There has been much controversy as to whether the Chinese influence in Indonesia has been detrimental or beneficial to the country. Before 1900 it was thought unquestionable that they exercised a pernicious influence over the natives, for the activities whereby they gained their wealth were more often parasitic than constructive. However, after that date the liberation of the Chinese from the ghettos, the abolition of the pass system, the recognition of Dutch-Chinese schools, and the improvement in their legal status gave the Chinese new opportunities which they have used to good advantage. Moreover, the abolition of the opium and the gambling farms in which Chinese money was employed has released their capital for productive enterprise, and they have for some decades been associated with the development of Indonesia's industries.[3]

Postwar disturbances in Indonesia have brought great hardships and difficulties to the Chinese. During the conflict between the Dutch and the Indonesian Republic there have been periods of confusion when the normal restraints of law and order have been suspended. At such times the natives' resentment against the Chinese as trade monopolists and usurers was further inflamed by charges of espionage on behalf of the Dutch, and there re-

[3] EDITOR'S NOTE. In Indonesia and Southeast Asia generally the natives are by choice farmers or fishermen, and are not attracted to business. Without Chinese enterprise and industry the area could never have attained its present degree of economic development and material prosperity. The Chinese discharge an essential function as shopkeepers, produce buyers, and providers of agricultural credit. Often all three roles are filled by the same individual. Price rings are formed which eliminate competition, and debtors are compelled to sell their crops to the creditor at less than the market price. The Chinese have much more business acumen than the peoples of Southeast Asia, and they have gained a degree of economic control over them that is far greater than their limited numbers would seem to indicate.

sulted tragic "incidents" such as that on the Tangerang River in June 1946 when 600 Chinese were reported to have been slain. The Dutch have on many occasions acted as protectors of the Chinese displaced in these disturbances, and many, perhaps a majority, of the Chinese of Indonesia feel that their interests lie more with the Dutch than with the Indonesians. On the other hand, it is to be remarked that within the Republican territory the Chinese are unmolested and that there are a number of Chinese in high positions under the Republic, including members of the government. But this is none the less a time of great trial for the Chinese of Indonesia, for they are liable to be caught between the upper and the nether millstones of Indonesian politics.

Indochina

According to Chinese official sources the number of Chinese in French Indochina was estimated at 427,000 in 1940. The census for Indochina for 1936 gave the number of Chinese immigrants as 326,000 and of Sino-Indochinese *métis*, or half-breeds, as 141,000 (based on counts of 1921 and 1931). The Chinese figures represent an estimate of the two classes added together.

Of the countries of Southeast Asia, Tongking and Annam have the longest history of intercourse with China and the Chinese. In the year 214 B.C. the first emperor of the Chin dynasty, Shih Huang-ti, conquered "Nam Viet" (the land beyond the southern border) and divided it into three commands. Until about 1000 A.D. Annam and Tongking were considered to be a part of colonial China. The result of the repeated Chinese invasions was that the country was very completely sinicized; but the coming of the French from about 1862 onward changed the nature of Chinese immigration, for it was henceforth to be mostly by sea and its volume was at the same time very greatly increased.

The French were not well disposed toward the immigration of Chinese, and a succession of restrictions was imposed to keep it within bounds. The effect of these restrictions was that the Chinese newcomers were largely confined to those recruited by Chinese businesses, the number of Chinese laborers and agricul-turalists entering the country being very small. The richer rubber-growing lands (the "red lands") were not alienated to foreigners by the French government. In Indochina once again the Chinese were the middlemen, and besides enjoying the lion's share of the rice trade, they were interested in sugar, cotton, fisheries, and other industries.

Intermarriage between the Chinese and the peoples of Indochina produced excellent results, especially in Cambodia where the Sino-Cambodians were virtually a new race. In health they were superior both to the Cambodians and to their Chinese fathers. A Chinese husband was considered a very good match for an Indochinese girl, especially since the immigrant from China was invariably more hard-working and provident than the native of Indochina.

The civil conflict between the French and the Vietnamese following on the Japanese surrender has been very detrimental to the security and interests of the Chinese. In Cochin China they have been largely concentrated in a few centers, owing to the French strategy against the guerrillas, since this concentration makes it easier to protect them by a military cordon. In Tongking business has been virtually at a standstill for long periods, and since the Chinese live by trade this has meant that they have lost much of their former prosperity.

Burma

The position of the Chinese in Burma is much less important than it is in the other countries of Southeast Asia. Their share in the trade, though considerable, is second to that of the Indians in the country. The nature of their immigration, too, has been somewhat different from that into Siam, Malaya, and Indonesia, consisting of what may be called the mountain Chinese, who came by the land route over the mountain passes from Yunnan, and the maritime Chinese, who came by sea from the ports of Fukien and Kwangtung. In the census of 1941 the total number of immigrant Chinese in Burma was 194,000.[4] According to the census of 1931, there were in Burma 86,000 Cantonese, 41,000 Yunnanese, and 66,000 from elsewhere in China, besides 104,000 Chinese born

---

[4] The census returns for 1941 were lost during the invasion, and only the racial totals by district have survived.

in Burma. It can be estimated, therefore, that there are now well over 300,000 persons of Chinese race in the country. Half of them are to be found within a hundred miles of the city of Rangoon.

Records of the earliest travelers to Burma mention the presence of small numbers of Chinese in various parts of the country. There is, however, no record of Chinese coming to Burma in large numbers before 1800, except in coasting vessels along the Tenasserim peninsula.

Chinese general merchandise shops are to be found in nearly all the cities and towns of Burma. Despite the Sino-Burmese riots of 1931, the Burmese regard the Chinese with affection, addressing them as *Pauk Paw* (next of kin), and everywhere there is greater intercourse between Burmese and Chinese than between Burmese and Indians. Intermarriage between the two races is common.

British Borneo

NORTH BORNEO (INCLUDING LABUAN), BRUNEI, AND SARAWAK

Chinese intercourse with Borneo is very ancient indeed, and in the fifteenth century the island is said to have been administered by a succession of Chinese governors. British interest in the island was somewhat later than that of the Dutch, and when the British established their settlements the Chinese followed immediately in their steps. Sarawak came under a British raja in 1841 and Labuan was established as part of the Straits Settlements in 1847; but North Borneo did not come under effective British control until 1885. Though the Chinese secret societies caused embarrassment to the local governments, the general opinion of the British administrator was that without the Chinese nothing effective could be done. Thus we find the superintendent of the 1931 census of North Borneo saying, "The one bright spot in all the adverse conditions (due to the trade depression) is the increase in the number of the Chinese, who can fairly be regarded as the mainstay of the commercial and agricultural population."

The latest estimates available give North Borneo 71,000 Chinese in a total population of 270,000 and Brunei 4,000 Chinese in a total of 30,000; while according to the census of 1947 the Chinese in Sarawak numbered 145,000 in a total approaching half a million.

The Philippines

Numerically the Chinese in the Philippines are inconsiderable compared with the total population (about 101,000 to 19,500,000 in 1948), but they have for hundreds of years exercised an influence out of all proportion to their numbers.

Under the Spanish regime (1565–1898) the Chinese suffered many vicissitudes. The Spanish in successive phases favored, oppressed, or merely tolerated them. Twice, in 1603 and 1639, they conducted a wholesale massacre of the "Sangleys" (as they called them from the Hokkien word for business), but within a short time after these bloody purges they were back again in their old numbers. One of the arguments against them was that they drained off the wealth of the Philippines, and of Mexico also, by their trade in cloth and other goods. All attempts to make them confine themselves to agriculture failed.

Directly the Americans took over the administration of the Islands in 1898, they extended to the Philippines the United States laws excluding Chinese. The numbers of Chinese nevertheless increased, partly by illegal immigration. It was estimated that before the systematic invasion of the business field by the Japanese after 1932, the Chinese conducted between 70 and 80 per cent of the retail trade, and a large proportion of the external commerce of the Islands. Among other things they had a virtual monopoly of the rice trade. Before the outbreak of the Japanese war it was estimated that Chinese investments in the Philippines reached one hundred million United States dollars. Since the liberation of the Islands from the Japanese, the Chinese (now that Japanese competition is eliminated) have more than regained their old trade position. The returns for 1947 show that the percentages of all trade done according to nationalities were as follows: Americans, 33.59; Chinese, 33.51; Filipinos, 22.70; and others, 10.20. This is in spite of the measures taken by the government to secure the transfer of the retail trade from Chinese to Filipino hands (Chinese stall-holders have, for instance, been excluded from the Manila markets).

It will be seen from the estimates of population given in the opening section of this chapter that although the Chinese in Southeast Asia are numerous and are on the increase, there is, except in Malaya and to a lesser extent in Siam, no threat that the native peoples will be swamped numerically by Chinese immigration. In Malaya, however, the latest census reveals that the fertility of the Chinese in the country is so great and the sex ratio so improved that even if no more Chinese enter the country the Chinese community will within a very few years greatly outnumber the Malays, whose fertility is less and among whom there is greater infant mortality.

The young nations or nationalisms that are seeking to establish themselves in this region of Southeast Asia are very conscious of the extremely powerful economic position of the Chinese, and they are aiming at reducing it in the interests of their own nationals. Nor is it with trade alone that the Chinese are identified, for in these postwar years it is the Chinese Communists who have shown the greatest energy in organizing subversive action, and in Malaya they have passed to open terrorism. It is likely, too, that the situation in China itself will be more and more reflected in these overseas Chinese communities. But in general retrospect there can be no doubt that the industry, enterprise, and endurance of the Chinese have played an indispensable part in the development of the countries of Southeast Asia, and that without them it would have been far less easy, if not impossible, to have utilized the natural resources of the region in the interests of the industrialized world.

Problems of
SELF-GOVERNMENT

NATIONALISM did not appear in Southeast Asia until the twentieth century. It is the product of a complex of influences, religious, political, intellectual, and economic. A very important underlying cause was the solvent effect of Western upon Asiatic civilization. Contact with the West brought about an economic, intellectual, spiritual, and social revolution in native society. Influences from the more advanced Asiatic countries like India, such as Gandhi's technique of non-cooperation, also played their part. This last factor is nothing new in the history of Southeast Asia. India has profoundly influenced its cultural and political life for nearly 2,000 years. The Buddhist temple of the Borobudur in Java and the ruined city of Angkor Wat in Cambodia are silent witnesses to this. The Moslem religion was brought by traders from India, and conquered the Hindu and Buddhist faiths which had come from India a millennium before.

The Revolt of Asia

The Koran teaches that true believers should never be under the rule of unbelievers, though the reverse is eminently praiseworthy. The Indonesian like the Malay takes his religion more lightly than the fanatical Arab; but in the present century he began to notice that in the Dutch East Indies the world was upside down. His perception was quickened by the modernist movement, which reached him from Egypt around 1900. This was an attempt to purify and strengthen Islam, so that the Moslems could hold their own under modern conditions. The movement had its anti-Christian side, and the work of Christian missionaries in Moslem Java provoked a reaction against them. In 1910 *Sarekat Islam* was formed. Originally its aim was to keep the Indonesians true to the religion of the Prophet. Within a few years *Sarekat Islam* entered the political field and demanded independence from Christian Dutch rule.

The Burmese are Buddhists, and their religion teaches the virtue of toleration. It also forbids monks to concern themselves with politics. During the last quarter-century both principles have been more honored in the breach than in the observance. In the pre-British period the King of Burma was a Buddhist and the church was a power in the land. All this was changed when the King of Burma—and incidentally the legal head of the Buddhist church—became an Episcopalian who lived in London. The monks resented their loss of influence, and they also had other grievances.

Persuaded by Christian missionaries, the British government refused to appoint the cleric who had been what one might call an ecclesiastical inspector-general of monastic troops. His duty had been to visit the monasteries and enforce upon the monks obedience to their vows. The disappearance of this official meant that the maintenance of discipline devolved upon the abbots. When they were strong and devout standards were maintained, and many Buddhist monks were truly holy men. A weak abbot meant decay of monastic discipline, and many monks were a scandal to the devout. Indirectly the British government was responsible for this and was blamed accordingly. The monks had another grievance: traditionally they had controlled education, and they had given Burma a high standard of literacy. Their control of the schools was one source of their great influence over the Burmese. The curriculum was narrow and the teaching methods prehistoric; and the monks were slow to change a system to which they had been accustomed for centuries. Influenced by Western educators the British set up state schools with a modern curriculum and with laymen, not monks, as teachers. Parents who wanted their sons to get on in the world sent them to the government schools, and the influence of the monks over the people began to lessen. This situation is not popular with any established church, and the hostility of many of the Buddhist monks was one reason for the growing unpopularity of British rule.

The Hindus in Burma aroused religious as well as economic hostility. From about 1880 onward the Burmese rice farmers fell more and more hopelessly into debt to the Hindu money-lenders. By 1930 farm debt was estimated at $200,000,000, and practically half the fertile rice lands were owned by absentee landlords through foreclosure of mortgages. The former peasant proprietors became tenants paying an excessive rent or else land-less farm laborers. The moneylenders were not Burmese but Chettyars, members of the Hindu caste of hereditary money-lenders. Hundreds of years of practice had made them experts, while the Burmese, who were just beginning to use money instead of barter, were children in their hands. So ruinous a revolution would have roused hostility in any event, but it was heightened since the moneylenders were foreigners of another faith. Reli-gious animosity aggravated the economic grievance, and it in-cluded the British as well since they protected the legal rights of the Hindus.

The conflict of religions has killed millions from the Roman expulsion of the Jews from Palestine to the Punjab massacres of 1947. Nationalism has been an equal breeder of wars; but when religion and nationalism are combined they produce a political high explosive of unique potency. The Buddhist monks concocted this mixture. They went into politics, which is forbidden by the rules of their order, and they became one of the most active elements in the Burmese agitation against British rule. Their slogan was "Burma for the Buddhist Burmese, and out with the Hindus and the Christian British." Monks were prominent in the fifth column which helped the Japanese invasion in 1941–42.

Western education has been one of the most powerful elements in the creation of Asiatic nationalism. It has provided the small educated minority that has taken the leadership in every country of Asia. No one can receive an American, English, French, or Dutch education without learning the ideas of nationalism and democracy. The United States in the Philippines acted deliber-ately, for it relied on the schools as its chief instrument in giving the Filipinos the desire to govern themselves in the American fashion. Stress was continually laid on ideals of freedom and democracy, and the work of the schools had a very great influence in spreading the desire for self-government and independence.

The British did not deliberately aim at training their subjects to want independence, but they realized that this was likely to be the ultimate result of establishing English schools. In the 1860's there was a significant debate in the council of the governor-general of India, the supreme government of the subcontinent. One of the members urged that the program of English education be abandoned, since it must inevitably create a hostility to British rule which might end in its overthrow. The council discussed the motion and decided that the member was very probably right. Then it voted not to abolish English education but to extend it. The majority felt that Britain's greatest contribution to the world had been democracy. Therefore she had no right to hide it from her Indian subjects, since it was her duty to give them the best she had. If the result was to destroy British control of India, that was regrettable but no justification for concealing the truth as Britain saw it. This was the British attitude, not only in India, but also in the tropical dependencies.

The French believed that knowledge of their culture would draw their colonies closer and closer to them, until metropolitan France and her empire became a single, closely knit unit. This goal was almost the exact opposite of the British policy of dominion status, or complete self-government inside the empire, with the right of secession. The Dutch of the twentieth century stood midway between the British and the French. They agreed that the élite of the Indonesians must be given a Western education and the East Indies progressive self-government. But always there was the determination that the final goal must be not independence but an equal partnership with Holland in a Dutch-Indonesian Union, both for the good of the Indonesians and of the Dutch. The colonial powers differed in their attitude toward self-government, but they all agreed that their subjects in the tropics must be given a Western education.

Asiatics were willing to undergo any privations to attend Western schools. In some cases a whole family would buy shares in a bright boy and all contribute to the cost of his education. Later when he had obtained a government post all his relatives would live on him when they were hard up. The driving force was not desire for knowledge but was strictly utilitarian. Only through Western education could a man escape from subsistence farming. Filipinos said that they wanted their sons to win release from the "very sad, sad life" of the rice farmers. Indonesians had perhaps an annual cash income of $25, and Indians an income of $30. (These sums do not give an altogether true picture, for the peasant is able to support himself and his family from the produce of his land. From his tiny income in money he pays his taxes and buys the few articles that he does not produce himself. But there is no disputing that agriculture means grueling hard work for part of the year in order to obtain the bare essentials; and Western influence has turned formerly unheard-of luxuries into necessities.) The only escape was to become a government official, lawyer, journalist, office clerk, or even—for this occupation was badly underpaid—a schoolteacher. For all of these callings a Western education was essential. The further it was carried, the greater the chances of sedentary employment. A high-school graduate was more likely to win the desired position than a boy who had attended only an elementary school, and a university graduate would beat them both.

The point is that the greater the amount of education received, the more certain it was to create ideological discontent. An Asian graduate of an English university, for instance, would have studied Burke on the American Revolution and John Stuart Mill on liberty and representative government. When he learned that democracy was the chief glory of Britain and the principal cause of her prosperity, it was inevitable that he should give this knowledge a local application. If democracy had made Britain what she was, why should not his own people govern themselves and prosper equally?

Western education has had an economic as well as an ideological result. It created the intellectual proletariat, the trained army of discontent. About 90 per cent of the people of Southeast Asia are still farmers or fishermen, and barely 10 per cent are urban. This means that there is a very limited scope for white-collar workers, because subsistence farmers cannot support too many of them. For instance, fondness for lawsuits has been a distinguishing characteristic of twentieth-century India and Burma. It gives a spice of variety to life, and might perhaps be compared with the autumn football season in the United States. But a farmer with a cash income of only a few dollars a year has to curb his passion. There is very little manufacturing, so that only a limited number of office clerks and technical experts are needed. An industrialized nation like the United States or Great Britain requires a vastly larger number of white-collar workers than the predominantly agricultural countries of Southeast Asia.

The Asiatic vastly prefers a literary to a practical education. The Philippines provide a typical illustration: out of the 76,000 attending secondary schools in 1938, only 9,000 were in the trade and 4,600 in the agricultural schools, while the very large majority attended the academic or literary high schools. In part this is due to the lack of openings; in a country that is overwhelmingly agricultural there is only a limited demand for engineers and trained mechanics.

Tradition also plays a determining role. By immemorial custom the man who sits at a desk has much greater prestige than one who works with his hands. The skilled mechanic often earns more than the office worker, but the majority of students greatly prefer the sedentary occupation. Years ago when manual training was first introduced in the schools of Ceylon, there were violent protests from the parents. They had sent their sons to school to learn to be clerks, and the education department was nefariously trying to turn them into coolies. Government employment is far more sought after than in Western countries. It is much more honorable than any other sedentary occupation, and the ambition of every clever schoolboy is to become a government official.

Education is not sought for the sake of knowledge, but for strictly bread-and-butter reasons. To a certain extent a Western literary education is a vocational training: governments and business firms do need office workers, but only a limited number of them. Most parents fail to realize this, or more probably, they feel sure that their own son is so much cleverer than other people's progeny that he is bound to obtain a position. So more and more students pour into the schools, and a diminished but still large army of graduates emerge from them. Before long supply exceeds demand, and the result is a surplus of educated unemployables. This is no deterrent; on the contrary it is a stimulus to further effort.

The history of Philippine education is typical. In the early days of American rule the demand for clerks was so great that anyone who passed the fourth grade of the elementary school was pretty certain of obtaining employment. By 1915 the fourth-grader had been superseded by the seventh-grader, and by 1925 he in turn had been eliminated by the high-school graduate. A few years later the clerkships went to the university graduates, or more accurately to the lucky ones among them. Students want diplomas and not learning, but with every raising of the standard of employment diplomas lose their value and more graduates are thrown on the scrap heap. In the topmost layer are the surplus B.A.'s and law school graduates. India has a special contribution, the failed B.A.'s. This is a title of distinction because the holder successfully survived the first two years of college work, and was brought down only at the final hurdle.

India also provides a name for this class, the intellectual proletariat. Its members will not do manual work because they are educated men and would lose caste if they worked with their hands. Also a literary education is one of the finest instruments ever invented to make a man unwilling to take anything except a white-collar job. So the intellectual proletariat remains in the towns, living hand-to-mouth, poor and discontented. Those of them who are lawyers do their best to foment lawsuits; but a population of peasant farmers cannot afford many court cases. "The Philippines are overrun with lawyers; in Indochina the annual output of lawyers is a menace to social equilibrium; under British rule the plague of lawyers is a general complaint; under Dutch rule, for special reasons, lawyers have been less numerous but now seem to be increasing" (Furnivall).

In Manila before the war many high-school graduates were forced to take minor clerkships at $10 a month, while a manual laborer received $15 a month. Lawyers and B.A.'s could aspire to a superior clerkship at $20 to $30 monthly. This was almost as much as the wages of a good chauffeur, except that he also received his board and room. In 1934 the Ceylon government advertised for

200 English-speaking clerks. The work would last only two months, the pay was $10 a month—and there were 2,000 applicants.

The intellectual proletariat exists in almost every country in Asia. It is bitterly discontented and blames the colonial government for its poverty. The government set up the educational machine, the student obeyed all the rules and collected all the diplomas; but he does not have the white-collar job for which his years and effort were spent. The government has failed to provide employment and therefore is obviously a bad one. It is also condemned for a second reason: the senior posts in the government services are largely filled by nationals of the ruling power. Educated natives covet these positions on account of the pay and because of the high social prestige of official employment. The obvious solution is to gain self-government and get rid of the foreign officials, so that every educated native of the country will have a position. Experience has shown, however, that the intellectual proletariat is so large that independence does not mean jobs for all.

Western education is a potent breeder of nationalism, both through what it teaches and because of the unemployed surplus it creates. Sometimes it produces men like Nehru or Sjahrir, who fight Western rule because of the ideas that they have learned from the West. At the other extreme it turns out the intellectual proletariat, the embittered army of political agitators.

Western economic influences have been another cause of nationalism, particularly among the agricultural nine-tenths. The old, pre-Western society was static; its one aim was to leave things as previous generations had formed them. The local headman was expected to maintain the customary law, and everybody was willing to help him to that end. There was no desire for a better and more comfortable existence, for nobody aspired to "progress." Instead of working for profit and advancement men preferred to tread in the path of their fathers, which was hallowed by religion. There was no inducement to produce more than was needed for consumption. If any villager had dreamed of asserting his individual rights, he would soon have been compelled to conform by his family and by community opinion.

This traditional mentality is now being gradually broken up, and society is losing its static character. The Western governments introduced the use of money, and they insisted that taxes be paid in cash instead of in rice and other crops. This forced a change in the old practice of farming for subsistence, since the peasant must now find money for taxes. In some countries the introduction of currency also led to an increase in agricultural indebtedness. The peasants were unaccustomed to the use of money and had little sense of its value. The moneylenders were astute businessmen who were adept in financial transactions, like the Hindu Chettyars of Burma and the Chinese moneylenders in the other countries of Southeast Asia.

Few calculations have been made of the amount of rural debt. There is general agreement, however, that it is very heavy and that it affects a large part of the peasantry. In Malaya and the Dutch East Indies the governments protected the peasants in the ownership of their land; but in Burma a large part of it came into the possession of the moneylenders. In the Philippines many of the Filipino farmers became debt slaves, and this situation was one main cause of the Hukbalahap revolt after World War II.

The growing number of landless farm laborers was another disrupting element in traditional village life. In Burma this was the result of the foreclosure of mortgages by the Chettyars. In Java it was due to the rapid growth of population during the nineteenth and twentieth centuries. On a smaller scale there is a similar situation in Annam in French Indochina. The decay of native handicrafts owing to the competition of cheap, machine-made goods forced many hand workers to find some other mode of livelihood. Since manufacturing was negligible, most of the increasing number of landless laborers had to earn a living from agriculture. The competition of too much unwanted labor has helped to keep wages low.

Java has a particularly serious problem because of its small size and remarkable increase in population. The island is about as large as New York State, and the population increased from 19,794,000 in 1880 to 48,416,000 in 1940. Today it is the most densely inhabited area in the world. It has 960 inhabitants to the square mile, nearly twice as many as in Japan and more than in the most heavily populated industrial countries of Europe. Twenty years ago it was pointed out that "the density of the population has more and more exceeded the producing capacity of native agriculture in its present state of development." Dr. J. H. Boeke estimated that before the war "65 per cent of the population of Java made their living from small-scale agriculture, and it was a bare living indeed. Of the remainder 10 per cent sought a livelihood in the cities, and 25 per cent stayed in the countryside, leading a hand-to-mouth existence. For this group coolie labor in Western-type enterprises was the main monetary recourse."

The traditional village economy has been changed by the building of roads and railways and the introduction of cash crops. Prior to the period of Western rule there were no roads worthy of the name. Often they were jungle paths, and in other cases dirt roads, hard as iron in the dry weather and bogs during the rains. Transport was by bullock cart or porters, which meant that costs of carriage were heavy. The only articles that it paid to move were those like spices, silks, and jewels that had high value in proportion to their bulk. It was unprofitable to transport such bulky commodities as rice because their low sale price would never have supported the heavy cost of carriage. Farm produce was sold close to where it was grown, and every community was to a large extent self-supporting. There was no point in the peasant's growing much more than was needed to maintain himself and his family because there was no market for it. This system had one great advantage: the peasant was practically immune from the effect of economic crises in the outer world. He might suffer from natural catastrophes like a failure of crops, but booms and slumps meant nothing to him.

During the nineteenth and twentieth centuries the government opened up the country by roads and railways; shipping companies, both coastal and oceanic, were developed. The economic isolation of the village was broken down, and the peasant was given a far wider market. It was easy and profitable now to send his produce to other parts of the country, or even overseas. With improvements in transport came the development of cash crops. The peasant was encouraged to grow for export, and not merely for subsistence. Sometimes the encouragement came from business firms, such as the Indian and British millers who exported Burmese rice. Other examples were the expansion of rice exports from Siam and French Indochina, and sugar and copra from the Philippines.

At other times it was the governments that were trying to raise the standard of living by encouraging the natives to produce cash crops for sale abroad. A notable instance was the success of the Dutch and British in persuading the Indonesians and Malays to grow rubber. Before the war native small-holders produced 40 per cent of the rubber of Malaya, and 50 per cent of that of the East Indies. Prior to the great depression the native growers in the East Indies (excluding Java) contributed 55 per cent of the total export of agricultural produce. This worked out at about $10 apiece, but small as this amount was it made all the difference to the Indonesian standard of living. The peasant's little farm gave him practically all he needed in the way of food, and what he made from the sale of his rubber or other export crop represented his cash income for the year.

This raised his standard of living; but it meant a break in the traditional village life, where no one worked for profit or tried to improve his condition. Now the peasant was exhorted to do precisely that. Once he was convinced there was money in it, he showed that he was no more indifferent to the profit motive than other human beings. The inevitable result of the change was that it destroyed the peasant's former economic immunity. He was caught up in the system of world economics. The price he got for his rubber depended primarily on the American demand, and that in turn was determined by the booms and slumps of the business cycle, of which the small-holder had not the dimmest conception. The effect of this dependence on world markets was brought out by the great depression. The peasants who had largely changed over to cash crops were in grave distress, while those who had stuck to the old system of subsistence farming fared much better. This was the situation in every country of Southeast Asia.

A money economy, farm debt, landless laborers, and dependence on overseas markets—all these have been changing the traditional village life and the mentality that went with it. Conservative peasants deplore the passing of the old order, and those who have suffered from the new dispensation are dissatisfied. The result is a feeling of restlessness and discontent, which is one element in the revolt of Asia.

The development of social services has been a very real benefit, but to some extent it has provoked a reaction against the colonial governments. From one point of view, social services in Southeast Asia can be described as forcing Asiatics to accept what they would much rather go without. It means imposing Western standards upon peoples who would prefer to be let alone. To take public health as an example, Asiatic villages are exceedingly insanitary. Drinking water is often drawn from shallow wells or ponds contaminated by sewage. Calls of nature are answered wherever the call comes. Garbage is left lying around, along with tin cans and broken coconut shells which collect water and form breeding places for malarial mosquitoes. All of this means hookworm and malaria certainly, and cholera and dysentery possibly. The European health officer draws up a model sanitary code and sets his health inspectors to enforce it, since otherwise it will be ignored. Americans sink artesian wells, and Filipino villagers prime the pump with water infected with cholera from a wayside pond. On British orders a village builds a model lavatory, puts the word "Welcome" over the door, and never uses it. Schoolteachers implore their pupils to be hygienic, and a British general dies of cholera because he drank a cup of coffee at a school reception.

The peasant profits from the social services and to some extent he appreciates the benefits. With all his conservatism he can finally be persuaded to adopt beneficial changes once he is convinced that they are helpful. It takes a long time, however, and during this century social services have descended upon him like a cloudburst. Sometimes in their zeal for improvement experts have forced the pace too quickly. The old village atmosphere of "As it was in the beginning, is now and ever shall be" has gone; and sometimes the peasant wishes that his Western government would leave him in peace.

The difference in attitude toward social services suggests another cause of nationalism. This is the divergence in point of view between Asiatic subjects and their European rulers in every phase of administration. Inevitably a European government acts in accordance with its Western principles, even though it tries to tone them down and adjust them to the ideas of its subjects. The West puts a high premium upon efficiency, while the Asiatic attaches more importance to leisure. He argues that only mad dogs and Englishmen run round in the midday sun. The Westerner condemns nepotism and bribery, while Asiatic public opinion expects an official to use his influence in favor of his relatives and friends in every way he can. "Squeeze," the Chinese term for bribes and other perquisites of office, is not confined to China.

The Asiatic is constantly reminded that he and his ruler look at life differently. Sometimes he feels that he would be happier with officials of his own race who shared his point of view. Lord Cromer, the British ruler of Egypt fifty years ago, declared that foreign rule is never popular however benevolent it may be. He added that only a fool would expect gratitude for benefits such as those which he introduced in Egypt. The generation that remembered the bad old days before the reforms might be grateful. Those who were born under the new dispensation took it for granted and thought only of the things they wanted and did not yet have.

World War II heightened nationalism in Southeast Asia as it did everywhere. The colonial peoples had trusted completely in the power of their Western rulers to protect them against invasion. These governments were utterly defeated by Japan, an Asiatic power. Western prestige received a blow from which it will never recover. Sir George Maxwell drew the picture very vividly for Malaya. "The general impression derived from all our information is that of Malay villagers everywhere throughout the peninsula watching for many months at the roadside . . . the long convoys of troops, lorries, and artillery proceeding northwards: of their amazement at the numbers and the stupendous strength of the forces, and of their unwavering belief in the Government. . . . In all this the Malays saw that for themselves, unarmed and untrained, there was no part that they could take. . . . Then something terrible happened. The roads were filled with cars carrying European women and children and wealthy Chinese and Indians all hurrying southwards, and in silent groups on the roadside the Malays looked on in bewilderment at the unending stream of cars. There were rumours of every sort of British defeat, but there was no news. . . . Then, only a few days later, southward came the mauled and battered remnants of the defending forces that so confidently had passed that same way a few months before, and the Malays knew that the end had come. . . . During those last days they did what they could, in the little ways that only were possible, to help the retreating civilians and military forces. But what they thought then will affect the Malaya of the future."

The Japanese retained all real power in the conquered countries, but they set up puppet governments composed of such nationalist leaders as were willing to work with them. These collaborators soon found that they had little real authority, but at least they had all the outward trappings of high office. This was a new and pleasing experience, and it increased the nationalist leaders' desire to enjoy the realities of power after the Japanese were defeated. The quiet life of the peasants was also radically disturbed. Crops and cattle were commandeered, and there was widespread use of forced labor. Particularly in the Dutch East Indies scores of thousands were rounded up and shipped overseas to build the Burma-Siam Railway, defenses, etc. Many of them never returned, and others came back ruined in health. Inevitably these shattering experiences profoundly affected the outlook of the peasants after the war.

The result of all these influences has been the growth of nationalism and the desire for independence. It is not surprising that this has been coupled with the demand for democracy. The nationalist leaders were familiar with the idea from their Western education. Moreover, the basic principle of democracy was majority rule, and applied to the tropical dependencies this meant that control of the government should be transferred to the people of the country, who were a good 99 per cent of the population. The colonial powers were themselves democracies and therefore sympathetic to a democratic appeal, while they would not have been favorable to a demand for the restoration of the autocratic rule of the old governing classes.

Freedom and Oligarchy

There has been an important distinction between the attitude toward nationalism and democracy of the Western-educated urban few and the agricultural many. The former were familiar with the history and theoretical working of these two ideas. The case was far different with the farmers; in the East Indies before the war it was estimated that probably not more than 200,000 Indonesians understood what state government meant. The average peasant had never traveled far from his village, and his whole life was bound up in it. His interests revolved around the crops, the taxes, and local matters. Everything beyond that was not his business; it was the concern of a vaguely comprehended thing known as The Government, which lived in the distant city of Rangoon, Bangkok, or Batavia.

From time immemorial life had been like that. In the old days the ruler had been a man of his own race and religion, a king or a sultan. Now he was a European, but the essence was the same. Always the government commanded and the peasant obeyed. Centuries of training had bred in him the conviction that authority came from above and not from below. It was not for the common man to give orders or tell the government what to do. Of course the peasant wanted his interests to be considered, but it was not for him to take the initiative. The ideal government was the benevolent despot who would find out what the peasant needed and see that he got it.

During the interwar period the British in Burma and the Dutch in the East Indies had been gradually transferring power from themselves to the nationalist leaders. The British had gone faster and further than the Dutch; and by 1937 the Burmese controlled the greater part of their own affairs. Male and female suffrage at eighteen had not, however, turned the peasants into conscious democrats; twenty years were far too short a time to counteract the tradition of centuries. J. S. Furnivall knows Burma as few Europeans do and is severely critical of British rule. In his judgment the prewar "villagers did not look beyond their village or care twopence who represented them. . . . The public in general took little interest in the proceedings in Council [the legislature]. The tie between the members and the constituencies, especially in rural areas, was very weak. The old hereditary aristocracy had been reduced to the dead level of the people by the abolition of [their posts as local headmen]. Its place had been taken, though not filled, by the moneylenders, predominantly Indian, and lawyers, now mostly Burmese though little if at all acquainted with village life. In the Council there was a high proportion of lawyers, not always of the best standing in the courts, and many of these became professional politicians. The electorate in general was apathetic."

Conditions varied in different countries of Southeast Asia, but broadly speaking, on the eve of the war democracy made little appeal to the peasants. There was an undercurrent of revolt against European rule, but while they wished for a change they did not know clearly what they wanted instead. With the Western-educated it was different; but there was a wide gulf between them and their fellow countrymen in the villages. The nationalist leaders drew most of their support from the towns and knew little of the problems of the peasant. He did not understand and was not interested in their speeches about the rights of the people, popular sovereignty, and the other principles of democracy. The result was that the nationalist movements probably did not have the support of more than about 10 per cent of the people.

On occasion the political leaders were able to win the backing of the peasants, but it was fluctuating and uncertain. When support did come it was not because the farmers had been led to believe in democracy. Instead, their Western-educated leaders used totally different arguments which would appeal to the villagers. A case in point was the promise of a new golden age which won Javanese peasants to the support of the Communist revolt of 1926. In fourteenth-century Java there was a powerful and prosperous kingdom, the empire of Madjapahit. Stories of its glory still survive, and the Javanese look back upon it as a golden age. The peasant is credulous, and agitators persuaded him that the emperor was returning and would revive the golden age. Farmers would all be prosperous, and for a small cash subscription they could buy positions at the court of the imaginary monarch.

The success of the Congress party in India affords another example. Originally it was a small, urban, middle-class party which made little appeal to the agricultural majority. Gandhi won for it the support of large numbers of the Hindu peasants, but he did not do it by using democratic arguments. Twentieth-century India has the same veneration for holy men as medieval Europe, and the signs by which they can be recognized are similar. A holy man must be deeply religious, indifferent to wealth, dress simply, eat little, and be afraid of no one. Anyone who consistently does these things obviously has divine inspiration, and this has been the source of his power over a devout and superstitious people. A European counterpart of Gandhi was Peter the Hermit, who did so much to arouse popular support for the First Crusade because men felt that God had appointed him as His messenger. Hindus looked upon Gandhi as the mouthpiece of their gods. When your gods told you to vote the Congress ticket, you did not disobey. It was an effective argument, but it cannot be called democratic.

Sometimes politicians with no pretentions to holiness won the country vote by promising that freedom and democracy meant no more crop failures and the abolition of taxes. In Ceylon, which is two-thirds Sinhalese Buddhist and the rest Hindu and Moslem, each candidate chose a color which he used throughout his campaign. It was printed on the ballot so that illiterate voters could pick out the man of their choice. One far-sighted Sinhalese chose yellow, the sacred Buddhist color. The mainstay of his campaign was his claim that Buddha was backing his election and had told him to use yellow as a sign of divine support. He also claimed that Buddha would give a special blessing to all who voted for the yellow candidate and a big black mark to all who voted against him. There was a landslide of votes for the man who so ingeniously adapted the democratic process to a rural environment.

Evidence is scanty as to the effect of the war upon the attitude of the agricultural majority. They appear to be decidedly more nationalist than before 1941, but they do not seem to wish to take an active part in government. That the educated leaders will develop this vague nationalism is undoubted; but whether they will be able to instill the democratic creed into conservative believers in a benevolent despotism is perhaps more doubtful. A great obstacle to change is illiteracy and the limited circulation of newspapers. For example, in the Philippines in 1938 literacy was estimated at 48.8 per cent of the population ten years of age or over, and about 45 per cent of the children of school age were attending school. About 14 per cent of the adult population were literate. Newspapers and magazines had a circulation of 1,500,000 out of the 17,000,000 Filipinos. In Malaya 90 per cent of the Malay and 38.4 per cent of all children were attending school. In Burma in 1940, 56 per cent of the males and 16.5 per cent of the females were literate. In the East Indies 40 per cent of the children were attending school in 1940.

It is not argued that literacy alone guarantees democracy, otherwise the Weimar Republic would not have failed in highly educated Germany. This example is balanced by the great success that the equally highly educated Dutch have made of democracy in Holland. Literacy can help to promote democracy, but alone it does not insure success. The ability to read enables people to seize an idea; but by itself it does not teach them to test and value it, and it may leave them easily susceptible to false propaganda. Literacy must be accompanied by development of the critical faculty. This is not the invariable result of a few years of primary education, which is all that the vast majority of children in the tropics receive. It can be said, however, that literacy is a sign, though not a cause, of social progress, and its low level in Southeast Asia does not favor the success of that most difficult of all forms of government, democracy.

The history of Western democracy seems to show that it is inseparable from the existence of the middle class. It was this class of business and professional men who established it in the first place. Then, dividing into opposing political parties, they acted as a mutual check, exposing one another's shortcomings with gusto and competing for the popular vote. The countries of Southeast Asia, however, have practically no middle class. In the Dutch East Indies, for instance, only 1 per cent are professional men and 5 per cent businessmen, while the rest are small farmers, fishermen, and laborers.

The reason for the absence of a middle class is that the colonial dependencies of Southeast Asia have a plural society. The controlling class both in government and economics are Europeans, combined sometimes with a minority of wealthy Chinese. The middle class of professional and smaller businessmen is largely Chinese, except in Burma where Indians take their place. The laborers are either natives of the country as in French Indochina, or else a mixture of natives and immigrants, as in Burma and the Dutch East Indies. The farmers and fishermen are natives of the country. Even in the independent state of Siam business has been almost entirely in the hands of the Chinese and of a few large European companies. The only exception is in the Philippines, where the mestizos, or Filipino half-castes, have a very considerable share of the control. In the Philippines in 1940 ownership of sugar refineries (the principal industry) was 55 per cent Filipino, 32 per cent American, and 12 per cent Spanish. Only one out of the eight large coconut oil refineries was in the hands of Filipinos. Spaniards owned 60 per cent of the tobacco plantations, and there were no large Filipino firms in the mining and cordage industries.

The Western colonial powers are relinquishing control of the governments in their dependencies, though they are trying to retain their economic interests. It is inconceivable that the native nationalists will permit political leadership by Westerners, though they will employ them as technical advisers. It is equally impossible to imagine their accepting the leadership of the Chinese, or of the Indians in Burma. One of the characteristics of nationalism in Southeast Asia has been the hostility shown toward them. They are alien in race, culture, and often religion, and there is growing opposition to their triple economic monopoly of moneylending, produce buying, and retail selling. This is the situation that always develops when an alien race seems to amass too high a proportion of the wealth of a country, as witness the persecution of Jews and Armenians.

It is significant that before the war the most overt action against the Chinese was taken in the Philippines, which were largely independent, and in Siam, which was completely so. In the dependencies the European governments protected the immigrants from the colonial peoples. Yet in Burma there were bloody outbreaks against the Indians in the thirties and after law and order collapsed during the Japanese invasion. In Malaya and Java the natives celebrated their liberation from the Japanese by killing Chinese. Incidentally, this is probably why the Chinese delegate in the United Nations has shown a covert sympathy with the Dutch in their troubled negotiations with the Indonesian Republic.

Since the local nationalists will not accept Chinese or Indian leadership in their attempt to establish democracy, there remains only a very small indigenous middle class of government officials, lawyers, schoolteachers, journalists, and businessmen. Beyond this group there is nothing but the great mass of peasants and laborers. There is little material from which to draw the essential talent for leadership. A further consideration is that if democracy is to succeed, there must be at least two well-organized political parties. They expose one another's shortcomings and enable the voters to choose between two governments. A single-party system is very apt to harden into a virtual dictatorship, as in the Philippines or China. Considering the small number of politically conscious natives in the countries of Southeast Asia, it is hard to see where they will find the material for both a government and an effective opposition.

The Chinese are an obstacle to the creation of democracy in still another way. They fill a vacuum, since someone must carry out their economic functions. Given their great business capacity and the native shortage of it, they will continue to be a power in the land, and economics influence politics. Professor J. R. Hayden's description of the prewar situation in the Philippines applies equally to the other countries included in this study.

"The Philippines has as its avowed political goal the creation of a representative democracy. The domination of the business of the country by a powerful, unassimilable foreign element in the population does not make this admittedly difficult task any easier. What would be the effect upon American local, state, and national government were three-quarters of the business men, including the bankers and the produce merchants engaged in the distribution of the basic foodstuffs, of virtually every city, county, town, and village in the land aliens who had no votes, no interest in government save to protect themselves from it or to use it, and no devotion to the political institutions of the nation? What would American politics be were 75 per cent of all taxes on business to be paid by this same group of aliens, who possessed no legitimate control over government agencies for the levying and collection of taxes and the regulation of business? Few indeed would say that the prospects for good government or democratic government would be bright under such conditions. Yet in the Philippines, which until three decades ago was an autocratically governed Spanish colony, precisely such conditions exist. . . . The ancient defense of this people [the Chinese], that of gold, may constitute a very real problem in the development of a sound democracy."

It can be argued that history will repeat itself and that political power in Southeast Asia will inevitably pass from the middle class to the peasants and laborers, just as it did in the West. It would seem truer to say that history repeats itself with variations, and that often the variations are due to the different racial characteristics and standards of values of the peoples concerned. The attempt to transplant democracy from the West to Asia is in its very early stages, and it is impossible to predict the later developments. Before long all the colonial dependencies in Southeast Asia will have self-government; but it cannot be taken for granted that they will also have democracy. The two terms do not mean the same thing. Russia has self-government, but only a Communist or a fellow traveler would call her a democracy.

Certainly at present the obstacles to democracy in Southeast Asia are serious. There is a tiny middle class, a smallish group of urban laborers, and a very large conservative peasantry, which wants a change but does not understand or believe in democracy. As an added complication there is a well-organized and wealthy alien element of Chinese, who act on the principle that almost all men have their price. At the moment it looks as if the Philippines and the countries of Southeast Asia will be governed by an oligarchy of the new, Western-educated middle class. This small group is the creation of the former colonial administrations, and in Siam of the absolute monarchy. At the present time it controls the governments of the Philippines, Siam, and Burma, and there are indications that the same development is taking place in the Indonesian Republic of Java and Sumatra.

Democracy in Practice

According to the terms of its constitution the Philippines are a typical, American-style democracy. No people, however, can adopt a foreign constitution ready-made; inevitably they must alter it to accord with their own racial characteristics and standard of values. Eventually they will produce a form of government which suits them far better than the original foreign import; but the final result is likely to be markedly different from the original model. Before the war under the late President Quezon the Philippine Commonwealth approximated to a semi-dictatorship. Judging by his unbroken electoral success his policy was approved by over two-thirds of the voters.

Professor Hayden gave the most important reason for this situation when he wrote that "the political institutions of the islands are still (and always will be) in large part the natural product of a tropical, Asiatic people who for three centuries were governed by Spaniards." The Filipinos were more thoroughly affected by Western influence and for a longer time than any other Asiatic people. Spain converted them to Christianity and gave to a small educated group the ideas of Western liberalism. The United States strove manfully for a generation to turn the whole nation into democrats. American influence went deep, but a generation was too short a time in which to carry out the transformation. There is a small minority who understand and are capable of working a democratic government. The majority are enthusiastic over the slogans but do not understand the spirit of it. Their actions reveal that they are still profoundly influenced by Asiatic racial traits that have not been greatly affected by American teachings.

Most Filipinos prefer a leader who will do their political thinking for them. One reason for the popularity of the late President Quezon was that he was a strong man who did not allow constitutional niceties to stand in his way. The people love oratory and prefer the most eloquent speaker; and especially in the country districts, they have not realized that their representatives should be held to account for their actions. As in other Asiatic countries politics is a matter of personalities rather than principles. Professor Hayden gave it as his opinion that "those familiar with Philippine politics are aware that a few men in Manila can almost overnight secure an apparently spontaneous clamor for almost anything from every municipality in the Archipelago; and that a week later they can produce an equally unanimous demand for the exact opposite." The Filipinos attach much less importance than the West to the qualities of efficiency and impartiality.

It would be hypocritical to claim that Western politics are free
from corruption and nepotism; but these characteristics are decidedly more widespread in the Philippines and in Asia generally.
There is a feeling that to levy tribute in reason is a legitimate per-
quisite of office, and Filipino public opinion does not strongly
condemn the political leader who takes advantage of his opportunities. The sense of binding obligation to relatives and friends
runs all through Filipino life and is not confined to politics. Often
this willingness to use one's influence springs from pure friendli-
ness, and not from the principle of "You scratch my back, and I'll
scratch thine." In the government services appointments and pro-
motions seem to depend about equally on merit and influence.
Every Filipino tries to find a political patron and protector. The
government services, however, are not merely a happy hunting
ground for relatives and friends of those in power; they contain
many able and conscientious officials who are well trained and
efficient.

The pure-blooded Filipinos are an attractive, easy-going race
without much foresight or thrift. About a tenth of the population
are mestizos, a cross between Filipinos and Spaniards or Chinese.
The mestizos were and are the governing class in the Philippines.
One reason is that the mixture of races produces a type that is
superior to the pure-blooded Filipinos in ability and the other
qualities that make for success. The quick wits have got control
over the slow wits. They hold most of the important positions in
government, the army, and economic life. The Filipino best known
to Americans, the late President Quezon, was a Spanish mestizo.
Most of the pure-blooded Filipinos are small farmers and laborers,
and a high percentage of them are heavily in debt to the propertied classes. In 1939 only 49.2 per cent of the peasants owned
their own land, 15.6 per cent owned part of it, and 35.1 per cent
were tenants, the majority being sharecroppers. The number of
tenants and sharecroppers is growing, the landlords being known
as *caciques*.

Often the *cacique* is descended from the Filipino aristocracy
of pre-Spanish days, and frequently he is a mestizo. Professor
Pelzer sums up his position accurately. "This same group retained
leadership after the coming of the Americans because it was the

educated element in the country. It was able to monopolize most of the advantages derived from the American regime and to obtain control over national as well as local political life. Hence these *caciques,* the landed aristocracy of the Philippines, having all the privileges that the possession of money and land may give in an agrarian community, are today in a position to exploit a large part of the rural population. In some provinces this part amounts to more than half of all the farming families."

The conditions of farming, together with the improvidence of the Filipino peasant, practically compel him to borrow from the *cacique,* who charges usurious rates of interest. Many tenants are so sunk in debt that they are debt slaves for life. The *cacique* is then able to order them to vote for his candidate. Landowner, usurer, and local political boss, the *cacique* is the mainstay of democracy, especially in the rice-growing areas. The politicians need his support to be elected, and it is significant how seldom any law has been passed that effectively curbed his power.

The governing class controls the Nacionalista or Nationalist party, which has been continuously in power since the first election was held in 1907. Occasionally the personal ambitions of rival leaders have caused a temporary split, but hitherto the factions have always reunited and the Nacionalista party has continued to rule the Philippines. It has a full campaign chest, it contains nine-tenths of the able leaders, it is supported by most of the newspapers, and it controls "patronage, the electoral machinery, the administrative departments, and to a lesser extent the courts."

Every attempt to build up an opposition political party representing the underprivileged has failed. They had neither money nor organization, and the leadership was amateur. Probably another cause of failure was that many of the debt slaves had no vote. The literacy qualification restricts the franchise to 14 per cent of the adult population. Often the poorest peasants could not afford to leave their children in school long enough to become literate. It is therefore probable, as Hayden pointed out, that the numerical strength of the opposition was greater than the number who voted for it. Several weak and unsuccessful revolts have taken place against the established order, such as those of the Sakdals before World War II and the Hukbalahaps after it. Communists played a part in them, but most of the rebels were debt slaves and tenant farmers who took up arms against agrarian abuses. Democracy in the Philippines has resolved itself into an oligarchy of the Western-educated minority.

Before the war the Burmese controlled the greater part of their own affairs. On paper the British governor had formidable reserved powers, but he rarely used them since he had orders to do so only under exceptional circumstances. The peasants took little interest in government, and political consciousness was largely confined to the towns. There were no parties in the Western sense of the term, but only fluid groups held, or not held, together by personal considerations. Often ambition would lead a section of a party to break away and join an opposition group, so that the leader could not be certain of the support of his followers. The result was that no ministry had a stable majority or knew how long it could retain power. The great game of politics was to combine enough separate factions to gain a temporary majority in the legislature. There was constant intrigue to obtain office or remain in it, and also a good deal of corruption.

Democracy seems to have operated in a partial vacuum, very largely divorced from the real problems of Burma, which were agrarian. The town-bred politicians knew little of rural questions, and the peasants were not much interested in their political representatives. The connection between the English-educated leaders and the agrarian majority was tenuous. Great allowances must be made for the political inexperience of the Burmese; but the fact remains that a generous installment of English-style parliamentary democracy produced a result remarkably different from its prototype in Great Britain.

The postwar Republic of Burma does not seem to be a promising experiment in the acclimatization of Western democracy in Asia. At the moment it is more like an Irishman's paradise, with everyone fighting everybody else. The old political parties were disorganized and discredited after the war. The dominant party was the Anti-Fascist People's Freedom League (AFPFL), which was formed by Aung San and other collaborators out of the resistance forces which they created after they broke with the Japanese.

Originally the party included many shades of opinion from Communists through fellow travelers and Socialists to moderates. An important element was Aung San's private army, the People's Volunteer Organization.

The AFPFL and particularly its leader Aung San had great popularity, especially among the youth of Burma. The party won an overwhelming majority in the election of 1947. Many of the polling booths were guarded by members of Aung San's party army; but this was not necessarily to intimidate the voters. The purpose may have been to prevent disorders by the rival party armies. Nearly 90 per cent of the seats were won by the AFPFL, over half of them without a contest. Apparently deputations of the People's Volunteer Organization interviewed the candidates of rival parties, and persuaded them that they did not really want to run.

Before long the AFPFL began to break up, and a multiple party system arose which suggested the prewar situation. As always, personalities counted for more than principles. There was the difference, however, that many of the postwar parties had their private armies and showed a growing preference for bullets instead of ballots. The moderate parties broke away, while the Communists were expelled and themselves split into two rival factions of Whites and Reds. Prime Minister Aung San and six other ministers were assassinated only three months after their victory at the polls, and a former prime minister, U Saw, was hanged for the crime. In 1948 the disintegration of the AFPFL continued. The fellow travelers joined the Communists, accompanied by the bulk of Aung San's People's Volunteer Organization and part of the small regular army. The AFPFL government was pretty well reduced to Prime Minister Thakin Nu's Socialist party. Next the Karens, who are anti-Communist but also anti-Burmese, threatened to attack the government unless Thakin Nu recognized their autonomous state. The government army is small, and quite a high percentage of the troops are Karens. A struggle for power is taking place between rival leaders, and it is plain that the outcome will be determined by hard fighting and factional maneuvers and not by an appeal to the voters.

A large part of Burma is controlled by the anti-government

forces and by thousands of dacoits (gang robbers). Part of the latter are honest gangsters, while others rob and kill under the banner of some political party. Dacoity was widespread and increasing for forty years before World War II. It was accompanied by a growing popular contempt for law. The Japanese occupation strengthened the trend toward lawlessness. Discipline had never been popular among the youth of the country, and it became still more lax. Many were trained on a semimilitary basis by the political parties. Inexperienced and impatient, they prefer short cuts and direct action to the slow processes of constitutional methods.

The AFPFL is itself partly responsible, for when it was struggling to obtain power after the war it organized and armed its followers to seize control by force if necessary. It instigated a political strike by the bulk of the police in 1946, and soon afterward gained control of the government. The party's policy was that defiance of authority and the threat of force would win power more quickly than constitutional agitation. It was easier to teach that lesson than to make the pupils forget it after the AFPFL had itself become the government. The successful strike of the police, for instance, undermined their discipline and their feeling that they were outside politics and loyal to the government of the day. This forced the AFPFL to rely upon the doubtful loyalty of the very imperfectly disciplined People's Volunteer Organization. When it went over to the Communists with part of the regular army, the existence of the government was endangered.

The years of fighting had left great quantities of arms in Burma, and many of these fell into the hands of the forces of disorder. The survival of Thakin Nu's government depends upon its ability to suppress the rebels and the dacoits and restore prosperity. Otherwise there is a grave risk that public opinion, tired of disorder and failure to govern, may swing heavily to the side of the insurgents. The prospects at the beginning of 1949 were gloomy. It seemed possible that the government might be compelled to share power with one Communist faction in order to gain enough strength to crush the other.

The leaders of the different factions are drawn from the English-educated minority. The peasants seem to have little influence except as they join one of the private armies or turn dacoit. Aung San and most of the older leaders of the AFPFL were honest and had a real idealism, but many of the younger men believe that to the victors belong the spoils. They feel that as members of Aung San's army they liberated Burma from the Japanese and the British, and that the country owes them a living. Government services are run on the spoils system, and no one can hope for a position of any importance unless he is a member of the AFPFL. The evolution of nationhood in Burma is a test case for the success of democratic government in the countries of Southeast Asia. Whatever the ultimate outcome, the immediate future seems to be that the Republic will be controlled by an oligarchy based on force.

The belief has been widely held that if the tropical dependencies were given their freedom they would set up democratic governments capable of fulfilling the functions of states, namely, maintaining internal order and security and protecting their independence. The British Labor government acted upon this assumption when it recognized the Republic of Burma; but the theory has not worked out in practice. Undoubtedly the widespread destruction caused by the war greatly increased the difficulty of establishing a stable government. Nevertheless, it would seem that the pace of constitutional advance has been too rapid, and that self-government has been given to a people who were not ready for it. It might be said that they had the desire but not the experience and training to manage their own affairs, and that the result is an acute attack of constitutional indigestion. Viewed in this light the present near-chaos in Burma is the understandable result of going too fast and too far.

The Indonesian Republic controls about a third of the population and something over a quarter of the area of the East Indies. Its territory includes a small part of Java and the bulk of Sumatra. The rest of the East Indies is in the process of being divided into a number of autonomous states. Their peoples are as nationalist as those in the Indonesian Republic, but they have their own island loyalties and they are afraid that if they entered a unitary state they would be dominated by the Javanese, who control the Indonesian Republic. They therefore favor the Dutch plan of establishing self-governing units with a large measure of state rights and joining them together in a federal union called the United States of Indonesia.

The governments of these new states are as inexperienced as that of the Indonesian Republic, but unlike the latter they have welcomed Dutch advisers and technical experts in setting up their administrations and reconstructing their economies. The available evidence seems to show that they are not democracies in the Western sense of the term. In all of them the population is made up of a politically conscious but inexperienced minority and a vaguely nationalist but unpolitical peasant majority; and the result is that the minority is in control. The Indonesian Republic has refused Dutch help, and has attacked its problems with its own unaided resources.

The constitution of the Indonesian Republic as drawn up in 1945 declares that President Sukarno is assisted by the cabinet and the Central National Indonesian Committee (KNIP), or legislature. It represents political parties, religious, youth, and labor groups—not the people directly. No elections were ever held, and the members were appointed by President Sukarno. He decided how many seats would be allotted to each of the numerous political parties, and varied their representation from time to time.

This power of appointment has given the president great authority over the popular representative body. The Republican government cannot be described as democratic; but on the other hand it has been living in a state of emergency since its establishment in 1945. The test will come when peace is restored and it can no longer be said that war or the threat of war makes it impossible to hold elections. Mr. Charles Wolf, who was American vice-consul in Batavia in 1946–47, takes a somewhat pessimistic view of the future. He considers that "the representative body in the Republic, while growing stronger and perhaps exercising a decisive influence in the Government, may perhaps continue to be largely an appointive body."

It would be wrong, however, to describe the Republic as a dictatorship. There are seven major and a number of minor parties, ranging from Stalinist and Trotskyite Communists to conservative

Moslem landowners. Most of them supported the government until 1948, when the Stalinist Communists and the factions associated with them began an armed revolt. Party membership appears usually to be small, and to be drawn from the educated minority much more than from the millions of rice farmers. The peasants however seem at least tacitly to support the Republic. Their motive appears to be a desire for independence rather than for democracy. Before the war the peasants were vaguely dissatisfied with Dutch rule, and this attitude was intensified by the effects of the Japanese occupation with its anti-Dutch propaganda. The peasants do not want the restoration of prewar Dutch control and prefer to be ruled by their own people. They have also been swayed by the magnetic personality and powers of oratory of President Sukarno; but at the same time they want peace.

The sense of nationalism is strongest among the educated minority, but it also exists among the rice farmers. Logemann, the Dutch colonial minister, considered that "in Indonesia this [nationalistic] movement is above all other considerations. One can indeed make a distinction and state that the broad masses of the population have hardly arrived at political awareness, and that among these broad masses nationalism is still only a spiritual awareness which is not of much practical consequence. If however one acknowledges the presence of any awareness, one must ultimately acknowledge the vitality of nationalism. I am convinced that there is not one man of influence in Java who is not a part of the nationalist movement in one way or another."

The growth of nationalism does not seem to have changed the prewar belief of the peasants that government comes from above and not from below. Mr. Charles Wolf wrote that "it appears that the Republic has a widespread support throughout both Java and Sumatra. But this popular support . . . is of a passive type. It is definitely not a participating support. The Indonesian people, in general and insofar as they can be spoken of as a unit, seem to prefer a government run by Indonesians. . . . On a national level, however, they have not reached the stage where they either wish or are able to take part in government. The Republican Government thus appears to be supported but not run by the Indonesian people. . . . the constituents of the Republic of Indonesia are, in a somewhat oversimplified sense, of two as yet only remotely connected types: the young and old intellectuals at the top and the poor, 'apolitical,' uneducated peasants and manual laborers at the bottom of society. Until this latter mass has been uplifted economically and socially, and until the gap between the two groups has been narrowed and bridged by an aggressive and flourishing middle class, Indonesian democracy will, at best, be shallow and uncertain. The completion of this mammoth task is likely to take several generations even under favorable conditions."

At present only about 11 per cent of the population are literate, compared with 48.8 per cent in the Philippines. The Indonesian Republic has ambitious plans to remedy the situation. The difficulty will be to find sufficient money, a problem which no colonial power was ever able to solve. The Americans in the Philippines spent about 20 per cent of the annual revenue on education. Yet they were never able to provide schools for more than 38 per cent of the children of school age, and the expansion of education did not do much more than keep pace with the rapid growth of population. The percentage of the revenue spent on education could not be increased without lessening the appropriations for health and other social services which were also essential. Java has the same problem of a rapid growth of population—about 650,000 a year—and it is difficult to see how it can do better than the Philippines, so long as it has to rely on its own financial resources.

Besides teaching millions of Indonesians to read the schools must train them to think, since otherwise they will be easy prey for demagogues. At present they are remarkably gullible in matters outside their own village affairs, which they understand well enough. It is also necessary to turn their political thinking upside down and convince them that they are the masters and not the servants of the state. The strong conservatism of the people will have to be overcome, and also their absorption in local affairs. They will have to be trained to consider the problems of 70,000,000 people instead of those of a village. So colossal a task will certainly require several generations.

As Wolf points out, another handicap is that there is practically no Indonesian middle class to lead the way. A large middle class acts as a check upon itself, since every child that is born into the world alive is a little liberal or a little conservative. Or translated into contemporary propaganda, a little progressive left-winger or a Tory right-winger, who is probably a reactionary if not a fascist. Meanwhile the peasants and laborers are gradually educated in their democratic rights and privileges until they too take an effective part in the struggle for political power. In Indonesia, however, there is very little between the Western-educated élite at the top and the vast majority of small farmers and laborers at the bottom. Of course the élite may gradually encroach on the economic preserves of the Chinese, for even such astute business-men could not ultimately prevail against Indonesian rivals who were given the full support of the state. It would be a slow process, however, and it would seem that it will be a long time before there will be a large middle class. Meanwhile the present political parties will continue to revolve around a limited number of leaders, professional party workers, and educated intellectuals, rather than drawing on mass support.

It is too early to say whether this new governing class will work toward broad-based democracy or will perpetuate itself as an oligarchy. Several of the leaders, like President Sukarno, have marked personal ambitions, but others, like ex-Premier Sjahrir, are firm believers in democracy. Moreover, there is an important difference between the Western-educated ruling group in the Indonesian Republic and those in the other countries included in this study. The governing class in the Philippines has economic and military as well as political power. In Siam the wealth of the country has been largely controlled by Chinese and West-erners, and in Burma by the British and Indians. The Siamese army, however, has been the real political power ever since the revolution of 1932. The situation in Burma is very confused, but Thakin Nu's government seems to be relying increasingly on the army to support its authority. In all three cases the ruling group maintains itself in office not only by its control of the government, but also by its military or economic power, or both.

In the Indonesian Republic the wealth of the country is owned by Europeans, Chinese, and Americans. The armed forces are only imperfectly under the authority of the government. As in Burma, there is a national army and also a number of separate party armies. They obey the orders of their particular party leader and not those of the Republican government. When the Stalinist Communists revolted in 1948, for instance, they were joined by several party leaders who took their armies with them. The Western-educated leaders of the Republic do not have the economic or military support for their political power that exists in the other countries. Nevertheless, one would hesitate to say that this rules out the possibility of an oligarchy in Java and Sumatra. Oligarchy means government by the few, and historically the political power of oligarchs has been buttressed by control of wealth, armed strength, or both. It seems conceivable, however, that an oligarchy might base its power primarily upon knowledge. The constitution of the Indonesian Republic provides for a democracy based on Western models. The governmental machinery and the fundamental idea of democracy itself are unfamiliar to the agricultural nine-tenths. They support government by the Indonesians, but they neither wish nor are competent to control it. The only people who understand the foreign import and are capable of working it are the small Western-educated group who created it. It seems possible that this monopoly of knowledge might enable members of the government to become an oligarchy, assuming that they gain sufficient control over their troops to prevent their overthrow by force, as the Communists attempted to do in 1948.

The military action by the Dutch in 1948 will not greatly change the basic factors outlined above, even if they find a group of more moderate nationalists to take over control of the government. The peasant will still be the peasant, with all that this implies of political power resting in the hands of a small minority. There will still be a multiplicity of rival political leaders with their parties. In a country where there are such stores of Japanese military equipment party armies are likely to continue. The government of the future will still have the problems of establishing control of the armed forces and creating a democracy. Its difficulties may well be heightened if troops of the former government carry on guerrilla warfare. To some extent this will be offset by Dutch administrative, technical, and military assistance, since one weakness of President Sukarno's government was the lack of trained personnel of all kinds. On the other hand, the use of Dutch help is likely to harden the determination of extreme nationalists and Communists to resist whatever government is set up. For a considerable time to come the Indonesian Republic will be ruled by a minority.

Nevertheless, there are so many unknown factors that it is impossible to be dogmatic. Much will depend on whether peace with Holland is restored quickly and the government set free to tackle the problems of reconstruction, including the establishment of firm control over its own armed forces. Another unknown quantity is whether the Communists are decisively defeated, or whether they will be strong enough to play the same role as in Burma. Still another unknown is whether the mass of the population will retain its present docile attitude toward authority. Democracy or oligarchy, the future of the Indonesian Republic is a question mark.

The constitutional monarchy of Siam is a military oligarchy, tempered by the rooted predilection of the people for a royal figurehead. The peasants, who comprise 90 per cent of the population, took no part in the revolution that overthrew the absolute monarchy. The revolutionaries, who called themselves the People's party, were a small group of Western-educated Siamese. Many were government officials, and the officers of the army and navy counted for most in the outbreak. Prior to the revolution the existence of the People's party was known only to people in Bangkok and to a few politically minded Siamese in the provinces. What really happened was that power was transferred from the king to an oligarchy.

Perhaps the most interesting point about the revolution was that the monarchy had created the instrument that was to overthrow it. A succession of enlightened despots had modernized Siam, establishing Western-style government services and armed forces. The reforms could not be carried out without the help of Western-educated officials. These did not exist in old Siam, but the monarchy built up a new, Western-educated middle class and appointed most of its members to official positions. The king's creation overthrew him in 1932. It is commonly said that Asia is revolting against the imperialistic control of the European colonial powers. This explanation does not cover events in Siam, which despite strong foreign influences was an independent state. The revolution in Siam was a revolt against the old order, which in this case was a native monarchy and not a foreign colonial government. The leaders of the revolt were as elsewhere the new, Western-educated class that had been created by the old regime.

The record of the Siamese oligarchy since 1932 has not been democratic, despite its professions that its purpose was to educate the peasants to take over control of the government. It is difficult to see how this training was to be acquired when twice as much was spent on the armed forces as on education, the press was strictly censored, and political parties were not allowed to be formed. There was a façade of democracy, but Dr. K. P. Landon described the regime as "a one-party system that has grown increasingly intolerant of opposition." The oligarchy divided into rival groups, there were various coups d'état, and the army has been the dominant political influence. It does not seem that democratic institutions have taken any real root in the country. What effect the growth of communism will have upon the oligarchy remains to be seen, but it will not improve the prospects of establishing democracy in Siam.

Chinese attempts to create a democratic republic go back to 1911; and their failure, after nearly forty years of effort, sheds some light on the difficulties which confront the countries of Southeast Asia. After the fall of the Manchu dynasty in 1911 the successful revolutionaries set up a republic. It failed because it was too great a break with the past and therefore unintelligible to the large majority of Chinese. As a result political power passed into the hands of the *tuchuns* or war lords. After their defeat by the Kuomintang a single party dictatorship was established under the leadership of Chiang Kai-shek. The entire party membership was less than 1 per cent of the Chinese population. The rival Chinese Communist government is also a dictatorship. China has passed from the autocracy of an emperor to that of two political parties, and those Chinese who wished to make her democratic have failed. This is not surprising, for as Professor Paul Clyde points out, the Chinese do not have a tradition of political democracy. "It is much nearer the truth to say that the Chinese do have a long and deeply rooted tradition of government *for* the people but certainly not *by* the people. This authoritarian tradition finds expression today in the party dictatorships of both the Kuomintang and the Communists."

The republics of South America have been the happy hunting ground of dictators ever since they were liberated from Spain in the early nineteenth century. Their experience also may throw some light on the probable development of Southeast Asia, although there are outstanding differences as well as similarities between the two areas. An important historical cause for the development of dictatorship was that Spanish colonial rule was completely autocratic, so that when the South Americans gained their freedom they had had no training either in political self-government or in administrative work. The ideological impetus and leadership came from a small group of intellectuals who honestly wanted democracy. The constitutions they drew up for the liberated colonies were based sometimes upon European models, but usually on that of the United States. The people who had to work the foreign import were complete amateurs, without the 150 years of training in political self-government which the Americans had received prior to their revolution.

After Spanish rule had ended, rivalry arose between the revolutionary leaders, and the victors (often army generals) imposed their control upon the new republics. An important contributory cause was that political parties were and are the personal following of outstanding leaders, and not parties in the American or British sense of the term. The parallels with Southeast Asia are striking, although some of the Asian countries start their independent careers under more favorable omens. The Philippines have had some forty years of training in democracy, and Burma and Indonesia rather less. Moreover, freedom was on the whole attained peacefully, though the chaos in Burma may furnish an opportunity to ambitious army leaders comparable to that provided by the long and destructive wars of liberation in South America.

One cause that has perpetuated the South American dictatorships has been the absence of a large middle class in most of the republics. The typical situation is a small educated group at the top, which provides the dictators, a great mass of peasants and laborers, and nothing much in between. Broadly speaking democracy is stronger in the republics that have a large middle class —the element that is so notably lacking in Southeast Asia. In most of the republics the peasants are the majority, and the rate of illiteracy is high. Their attitude toward politics, however, differs markedly from that of the Asiatic farmers. The South American peasants do not prefer government from above, and they are not absorbed only in village affairs. They take a keen interest in national elections, and they seem to be less open to demagogic appeals than Asiatics.

This has not sufficed to prevent dictatorship, which has usually come from the educated governing group. Often but not always this same minority controls the wealth of the country, a contrast to most of the countries of Southeast Asia. On this point the Philippine Republic offers the closest parallel. It also resembles South America in the high percentage of sharecroppers among the peasants. Usury, however, does not appear to flourish as it does in the Philippines, and there is no equivalent to the *cacique*. Nevertheless, there is a feudal submissiveness of the tenant farmer toward his landlord that is a partial substitute for *caciquism*.

The army is a far more important political force in South America than in Southeast Asia, except for Siam. The officers usually belong to the governing class, and most of the dictators have come from their ranks. There is a tradition that the army is the savior of the state, not merely its defense against invasion. The normal practice is that the intellectuals start a revolution, the army takes over control, and its general is the next dictator. It is obvious that Southeast Asia will not be a duplicate of South America, but the two have a good many points in common.

There is a natural tendency for each Western democratic nation to assume that the form of government it has evolved will be copied by the newly emancipated countries of Asia. This belief is strengthened by the vocabulary of the Asiatic political leaders and the phraseology employed in the constitutions which they have drawn up. All of them proclaim themselves to be democrats, talk about popular sovereignty, and state that the new governments are the servants and not the masters of the people. The difficulty is that the form of government in each country has been molded by its own particular history, social and economic organization, racial characteristics, and political ideas. Americans would be far from happy if they were compelled to adopt the British form of government, and the British would be equally dissatisfied if they found themselves living under the constitution of the United States. Neither Americans nor British have the slightest desire to copy the French variety of democracy. The French regard the Anglo-American two-party system as undemocratic, and gravely fear that General de Gaulle's demand for a strong executive somewhat after the pattern of the American president and a lessening of the powers of the lower house might lead to a dictatorship. The United States, Great Britain, and France are all democracies, but each has evolved the variety that is most congenial to it.

The Asiatic peoples have their own peculiar history, political ideas, and social and economic organization, and these differ greatly from those of the Western world. What they are today is the result of centuries of evolution, and no people can throw off its past like a worn-out suit of clothes. Old traditions die hard, even when they are held by peoples who pride themselves on being progressive and enlightened. Most Asiatics, however, are conservatives and proud of it, and are less ready than Westerners to abandon their inherited ideas. The new forms of government in Asia will not be mere copies of Western imports. They will be profoundly affected by all the complex influences which are the product of Asiatic civilizations. It is certain that the result will not be a revival of the traditional forms of Asiatic government. There will be no resurrection of the despotic god-kings of Siam or the vanished autocrats of Indonesia and Burma. The evidence suggests that the governments of the future will be neither a revival of the past nor a wholesale adoption of Western ideas. They will be a combination of the indigenous and imported, and different from both of them.

Indirect Voting

The greatest single obstacle to the establishment of democracy has been the unpreparedness of the peasant majority for this form of government. It seems arguable that this was accentuated by the introduction of the system of direct voting in the American and British, though not in the Dutch, colonies. Some of the members of the prewar Volksraad in the East Indies were elected by indirect voting. The Dutch allotted to themselves far too many representatives—twenty-five out of sixty; but this was the result of official policy and not a necessary part of the system of indirect voting. French Indochina had direct voting, but the voters were so few and carefully chosen that it may be left out of the discussion. The Anglo-American assumption was that the farmers of Burma or the Philippines would soon react in the same way as those of the United States and Great Britain. It ignored the facts that the Asiatic peasant believed that central as opposed to village government was an omnipotent and incalculable affair which he had no right to direct, and that he neither understood nor cared about the parties and policies that agitated the town politicians who solicited his vote. Add that he was slow to change and that his gullibility was great. Inevitably direct voting did not give the same results in Asia as in the West.

The Asiatic villager is shrewd in matters which come within his own experience. He knows what he wants within the ambit of local affairs, and he has a very exact knowledge of his fellow villagers, since in a village everyone knows everything about everyone else. He requires no training in voting for a fellow villager—a very different matter from being asked to vote for some unknown person to be a member of a national legislature of which he understands little or nothing. The peasant's life is far more bound up in village affairs than with dimly understood national problems.

Usually a tropical dependency is divided into states or provinces, each of which is composed of a number of districts. The administration of the district is controlled by an official, sometimes called a district officer, who is responsible to the governor of the dependency. The district is made up of a varying number of towns and villages. The district officer directs the administration of the latter and sometimes that of the former. The members of the town board or council represent the local population, and the chairman is sometimes elected and sometimes a government official. Usually the village headman is appointed by the government and is a salaried official; sometimes he is elected by the villagers, and he may be assisted by a council of local notables. The headman has power to decide minor civil and criminal cases and to control local matters such as the repair of roads, building of schools, and collection of taxes. Frequently the headman has ceased to be the trusted and influential leader of his community. Instead he is the agent through which the colonial government imposes on the village its mysterious and unwanted policies on health, agriculture, and other matters. The government is entirely official, the chain of responsibility stretching from the village headman through the official hierarchy to the governor.

The establishment of self-government does not affect the administrative machine. All that happens is that a Western official who has spent years at his job—the treasurer, or the director of education, or the chief medical officer—walks out of his office; and in walks an Asiatic, frequently a lawyer or journalist, who is a leader of the majority party in the legislature. Policy is now determined by the new minister instead of by the former bureaucrat; and gradually Asiatics replace Westerners in the government services. The administration continues to be a centralized bureaucracy, controlled by the Asiatic executive or cabinet in the capital of the colony. There is no elected self-government in the rural areas, and the role of the peasant is limited to casting his vote at intervals for some unknown Western-educated townsman who is seeking election.

Sir George Maxwell suggested that the position could be improved by a combination of indirect voting and decentralization of authority. The villagers might elect some of themselves to a village council. Acting under the chairmanship of the headman the council would carry out the functions of government at present discharged by him alone. Its most useful duty could be to carry out schemes for village sanitation. Each village council would elect some members to a district council. This body would work with the district officer in controlling the affairs of the district. As the elected members gained experience the powers of the district officer would gradually decline. The district councils would elect members to the state or provincial council, which would gradually replace the official who now controls the administration of this area.

The state councils in turn would elect the members of the central legislature. Each town would have an elected council that would manage municipal affairs and also elect some members to the council of the district in which it is situated. There are few large cities in Southeast Asia, and their elected councils would elect members to a state council or perhaps directly to the national legislature. The number of members that a village or town council would elect to a district council would be determined by the proportion existing between the number of village or town voters to the total number of voters in the district. The same ratio would fix the number of district representatives in a state council, and of state members in the central legislature.

The first advantage of this proposal is that the peasant would take a greater interest in village affairs, since as a voter or member of the council he would have a voice in controlling them. Those who served on the council would receive a training in administration. The absence of this training has been one of the weaknesses in the democratic governments already established. Many of the cabinet ministers in Burma or Indonesia have never even been members of a town council. The operation of government would be improved if in time their successors were men who had already served an apprenticeship in the less important councils. Precisely this training was one important reason why the English parliament in the seventeenth century was able to take over control of the executive from the king and govern successfully. The members of parliament who broke the royal absolutism of the Stuarts were no novices in administration. For several centuries they and their forebears had controlled local government in the counties, towns, and parishes. The kings of England had laid this burden upon their subjects as an unpaid duty to the state. The result was that when the English people decided to control their own government they had the trained ability to do it successfully.

The second advantage of indirect voting is that the villager would know exactly what he is doing. He would cast his vote only once, for the members of the village council. He would be thoroughly familiar with the local issues and the personalities of the candidates. If he were asked to vote for A when he felt that B would suit him better, no one could persuade him to vote for A. The voting would be far more intelligent, and there would be a heavier poll than at present. Also self-government in the village would grow from it to the district, the state, and the whole country.

Pressure could perhaps be used on the villagers in casting their votes. This is already done in the Philippines, for instance, under direct voting, so the case is as broad as it is long. It can also be objected that whenever a central legislature has been elected by indirect voting there has been a lack of responsibility. In case of misconduct appeal to the people is impossible, since they do not directly elect the legislators. The only recourse is to the state councils (themselves elected indirectly) which choose the national legislature. Experience has shown that this form of control is ineffective. On the other hand, appeal to the whole electorate under the present system of direct voting is also ineffective. The peasant majority of voters lack interest in and understanding of democracy, and they do not hold their representatives to account. There is irresponsibility under either system; but there seem to be sound reasons for expecting good results from indirect voting, while direct voting has not been a success.

Unions and Trusteeship

Proposals have been made for a union of the countries of Southeast Asia and the Philippines. One suggestion is that they set up councils for the joint control of defense, economics, and finance. Another plan is for a political federation. A less ambitious scheme is that of the small, left-wing Malay party which would like Malaya ultimately to join the Indonesian Republic of Java and Sumatra, although the large majority of the Malays have shown no interest in the idea. Conceivably there may someday be a union between Malaya and the United States of Indonesia that the Dutch are in process of establishing. A great part of the Malays of the Peninsula are descended from immigrants from the East Indies. Furthermore the Indonesians and Malays are linked by ties of race, religion, and culture, though this does not apply to the Chinese and Indians who are three-fifths of the population of Malaya.

The prospects of a wider union of Southeast Asia and the Philippines seem more dim and remote. The six countries concerned have little in common save geographic propinquity and the fact that the overwhelming majority of their population are peasants. The forces that work against union are numerous and powerful. The Malays, Indonesians, and Filipinos (if one goes far enough back) are the only ones who have a common racial origin and, in the case of the Malays and Indonesians, the same language. There is no common culture, for some derived their civilization from India, while Annam was powerfully affected by China and the Philippines by the United States and Spain. Religion is to some extent a barrier, since the Malays and Indonesians are Moslems, the Burmese and Siamese Buddhists, and the Filipinos Christians. The whole area has never formed a single state, so that there is no tradition of unity. On the contrary, the countries are divided by memories of long-standing hostility. Burma and Siam were enemies, as were Siam and Cambodia. The Malays' experience, renewed in World War II, has been that Siam's attempts to conquer them were ended only by British protection.

Rising nationalism has added a new element of disunity. A good illustration is the Dutch East Indies, where after the war the Indonesian Republic tried to assert its control over the whole area. The inhabitants of Borneo, Celebes, and the other islands had developed strong insular loyalties. They refused to agree to too close a union, fearing the Javanese would dominate them by their superiority in population, wealth, and degree of civilization. This was one reason why the other islanders supported the Dutch. It did not mean they were willing to restore prewar Dutch control, or were less determined to govern themselves. As the weaker side they wanted Dutch help against the claims of the Javanese. The result is that Indonesia will be not a union but a federation of about a dozen states, each of which controls its own domestic affairs.

What has happened in the East Indies applies even more strongly elsewhere. In every country the desire is for complete independence to manage its own affairs, without any outside interference or control. Sometimes, as in Burma, this has been tempered in the minds of a few far-sighted leaders by the realization that absolute freedom may be an expensive luxury in the postwar world. The late Aung San and his successor Thakin Nu would have liked to abandon the project for a Republic of Burma and accept dominion status in return for British protection. They had preached the doctrine of independence so successfully, however, that they did not dare depart from it. Nationalism is in the ascendant, and it runs counter to any idea of union. This would have to be imposed from outside, and it would be an artificial creation without effective local support.

Economic influences work in the same direction as the political factors. Roughly speaking, the countries of Southeast Asia do not complement one another, but are competitors in the world markets. They are producers of raw materials and foodstuffs such as rubber, tin, copra, and rice. There is need for coordination of production in the general interest, but similar and competitive economies are an insecure basis for union. It is also doubtful whether union would greatly increase security. One reason for the Japanese conquest was that almost all munitions had to be imported. Little can be done to remedy this weakness, since Southeast Asia and the Philippines do not have the natural resources necessary for the development of heavy industry on any significant scale. The area will continue to be incapable of defending itself against a great power, and will have to depend for its protection principally on the United States and Great Britain. The analogy might be drawn of the South American republics and the United States.

The six countries can give mutual help by abandoning any ambitions to annex one another's territories, and by refusing to provide an aggressor with bases for an attack. Leaving out all discussion of the motives that led the Siamese government to join Japan in World War II, its actions provided a good example of what not to do in the general interest. Naval and air bases should be provided for the great powers protecting the area, such as those that the Philippines have granted to the United States. Except in these ways, however, it is hard to see how defensive alliances between six weak countries would strengthen local security.

United Nations trusteeship of the tropical dependencies has been rejected by the colonial powers and would be opposed by the inhabitants. The former offered to submit to the United Nations for information purposes annual reports on economic, social, and educational matters. They promised to develop self-government and free political institutions. They did not undertake to supply information on these last, however, and they refused to submit their dependencies to United Nations supervision and control.

Some members of the United Nations, particularly Russia, India, and the Philippines, made reiterated attempts to compel the colonial powers to reverse their stand on these points. The colonial powers have refused to give way on the ground that the claim to intervention is contrary to the terms of the United Nations Charter. Russia supports the campaign as the pretended champion of the colonial peoples throughout the world. In this as in other respects she has turned the United Nations into an agency in her campaign against the Western powers. British delegates have pointed out the hypocrisy of the Russian attitude in, for instance, expressing horror that the peoples of Malaya do not have the self-government that Soviet policy denies to every country in the Russian bloc. The colonial powers decline to provide ammunition for further attacks.

Conflict with Russia is only one reason for the attitude of the colonial powers. Ever since 1917 the aim of British colonial policy has been the progressive establishment of self-government. Great Britain has hoped that the goal would be dominion status within the Commonwealth. The right of secession has been admitted, however, and no attempt was made to compel Burma to abandon its intention of becoming a republic. The rate of constitutional advance in the tropical dependencies has been uneven, owing to the very great differences in degree of civilization, political development, and wealth. British policy has been to transfer power to elected representatives of the colonial peoples as fast as it was possible to do so. The chapter on Malaya gives one illustration of the difficulty of the problem. Holland and France have also accepted the policy of colonial self-rule, and all three nations refuse to permit United Nations interference.

The colonial peoples themselves would oppose United Nations trusteeship. Their general tendency has been to believe that they are capable of full self-government without a period of apprenticeship, and that the policy of self-rule on the installment plan was merely a device to keep them in subjection. Burma, Ceylon, and India illustrate this attitude. Asiatics would not be satisfied with the substitution of international for national government, because what they want is freedom from all control. Trusteeship would be regarded as a device to thwart their aspirations. The Western-educated in each country also wish to replace the European officials. In this regard it is necessary to remember the immense prestige attached to government service in Asia. Particularly in the British Empire, the policy for years past has been to substitute natives of the country for European officials. Trusteeship would mean that an international team of administrators would descend upon the colony. Their intentions would be of the best, but every local candidate for employment would consider that they were thwarting his ambitions. The United Nations officials would start their careers with the ill will of all the educated natives in the dependency.

On technical grounds it is questionable how well officials of different nationalities would cooperate, since each state has its distinctive colonial policy and is convinced that it is better than that of any other colonial power. The Americans emphasize the rapid establishment of democracy, and believe that education is the best means of attaining this end quickly. The British have the same aims, but their advance toward self-rule is less rapid. They have also held that the creation of a higher standard of living through health, agricultural improvement, and opening up the country by roads and railways is as important as education. The Dutch have much the same attitude as the British, but they have been slower and more cautious in transferring political power. The postwar French policy has been to grant self-government, but with the proviso that the colony is to remain an integral part of the French Empire instead of attaining virtual or complete independence, like Ceylon and the Philippines. A Russian United

Nations official would doubtless hold the peculiar Soviet views about democracy. Some writers have suggested that Japanese and Chinese officials should also be added to the collection. Judging by Japan's behavior in her prewar colonies and the domestic policy of Chiang Kai-shek, one wonders how accurately they would interpret the four freedoms.

Officials would not change their convictions merely because they were employed by the United Nations. Each man would continue to feel that his own nation's standard of values was the best. A unified and consistent policy is essential to the success of colonial administration. Nothing is more unsettling than changes which leave the native with the bewildered feeling that the government does not know what it wants, and that he himself can never guess what is going to happen next. But this is what would occur with an international personnel where the members were pulling half a dozen different ways at once.

Nation-Building Services and Finance

The mere establishment of political self-government in the tropical dependencies is not enough. It will have little reality unless it is based on a foundation of economic stability and a higher standard of living. Constitutional reforms did not solve the Burmese problem, since a large part of the farmers were hopelessly in debt to Indian moneylenders. The postwar Communists have enlisted a good deal of peasant support through their slogan of "down with usurers and tax collectors." The establishment of democratic institutions in the Philippines has not satisfied the demands of the debt slaves. The creation of a United States of Indonesia will not mean a great deal, as long as the standard of living of a large part of the population depends on the sale of their products in world markets, where prices can change with devastating rapidity. Nationalist leaders and the governments of the Western powers agree that there is an urgent necessity to improve material conditions. One of the many things that needs to be done is to expand medical services, for one reason for the present low productivity is the lack of energy caused by such diseases as hookworm and recurrent attacks of malaria. The peasant would also benefit from improved farming methods and cheap credit. The overpopulation that is one cause of poverty in Java and parts of French Indochina could be alleviated by migration to underpopulated areas and birth control.

All these methods and many others were followed by the pre-war colonial governments in their attempts to improve conditions. They never had enough revenue to do the work properly. The postwar governments, both colonial and independent, have ambitious plans to expand what India calls the nation-building services on a scale that will eclipse prewar efforts. Once again the obstacle is lack of money. The typical Asiatic taxpayer is a sub-sistence farmer who supports his family from the produce of his farm, but who has a very tiny cash income from which to pay taxes and to buy such things as he does not make himself. In Java it has been estimated to be about $25 a year. This means that the revenue from taxation is small, and there is only limited scope for floating domestic government loans.

The bulk of the money has to be obtained abroad. The Indo-nesian Republic, for instance, would like to borrow about $400,000,000 to finance its program of expanded social services, migration, and industrialization. Separate from this is the cost of restoring war damage, which at 1938 prices is estimated to be $1,650,000,000 for the whole of the East Indies. The Dutch have spent about $333,000,000 for reconstruction, but neither Holland nor France is in a position to lend much to its dependencies.

Great Britain has been giving financial help to her tropical colonies to an increasing degree since 1929. Under the Colonial Development and Welfare Act of 1945 she granted $480,000,000 to be spent over a ten-year period. This will supplement the amounts provided by the dependencies from revenue and loans. The British grant is to be spent principally on health, education, and economic development, such as improvement of native agri-culture, roads, railways, and harbor works. Malaya is receiving its share of this amount, but Burma is of course not eligible since it is not a part of the empire. In 1947, however, Great Britain gave it $122,000,000 for rehabilitation. The United States granted the Philippines $620,000,000 for reconstruction, and in addition lent $75,000,000. Other tropical countries hope to obtain American loans, or else interest foreign capital in the development of their natural resources. The governments of the tropics cannot carry out their policies without foreign financial aid on an extensive scale.

A great part of this will have to be provided by private business, and much misunderstanding exists on this point. The foreign investor is often pictured as a ruthless exploiter, and the conclusion is sometimes drawn that he should be debarred from the tropics. Alternatively, the pariah might be admitted, but he should be comprehensively taxed and controlled so that his profits would be reduced to a minimum. This overlooks the foreign capitalist's side of the story. He is not a philanthropist, but an individual who is as strongly influenced by the profit motive as trade-unionists and most other normal human beings. The tropical investor is not the sinister and soulless millionaire he is sometimes pictured to be. Very often he is a small investor with a few thousand dollars to lend, and he has put it in a tea, rubber, or tin company because he thinks he can secure a higher return than if he invested it in his native country. The point is that he wants what he considers a satisfactory dividend, and if he can't get it he won't invest. The hard reality is that without his financial cooperation the countries of the tropics cannot expand their economic development, or repair the damage done during the Japanese invasion and restore existing enterprises to their prewar level of productivity.

With the exception of the Filipino mestizos the natives have never been interested in becoming rich or developing their own natural resources. They have preferred to remain farmers or fishermen, they have limited inclination or capacity for business, and they are not noted for thrift. A goodly percentage of the debt that burdens the peasants was incurred from sheer extravagance, and not for legitimate agricultural purposes. This attitude explains why the wealth of Southeast Asia is controlled by Westerners and Chinese. They had the capital, the business capacity, and the technical knowledge that the natives lacked, and it was they who developed mines and plantations and built up trade. Merely because the natives are acquiring self-government does not mean that they will suddenly display characteristics of which they have given limited evidence in the past. A long time will elapse before they have accumulated enough capital to finance themselves the development of their resources. Until then the foreign investor will continue to be indispensable.

Social services are very expensive, as witness the estimated cost to the taxpayer of the proposed American national health service. It is no accident that these services originated in the industrialized nations of North America and western Europe, where there was the basis of taxation to pay for them. The accumulations of wealth and the average income were so much greater than in Asia that enough could be collected in taxes to support the cost. Nevertheless, one has heard of teachers' strikes and other manifestations which showed that the taxpayer was unwilling to add to his burden.

In the tropics the average man is a subsistence farmer with in many respects antiquated methods. The condition of agriculture is roughly comparable to that of fifteenth-century Europe. In other words modern, Western social services were set up in the tropics on the taxable basis of medieval agriculture. There simply was not the money to pay for them. If the governments relied on what they could extract from the local inhabitants, the country would have had practically no social services until doomsday. Because there were no social services the standard of living could not have been raised—and with it the capacity to pay heavier taxes—and therefore there would continue to be no social services. The only way to break this vicious circle was to persuade the foreign capitalist to invest his money in some profitable enterprise and then tax him. Benefiting the natives was not of course the only motive of the colonial governments. They considered that foreign capital had the right to develop the largely untouched resources of the tropics. By encouraging investment they were killing two birds with one stone.

The British and Dutch particularly followed this policy. First of all they built roads, railways, and harbor works, because no one will develop, say, a rich tin mine, if there is no way of getting the ore to a seaport. Incidentally the opening up of the country also helped the natives to sell their products abroad, instead of producing for a small, local market as previously. Eventually the foreign investor put his money into tin, rubber, oil, teak, or whatever natural resources promised a profitable return, and the colonial treasury went into action. In the prewar Dutch East Indies it was estimated that the foreign capitalist furnished over half of the taxes and more than a third of the total revenue, while government enterprises and the 71,000,000 Indonesians provided the remainder. In other words the foreigner paid for a good part of the social services that benefited the Indonesians. It is also true that the investor profited, since healthier and partially educated native workmen were more efficient. It is a mistake, however, to believe that the social services were merely a Machiavellian device to increase the profits of the foreign capitalist. The colonial governments had a genuine desire to improve native living conditions.

Prewar Malaya was a good example of this policy of collecting most of the revenue from foreign investors. The bulk of the export tax on tin and rubber was paid by them. Moreover, these were not taxes that they could pass on to the overseas consumer, since the world price of tin and rubber was not determined by their exports but was fixed independently of the prices at which they must sell to make a profit. Foreign enterprises paid a large part of the import duties as well as death duties and annual land rent on plantations and mines. The government obtained further revenue from its ownership of the railways and its partial ownership of the electric power industry. There was close correspondence between the amount of revenue received from these sources and the world demand for tin and rubber. When there was a boom the revenue rose and social services expanded, while a slump in tin and rubber was reflected in a sharp fall in revenue and contraction of the government services.

Foreign Capital and Freedom

Foreign enterprise in the tropics has been condemned as a sign of colonial status, on the ground that the profits are drained away for the benefit of shareholders overseas instead of being kept in the country. If drain is to be the criterion, then Canada has a colonial status toward the United States. In every industry many firms are branches of American businesses or controlled by them, and for years past there has been a very heavy annual drain of profits to the United States. This is the price Canada has to pay for the development of its natural resources, since it lacks sufficient native capital to finance its own exploitation. Prior to World War I the United States was in the same position as regards Great Britain. The drain is not a stigma of inferiority, but an economic phase through which an undeveloped country has to pass.

Another criticism is that foreign capital is too lightly taxed, and that too little of the profits are retained for the expansion of the social services. The assumption is that tropical enterprise is immensely profitable, and it is easy to point to tin and oil companies that have paid high dividends in good years. It is equally easy to instance others that have paid the shareholders very little or have gone bankrupt. Far from being an easy road to El Dorado, investment in the tropics has been a gamble, where some have been lucky and others have not. In addition to extreme fluctuations in price, tropical production has certain risks peculiar to itself. Malaria and other diseases have in the past wrecked many promising enterprises; and while nowadays they can be held at bay successfully, this is done at a heavy cost from which industries in healthier parts of the world are free. Tropical agriculture has its own special problems which differ from those of Western agriculture. The history of rubber is a good illustration. The problems were to acclimatize on the plantations of Southeast Asia a tree which grew wild in the Brazilian jungles; to discover the best methods of cultivation, tapping, and increasing the yield; and to find out the cause and cure of the various diseases which attacked the tree. The solution, by a combination of trial and error and elaborate scientific investigation, has been costly.

Few studies have been made of the average profits of tropical enterprises over a long period of years. The scanty information available confirms the belief that they have been less profitable than is commonly supposed. An analysis of the figures relating to some two hundred Malayan rubber companies, whose issued capital amounted to $170,000,000, showed that their average dividend over their whole life was 7 per cent. In many cases capital was written down after heavy losses; in others shares were issued in prosperous times at a high premium; and very often profits were plowed back into the business. As a result the money invested was about half as much again as the issued capital, and on the money invested the dividends represented a return of roughly only 4.5 per cent. Major Orde Brown, labor adviser to the British colonial office, reported that in 1940 the twenty principal tea and rubber companies in Ceylon paid dividends varying from 7 per cent to 28 per cent, and in one case 55 per cent. But when these figures were adjusted to a payment on total capital invested, together with reserves put back into development and improvement, the 55 per cent fell to 14 per cent, and most of the companies proved to be paying from 9 per cent to 12 per cent. Major Orde Brown pointed out that "these companies are the most successful survivors, and do not reflect the situation of the poorer propositions, or of course those that have failed and fallen out. . . . Tropical products are in fact highly speculative as a whole, and their attraction is largely that of a gamble."

Before the foreign capitalist will run the risk he wants reasonable assurance that he will receive a higher return on his money than if he invested it in his own country. Failing this there is no point in incurring the heavy expenses and dangers of loss. In the past one important attraction has been that taxes have been lower in the dependencies than at home. They are susceptible of increase, but subject to the qualification that if they are raised too far further investment will stop.

The postwar governments intend to increase taxation to help pay for enlarged social services. There are plans for semi-socialistic regimes. The Indonesian Republic, for instance, proposes to nationalize communications, public utilities, and banks, and to direct imports and exports. This is not a new departure, but is an extension of prewar Dutch policy.[1] Other companies will be returned to their prewar owners, but will be subject to more stringent control designed to raise wages and improve working conditions. The Republic has very few Indonesian technical experts and business executives. It must depend on foreign companies to

[1] The former Dutch government of the East Indies engaged in business on a considerable scale. It developed railways and coal mines, was the principal tin producer, was interested in the provision of electricity and water power, controlled most of the forests and the manufacture of salt, had a monopoly of pawnbroking, and provided farm loans on an extensive scale. The profits from these enterprises helped to defray the cost of government. After the abolition of the Open Door in 1933 the government directed imports and exports.

provide this indispensable assistance and to train Indonesians to fill these positions. Foreign capital is willing to operate under these conditions. It does not object to the substitution of native for foreign employees as long as they are competent—in fact, there is a large saving in salaries. Foreign investors do not oppose the grant of political independence, always providing that the new regime respects their rights. In return they stipulate that they be allowed to earn what they consider a reasonable return on their money. They also require the maintenance of law and order, legal security, and stability.

The nationalist leaders say that they are willing to restore property to its prewar owners, except when it is nationalized after compensation has been paid. They also admit the necessity of attracting additional foreign capital. They are afraid, however, of economic domination from abroad, and there is resentment that the development of natural resources has been almost entirely in the hands of foreigners. Moreover, many of the leaders are interested only in politics and do not understand economics. The Siamese government believed that by forcing Chinese out of business it could turn Siamese rice farmers into shopkeepers. The Burmese government has begun to nationalize British companies, without first arranging the amount to be paid for the properties. It admits that it has no money to pay compensation, and suggests that the owners accept bonds which will be redeemed if the government wins the civil war, rebuilds national prosperity, and eventually is able to collect enough taxes to balance the budget. In the opinion of the British Labor government the compensation offered is inadequate. Yet Burma does not have the money to make good the immense destruction done during the war, nor are there Burmese who have the training to operate the companies when they have been rehabilitated. In fact, a member of the Burmese government made an appeal for the investment of new foreign capital. This might be described as robust optimism; but it is unlikely to justify itself until the government restores order and adopts a more reasonable policy toward the foreign businessman.

If the demands of foreign capital are not met further investment will cease, and investors will use all their influence with their governments to safeguard their interests. Pressure might take the form of refusing to allow the new Asiatic governments to float foreign loans. The effect would be to postpone indefinitely their ambitious plans for improving the condition of their people. In Burma it is probable that it would be impossible to restore even the prewar standard of living. The Indonesian Republic would be very vulnerable to economic pressure owing to the dense population of Java. There is not enough land to support the people by agriculture, and before the war 25 per cent of the Javanese depended mainly on Western enterprises for their livelihood. The continuance of these industries is a matter of life and death to 12,000,000 people, and only the foreign owners are in a position to do this, since they alone have the capital and the managerial and technical knowledge that are necessary for efficient operation. In the rest of the East Indies (the part that is cooperating with the Dutch) the eviction of foreign capital would not have so devastating an effect upon the population, but it would completely disrupt economic life. Moreover, the governments would lose the high percentage of their revenue that came from foreign enterprises.

The Philippines and the countries of Southeast Asia either have self-government or are in the process of gaining it. Political freedom does not mean economic independence, however. Eventually they will acquire the native capital and technical skill to develop their own resources; but the history of Canada, India, and South America shows that this will not take place quickly. Until then these countries will have to depend upon foreign capital, and it cannot be had without paying a price. It is equally true that the Western world needs Southeast Asia as an outlet for investment, as a source of raw materials, and as a market. If either side is intransigent both will suffer for it, and only the Communists will profit. If the new Asiatic governments make a fetish of independence, they will remain economically depressed and politically unstable. Western capital will also make a serious mistake if it refuses to accept a reasonable measure of control. Cooperation is in the best interests of both Asia and the West, for each can provide what the other badly needs.

Southeast Asia in
WORLD ECONOMICS

Some Difficulties of Forecasting the Economic Future

WHAT part Southeast Asia will play in world economics during the second half of the twentieth century will depend upon the interplay of strong forces, many of which are highly volatile and almost wholly unpredictable. Just to mention a few of the imponderables will be sufficient, perhaps, to suggest the complexities of forecast.

Never before has the concept of *political* economy been more important than now in the Far East. In a world dominated in considerable part by Communist Russia, Socialist England, the combination of New Deal welfare economics, pressure groups, and large corporations in the United States, and a host of international agreements for the control of raw materials, the conscience or the whims of persons temporarily at the head of government agencies will do much to mold and shape' economic developments. The mass behavior of people is difficult enough to forecast, but the law of averages makes it more often predictable than the decisions and actions of individuals who are in positions of great authority.

By the Philippines Act of 1946 the United States presumptively has set part of the political climate in which an independent Philippine economy is to develop until 1974. For the first few years, until 1954, the free-trade conditions of the dependency period are to continue. Then for twenty years there is to be a gradual reduction of tariff advantage to the Philippines. This will be of some continuing advantage throughout the quarter-century unless, perchance, the United States should adopt a free-trade policy with the rest of the world. The possible economic impact of this act between 1954 and 1974 will be discussed later in the chapter, but it must be kept in mind that subsequent sessions of the American congress may see fit to modify its terms in less than twenty-eight years.

A working agreement between the United States and the Philippines has been reached earlier than similar ones between the Netherlands and the Netherlands Indies or between England and Malaya. Just what these are to be still remains to be seen. Whatever the final political arrangements between metropolitan country and colonies in these cases, they are not likely to be so important to world economy as in the case of the Philippines, since the United States rather than the metropolitan country is the principal buyer of the materials exported from each area.

It is not alone in the field of political control that the imponderables lie. The industrial revolution that has been proceeding with inexorable force for one hundred and fifty years appears to be well into a new phase, the chemical revolution. Throughout the industrial revolution the use of power and machinery has greatly increased the physical output of those who have embraced industrialization. Ever since World War I, at least, the technocrats and others have predicted that soon the use of power techniques would have been carried so far that the world would be flooded with goods and there would be little or nothing left for the masses of the population to do—nothing, at least, that had economic value or meaning. To some extent that philosophy of the danger of over-production entered into the American WPA program during the 1930's.

Fortunately industrialization has proceeded most of the time at a rate slow enough so that its products have been consumed without causing insurmountable difficulties. Now, however, many are predicting that chemistry and physics are about to lead to far more drastic and rapid changes. Rayon and nylon already have played havoc with the silk market. Synthetic rubber permits independence from a supply of natural rubber. Synthetic vitamins can be used materially to modify the requirements for farm-produced foods. These changes already have occurred. Many more like them doubtless are to follow. The impact of synthetic fabric and rubber hits directly on the Far East, since silk and raw rubber have been principal industries there and have furnished a large part of the interregional trade and purchasing power gen-erated in the Far East. Synthetic vitamins and other food materials may, perhaps, be of considerable future aid in overcoming the shortage of farm-produced food supplies in the Far East.

These changes in direction and tempo of the industrial revolution come just at a time when various peoples in the Far East are contemplating industrialization. Will their undertakings follow the patterns of the past and present, that is, the use of power and mechanical processes? If so, will they soon become obsolete in favor of chemical processes? Or will they largely skip over the power revolution and enter the chemical and atomic age direct? Can they, in fact, develop both the technical know-how and the essential auxiliary facilities for communication and transportation sufficiently to do either?

It is much more difficult to board a train already at full speed than one standing in the station ready to start. So it may prove for the countries of the East as they undertake the development of industry. In this country we developed railroads and highways in advance of population and goods. Conspicuous in the early history of our transcontinental railroads were the sparseness of population and the dearth of tonnage. There was ample good agricultural land on which farmers could produce even with extensive methods far more food than they and their families needed. Consequently the entire local population could be well fed and a tonnage of food made available for interregional movement, while a considerable number of persons were free for other tasks. One of the outstanding facts in the development of this country has been that a continuously declining fraction of our workers has produced sufficient food so that the rest of us could go well fed about other tasks.

Not so in many parts of the Far East. There a very high proportion of all workers are required in agriculture to provide even the present comparatively low dietary. Nor is there surplus food elsewhere in the world that can easily be moved to this area in exchange for other things. Unless or until there is an important change for the better in total world food production, it will be difficult for many parts of the Far East to spare laborers from agriculture in order to develop industry. A comparison of the value of agricultural products per person engaged in farming between the United States and the Far East shows American workers to be over five times as productive. This fact goes a long way toward explaining American ability to supply labor for intensive development of industry. The possibilities in the Far East are by no means so hopeful.

The point just made may seem to contradict the oft-repeated statement that labor is the most plentiful and cheapest thing in the Far East. So it is, in a sense. Labor is cheap in China and some other parts of the Far East because its productivity is low. The product of each man is small because he must work with hand tools at farming a very small parcel of land. This he must do endlessly and intensively to eke out a small ration of food, and in the doing he obtains a high total yield per acre of land. Unless nearly 90 per cent of the Chinese population stays everlastingly at this work someone must go hungry, and perhaps they do anyhow. Each person pulled away from agriculture to industry tends to reduce the total food supply and increase the hunger, since the land cannot be made to produce more per acre.

While this condition does not occur with equal severity throughout all parts of the Far East, it does in enough of it to make the problem of industrialization very different from what it ever has been in this country or what it was in Europe in the early nineteenth century. How it will be resolved remains to be seen. Perhaps in part by the chemical revolution, through the production of synthetic foods, thus freeing some peasants from the land. Perhaps in part and temporarily through the development of lands not now used to capacity in the Philippines and in parts of the Netherlands Indies. Unless, however, a positive check on population growth is developed this latter will not give more than temporary relief.

Certainly there is the possibility of adopting some of the techniques of Western agricultural production, thus increasing the output per worker and freeing large numbers for other lines of work.

Agricultural experts from this country who have studied the situation at first hand are convinced that adaptation of American methods in the production of rice, for example, could be employed in parts of the Far East with a considerable decrease resulting in the number of workers needed to produce that important food staple. Experiments and demonstration farms occur both in Siam and in French Indochina. In the latter country an American implement firm successfully established a demonstration farm some years before the war, and in Siam a firm of Chinese started cultivation on a large scale with the use of machines. This experiment was so successful that 30 men were able to till 600 acres of paddy that ordinarily would have required 300. If such demonstrations were copied widely a great supply of labor would be released from agriculture.

The fact remains, however, that no such change has occurred on any large, national scale anywhere in the Far East in spite of the many and diverse forms of political organization that exist there. Neither under the nominally independent governments of China and Siam, the colonial governments in French Indochina, Burma, Ceylon, and the Netherlands Indies, nor the dependencies in Malaya and the Philippines have any important increases occurred in the production of rice per worker. The yield per acre increased between 1920 and 1940 by 50 per cent in British Malaya, by 30 per cent in Taiwan, and by 20 per cent in Ceylon; and total acreage devoted to rice also increased in much of the area, but not the yield per worker. This latter could come about, apparently, only as the result of fundamental changes in land-ownership and the organization of farm and family life. None of the forms of government in force throughout the Philippines and Southeast Asia has brought about such changes. Perhaps the reason lies deeply imbedded in the psychology of the people themselves.

Japan has made available fairly large numbers of workers for industry in spite of a shortage in domestic food supply. This has been made possible, partially at least, through the importation of food. In the prewar decade, for example, at least 15 per cent of the rice consumed in Japan proper came from other areas, largely from Korea and Formosa. In addition, substantial quantities of beans were imported from Manchuria and of sugar from Formosa. Even with these importations of foodstuffs the percentage of gainfully employed persons who were working in agriculture was over twice that in the United States, while the physical production per agricultural worker was less than one-third of ours.

Unless or until some important changes occur in world food supply it will not be possible for Southeast Asia to import food from other areas to the end that workers may be shifted from agriculture to industry, for the simple reason that there are no present sources of surplus supply; so Japan's method appears not to apply there. Mechanization of agriculture would seem, therefore, to be the only solution to this problem, and this is likely to come very slowly. Before the end of the century, however, great changes may occur in this regard. As they develop the stage will be far better prepared for industrialization.

Perhaps enough has been said to clinch our original point, namely, that the part the Far East is to play in world economics depends upon many variables. This much we know: in sheer numbers there is a population in the Philippines and Southeast Asia somewhat greater than that of the United States; in all of Asia well over half of the world's population lies; and during the past 300 years (since 1650) the population of Asia has increased at almost the same rate as has that of the entire world, even though it has not been industrialized.

Since 1800 the per capita consumption in the United States appears at least to have doubled, although accurate measurement of such phenomena admittedly is difficult. In a considerable part of Southeast Asia, in contrast, the scale of living (and even its detailed form) has remained virtually unchanged. This contrast has led to "divine discontent" in parts of Asia, notably in Japan, but also, and especially since World War II, in parts of the Philippines and the Netherlands Indies. Now the peoples of several parts of Southeast Asia are aroused against what they choose to consider a shortage in their share of world resources. A generation ago Lothrop Stoddard crusaded for the idea that once the people of the Far East became conscious of relative scales of living and distributions of resources they might rise in a world-shaking revolution that would be impossible to control. Jealousy, fully aroused, is a terrible force, and what influence it may play in determining the place of Southeast Asia in world economics in the future is hard indeed to predict.

The Raw Materials of an Economic Order

Before going directly to a discussion of the economics of Southeast Asia it may be worth while to take a short airplane excursion to view in perspective some of the interrelations with which we are concerned. The raw materials with which a commonwealth is endowed will do much to determine its future. The raw materials of an economic order are of several sorts, and an understanding of their potentialities requires viewing them in perspective. In this connection I propose to use the term "raw materials" in a broader and more inclusive sense than sometimes is the case. First I want merely to list or define the sorts of things that seem important to economic development. Later each sort of raw material will enter into the discussion of Southeast Asia in somewhat more specific terms.

Of first importance, perhaps, are the people themselves, since it is they who will manipulate, develop, trade, or otherwise use all the other resources. Clearly it is not enough merely to count these people. Their customs, habits, mores, and ambitions may be much more important than their numbers. Perhaps the greatest contribution of the temperate zone has been the temper and ambition of those nurtured there. The lands of "mañana" have produced men and women who do some things with surpassing excellence, but in total their contributions to world change have been comparatively slight. Most of Southeast Asia lies outside the temperate zone and its people, as raw material for an economic order, must be rated accordingly. Latitude has much to do, perhaps, with Japan's almost successful attempt to dominate and coordinate the Far East. The powerful force of human nature still might make that effort successful before the end of the century.

Closely allied to the people themselves are the political and economic institutional arrangements under which they live. These arrangements form a sort of framework within which all the other resources may be manipulated into many kaleidoscopic patterns.

Matters of ownership, the rights accruing to owners, the methods by which these rights may be transferred, the concepts of fair trade and of good will are illustrative in this field. The discovery that debt is a negotiable instrument has been called one of the greatest discoveries of any age. To what extent, one wonders, have the people of Southeast Asia seen the implications of this discovery? Will they use it in the future as an aid in establishing huge corporations under concentrated ownership and management in accord with the prewar Japanese pattern? Or will they use it as a method of decentralized ownership with bonds held by thousands of individuals, even when efficiency calls for concentration of operation, as in the case of such institutions as the Bell Telephone System in this country? Or will they so legislate as to close off that particular road to concentration of the decision-making function in industry under either of the two patterns just mentioned or any other?

The most commonly accepted single measure of raw material for economic development is an inventory of the natural resources. These include land, mineral deposits, water and power supplies, and so on. Certainly access to these things is imperative, but England long has proven that they can be obtained through trade, as the United States has also found more recently; witness the dependence of our automobile industry on rubber and our food-canning industry on tin, of neither of which we possess any natural source. It is significant and informative, perhaps, to note in this connection that in the United States in 1939 the products of farms, forests, and fisheries accounted for only 8.4 per cent of the national income, while the products of mines added only 2.6 per cent. The total value of the annual production from these great groups of natural resources was only 11 per cent of the total national income.

Even in 1945 during the wartime shortage of food supply this combined total rose only to 11.6 per cent. In this country, at least, retail trade contributes much more value to national income than does the production of all the natural resources used directly as raw materials of industry. England, and to some extent Japan, have found that they can profitably trade products of their labor in fabrication for ample supplies of those natural resources which they do not have at hand. While it must be pointed out that this ability sometimes has been associated with a colonial system, this has not been so in our own case.

People, as labor supply, are thus a very important raw material in a modern economic order. Important in its evaluation are the skills already possessed, including those required for organization and management. Casual observation suggests that these latter are and may continue to be one of the bottlenecks of industrial development in Southeast Asia. At least it has been true so far that foreign entrepreneurs have been of major importance—Chinese, English, Dutch, American, and Japanese. Not only have these foreigners played the role of decision makers, but to a considerable degree they have furnished the necessary capital and taken the business risks. The economic future of Southeast Asia will depend in no small measure upon the extent to which foreigners continue to play these roles, or on the rapidity with which competent management develops from among the native population. The other types of skills are, perhaps, less critically short in Southeast Asia, but it should be recalled that many workers have been imported, into Malaya at least—Chinese to work in the tin mines and Tamils from India for the rubber plantations. These importations have not resulted from shortages in the quantity of local population, but from its inadequate quality as labor.

Finally, the present capital plant is an important ingredient among the raw materials of an economy. Perhaps most important in this field is the transportation system, without which regional specialization cannot proceed. Much of the Far East is woefully short of transportation facilities, China furnishing the extreme example of this shortage. This is a difficulty that can be corrected neither easily nor quickly, although recent experience with air transport suggests that perhaps it is easier than we think. Southeast Asia also is short of industrial equipment. Such equipment requires steel. Southeast Asia has little steel, and world capacity is in high demand at present and can be purchased, if at all, only at high prices.

Even if steel and other capital goods could be purchased they would have to be paid for by someone. In the past this has been done for Southeast Asia very largely by foreigners. For example,

prewar estimates suggest that the private ownership of non-agri-
cultural capital in the Netherlands Indies was distributed among
the citizens of different countries about as follows: Holland, 52
per cent; native, 19 per cent; Great Britain, 9 per cent; U.S.A.,
8 per cent; China, 7 per cent; and other, 5 per cent. Much of this
investment is in tin mines and smelters, but it also provides the
capital for other manufacturing and commercial enterprises. Even
in agriculture only about 60 per cent of capital investment was
held by natives.

In British Malaya foreign investments were estimated as exceeding $450,000,000, about 70 per cent of which were held in the
United Kingdom. In the Philippines the investments of citizens of
the United States amounted to about $550,000,000, which was
about one-quarter of all United States investments in the Far
East. In French Indochina foreign investments amounted to
about $400,000,000, over 90 per cent of which was held in France.

If the flow of foreign investment were to be cut off it is difficult to foresee any rapid development of capital from the savings
among the native population in either the Philippines or Southeast Asia. This is so because the incomes of the great mass of the
native population are well below the level at which savings and
investments start in this country. Moreover, these natives have
shown little tendency in the past to make capital investments.
Thus while foreign participation in the financial development in
Southeast Asia has been called "ruthless imperialism" by some, it
has been largely responsible for such modern industrial development as has occurred. Without such participation the rate of industrial change throughout the area might well carry out the
old adage that the East is not to be hurried.

The Present Economic Situation in Southeast Asia

So much has been said in the chapters on the individual countries that it is not necessary here to do more than summarize and
draw some implications from the economic conditions in the area.
The reader may refer to the earlier chapters for details, so here
let us be brief.

The conspicuous characteristic of the entire area is its plural
economy. Each separate country is composed of two or more social

groups living side by side, but without mingling, and governed in the main by a single government. This condition is less in evidence, perhaps, in the Philippines than elsewhere in the area; but if this is a difference it is one of degree only for the mestizos play a part in the Philippine economy far out of proportion to their numbers. Even in the independent state of Siam the natives, the Chinese, and the Europeans live in essential isolation from each other, each group performing a separate function in the economy. In Malaya a considerable part of the work on rubber plantations and in the tin mines is done by Indian and Chinese workmen who live quite apart from the natives. Of course, this same phenomenon is found to some extent in our own South where the Negroes and whites do not mingle, and in eastern Canada where the French and English tend to live quite separate lives. Perhaps, in fact, this sort of plural society is more nearly the rule than the exception, but certainly it is conspicuous and important in Southeast Asia.

Among the conditions that both give rise to and account for the plural society in Southeast Asia is the fundamental difference in temperament, ambition, and aroused desire for material gadgets on the part of the rank and file. The natives of Southeast Asia appear, in general, to be much simpler in their pattern of wants than are the Europeans. Perhaps this results from the long-time influence of climate already referred to. At any rate, it is likely to have a continuing influence upon the uses of resources and the resulting pattern of production throughout the area.

Few, if any, of the great types of civilization have originated within twenty degrees of the equator, while all of the Philippines and Southeast Asia lie within that zone. In fact, most of the area we are considering lies within ten degrees on either side of the equator, a region in which it appears that as yet no important industrial development has occurred. While this is not positive proof that no such developments will be made there during the next fifty years, it strongly suggests such a forecast since, after all, when the past is highly consistent its pattern is likely to continue.

Analysis of economic efficiency the world around shows it to have been especially influenced by climate, diet, density of population, and disease. Each of these factors appears to be working against the development of economic efficiency in Southeast Asia. The climate, mostly hot and humid, tends to produce lethargy and inertia among humans, except in the matter of reproduction which appears to be stimulated. The combination of climate-induced laziness and high birth rate leads to overpopulation relative to the produced food supply. The resultant inadequate diet leaves individuals easy prey to disease. Such economic progress as has come in the area has been due in considerable measure to the whiplashing leadership of foreigners from the temperate zone. This has been the essence of the plural economy.

Even in the Philippines, the part of the area farthest removed from the equator, fifty years of relatively beneficent American tutelage has produced few striking cultural or industrial developments. The educational system which we installed and of which we thought to be proud has left about 50 per cent of the population illiterate. Only 14 per cent have gone beyond the elementary schools. The modal schooling is only three years and, presented as it has been in English, it has not even given the masses permanent literacy in that language. Even so, the educational status appears to be much better in the Philippines than elsewhere in Southeast Asia. Beginning in 1940 the Tagalog language has been substituted for English so that progress may be more rapid in the future, although of that we cannot yet be certain. If, as now seems likely, American and European leadership is to play a diminishing role throughout Southeast Asia the chance of Western industrial development may be reduced still further because of lack of educated personnel.

Western medical practice and sanitary measures have been introduced into many parts of Southeast Asia, lowering the death rate. The most obvious direct result has been to intensify the pressure of population upon land resources and the food supply. The dietary standards almost everywhere throughout Southeast Asia are inadequate in quantity and poorly balanced. Consequently the diseases of malnutrition are very prevalent.

Not all of the arable land in the area is cultivated intensively. Especially in the Philippines and in some of the outer provinces of the Netherlands Indies there is room for considerable expansion. Concerted and persistent efforts have been made for some years, especially since 1931, with the aid of government cajolery if not actual coercion, to induce part of the native population in Java, where the density is over 800 per square mile, to move onto new land in the outer provinces. It seems to be illustrative of the inertia of the people that these efforts have met strong opposition, perhaps because of ignorance and fear of the unknown. The fact that land was available on some of the islands was well enough known so that consideration was given in 1940–41 to a plan to make some of it available for Japanese expansion. Such a plan, while doubtlessly well intentioned, could hardly have averted a war with Japan; but it would have put her in a far more strategic position to dominate the Orient. The fact that it even was proposed is evidence that the density of population on Java could be lessened if the natives there were adventuresome enough to pioneer in new territory. The fact that they have not done so highlights an important difference between the people of Southeast Asia and those who pushed westward across the North American continent.

The Dutch have tried throughout their administration of the Netherlands Indies to make the islands an integral and equal part of the realm. In political organization they have succeeded rather well. The People's Council was established thirty years ago in 1918. A full-fledged legislature came ten years later. But the small group of civil servants still must urge and prod the population into physical and educational improvement.

The population of the Netherlands Indies has increased from under ten million in 1845 to over seventy million in 1948. It is doubtful, however, if production has kept pace with population—if, that is, the people as a whole are as well fed today as they were before World War I. Furnivall has summarized the situation as follows: "The Dutch themselves, however, are dissatisfied with what has been achieved. A very interesting, though pessimistic review of the economic history of Netherlands Indies has been given by Dr. Boeke, formerly advisor for Cooperative Credit in Java, and now Professor of Tropical Economy in Leiden. Raffles and Muntinghe, he says, thought to improve the condition of the people by encouraging peasant cultivation; Du Bus by encouraging State production; then the liberals looked to freedom of enterprise as the key to prosperity and, after a campaign of fifty years knocked off the last fetters from the cultivator by substituting capitation tax for compulsory services; finally the ethical movement aimed directly at building up the economic position of the people. Yet the reports on the Economic Enquiries of 1924 and 1926 lead him to conclude that, despite all this benevolent activity, the cultivator eats rather less well than before the war, and can obtain less for his surplus produce, while his emancipation from compulsory service has done so little to improve his economic position that he cannot even pay the tax in money which was substituted for compulsory service."

It seems almost crystal clear that the rank and file have not yet been sufficiently impressed by economic progress, as Americans and Europeans understand the term, to strive for its advantages. Perhaps they are right in concluding that not all of its vaunted advantages are worth striving for.

This natural resistance to the Western type of aggressiveness apparently is illustrated also in the Philippines. There it is estimated that only about 50 per cent of the arable land was under cultivation in 1938. Food for several millions of underfed people throughout Asia might have come from the additional acres. Or lacking a profitable market for such surplus food, a wider adoption of American mechanized agriculture might have freed many Filipinos for industrial developments. Leadership, vision, and energy appear to have been inadequate to find ways and means by which to undertake such developments. One can but wonder whether or not the increased political independence now coming to these countries will lead to fuller and more efficient use of available resources. Responsibility often develops latent powers. Perhaps it will do so now in the Philippines and Southeast Asia, but the history of lands near the equator is against it.

The Importance of Imports and Exports

The foreign trade of Southeast Asia has some characteristics that are of peculiar importance to the area itself and to the rest of the world. In the first place the exports include, as an important part of the total, certain raw materials, such as natural rubber, tin, and some oils with unique properties, not readily available from other parts of the world. These raw materials have contributed in a major way to the Western economy and especially to that of the United States. Without them it would have been impossible for automobile use to have reached its present high level nearly so quickly. Nor could the food-processing industries have developed around the canning process without the ample supplies of tin which have come from the area. The cutting off of these two materials at their source during World War II posed some problems of great difficulty for the Allies. The recovery of export totals of rubber and tin indicates clearly that the war was not long enough for the rest of the world to find ways to get along economically without them.

In the second place there has been a continuous and substantial export balance of trade from Southeast Asia. In 1939 this excess amounted to about $250,000,000 or approximately $2.00 per capita for the entire population of the area. The primary cause of the excess was the necessity of paying the earnings upon landownership and other capital investments of foreigners, largely in England and the Netherlands although to a lesser extent in China, the United States, and Japan. Thus the export balance resulted in European credit in the United States, since much of the surplus export came here. With these credits Europeans, including the British, were able to buy a considerable volume of goods from us in excess of the value of goods which they sent directly to us.

It is not yet clear to what extent the British and the Dutch have lost their investments in Southeast Asia, but there seems to have been sufficient change in ownership to modify in an important degree the directions of triangular trade from that which took place before the war. Temporarily, to be sure, we are exporting to Europe more than our prewar totals, but that is because of the Marshall Plan in aid of European recovery. When that plan has run its course it is doubtful that Europe will have any purchasing power to take the place of that which previously originated in the excess of exports from Southeast Asia.

The $2.00 per capita net exports may seem somewhat insignificant. It is, in fact, almost exactly our own average per capita net export during the thirty-five years 1913–1947 inclusive; it is only about one-third of our net balance in 1947. There are, however, at least two important differences in the two cases. We are a relatively rich people with a comparatively high per capita production, while the people of Southeast Asia continuously are close to a subsistence basis. Moreover, during the thirty-five year period our net exports paid off our foreign obligations and left us a creditor nation, while in the case of Southeast Asia the net exports have barely sufficed to service the foreign investments without reducing them. To some extent, to be sure, the foreign investments provided machinery and power equipment with which production was increased, but in considerable part they represent merely foreign ownership of land which does not change materially the production and thus provides no additional income with which to pay the land rent to the foreign owners.

The two most important exports from Southeast Asia from the standpoint of total value have been rubber and tin. The future of each of these is highly unpredictable. In the years between the two world wars each of them was subjected to a series of experiments in national and international control of supply. Rubber exports from British territories in the Far East first were regulated under the Stevenson Act. This move was initiated because the quantity of rubber available relative to the demand was so high that the price was forced down to a wholly unprofitable level. About all the Stevenson Act accomplished, however, was to arouse resentment on the part of American buyers against the British and to develop an increase in the Dutch share of the total world market from 16 to 33 per cent. The British share fell from 75 to 52 per cent.

In 1934 there was established a world rubber cartel. A second agreement was signed in 1938. The International Rubber Agreement formed the basis for this cartel. It was signed by Britain, the Netherlands, France, and Siam. The main features called for a quota set every four months on the amount of rubber that could be shipped from each country. A committee appointed by the participating countries administered the pact. The principal consuming countries were represented on the committee by nonvoting advisory members. The function of this committee was "to adjust in an orderly manner supply to demand and maintain a fair and equitable price which will be reasonably remunerative to efficient producers."

These instructions contain some words with great flexibility, depending for their meaning upon the temporary temper of the committee members—for example, "reasonably remunerative," and "efficient producers." Arbitrary as opposed to objective standards are the only ones that are possible in such cases, and there is certain to be much political jockeying in their establishment. So far they seem to have been set in the immediate interests of producers and somewhat against the interests of consumers, not only in the case of rubber but whenever international cartels have been used. History has proven, however, that it is difficult to administer such cartels in the long-run interests even of the producers.

The desire for this sort of control over supply grew out of an excess of production relative to demand. While the international rubber agreement was signed in 1934, the excess of production was by no means entirely a depression phenomenon. The Stevenson Act, which the British unsuccessfully had urged the Dutch to join, was in effect during the prosperous 1920's. As early as that, increases in production had been greater than even the expanding automobile use could absorb. Thus it appears that Southeast Asia had pushed the development of one of its most important export industries beyond the point of profitable use of resources during the period between the two world wars. Throughout this period there was strong competition among producers within Southeast Asia, but relatively little from outside sources of supply.

During World War II a new and potentially very strong form of competition arose. The necessities of war led to rapid furtherance of work already under way in the commercial development of synthetic rubber. In 1946, one year after V-J day, the United States consumed 1,100,000 tons of rubber, 85 per cent chemical and only 15 per cent natural. Thus it had been proven that the world *could* be largely independent of natural rubber.

It now appears that in 1948 natural rubber again held the dominant position. World production for 1948 was estimated at

1,745,000 tons, about 75 per cent natural and 25 per cent chemical. Of this the United States will use about 55 per cent. Other principal users will include the USSR, 13 per cent; United Kingdom, 12 per cent; France, 6 per cent; Canada, 3 per cent; and all others, 11 per cent. Thus it appears that natural rubber producers have staged an important market comeback in a two-year period. The United States alone is expected to consume about 580,000 tons of natural rubber against 390,000 tons of chemical rubber in 1948. It also is believed that since certain backlogs of demand have been filled, the United States consumption in 1949 will not be over a total of 920,000 tons, or 50,000 tons less than in 1948 and nearly 100,000 tons less than in 1946.

The United States military authorities and the manufacturers of chemical rubber would be reluctant to see the production of chemical rubber fall below its present level of from 350,000 to 400,000 tons. As long as threats of war continue it seems unlikely that our production will be permitted to fall below that level, even though some government subsidy may be required to keep it at that figure in competition against natural rubber.

The rubber producers in Southeast Asia are certain to attempt to get as high a proportion of the total market as possible. They are convinced that the introduction of higher yielding trees and other improvements in the techniques of production will permit them to undersell the producers of chemical rubber in a free world market. Present estimates indicate that one and one-half to two million tons of natural rubber can be produced in the Far East at costs that will permit it to be laid down in New York or Los Angeles at perhaps 7 cents a pound; while United States chemists and technicians predict costs of synthetic rubber of about 8 or 9 cents a pound. This seems to give a financial advantage to natural rubber, but neither the United States military nor the United States tire manufacturers want ever again to be wholly dependent upon a foreign source that either may be lost entirely through war or may put on a squeeze through restriction of export.

There are two important reasons which explain, perhaps, the rapid postwar recovery of a large share of the market for natural rubber and the corresponding drop in the market for chemical rubber. In the first place, as just pointed out, the former is cheaper than the latter. In the second place, chemical rubber has not yet been accepted as equal in quality to natural rubber. Experts appear to agree that some cost difference in favor of natural rubber will continue at least for some years. On the other hand, expert opinion is agreed that in the manufacture of rubber goods of all sorts a total of at least 75 per cent of chemical rubber could be used as raw material without any deterioration in the quality or performance of the final product. Some goods might still need to be made entirely of natural rubber, but others might better be made entirely of chemical rubber.

In total, the 75 per cent figure is believed by many technically competent persons to be too low rather than too high. The early experience with synthetic tires, however, was sufficiently variable and unsatisfactory so that consumers may be hard to convince of this fact. They want "the good old natural product," even though present know-how may permit tires of superior quality to be made with a high percentage of chemical rubber. In spite of present cost differences and consumer preferences, however, the American manufacturers of chemical rubber, urged on by the advocates of preparedness and self-sufficiency, will make a strong bid for a sizable part of the total market.

Thus the competition which is shaping up seems likely to result again in overproduction. This well may lead to a revival of an International Rubber Agreement, but this time the United States must be asked to join the agreement not only as a principal consumer, but as an important producer as well. Moreover, this importance is not limited to the supply of chemical rubber, since in addition the importance of American-owned plantations in Liberia, Brazil, and perhaps some other areas already is considerable and will increase during the next decade.

In view of all these circumstances it appears unlikely that Southeast Asia can hope to increase its export of natural rubber. In fact it seems more likely that there will be some decrease, even if the United States under a Republican administration does not impose a tariff in favor of American-produced rubber. This latter certainly is not an impossibility if the threat of war continues. If such a policy were established by our government it would create a very serious economic problem both in Malaya and the Netherlands Indies.

The situation in French Indochina calls for an additional word. By the terms of the International Rubber Agreement of 1934 Indochina was not given an export quota as were the other producing areas. Rather, Indochina was given exclusive rights to the French market for rubber in exchange for an agreement to sell no rubber outside the French Empire. If this condition is retained in future agreements, rubber producers in Indochina will be less affected by any increases in American production than will those in other parts of Southeast Asia. Incidentally, this arrangement was in keeping with much of the French colonial policy: the colonies were considered as so closely bound to the empire that their products "belonged" to the mother-country in a very special sense.

Tin, likewise, has a prewar history of production in excess of demand. Control schemes progressing from little to great authority were used almost continuously from 1920 to the outbreak of World War II. During the five years just prior to the war an International Restriction Plan was in operation with sufficient force to hold the price essentially stable at £230 per ton, although it had been as low as £104 in 1930–31.

Because of the characteristics both of demand for and supply of tin, it is an unusually interesting and successful example of centralized control. The demand for tin comes mainly from two uses, namely, as a bearing metal for high-speed machinery, and as tin plate in the food-canning industry. In each of these cases a doubling or trebling of the price of tin makes little measurable difference in the cost of the finished consumer goods—automobiles, for example, or canned peas. Consequently when the cartel manipulated supply so as to hold the price at £230, no one bothered to search for substitutes or in any other manner to reduce their use of tin—the demand proved to be highly inelastic.

The supply of tin likewise has some interesting characteristics. In Southeast Asia it is produced from surface mines with comparatively low-cost dredging operations. During the 1930's British Malaya produced nearly 40 per cent of the world's supply, the Netherlands Indies nearly 25 per cent, and Siam an appreciable amount by means of this type of operation. In contrast, Bolivia produced nearly 25 per cent of the world's total from deep mines at much higher cost. Other deep mine operations occurred on a smaller scale in Nigeria, China, and Cornwall. Thus the different regional parts of the industry had widely different costs, and there seems to be no question but that Southeast Asia could have supplied the world demand at prices considerably below those actually maintained during the last half of the 1930's. When the price first reached £230 in August of 1933 the production quotas were restricted to 35 per cent of 1929. From that low point they rose gradually until they reached 90 per cent in January 1936.

During the years in which this cartel was in the making two important areas of disagreement arose. The first was between the low-cost and the high-cost producers. Pressure by strong political and trade groups finally resulted in an agreement to hold the quotas low enough to permit working of the Bolivian mines, partly in order that Bolivia would have an item of export with which to finance the importation of goods, and partly to furnish Bolivian tin ores to British smelters that were adapted only to their use. Incidentally, the United States was greatly embarrassed at the outbreak of the war in the Far East in having a nearby source of tin ore, but no smelters in which it might be used, at a time when transatlantic shipment to England would have been very hazardous even had ships been available to undertake it.

The second principal area of disagreement arose between the new and the established producers. The most conspicuous case, perhaps, arose when producers in Siam undertook to enter the competition for markets. They had not been considered a factor of sufficient importance to be included in the original international quota agreement, but in 1935 they actually were supplying between 10 and 20 per cent of world production and were threatening the success of the cartel. Consequently they were persuaded to join the scheme with a fairly liberal national quota. This case illustrates the generalization that no such control scheme can be successful for long unless the entire supply, both present and potential, is included.

During the postwar period it would be possible, from a cost

standpoint, for Southeast Asia to squeeze out of the market all other tin-producing areas. It seems unlikely, however, that this will be done, for two principal reasons. In the first place, when the demand for a commodity is highly inelastic as in this case, a smaller amount actually will sell for more total money than a larger amount. Moreover, in the case of tin the smaller amount will cost less to mine and will leave more in the ground for future sale. Consequently as long as international quotas can be maintained the operators in Southeast Asia are better off on two counts, namely, they can expect a higher annual revenue from restricted than from unrestricted sales, while at the same time more tin would be left in the ground for future sale.

In the second place, the United States now is in a position to use Bolivian ore. Apparently refinery costs in our war-built plant on the Gulf Coast, which handles Bolivian ore, are higher than those required for reducing local ores in Malaya and the Netherlands Indies. Again, however, it may be pointed out that cost is not so important in the case of tin as is the assurance of a supply, and even if some continuing government subsidy is needed our plant is likely to remain in active operation. Consequently, as long as a threat of war continues we shall find it expedient from a defense standpoint to keep the Bolivian mines in operation. The time may come again all too soon when that supply will be highly important to us and, fortunately, this time we shall be in position immediately to use it.

There is, however, a factor that is tending to reduce the total demand for tin. The quick freezing of food is in keen competition against the canning industry, and even within that industry the use of glass containers is in competition against tin. It is too early to tell how much these developments will curtail the use of tin, but they could seriously affect the export income of Southeast Asia.

When all the complex factors that are likely to affect future demand for these two products are considered, the prospects for maintaining their present level of export value does not seem too good. For that export value to increase as rapidly as will population in Southeast Asia is still less likely. In other words, the purchasing power of these commodities per capita of population in

Southeast Asia is much more likely to fall than to rise during the next several decades.

In Malaya, especially, any reduction in the export of tin and rubber would have an important effect on total foreign trade. In 1939 these two commodities represented nearly 75 per cent of all exports. The remaining 25 per cent was divided among a long list of things. For many of these, increased export is not to be expected; rice, sago flour, and fish are examples, representing in 1939 about 3 per cent of total exports. Copra, coconut oil, and palm oil, also representing about 3 per cent of total exports, might be increased in production, but they would meet the competition of both the Netherlands Indies and the Philippines. It is difficult to find in the list of present exports any items the increased export of which would be likely to offset any large drop in the sale of tin and rubber.

The Netherlands Indies are not so dependent upon the export of these two principal commodities. In 1939 they represented only about 35 per cent of total exports. Petroleum products accounted in that year for about 20 per cent of the total, and this item has possibilities for considerable expansion. Tea furnished about 8 per cent and the special tropical oils about 5 per cent of all exports. Probably the sale of the former will increase slowly if at all, but the latter may be subject to considerable increase. Sugar accounted for 10 per cent of total exports. This item is subject to periodic if not continuous overproduction throughout the world. Consequently it is doubtful that any important increase in export revenue can be expected from this source.

While tin and rubber have not been important export items for the Philippines, in some respects the Filipinos face more serious problems of readjustment of foreign trade than do any other peoples in the area. The cause for their present plight lies in the changes which their complete independence will bring following 1954 in their commercial relations with the United States. For thirty years the United States has followed a contradictory policy toward the Philippines. On the political side, the aim has been increasing self-government. On the economic side, in contrast, the policy of free trade between the United States and her dependency has created so complete a state of economic dependence that it even is doubtful whether political independence really is possible.

One effect of the free trade policy is indicated by a comparison of the exports from the Philippines before and after 1909, when it was established. From 1902 to 1909 the average annual export was about $31.5 million, of which 38 per cent went to the United States. From 1909 to 1914 average exports rose to $46.6 million, of which 43 per cent went to the United States. In the four-year period from 1919–1922 the corresponding figures were $112 million and 62 per cent, while in 1929 they were $164.5 million and 76 per cent. Philippine trade in the twentieth century shows not only a remarkable growth in total exports but also in the importance of the American market. This latter was built up with the aid of free trade, and the gradual reduction of that advantage, which is scheduled to start in 1954, may prove to be embarrassing in the extreme.

Examination of the products exported shows an important change, also, in their relative importance. Prior to 1909 Manila hemp, or abaca, and manufactured cordage were by far the principal exports, in some years making up 70 per cent of the total. In 1937 they were only 15 per cent of the total, and their value was only about half as great as in the earlier period. In 1937 the two principal exports were sugar, which was 38 per cent of the total, and coconut products, which represented 30 per cent. In the future the latter will be subjected to growing competition from Malaya and the Netherlands Indies, as already pointed out, and at present the products from the Philippines seem of somewhat inferior quality when compared to those from the other two areas.

After 1954 Philippine sugar will be subject to United States tariff so that its present share of the American market will be in very real jeopardy in competition against, for example, the Cuban producers. Perhaps an international cartel may be invoked to save some part of the American market for the Philippines. Lacking such a move it appears inevitable that Philippine exports of sugar will fall sharply, especially since essentially all of their sale in recent years has been in the United States.

This brief review of the prospects for export trade from the Philippines and Southeast Asia generally points to the conclusion that the export value of basic raw materials, the products of farm and mine, is more likely to fall than to rise in coming decades, at least on a per capita basis. Petroleum products and the unique tropical oils are almost certain to be exceptions to this generalization, but their increase may well be quite inadequate to offset the decrease in other items, especially in the cases of the Philippines and Malaya. If this forecast is even reasonably correct it suggests exploration of other sources of regional income. In this connection attention turns naturally to the possibilities for industrialization within Southeast Asia.

The Prospects for Industrialization

In this postwar era two strong but contradictory forces are in clear evidence. On the one hand is the apparently awakening desire for a higher scale of living. On the other hand is the expectation that the income accruing to Southeast Asia from the export of its principal prewar products will diminish, at least on a per capita basis. Because of this second circumstance the first must depend upon a program of economic expansion. To accomplish this, consideration turns at once to industrialization as one of the most promising fields available. This the British already have attempted to foster through their Colonial Development and Welfare Acts of 1940 and 1945. So far, however, their most vigorous efforts are being directed toward the colonies in Africa rather than Southeast Asia.

The question of adequate native leadership for industrialization already has been raised. Industrial development generally is a slow process even under aggressive leadership. When one recalls, for example, the aggressive spirit *and* the slow progress toward industrialization in southern California from 1900 to 1940 the truth of this adage is emphasized. The impact of the second World War was needed to add to the conglomeration of specialized farming, haven for old age, and Hollywood a really substantial body of income-producing industry. The combination of forces needed for the industrialization of Southeast Asia still is in an amorphous state. What spark will serve to crystallize them —and when—is uncertain. But the forces are present, and the process may go a long way forward before the close of the century.

There is reason to expect that governments will play a larger

part in economic developments during the next fifty years in
Southeast Asia than they have during the past hundred years in
the United States. There are several reasons for this expectation. World trends are toward government participation. The
large-scale industrial developments already established, against
which new areas must compete, almost require large-scale operations for successful competition. This, in turn, often can be
provided more quickly with the aid of government financing,
which leads to government supervision, control, and perhaps actual operation. The temper of the people around the world seems
to be against huge private concentration of ownership, as witness
the attempts to break up the Zaibatsu in Japan. The easiest alternative in countries where 90 per cent of the population have no
funds to invest in bonds or stocks is, perhaps, government ownership "for all the people." Probably Russia has developed industry
faster under government control than would have been possible
under private capitalism there. And so we well may expect industrialization in Southeast Asia, if it comes at all rapidly, to exhibit a
degree of government participation larger than we are used to or
believe we like in the United States.

A principal purpose of industrialization in Southeast Asia
would be to provide a profitable income to the workers in industry. Manufacturing industries differ greatly in the wage opportunity which each provides, that is, in the amount of value that
is added to the raw material and distributed to wage earners as
a result of the manufacturing process. This factor should have a
bearing on the choice of industries undertaken within a country
seeking profitable employment for large numbers of workers.

In the United States all manufacturing industries, on the average, distributed directly to wage earners 15.7 per cent of the
total value of their finished products (1939 data). The industries
that are most prominent in Minnesota, however, paid out in
wages a much smaller portion of the value of products, namely,
in butter-making, 3.7 per cent; in sugar refining, 4.1 per cent; in
flour milling, 4.3 per cent; and in meat-packing, 6.7 per cent. This
type of industry provides wage incomes for only a relatively small
labor force and, consequently, would not go far toward solving
the problem of overpopulation or low total income in the Orient.

In contrast, some of the industries that seem natural for Southeast Asia because of either a local supply of raw materials or developed skills fortunately could absorb a large labor force relative to the value of the raw material used and of the finished product. Based on United States experience in 1939 the following ratios pertain:

WAGES AS PER CENT OF VALUE OF PRODUCT

Hotel Chinaware 49	Textile Mill Products 23
Total Pottery Industry 38	Cigars 21
Embroideries 25	Rubber Products 18

From the standpoints both of employment and of availability of raw materials, therefore, these are industrial fields the expansion of which in Southeast Asia merits careful consideration. These are fields, however, in which in the main production already is well developed in other parts of the world and specifically in the United States. Competition for world markets would be keen. If, for example, the Netherlands Indies undertook to market automobile tires instead of crude rubber, strong interests in the United States would move toward further use of synthetic rubber and perhaps also toward tariff protection against the importation of tires. The tire market would not be an easy one for manufacturers in Southeast Asia to enter or exploit. Neither, perhaps, would any of the others in the above list.

Thus the conclusion seems inevitable that the road to industrialization of Southeast Asia will be long and rough. The obvious obstacles include possible lack of leadership, difficulty in freeing the people from the pressing job of obtaining a food supply so they may work in industry, overcoming a considerable degree of lethargy or contentment with present status, and ruthless competition from areas already industrialized. That the trend toward industrialization will override these obstacles in time seems certain, but that the pace will be slow is almost equally sure.

Suggested Reading

The Annals. *World Population in Transition.* Vol. 237. January 1945.
Abelarde, Pedro E. *American Tariff Policy Towards the Philippines.* New York. 1947.
Bisson, T. A. *America's Far Eastern Policy.* New York. 1945.

Boeke, J. H. *The Evolution of the Netherlands Indies Economy*. New York. 1946.

Callis, H. G. *Foreign Capital in Southeast Asia*. New York. 1942.

Christian, J. *Modern Burma*. Berkeley. 1942.

Cressey, G. B. *Asia's Lands and Peoples*. New York. 1944.

Furnivall, J. S. *Netherlands India*. New York. 1944.

Gull, E. M. *British Economic Interests in the Far East*. New York. 1943.

Holland, W. L. *Commodity Control in the Pacific Area*. Stanford. 1935.

Hubbard, G. E. *Eastern Industrialization and Its Effect on the West*. London. 1935.

Knorr, K. E. *Tin under Control*. Stanford. 1945.

————. *World Rubber and Its Regulation*. Stanford. 1945.

Mason, Edward S. *Controlling World Trade*. New York. 1946.

Mitchell, Kate. *Industrialization of the Western Pacific*. New York. 1942.

Porter, Catherine. *Crisis in the Philippines*. New York. 1942.

Robequain, Charles. *Economic Development of French Indo China*. New York. 1944.

Shepherd, Jack. *Industry in Southeast Asia*. New York. 1941.

Stocking, G. W., and M. W. Watkins. *Cartels or Competition*. New York. 1948.

Tsang, Chih. *China's Post War Markets*. New York. 1945.

Wickizer, V. D., and M. K. Bennett. *Rice Economy of Monsoon Asia*. Stanford. 1941.

INTERNATIONAL RELATIONS
in Southeast Asia

❖

SOUTHEAST ASIA has become more significant as mighty forces clash in that strategic area. The demand for social justice struggles against privilege. Economic development challenges centuries of backwardness. Tolerance rises against bigotry. Peoples not yet free vie with the great powers from over the seas to establish new relationships which will bring more of the freedom and the prosperity that the Western world has long guarded for itself.

Dependent peoples differ in no essential human characteristics from those who enjoy independence. Peasants and fishermen, sailors and merchants, taxi-drivers and dancing girls laugh at the pleasures and cry from the pains of their own environment. Even in the lethargy of the tropics, they appreciate the good things of life and feel resentment against their poverty. They are aware of the gap which divides them from the "foreign masters," and they are beginning to believe that something can be done to narrow it.

These peoples are learning what we Americans also had to learn the hard way—that they cannot afford to be complacent, that in union there is strength. They believe that now is the hour to apply joint intelligence and mutual effort to their problems and to challenge innumerable conditions which they had heretofore accepted and endured.

Fundamentally their problems are economic in nature—too many people and too little land. Even in the name of law and order, it would be wrong to try to stabilize the existing divergence between the rich and the poor. Law and order are not the sole ends of political development. Opportunity for progress and improvement is at least as important as the right of property.

The current conflicts in Southeast Asia are not clear-cut clashes between right and wrong. Every situation is shot through with complexities and imponderables. It is never a case of a completely good, democratic nationalist movement versus a completely bad, fascistic exploiter; nor of a completely bad, communistic revolution versus a completely good and benevolent protector. No one power can claim a corner on wisdom or magnanimity. Japan and the Third International in their turn sharpened the grievances; they did not create them.

Psychological and cultural factors intensify economic and political struggles. Ancient races are proud of their inheritance, and they intend to preserve their heritage as the "Eastern ocean into which Western streams must pour." They are determined to be the masters of their own destiny and no longer pawns in the game of power politics. They will cling to their old customs as they choose, and they will modernize at a rate of speed which suits their own convenience. They have a way of sabotaging any impatient outsider who would try to hurry the pace. On the other hand when they adopt new ideas they utilize the tremendous inertia of the masses to set in motion forces that Western interests would sometimes prefer to keep stationary or silent.

The art of international diplomacy is the accomplishment of wise adjustments. The prestige of a nation rises when it adjusts its policies to the aspirations of the most people. Prestige falls when the states and their governments get out of tune with popular demands. In the clash between overseas "imperialists" and their distant wards, whatever the first loses the second gains. The erasure of German power in the Pacific after World War I, the eclipse of Japan and the plight of the United Kingdom, France, and the Netherlands during World War II, the withdrawal of the United States from the Philippines—all prepared the stage for the emergence of local leaders who have captured the imagination of the masses.

If Southeast Asia is astir with the desire for national determination, instead of being an amorphous mass of village and tribal units, it is because of Western thought and technology. If it reaches its goal it will be through borrowing more, not less, from Western teachers and Western examples.

The great powers do not by any means present a united front or a common attitude toward colonial problems. The British look upon the French and Dutch as stiff-necked. The Americans regard the British as scheming and selfish, and the Russians consider the whole lot as exploiters and bandits.

Every great power is primarily concerned with its problems at home and places its own strategic and economic needs first. Even a mother-country which has itself suffered under the heel of an invader is more interested in justice than in mercy in its relationships with its overseas possessions. It considers the historic responsibilities and interests of its own nationals more important than the needs of its colonials. It doles out to its dependent peoples only those energies and goods which are surplus or directly contributory to its own welfare. It expects from them a minimum of trouble and a maximum of sympathy and support in its own struggle to recover.

Overseas policies are conditioned by domestic politics. Socialists and Catholics in the Netherlands divide sharply on the issue of empire. French Communists and de Gaullists have radically different ideas for the future of Indochina. Economic pressure groups in every country favor foreign policies that contain the promise of privileges or profits. Once a liberal party arrives in power, its liberalism suffers from the demands of its responsibilities. The British Labor government is infinitely more cautious than the British Labor opposition party. Bevin sounds remarkably like Churchill when explaining British colonial policies to the House of Commons.

It is assumed that the objectives of foreign policies are peace, security, and welfare. Nations differ in their definitions of these objectives and in the relative importance which they ascribe to each one of the three. But all nations, including the United States, protest that no matter how their behavior patterns might be conditioned by geographic or historical factors, their particular policies are dedicated to the achievement of peace, security, and the best possible welfare for all.

The preference for peace is universal. The more a nation enjoys the good things of life, the livelier is its support of peace. It is idle to accuse the capitalist nations of preferring profits to peace; two bitter experiences have driven home the unescapable truth that the costs of war obliterate the apparent or temporary gains of any class or group. Some nations have learned that the unbridled quest for power leads only to destruction. Peace has been proved to be more precious than profit or power, but it is less desirable than the preservation of principle. It is a valid objective only as long as it is inseparably coupled with the continuing existence of the principles in which a nation believes and under which its people prosper.

The quest for security in the past has prompted every nation to develop and to seek reliance upon its own strength. In the modern world, security has taken on a new meaning and called for new techniques. Armaments are useless, except for the strong, and security for one is bound up in security for all. A local conflict anywhere has the inherent danger of involving the great powers, and if the great powers fight the whole world is a potential battlefield.

Security is more than a negative freedom from danger. In a positive sense, it implies a condition of society where peace and freedom are assured by the combined action of all, where all economic and financial resources are devoted to the common welfare, and where disputes are settled by diplomatic or judicial means. Those who have the power must be ready to use it instantly and unselfishly in the service of a common interest whenever and wherever threatened. Utopia perhaps, but this is the concept of security that every nation seeks.

Welfare, as the third objective of foreign policy, is the promise of a better world. To some it means more luxuries, to others it implies economic self-sufficiency, and to unnumbered millions it is the mere hope for a decent standard of living. Political parties derive their strength from their social programs. Nations choose their friends and enemies largely on the basis of ideological compatibility.

Every nation has discovered and admitted the necessity of basing their short-term "realities" on long-term "ideals." Men are both realistic and idealistic. They may infringe their ideals by their actions, but their lives are given direction and purpose by the ideals they cherish. They instinctively demand that their governments devote themselves to the pursuit of high ideals, even though expediency demands an occasional departure from the course or a trimming of the sails.

There is no single road which leads directly to the achievement of these objectives. Nations traditionally have neglected to pry into the secrets of successful cooperation toward common goals, but have relied upon methods of war and diplomacy to settle disputes as they arose. Some nations are now disposed to shift their sights and seek mutual understanding in a freer exchange of information, a broader basis for trade, and an expanded program for travel and study abroad. They hope that through their new instrumentality—the United Nations—they will discover more efficient ways and means to preserve the peace, to guarantee security, and to promote the public welfare, particularly in the backward areas.

The Rights and Interests of Indigenous Peoples

Southeast Asia is home for more people than there are in the United States. Their rights and interests take precedence over the rights and interests of the Western powers there, even if the latter are supported by four centuries of legal documentation. What may seem to the Western powers as impersonal items of policy may be looked upon in the dependent areas as personal insults or tragedies. Questions of profit or loss for the West are matters of life and death in the East. No matter how much Singapore means in the defense of the British Commonwealth, or Java to the prosperity of the Netherlands, or French Indochina to the prestige of France, all three places mean more than these things in human values to those who regard these outposts of empire as the land of their birth.

Southeast Asia is a region of divergent peoples. They have little in common except that all are weak and under foreign control in varying degrees. Their nationalisms are distinct, ranging from that of the Malays, who are perhaps the least democratically minded people on earth, to that of the Siamese, whose extremism increases with the years. Socially they vary from cannibalism to the most lofty and enlightened levels of human thought; economically they range from a Stone Age culture to a highly developed economy on the Western model.

The changing nature of their society is the most important factor in the power relationships in Southeast Asia. The masses have been separated from the ruling groups—in education, wealth, and political status. They now demand a greater voice in their own destiny. They have learned about the right of self-determination. They insist that the Atlantic Charter must apply to the Pacific and that the grandiose sentiments that were created primarily for Europe must also extend to Asia. They want a greater share of their own wealth for themselves, not as charity but as their right. The riches of the Indies stir Western imaginations—but to millions in that part of the world "even the tawdriest gewgaw in the five-and-ten-cent store would be wealth beyond dreams of avarice."

They lived in comparative contentment and isolation until the modern world broke down the barriers and brought them glimpses of material prosperity. They discovered a new and attractive political philosophy, and they wanted it for themselves. They asked for more guidance, less ordering; for more education and less domineering.

As they organized and developed movements for independence, they encountered major limitations upon their individual freedoms of speech, press, and assembly. They found little sympathy and few friends in the Western world. They turned to Canton and to Moscow, where they received paper support but no guns or dollars. Then they considered Japan. Because of its victories over China and Russia, because of its successful fight against its own international bondage, and because of its acceptance into the ranks of the great powers, Japan was regarded as a potential help in the struggle for freedom.

Daydreams about Japan's potential for help took on a different hue when the Japanese unleashed World War II in Southeast Asia. How could Japan be accepted as a liberator when it was acting worse than the worst imperialist in China? Japan's slogans, "Asia for the Asiatics," "The New Order," and "The Co-Prosperity Sphere in Greater East Asia," had a hollow ring when tested against the hard steel of the Japanese sword.

The impact of Japan shook established internal institutions and made it impossible to turn to Europe for help. At first, the dazed masses "accepted the exchange of one set of foreign masters for another with little more than a shrug of their fatalistic shoulders." Some chose to cooperate with Japan; some took to the hills. But whether collaborators or guerrillas, they came to think more than ever in terms of their own national advantage. As former leaders of the independence movements were released from jails or brought back from exile, they used the press and radio—or in some cases dangerous secret meetings—to sharpen the nationalistic consciousness of the masses. More people were brought into the political swim, and more were given jobs in local administration. More found in politics a means of livelihood, and more were given military training and drilled in the use of guns.

Their minds were poisoned against the return of their former masters. They were wooed with promises of self-government or gifts or independence. It was a mockery, but it necessitated a new consideration of the nature of independence. It forced the triumphant West, on its return, to grant at least as much independence as had been obtained under the Japanese. The burden of proof was placed on those who assumed the right to rule over anyone else, and not upon those who demanded the right to demonstrate their capacity to govern themselves.

The peoples of Southeast Asia admitted the need for the continuing military protection of the West, but they asked whether it could not be given more effectively by an international organization than by the re-establishment of imperial structures. They questioned whether independence, complete aloneness, was to be preferred to self-government within an interdependent commonwealth system. They feared that independence might be harmful if it meant only the freedom to sink or swim. They knew that it would not be easy for a new and helpless nation to keep its head above the swirling waters of international turmoil. They saw the unfortunate difference between independence for the nation and freedom for the individual, and they reasoned that they might suffer more under their own ruling groups in new positions of power than at the hands of their accustomed rulers.

There was never any question about Siam's regaining its complete independence. The militarism of Phibun Songgram was discredited and the flirtation with Japan was ended. After accounts were squared with the British and the French, after territories were returned to Indochina, to Burma, and to Malaya, Siam returned to its old ways of seeking advantage for itself by playing off the interests of one great power against the other.

Burma negotiated its independence with the United Kingdom and became the first country since 1776 to sever completely its connections with the British Empire. Britain retained no strategic bases in Burma, received no preferential trade position, and kept no control over Burma's policy as an independent state. On a temporary basis, Britain agreed to send a naval, military, and air force mission to Burma, and to provide training facilities for Burmese forces. Burma is not to receive defense missions from any government outside the British Commonwealth. Pending the negotiation of a definitive commercial treaty, Burma guaranteed that it would not take any action prejudicial to British commercial interests in Burma without prior consultation with the British government. If official policy "should involve the expropriation or acquisition in whole or in part of existing United Kingdom interests in Burma, the Provisional Government of Burma will provide equitable compensation to the parties affected." Britain undertook to write off $15,000,000 of the Burmese debt, while the balance is to be paid off in annual installments after 1952.

The Philippines were granted independence on July 4, 1946. The new Republic was by no means a slavish imitation of its American model. The government was more centralized, and the state had more powers over the individual. President Quezon once explained that "the United States' Constitution is predicated on the inalienable rights of the individual to life, property, and the pursuit of happiness, but under our constitution, what is paramount is not individuals. It is the good of the state, not the good of the individual, which must prevail." Pursuing its own independent way, the Philippines negotiated a treaty with the United States concerning joint use of bases in the Islands and providing for American military assistance and training of Filipino troops. The Philippines opened diplomatic and consular establishments throughout the world and plunged with vigor into the work of the United Nations.

The Netherlands East Indies, French Indochina, and Malaya are still non-self-governing areas. Malaya does not object strenuously to an improved status in the British Empire, but Indonesia and Indochina seethe with resentment and rebellion. Even if they are not successful in their fight for independence, their perpetual unrest weakens their overlords and makes it impossible for them to derive profits from their possessions. What good is an overseas empire that is a drain on the national budget and a source of worry and frustration? Furthermore, the strategic value of an insurgent colony is less than nothing because it will at the first opportunity sell out to an enemy of the mother-country in the interest of its own independence. A Yankee soldier on the Stilwell Road remarked, "There were more Burmese knives in the British backs that there were in the backs of the Japanese."

Nationalist leaders in all these countries are faced with new responsibilities. Their experience and strength have been gained in opposition and sabotage. Now they are called upon to assume administrative responsibility and preserve the order they have been prone to disturb. They must work for unity. They must satisfy the peasants and workers, but they dare not alienate completely the landlords and the bourgeois to whom they must look for economic leadership and financial support. They must think constructively. They must dare to call upon their followers for sacrifices instead of feeding them with palatable but impossible promises. Most important of all, they must develop dexterity in the arena of diplomacy, into which as colonials they had not even been permitted to enter.

Historic Interests and Policies of the Great Powers

Rights and interests of the great powers in Southeast Asia are more than matters of dollars and cents. In the prewar scheme of things the United States, the United Kingdom, the Netherlands, and France had important territorial interests and military and naval bases. Eight powers had eighteen jurisdictions in the islands of the Pacific which extended from Hawaii to New Guinea. Private investments made possible the development of agricultural, forest, and mining resources and the beginnings of industrialization. Loans to governments afforded native employment and contributed to the public welfare in the form of highways, railways, sanitation projects, and irrigation reservoirs and canals. Outbound ships carried cargoes of rubber, tin, coconut products, crude petroleum, quinine, lumber, and spices. Inbound steamers brought automobiles, machinery, cotton textiles, gasoline, iron and steel, paper, and different varieties of food.

The United States enjoyed the major proportion of this trade, and through it poured millions of dollars in profits into the pockets of the European investors. Everybody gained, because those profits came back to the United States eventually in the form of payment for surplus American exports to Europe. Southeast Asia has always been a vital factor in contributing to the high level of world commerce.

Shipping routes converge at Singapore; international air routes have essential bases at Manila, Bangkok, Singapore, Batavia, and Hong Kong. Submarine cables, anchored at a dozen places in Southeast Asia, carry commercial information and provide for the fast flow of news between East and West. A network of world-wide radio communications has key stations in the political and trading centers.

Intangible and cultural interests cannot be reduced to material values, but they contribute to the security, the welfare, and the prestige of the imperial powers. Schools and hospitals are often dedicated to the memory of some international philanthropist. Many colonial officials are better known for their humanitarian activities than for the quality of the performance of their routine responsibilities.

Every imperialistic nation thinks of its own empire as decent and proper, and as a valuable cog in the cumbersome machine of progress. Any shortcoming is excused as unfortunate but probably unavoidable, the sort of thing that is likely to mar any long record of activity. Without overseas exploitation both sides of the world would be poorer; with it, the whole of mankind is richer. Empire means more to government officials, military strategists, investors, businessmen, labor leaders, and idealists who take a direct interest in its affairs than it does to the man on the street; but the future of empire has a tangible and perhaps commanding relationship to everybody's pocketbook and military service.

Intrepid mariners in the service of Spain or Portugal first linked Asia to Europe. Their skill in seamanship was not equaled by royal statesmanship. The flag of His Catholic Majesty disappeared from the Philippines, but only after more than three centuries of intercourse and domination. The memory of Spanish and Portuguese sailors, fighters, and traders is unsavory, if sometimes gallant, on the China coast; but the stamp of Spain's civilization is more permanent than the legacy of her politics or commerce.

The British, the Dutch, and the French built upon the pioneering work of their Latin predecessors. They continued explorations, multiplied colonies, extended their conquests, and enlisted the energy of the entire nation in exploits which in Spanish times had resulted from some single individual's fanatical devotion to the search "for God, for glory, or for gold."

Great Britain has been a major Pacific power since the days of Captain Cook. Its interests equal, and in some respects exceed, those of the United States. It maintains the closest ties with the Pacific dominions, and those links are likely to become stronger rather than weaker. Great Britain still has colonial responsibilities in Hong Kong, Malaya, North Borneo, and Sarawak, and in the islands of the western Pacific.

British security has rested upon sea power. The British fleet regarded Hong Kong and Singapore as its impregnable bases in the Far East. Hong Kong was obtained in 1842 and grew rapidly in importance because of its excellent harbor, its political and strategic position off the coast of South China, its shipping and air connections, and its facilities for trade and finance. The British agreed not to increase their fortifications in Hong Kong as part of the Washington treaties of 1922. They developed Singapore as an alternative and completed the George V graving dock there in February 1938. The sentiment at the dedication exercises was that the empire in Asia was at least safe, let the Japanese do what they would.

The Singapore base seemed to afford adequate protection for the sea routes in the Pacific. These extended from Vancouver to Dunedin and from Shanghai to Sydney. Singapore was the nodal point in these ocean highways and was the gate to the British sphere of interest in the South and West Pacific.

The historic commercial interests of the British consisted of their trade, banking and insurance enterprises, shipping, and capital investments. One per cent of British overseas investments were in Hong Kong and another 3 per cent in Southeast Asia. The British investments were small but important in the Philippines and French Indochina, substantial in the Netherlands East Indies (primarily the Royal Dutch-Shell Company), and dominant in Siam, Burma, and Malaya. These commercial interests brought a contribution to British economy that was large enough to justify an important effort to keep them. Their loss would make a serious dent on the credit side of the balance of trade, throw many British workers out of their jobs, and disturb seriously the foundations of the British standard of living.

The British considered high among their interests the promotion of social welfare, a rising standard of living, a more balanced and progressive economy, and the organic growth of self-government throughout all their colonial territories. Their progressive attitudes contributed substantially to the enlightened doctrines of partnership and accountability which were later incorporated into the Charter of the United Nations.

The main lines of Britain's policy before World War II are quite clear in the light of her interests. The British supported the Open Door in commercial relations because foreign competitors could not match them in manufacturing skills or trade advantages. The anti-Russian policy at the turn of the century resulted from the British fear of the political consequences of the trans-Siberian railway. Land communications to East Asia removed Russia from the range of the British dreadnoughts, so Britain sought a new balance of power aimed against the tsar.

After the collapse of Russia in the Russo-Japanese war, Britain turned against a new rival and a new enemy, Germany. The alliances with France, Japan, and Russia were intended to offset the challenge of the kaiser. When he in his turn disappeared from the seats of the mighty, Britain sought her security in the world system created by the Treaty of Versailles. She joined the League, the Permanent Court of International Justice, and the International Labor Office, and took a leading role in the work of the technical commissions. She pursued parallel policies with the

United States until the eve of the war against Germany, Italy, and Japan.

The interests of the Netherlands are exclusively in the Indies. They lie in the defense triangle between Singapore, Manila, and Port Darwin and therefore constitute a vital concern both to Great Britain and the United States. The Dutch did not have the manpower or the equipment to provide defense against the invader, and Dutch strength has never been more than sufficient to preserve internal order. The security of the Netherlands Union cannot be guaranteed by the limited resources of the tiny mother-country.

It has been estimated that from one-fifth to one-tenth of the entire Dutch population depends on the industry and trade of the Indies. Ties with the colonies intrude into every sphere of life. The Dutch have invested $1,500,000,000 in the Indies (compared with the British $200,000,000, the Chinese $150,000,000, and the American $100,000,000), and they derive ordinarily an annual income of $150,000,000 from these investments in the form of profits, interest, wages, salaries, and pensions. The foreign trade of the Indies reached $1,000,000,000 in the boom year 1929, but it fell to half that amount before World War II. As the share of the Dutch declined, they abandoned free trade and resorted to the usual practices of discrimination and restriction.

Dutch policies in the prewar era followed those of the United Kingdom. The Dutch enjoyed some freedom of action as long as a semblance of peace was preserved; but they lost all power and initiative when the Nazis invaded their homeland. The government-in-exile fled to London and managed to keep a tenuous grip on its overseas storehouse. Even that disappeared when the Japanese hoisted their flag over the governor-general's palace at Batavia.

The French populace has never been enthusiastic about colonialism and has entrusted its overseas interests to kings or presidents, bishops or aristocrats. It has always regarded colonies as places for government employees, merchants, adventurers, missionaries, and ne'er-do-wells. It does not mind too much that Indochina is all that has been salvaged from centuries of disastrous warfare in Asia.

Indochina is one-third larger than France and borders on Siam and China. It has been incorporated into the French Empire by a succession of subtle diplomatic devices. The French would help one local potentate against another and demand a concession as the price for their help. They would convert that concession into a territorial right, expand the territorial right into a protectorate, and if possible, follow up the protectorate status with direct annexation.

For security, France depended upon native troops under French command, an inadequate naval force in East Asia, and a military tradition. She strengthened her land frontiers with China, poured millions into the Camranh naval base, and began the manufacture of small arms and ammunition on Indochina's soil. In spite of last-minute preparedness efforts, the French collapsed completely when struck by Germany and Japan.

France was completely mercantilist in her commercial policies toward Indochina. The colony existed for the well-being of the mother-country. It was one of the best-paying of all colonies and was a lucrative outlet for French capital and commodities. Foreign investments and foreign trade were small when compared with the Netherlands East Indies, but they were designed with the overwhelming purpose of profit for France. The French administrative staff was buttressed with experts in banking, industrial development, and commerce.

France prided herself on her *mission civilisatrice*. She claimed for herself "nationalism, peace, science, humane treatment, hospitals, schools, respect for local traditions and for the intellectual and social evolution of the natives." She afforded special diplomatic protection for Catholic missionaries and gained good will because of the traditional French courtesy, lack of color prejudice, and innate skill in the conduct of human relations.

French policies have been based on selfish and cold-blooded diplomacy. The French carved out their sphere in South China, while protesting faith in the Open Door. They led in the fight for democracy at home while exercising the most calculated imperial privileges abroad. They were the chief architects in the pre-1914 combinations against Germany and were so preoccupied with preserving their own existence in Europe that they had little energy or resources for problems in Asia.

The French never displayed any sympathy for the Chinese Republic nor for the national achievements of Chiang Kai-shek. Chinese success was potent wine and it might intoxicate the Annamites. A native uprising was the last thing in the world the French desired, and they were apprehensive about the prospect of any unified China. The French wanted law and order in China and none of the revolutionary tactics which jeopardized life and property. They hated liberalism and particularly the communism of the early twenties which aimed its darts at imperialist masters.

France was the cornerstone of the League of Nations, but she refused to become overly exercised when the collective system was threatened in Asia. France seemed content to let relationships in East Asia drift along without too much fuss, provided always that the strong powers should intervene to protect their legal positions against the aspirations of awakening native populations. France insisted upon her prerogative of dealing with Indochina in her own way without external meddlers, and was prepared to recognize as legitimate the same insistence on the part of Japan in China.

For a brief time the Socialist government of Leon Blum embarked upon an enlightened colonial policy. It promised more democracy and self-government for Indochina and instituted a comprehensive program of housing, flood relief, and agricultural assistance. These liberal inclinations were buried with collective security. France was obliged to abandon its New Deal in Indochina and to look to its allies to keep Japan in check.

The United States built its interests in Asia in a manner diametrically opposed to the methods of France. Americans seemed unable to appreciate the value of the Pacific area to their own security, and they never pursued a Machiavellian plan to utilize their overseas assets for an exclusive national advantage. Individuals plunged into trade adventures or placed their investments wherever there was hope for an honest penny. They would have recoiled before any suggestion of regimentation. If they made profits for themselves, they were quite content to let the government ponder the overall political perplexities of their free enterprise. They made money from sugar; the government could worry about the consequences of tying the Philippines to the American market. They placed the government in a constant dilemma, deciding just which individuals' interests most nearly approximated American interests.

In spite of the fact that the blue Pacific washed American shores, Americans were on the whole singularly unimaginative about the distant horizons. The whalers, the missionaries, the merchant-adventurers, and the beachcombers were the exceptions. The westward movement of the prairie schooners across the great plains and the westward voyages of sailing vessels around the Horn or from Boston to Panama were dual aspects of a common national surge. It exerted its force beyond California and carried "the American way of life" to Alaska and to Hawaii.

The Spanish-American War generated enthusiasm for further adventures and gave birth to the concept that the Pacific should be an American lake. Americans acquired Guam and the Philippines as the reward of their victory, and they took title to a part of Samoa. They lost their appetites for expansion as they learned that imperial responsibilities were heavy and development schemes costly. Americans were embarrassed by internal conflicts of opinion over whether they were morally justified in having an empire, whether it paid, and whether it was a military asset or liability. In the midst of their indecision and vacillation, they proceeded (with a great deal of satisfaction) to utilize their island pinpoints at Midway, Wake, Howland, Baker, Canton, and Enderbury as commercial air bases. At the same time they refused to spend the money required to build up an impregnable naval and military position, and they counted upon their diplomacy to halt the advance of Japan.

American commercial interests in Southeast Asia are comparatively slight. The automobile industry created an unusual demand for rubber; but the promise of synthetics has blighted the dreams of the producers of natural rubber. The American market for tin has also been reduced by the discovery and use of tin substitutes. World shortages of fats and oils have been overcome —greatly to the chagrin of Southeast Asia—and the monopoly of quinine has lost much of its advantage because of the medicinal value of atabrin. American producers and consumers of the capital crops of the tropics—sugar, bananas, pineapples, tobacco, tea, and coffee—can look elsewhere if the political climate promises to become unhealthy for their trade and investments.

American investments in Southeast Asia were scarcely more than $250,000,000[1] before World War II. They covered the entire gamut of government loans and private enterprise. America usually found the Philippines among its first ten customers in international trade, and it always looked to the Islands and their neighbors for 10 to 15 per cent of its vital imports. Americans were unwisely disposed to discount or overlook the value of the wealth in Southeast Asia, because they were continually dazzled by immediate profits in Japan or long-run dreams of fortunes to be made in China.

More than any other nation, the United States has magnified the value of its intangible interests. It prides itself on its cultural achievements and its contributions to educational and missionary enterprises. It lists the attainment of "orderly processes" in the conduct of international affairs high among its interests, and it repeats time and again its conviction that principles and ideals are more precious than silver and gold.

The principles that apply particularly to Southeast Asia are those identified as the American way of life since the days of the Bill of Rights in the Constitution and the Declaration of Independence. All men have the right to life, liberty, and the pursuit of happiness. All men have the right to be free from outside domination or discrimination based upon race, descent, creed, class, or previous condition of servitude. All men have the right to equality before the law, equality in economic opportunity, and to complete mobility in the social scale. Any mother's child can be president some day. All men have the right to an education, a representative, democratic form of government, and the four freedoms. In the words of Secretary Hull, "All peoples who are prepared and willing to accept the responsibilities of liberty are entitled to its enjoyment."

The policies of the United States have been born of the wedding of sincere idealism and practical diplomacy. They manifest the characteristics of both parents, but they are never the complete image of the one or the other. Historically, the United States has been an active participant in the conflicts of Asia. It has never taken shelter behind a cloak of isolationism in relation

[1] EDITOR'S NOTE. This estimate differs from the one given in Chapter I, which is based on Callis' study, *Foreign Capital in Southeast Asia*.

to that part of the world. It has championed the Open Door and the administrative integrity of China, and it has opposed the policies of Russia and Japan when they rode roughshod over the rights of others. It cooperated with the League of Nations, sponsored the Washington Conference, and sired the Pact of Paris. It took a firm diplomatic position with its pronouncement of the Stimson Doctrine. It made every concession it reasonably could in limitation of armaments conferences before it embarked upon its tardy defense program in the late thirties.

The United States and the great powers of Europe did not have a monopoly of the foreign rights and interests in Southeast Asia before World War II. Three Asian nations also had to be considered: India, China, and Japan. India and China had not achieved great power status—India had not even been granted dominion status—but they exerted tremendous political influence because of their huge size, their geographic nearness, and the numbers of their nationals who had settled abroad. India was preoccupied with its own struggles against Great Britain, and China found that all its strength was still insufficient to repel the invader. Both countries were conscious of their neighborhood and of their cultural affinities with peoples in Southeast Asia; but they realized they would have to wait for some time before they could translate their material and cultural interests into political advantages.

With Japan the case was entirely different. She was young, strong, and growing. She had emerged from her isolation, copied the West, increased her economic and military strength, and adopted the Western rules of the diplomatic game as her own. Japan too sought security and welfare, and added equality as her third objective. She combined the methods of peace and war, first, to win a place for herself in the ranks of the great powers, and second, to launch upon an independent imperial career of her own. She protested against discrimination on the part of the United States and some of the British dominions, while she was herself discriminating against all comers in China. She propagandized for an Asian Monroe Doctrine. In the name of security, she sought domination over Korea, Manchuria, China, and the islands of the Western Pacific. Possessed as she was with a gov-

ernment controlled by the military and a docile people steeped
in traditional beliefs in their divine· origin and their superiority
to other peoples, Japan followed an unswerving policy of expansion which led her to disaster.

As soon as Japan achieved her announced territorial objectives
in China and proclaimed the establishment of the New Order
(November 1938), she turned to Southeast Asia. She reasoned that
her need for self-sufficiency demanded an advance to the south
under the "joint efforts of diplomatic skill and national defense."
With the advent of the war in Europe, Japan became increasingly
arrogant in her relations with the Western powers. She sought an
understanding with the USSR and a settlement in China. She believed that she could take advantage of the deadlock in Europe to
take decisive steps to the south.

In 1940, as soon as the Germans overran the Low Countries,
Japan expressed a special interest in the *status quo* in the Netherlands Indies, and brought pressure to bear on the hapless Dutch
government to increase its exports from the Indies to Japan. She
warned French Indochina that she was determined to wipe out
at any cost all obstructions to building the New Order in East
Asia. She forced Indochina to agree to suspend all pro-Chinese
activities, including the supply of munitions and war materials
to China, and to agree to the dispatch of a Japanese military mission to northern French Indochina.

Since Japan's determination to extend her dominion entailed
the risk of war with France, the Netherlands, and even Great
Britain and the United States, it seemed expedient to conclude a
non-aggression pact with the Soviet Union and to sign a definitive alliance with the Axis powers. Throughout the summer of
1940 Japan maneuvered to increase her diplomatic pressure on
French Indochina and the East Indies, and to obtain German
assent to her occupation of the French Pacific possessions and outright annexation of the mandates.

In September the Tripartite Pact was signed. Japan regarded
the alliance as a necessary step in her preparations for military
action. She practically committed herself to war against her
European adversaries and expressed her willingness to wage war
against the United States. The alliance was presented to the pub-

lic as defensive; but the whole tenor of the discussions before the privy council showed clearly that the three powers were determined to support one another in aggressive action whenever this was considered necessary in furtherance of their schemes.

Japan set to work in earnest to build a Co-Prosperity Sphere which would include eventually French Indochina, the Netherlands East Indies, the Straits Settlements, British Malaya, Siam, the Philippines, British Borneo, and Burma. (India, Australia, and New Zealand were afterthoughts and added later when Japanese hopes were brightest.) In the excitement of her ambition, Japan offered to mediate for settlement of the European war if Great Britain would recognize the Co-Prosperity Sphere. Japan suggested a non-aggression pact with the United States which would exchange American recognition of "the Sphere" for a Japanese promise to respect the independence of the Philippines. In the midst of all this hysteria Shigemitsu was the only Japanese official who counseled caution, lest the British turn the tables on the Germans and thus destroy the whole dream house which Japan was building.

In the fall of 1940, Japan negotiated protective treaties with French Indochina and Siam and planned to stir up or utilize independence movements in French Indochina, Malaya, and Burma. Japanese military leaders began to prepare for attack. They conducted aerial surveys, completed hydrographic maps, printed occupation currency, and organized a Total War Research Institute to make appropriate studies. They stepped up fifth-column activities; they accelerated the armaments program; and they increased the fortifications on the mandated islands.

Japan exerted every effort to gain a stronger foothold in the Netherlands East Indies. The attitude of the Dutch was very cool to her proposals, and two economic delegations to the Netherlands East Indies were not able to persuade them to accept Japan's terms. The Dutch stiffened their attitude as a result of a growing confidence in their own capacities and the benevolent policies of Great Britain and the United States. Negotiations broke down in June 1941.

Japan planned her attacks all the while she carried on negotiations in Washington. By the time Admiral Nomura arrived there, preparations for an attack upon Singapore were rapidly progressing. By July 1941 arrangements were completed. Troops began practicing landing operations and storming pillboxes. Three divisions were prepared for action against French Indochina. After Vichy France accepted an ultimatum on July 24, 1941, Japan sent 40,000 troops to Saigon and Camranh Bay. She desired to secure bases for an attack upon Singapore preliminary to a campaign against the Netherlands East Indies.

This action on the part of Japan stimulated decisive American countermeasures. The United States froze the assets of the Axis, stopped trade between Southeast Asia and Japan, and created the United States Armed Forces in the Far East, with General MacArthur in command. The sparring match ended—the fight began.

Japan needed oil. The Netherlands East Indies were the target. In September the weather was favorable for attack. The Americans were still unprepared, the British were helpless, the Germans were swarming over the plains of Russia. The amphibious war games of the imperial army and navy foretold spectacular results. Tojo was impatient, Konoye hesitant. Tojo said, "I do not wish to discuss matters with Konoye; I am not sure I shall be able to control my temper." Tojo became prime minister and Nomura in Washington sorrowfully declared: "I am already a dead horse. For me it is too painful to continue in a deceptive existence, deceiving myself and others."

On November 10 the Japanese carrier task force was ordered to rendezvous in the Kuriles for its attack on Pearl Harbor. Combined Fleet Operation Order No. 3 of the same day fixed December 8 (Tokyo time) as "X" day both for Pearl Harbor and Singapore. The Japanese landing force appeared off Kota Bahru two hours and forty minutes before the attack on Pearl Harbor, and the Japanese bombers were over Singapore within the hour after the strike against the American fleet.

Japan had an unexcelled opportunity to guarantee her security and welfare by adopting an intelligent policy in Southeast Asia. Instead, she overplayed her hand. She might have inspired native peoples by becoming their friend and leader, but she chose the role of master and butcher. She might have become the great liberator. On the contrary, she turned back the hands of the clock.

She confounded confusion and destroyed such bases of individual dignity, freedom, and prosperity as already existed.

When the tide of Japanese aggression receded, it left the beaches strewn with litter and debris. They were the same beaches with the same sands; it was the same ocean with the same crosscurrents washing the same shores. But the mess had to be cleaned up before work on the breakwater could be started again and the harbor considered safe.

International Relationships after World War II

Japan's war lasted three and a half years. Within three and a half months, she had exploded the myth of Western invincibility and annihilated the prestige of the Western powers. Japanese planes sank mighty battleships, Japan's fleet dominated the South Seas, and Japan's armies were victorious in the Philippines, Malaya, Burma, and the Netherlands Indies. French Indochina collapsed without a fight, and Siam allied itself to Japan. Japan treated her white prisoners of war with a calculated indignity and barbarity that was designed to strike awe and trepidation into the hearts of the hapless inhabitants. The complacency, disunity, and unpreparedness of the West made the Japanese look stronger by comparison. There is no way to overemphasize the psychological amazement of seeing Japan's soldiers on guard, while strong, husky whites who had been accustomed to giving orders all their lives were lined up behind barbed wire fences and forced to humiliate themselves to receive their daily bread. As their own bodies wasted away, they symbolized the withering position of the West in Southeast Asia.

During those three and a half years of warfare, Southeast Asia was isolated except for short-wave radio or daring agents who brought news, hope, and promises from the outside world. Japan set up political administrations which gave the semblance of representation to the local populace but reserved real power for herself. Japan exploited the resources of the occupied areas for her own exclusive military benefit. Her radios, movies, magazines, and papers provided a constant barrage of propaganda which blasted the enemy, praised Japan, and tried to drive home the idea that Utopia could only come when she had won the war and made Asia safe for the Asiatics.

Japan's actions and policies became more brutal as the United Nations launched their counterattacks. Bloody fighting drove the Japanese out of the Solomons, New Guinea, Halmahera, and eventually the Philippines. Bombers and submarines sank transports and merchantmen, and the American navy sent practically every Japanese fighting ship to the bottom. Strategic bombers rained fire on the Japanese homeland. Combined Western military might stopped the flow of resources from Southeast Asia to Japan and had just begun the systematic mopping up of Japanese troops when surrender intervened.

Straggling, hungry, desperate Japanese forces in Burma, Malaya, French Indochina, and the Netherlands East Indies wandered about for weeks after the surrender in Tokyo Bay, waiting for the Allied forces to take them in hand. Some of these units remained subject to their commanders and maintained discipline. Others terrorized the countryside and sold or gave away their guns and munitions to whoever demanded them or offered a price for them. Still others hired themselves out as mercenaries to do the hatchet work for gangsters, rioters, "nationalists," or even the returning victorious armies. In Indochina, Japanese effectives were found among the troops of the French, the Annamites, and the Chinese.

As an editor of *Newsweek* (Harold Isaacs) expressed it, "The war settled nothing but Japan's attempt to master the continent. The war drew all the tangled threads of the past into a hard, swirling vortex, then flung them free again to assume new shapes and new combinations, and to create new patterns of conflict." The tempo of the "Revolt of Asia" speeded up. The Rising Sun suffered total eclipse and the nascent strength of India, China, Australia, and New Zealand emerged. The British, Dutch, and French lost their grip on their distant empires. The United States gained military ascendancy in the entire Pacific basin. Russia reentered the Pacific stage, taking over the role of the tsars, and contested with the United States to fill the political vacuums and satisfy the appeals of the teeming masses. None of the colonial powers came out of the war with sufficient manpower, weapons, or wealth to restore the *status quo*. None was able to avoid recognition of the deep-seated changes, but none was quite willing to admit the errors and the debts of the past and adopt a completely new approach to relationships in Southeast Asia.

The Asian peoples thought that they would receive immediate help. They expected the benefits of the Atlantic Charter and the immediate fulfillment of wartime promises. As Sjahrir, in Indonesia, said: "We have learned to handle instruments of power, but we do neither worship nor swear allegiance to power. We have faith in the future of humanity, in which a life based on humane principles will no longer be suppressed by power, in which there will be no wars and no reason for hostility between human beings."

Recognizing the necessity for protection, they looked to the United Nations. Anticipating their own need for cheap consumer goods, they asked for outside help to create an industrial machine of their own. They drew up plans, modified them, revised them, and put them in operation. In the enthusiasm of their liberation, they dreamed of accomplishing in a few years more than they had achieved in centuries. They were free. In Gandhi's words, they had gained the fifth freedom—the fundamental freedom to be free—and they meant to convert their pent-up energy into rapid modernization and industrialization. It was certain that they would never again be content with a bowl of rice per day or a menial role in a white man's paradise. Neither religious differences nor different nationalist aspirations could thwart them in the fulfillment of their social, political, and economic revolution.

As the people of Southeast Asia analyze their own position, they naturally think first of their own suffering and their own determination. Then they look to their neighbors, and after that to the nations beyond the seas. They regard Japan as a nation in eclipse, but not in the limbo of forgotten things. When she first talked of a hundred years' war, no one listened. A Japanese officer said, "When our schoolboys read about the War Of Greater East Asia, they will not read about defeat. They will read about the glorious fifty-five days' march to Singapore and the holy sacrifices of our wild eagles. Our aims in Asia are righteous aims—and the history of Japan is long."

Japan has lost her power to wage war in the foreseeable future; but she is learning valuable lessons in industry, science, transport, and even agriculture from the Americans. Japan is avidly absorbing American know-how and she will have a long lead in all these fields over her Asiatic competitors whenever she re-enters the family of nations. A former representative of the British Commonwealth on the Allied Council in Japan says: "There may have been a great deal of bunk in the propaganda slogan 'Asia for the Asiatics' but it still has meaning and life for most Asiatics. If it should ever become a powerful political weapon against Western interests, it is likely to be under Japanese leadership. Moreover, Japan's economic destiny would appear to lie mainly in East and Southeast Asia."

In many respects Japan is missed in Southeast Asia. Her cotton textiles were cheap, her trinkets were interesting, her fish were very good, and her ships were beautiful and useful. The combined efforts of the Allies and the native peoples have not been able to fill the vacuum created by the collapse of Japan's economy. She needs to make a living for her millions. Her traders and industrial workers might be welcome if they were to come again without benefit of militarism. They could fill empty shelves, work in new factories, operate camera stores that would be camera stores, and contribute in a hundred ways to an improving standard of living.

Suspicion lingers on that Japan is the "same doll in a new dress." The emperor, despite all efforts to democratize him, is still the Son of Heaven in the hearts and minds of the overwhelming majority of the Japanese people. He is more human and more powerful in his new status. He preserves and symbolizes national unity, and he might restore Japan to the leadership which blundering admirals and generals lost. Militarists are discredited, not for the suffering they caused, but for the catastrophe they brought upon the nation. Japanese, more than others, seem to love a parade of tanks and guns and goose steps. They would flock to enlist in American forces if the ranks were open. It is touch and go whether Japan has renounced forever her faith in the sword, particularly since it looks to her as if God is still on the side of the nation with the strongest battalions.

Inside Japan the liberals and progressives face the same crises which drove them to prewar fanaticism. They have learned new lessons about democracy and the rights of the individual. They will not let go the privileges they won unless—repeat, unless—the life of the nation is at stake. Even the Left in Japan is patriot first, party or trade-union member second. Japan has a new mission, to lead in peace instead of war; but the concept prevails that she has a mission. Communists do not preach internationalism—they advocate more intense nationalism. They demand the withdrawal of the occupation forces for the sake of their own national prestige. They do not say it in public, but they know Russia has little chance of exerting influence as long as the occupation is successful.

But if Americans tire of the job and refuse to live up to their responsibilities, that would be the opportunity for America's opponents to assert themselves more vigorously. Japan would then play both ends against the middle—avoid exclusive commitment to either and utilize her new-found power to increase her strength at home and to fish again in the troubled waters of Southeast Asia. Discontent among dependent or newly independent peoples would give a plausible opportunity for extreme nationalist groups in Japan, economic as well as political, to raise again the cry, "Asia for the Asiatics."

Japan is no longer thought of as the former enemy but has achieved the enviable status of everybody's potential ally. The pressure for a treaty grows. The feeling is that Japan should not be kept down, but should be helped to get up. The risks are not to be minimized, but the conviction is not to be denied that the recovery of Japan is vital to the recovery of Asia. Postwar treaty control must deprive Japan of the material means to renew aggression, guarantee the framework for continuing reforms, replace a power with a welfare economy, and inculcate a changed outlook that will respect the dignity of the individual and the rights of other nations. Beyond that it is a devout hope that Japan will use her newly won position in the pursuit of policies mutually beneficial to the whole of Asia, rather than in the resurrection of any imperialistic ambitions or aggressive adventures.

It was popular toward the end of the war to think that the nations of western Europe had gone down for the count. It was said that France was through, the Netherlands was crippled beyond help, and the British Empire had outlived its allotted span. It is remarkable how those countries have demonstrated their vitality and struggled to regain their shattered prestige.

At Yalta, Prime Minister Churchill emphatically told Marshal Stalin that he was not prepared to preside at a dissolution of the British Empire. His Conservatives writhed as the Labor party set about making international adjustments according to its own lights. The cry of "scuttle" was a nasty epithet, but it disappeared as most Britons became convinced that the Labor government was right in abandoning the old forms of empire in favor of free association.

Great Britain's major dilemmas resulted from her economic crisis. The war had cost billions in attrition and ordinary wastage. Before the war Great Britain had assets of $20,000,000,000 abroad. During the war she was obliged to liquidate half of them. In addition she became a debtor for another $20,000,000,000 that other nations had accumulated in London banks. Her own struggle for existence became desperate, in spite of her "glorious" victory. Imports were necessary to live, and there was too little of British exports, shipping, and income from overseas investments to pay the bills. Lend-lease expired precipitately, and the American loan provided only a temporary and expensive expedient. Great Britain subjected herself to a regime of austerity, cut down her expenses, marshaled every dollar, and pared her overseas commitments.

She mustered out soldiers to work in the mines. It was more important to increase the supply of coal than to provide an extra measure of defense. The budget for the services necessitated drastic reduction in the occupation forces in Germany and complete withdrawal from Japan. The bases at Hong Kong and Singapore were slighted. The British were faced with virtual withdrawal of their fleet from Eastern waters and the sacrifice of the entire air arm east of Suez.

The economic crisis at home provided new demonstrations of the value of Commonwealth relations. The Dominions paid part of the defense bills that had been borne primarily by Great Britain before the war. They were generous with loans, credits, and gifts. The preferential tariff agreements guaranteed a steady exchange of food and raw materials for manufactured products. Thus financial burdens were equalized, and the Commonwealth as a unit was strengthened.

In the realm of foreign affairs Great Britain consulted continuously with the Dominions. In the matter of making peace in Europe, in determining attitudes toward Germany or Japan, or in presenting the British case at international conferences, there appeared to be complete cooperation. Not that the Dominions sacrificed any independence of judgment—on frequent occasions the foreign minister of Australia, as the spokesman of the middle powers, took violent exception to the procedures and decisions of the Big Three. An Australian regularly represented the British Commonwealth on the Allied Council in Tokyo, and a Commonwealth conference met at Canberra to establish a common policy in treaty-making with Japan. Each member of the Commonwealth had as many internal differences of opinion as Great Britain herself, but postwar "British" policy was a composite of the entire membership of the Commonwealth.

The British looked to the United Nations as the great hope for postwar peace, security, and prosperity. In spite of their blasted hopes in the earlier League of Nations, they considered collective security the only effective replacement for the *Pax Britannica*. They had no appetite for the polarization of international relations into Russian and American extremes. The British had little love for the Russians and disliked the prospect of a Europe united under the hammer and sickle. They appreciated American help and understood the strength of the American reservoir of power; but they felt an inner repugnance at becoming in their turn a British rowboat in the wake of an American battleship. They were determined at all costs to retain their independence of judgment and their freedom of action. They insisted upon their own formulas for the Socialist solution of internal problems and the remolding of their interests overseas.

British interests in the East have traditionally been guarded by the "life line" through the Mediterranean and the Suez Canal and by the magic circle of imperial naval bases that runs from South Africa to India to Malaya and Australia. Typical British sentiment has been "God help the Empire if the Germans or the Russians ever break the life line." The British counted upon their own bases, the strength of India, and their friendship with the Moslems to protect the shore sides of the path patrolled by the Royal Navy.

The traditional pattern of security was shattered by World War II. The Mediterranean was closed and the Suez Canal became useless. The development of atom bombs and air power revolutionized the approach to problems of defense. The British sought a new route to the Indies. They looked upon Kenya in East Africa as a replacement for bases in Palestine and the eastern Mediterranean; and they planned a string of bases across Africa north of the equator as an alternative life line. They would develop in Africa new footholds to take the place of those they lost when they withdrew from India, Burma, Iran, Egypt, and Greece.

The British have no intention of abandoning or even diminishing any of their vital interests in the Far East. The term "Far East" itself reflects the age-long paramountcy of the British in that area, because Japan, China, and Hong Kong are the "Far East" only from the British point of view. The British may change the nature of their commitments or modify their tactics to suit the circumstances, but they think fundamentally in terms of recouping and expanding their permanent influence and power.

The British after the war pursued modest and mature policies in both Japan and China. The guns of the British fleet were less loud than those of the American in the Pacific victory, so it seemed more becoming for British voices to be less strident than American in administering the peace. One British spokesman said: "I rather like the occupation of Japan. It seems that the Americans have done the same things we would have done, and it hasn't cost us a penny." The British have given silent support to most American policies, they have put themselves on record when they have objected, and they have avoided committing themselves in the eyes of the Japanese. The British have received the advantages implied in every American decision without having to bear the responsibility for having made it. This is a reversal of the customary British-American relationship in China. There the British have been the historical leaders. The Americans enjoyed the benefits of the British concessions, but the British bore the brunt of Chinese anti-imperialist charges.

The British have maintained discreet silence in matters of Chinese policy since the war. They avoided any one-sided endorsement of the Kuomintang and resisted its pressure to force them to put a clamp on the activities of the Chinese liberals and Communists in Hong Kong. The British were not involved as the Americans were in sending economic aid, lend-lease supplies, surplus goods, and military missions. Thus they escaped the antiforeign attacks of both the Kuomintang and the Communists. The Kuomintang blamed the Americans for "too little and too late," and the Communists criticized them for making a travesty of their own traditional policy of non-interference in the internal affairs of another sovereign state. The British followed a "hands-off" course, regardless of their own personal feelings, and were in a position to resume trade with whichever side might win.

When British fortunes were lowest, they were faced with Chinese intimations that Hong Kong should be returned to China. Hong Kong's population is Chinese, except for the 20,000 Europeans who live in comparative luxury above and apart from the masses. The British title is founded on the unpopular right of conquest. The Chinese argued that Hong Kong was a feudal and comprador stronghold, a hide-out for political refugees, and a center for rebellious activities. They contended that the Chinese in Hong Kong had no political rights and no hope of a free or prosperous future.[2] The Chinese arguments lost their force as conditions deteriorated in China, and as of old the Chinese men of means took their families and their concubines and crowded the ships and planes headed for the British colony.

Chinese merchants and investors have an economic haven in Hong Kong. They warehouse their goods, they keep their money in the banks, and they engage in business or even smuggling, if it promises to be lucrative enough. They like the protection of the law and the sanctity of contracts in Hong Kong. They have the best of both worlds. They go to and from China exactly as

[2] EDITOR'S NOTE. Since the war Britain has been working out a form of self-government for Hong Kong. One great difficulty is that the colony has a floating population: not much more than a third of the Chinese remain more than ten years before returning to China. The legislature now has a popular majority.

they please, and in the colony they have personal safety and a stable currency.

To the British, Hong Kong is no longer esteemed as a tenable base. The events of Christmas day, 1941, proved that it is at the mercy of the power that controls China. However, it is a valuable trading center and outpost of empire. Respected old firms have their headquarters there, and newer firms are moving to Hong Kong from Shanghai.

The colonial conscience of Socialist Britain finds it difficult to overcome deeply rooted attitudes and behavior patterns. Hong Kong is such a special problem. The governor may be a benevolent despot, but it requires a firm hand to control the political tides to which the colony is exposed. The British have brought good roads, a magnificent harbor development, and hospitals and schools (for those who can pay the bills); but they have not brought any coordinated program for social insurance or self-government. Some Britons hold the opinion that even in Hong Kong old-fashioned colonialism is living on borrowed time. "Hong Kong is the shop window of Great Britain in China, and behavior on that small stage can do much to make or mar policy on a vaster one. A progressive democratic community in Hong Kong would have great repercussions in China." With all the complications of foreign policy elsewhere, the British official attitude is cautious and sporadic with regard to the colony. But it is predicated on the assumptions that the naval importance of Hong Kong is gone, that its economic prosperity is tenuous, and that its great challenge is to show China what Britons at home have learned about the "middle way."

Postwar British activities in India and Burma have been characterized as "the most far-sighted pieces of imperialism we have done for a generation." The withdrawal from India renders possible a new and beneficial relationship between Britain and an independent India that may well be far more profitable to the British Commonwealth than all the years of the old-fashioned raj.

Great Britain did not have the support of Gandhi's All-India Congress party during the war, and it faced the enmity of Subhas Chandra Bose and his Free India Army from Southeast Asia. Still Great Britain received so much help from India that she was obliged to liquidate all her net assets in India to pay the bills. In addition she was obliged to borrow and obtain credits from India amounting at the war's end to $5,000,000,000. Obviously the continuation of the colonial status was impossible.

Great Britain, in March 1946, sent Lord Pethick-Lawrence and Sir Stafford Cripps to work out with the representatives of the Congress, the Moslem League, and the princely states a constitutional regime to which the British could turn over power. Bitter differences of opinion resulted in communal riots and violence. The British had every opportunity to plead the necessity for the continuation of their rule, but the government decided against it. In February 1947, Prime Minister Attlee announced that "His Majesty's Government wish to make it clear that it is their definite intention to take the necessary steps to effect the transference of power into responsible Indian hands by a date not later than June 1948."

On August 15, 1947 the British relinquished their paramountcy over the princely states and transferred their power to Moslem Pakistan and the Hindu Union of India. Both were given complete sovereignty. They were to work out their internal destinies and choose freely whether they wished to remain within the British Commonwealth. India was given her freedom. One observer wrote: "No Bell-Tydings Act was passed to ensure that Britain should be on a parity with the Indians, and plans were made for a complete evacuation of the British army."

British policies in Ceylon and Burma were equally far-sighted in effect, even though they may have been forced upon the government by circumstances beyond its control. On February 4, 1948 Ceylon became a full-fledged, self-governing Dominion. Under the terms of the 1947 defense agreement Great Britain was given the right to station British troops on the island, and the Royal Navy retained the use of its base at Trincomalee.

During the war, Great Britain dreamed of "assisting Burma's political development until she can sustain the responsibilities of complete self-government within the British Commonwealth." On liberation, Great Britain presented a plan to return to the *status quo ante* 1941, provide for a slow tempo toward autonomy, preserve a special position for the Karen states, and keep prime power in the hands of a British governor who would be properly limited by a Burma legislature. Here again, Mr. Attlee recognized the innate dynamite of Burman nationalism, and agreed to grant Burma the same privileges that he had given to India. On January 4, 1948 the last British governor formally handed over full political control to the new Burmese government. Great Britain salvaged a significant amount of good will, a satisfactory economic interest in Burma, and a defense treaty that permitted her to maintain a military training mission in Burma until 1950.

Great Britain was obliged to "eat bitterness" in her relations with Siam. The British smarted under the Siamese declaration of war against them, the Siamese activities on the Malay and Burma borders, and the treatment given to British nationals and concession-holders during the war. The British were disposed to hold the entire nation guilty for the acts of its government, and were not inclined to listen to American suggestions to treat the Siamese with leniency. The British-Siamese treaty of January 1, 1946 obliged the Siamese to pay arrears of loans and pensions from their blocked funds, restore Allied property with compensation for losses and damages, turn over 1,500,000 tons of rice as indemnity, sell all their rice at an agreed-upon price, and accept a policy of non-discrimination against British interests. Siam further agreed to join the United Nations, participate in regional security pacts, and negotiate supplementary agreements covering shipping, air traffic, and air and naval bases. The intransigence of the British has had an adverse effect on their influence in Bangkok, and has caused a substantial drop on their share of international trade and investments in Siam.

British policies in Malaya and the colonies adjacent to Southeast Asia reflect the Socialists' desire to ease the life of the colonials and gain friendly allies and partners in place of unwilling vassals. Allotments under the Colonial Development and Welfare Acts call for direct allocations for roads, port improvements, and health and sanitation programs. Millions are to be spent for higher education and training colonials for more important posts in the government service. Research councils and advisory commissions have been appointed to assist the colonial office in its schemes for marketing controls, crop insurance, and price stabilization. This program is a partial answer to native unrest.

In Lord Hailey's words, pronouncements on British colonial policies are usually "platitudes about our intentions and beatitudes about the future of colonial peoples." At the end of the war, Britain recognized the necessity of paying serious attention to the demands of the colonials, and saw in the colonies new sources of help in coping with the economic crisis. Increased production there would fill gaps in the skimpy British diet, earn larger supplies of dollars, and provide markets for export goods. Pressure from Britain's critics forced the pace, particularly in areas of direct concern to the United Nations.

In the very early days of imperialism, the British considered it to be the natural order of things that parts of Asia should come under the dominion of the more enterprising West. Colonies were regarded as properties to be farmed entirely for the benefit of the mother-country. It was a significant step forward during the nineteenth century to add the concept of moral trusteeship for the welfare and advancement of the colonial peoples. World War II accentuated the objective of self-government, which had been accepted after World War I. The British believed that it would be premature to grant self-government before it was reasonably sure that a colony could provide a representative legislature and a competent executive.

The British entertained an honest doubt whether self-government would bring greater contentment or provide a better guarantee for social and economic progress. It was indisputable that economic progress was essential. Therefore the resultant policies admitted the advisability of eventual self-government, but emphasized the greater importance of immediate economic assistance. Self-government would be granted where it could not be resisted, but otherwise it would be withheld until a native majority had reached a stage of development that would enable it to take its own share in the exercise of its political rights.

The British did not hold up the ideal of independence. They preferred their former colonies to remain as self-governing units within the framework of the Commonwealth. But they offered the choice to the colonies to sever connections if they preferred. It was the British objective to "make them conscious of the value of connections with us; to make them prize our ideals even if they have different traditions, a different social structure, and a different outlook on life." The final curtain has rung down on the era of the white rajas in the British portions of Southeast Asia, but with local populations backward or split into antagonistic factions, enlightened British rule can be expected to continue indefinitely. The British have demonstrated an ability to keep in step with the march of progress that has at least temporarily strengthened their international position.

This is more than can be said for the Dutch and the French. On December 6, 1942 the Queen of the Netherlands stated that Dutch policy would look to the creation of "a commonwealth in which the Netherlands, Indonesia, Surinam, and Curaçao will participate, with complete self-reliance and freedom of conduct for each part regarding its internal affairs, but with the readi-ness to render mutual assistance. . . . This would leave no room for discrimination according to race or nationality." The Dutch looked forward to the creation of a partnership as a solution which would give complete satisfaction to a national conscious-ness that promised to become unmanageable as a result of the Japanese occupation.

On August 17, 1945 a constituent assembly at Batavia, called by the Japanese, proclaimed the end of 350 years of Dutch rule, declared independence, and set up the Republic of Indonesia. For thirty days the Dutch were helpless. Terrorism swept the countryside. On September 17, the British arrived, accompanied by the Dutch and their Ambonese auxiliaries. For more than a year, fighting continued while the Dutch and the Indonesians negotiated. When the Linggadjati Agreement was initialed, the British pulled out. They had not relished their assignment and were glad to end their thankless task. When General Sir Philip Christison landed, he is reported to have said, "We did not come to give this country back to the Dutch." It was his task to effect the surrender of the Japanese and restore law and order.

By the terms of the Linggadjati Agreement, the Dutch recog-nized the Republic of Indonesia as part of the United States of

Indonesia, which would also include Borneo and East Indonesia as separate states. All would remain within the Netherlands Commonwealth. The problems of police power and the actual degree of Indonesian independence were vaguely treated, and disputes over interpretation led to police action in the summer of 1947. The Dutch army in Indonesia had grown to 100,000 men by that time, and its action was spearheaded by a marine commando division trained and equipped in the United States. The Dutch occupied Republican territory, alleging bad faith and communism. The Republicans resorted to scorched-earth tactics.

The Dutch were not pleased with United Nations interference with their domestic affairs. But they were a small nation and amenable to international pressure. Their recovery in Europe depended upon American good will and loans. Therefore they entered into new negotiations and signed a truce agreement aboard the USS *Renville* on January 17, 1948. Each side quickly accused the other of violating the terms, and the Dutch resorted to new police action in December 1948.

Their military action brought discouraging results. As their own liberal leaders predicted, it generated countermeasures and intensified the bitterness of the nationalists. Partnership as equals might have been acceptable and workable in 1945; it was impractical and unacceptable in 1949. The Dutch still talked of an Netherlands-Indonesian Union, a federal interim government, and an accelerated transfer of their power to a representative federal government earlier than July 1, 1950, the date specified by a resolution of the Security Council. But their promises do not ring true in Indonesia. They are looked upon as masks for a stubborn insistence upon the retention of Holland's vital stake. The Dutch cannot lose Indonesia and keep their status in Europe. Yet they have not been sufficiently astute to win the Indonesians as friends, nor sufficiently strong to keep them in line as "unwilling vassals." Dutch security, peace, and welfare are all jeopardized as long as civil disorder continues to disturb the "dull equator."

The French have been no more successful than the Dutch in re-establishing their international position in Southeast Asia. From the fall of France to V-J day, French Indochina was the major operations base of Japan. The Vichy colonial administration rendered satisfactory service to the Japanese army until March 9, 1945, when the Japanese interned French officials and soldiers and declared the native governments of Annam, Cambodia, and Laos independent of France. The government of Annam included Tongking and Cochin China in its jurisdiction.

The Free French forthwith issued a declaration at Brazzaville that they would create a federal Indochinese state as an integral part of the French Union, having economic autonomy but with its foreign interests represented by France. Five months later, when Japan collapsed, the anti-Japanese and anti-French Viet Minh proclaimed the independence of Viet Nam (Annam, Tongking, and Cochin China). The French and the British returned to Indochina between September 1945 and January 1946 to restore Indochina to its rightful sovereigns, but the native peoples welcomed the would-be liberators as enemies. The French explained the hostile attitude of the Vietnamese as due to Chinese looting, Japanese propaganda, and American bombing. When the Chinese occupied the north, they looted indiscriminately; and when the Americans bombed the Japanese military installations they destroyed everything from the work animals to the works of art. At a later date, communism was blamed for the bitter anti-French feeling, and the Vietnamese were accused of being drunk with liberty.

Viet Minh propaganda leaves no room for doubt concerning its motivation. It accuses the French of causing misery and famine by their exploitation. It speaks of French "poison," "corruption," "slavery," and "terror," and asks: "Is civilization culture or obscurantism; is self-government treason or patriotism?" The Viet Minh posted signs on the telephone poles which said: "Anyone who cooperates with the French will be shot on the spot."

Nothing daunted, the French proceeded methodically to restore as many as possible of their lost rights and interests. They negotiated a treaty with Cambodia which recognized its autonomy, but provided that the king should receive a French commissioner as a personal adviser and as a representative of France and the Federation of Indochina. The French then signed a *modus vivendi* with Laos, creating a separate kingdom there.

They explained that this arrangement resulted from the necessity of protecting Laos from the Annamites on the east and the Siamese on the west. France then made boundary adjustments with Siam which returned to French Indochina the territories previously ceded to Siam under Japanese auspices.

France next negotiated a very important treaty with China. Following the wartime British-American lead, she abandoned the old, unequal treaties and sought a new basis for good neighborliness, friendship, and alliance with China. The treaty provided that French troops should replace Chinese in North Indochina, and agreed that the Chinese should have the traditional advantages of the congregations or communities in Indochina. It established a customs zone at Haiphong, provided for a customs accord to be signed at a later date, and fixed the terms for an anticipated repurchase of the Chinese section of the Yunnan Railway.

In March 1946, the French signed a treaty with Viet Nam recognizing it as a free state with its own government, parliament, army, and finances, forming part of the Indochinese Federation and the French Union. France agreed to a referendum on reuniting the three provinces into Viet Nam, and Viet Nam promised not to oppose the French army when it should arrive in the north to replace the Chinese. The problem of the referendum was not settled satisfactorily, and "someone" fired on the French the moment they arrived in Tongking.

Negotiations between Viet Nam and France bogged down on the question of complete independence or commonwealth status. The French wanted to talk about their properties, a customs union, consular representation, and integration of communications. The Vietnamese were more interested in their democratic liberties and the satisfaction of their nationalist aspirations. Neither party showed sufficient tolerance or understanding to prevent a bloody war in Indochina. No one is secure, and no one can undertake successful social and economic reforms as long as the fighting continues. The president of the French council of state expressed his government's point of view: "Nothing has been spared to reestablish agreement with Vietnam. It is our duty to do everything to protect French lives and interests, the blood of our children, and that of a people whom we recognize as having the right to political liberty, and which ought to have its place in the French Union. We have been placed in a position where we must stand face to face with violence. Our soldiers and our friends can count on our vigilance and resolution. These harsh realities will not change our principles. The old colonial system has been resolved. In our republican doctrine, colonial possession only achieves its destiny when it ceases to exist, the day when colonial peoples are able to govern themselves."

On another occasion he added: "This war has been imposed upon us—we did not wish it—we do not wish it. Some time we will be able to sit down with representatives of the Annamite people with whom we shall be able to speak the language of reason. France will not fear the union of the three Annamite countries any more than she will fear the independence of Vietnam in the French Union."

These words have a curious unreality. It would seem that France, with her hands full at home and with her international prestige as low as it has ever been, would take her cue from the British and either leave a territory where she is not wanted or give some proof that her policies and troops are vital for the well-being of Indochina. Until she does one or the other, she is missing opportunities to boost her international stock and reestablish friendly contacts with people who are determined that they can do without her.

Like France, China has had difficulty in carrying the weight of international affairs that history and geography have assigned to her. During the war she pretended to great-power status. New agreements with the United States and Britain abolished the last of the unequal treaties. Representatives of China attended international conferences, and she was considered one of the Big Four in discussions about the future of Asia. Beneath the pretense, however, the power position of China was slighted. She was given little voice in decisions of strategy. At the Yalta Conference, which disposed of part of her territory, China was not invited to be present, nor even informed that Chinese questions were to be discussed.

China's main international problem is to achieve the "stable and effective government," or "the free, united, and democratic China" which the international notes talk about. China in turmoil is more an invitation to others to interfere in her affairs than a threat to intervene in the affairs of others. However, more than one official in Southeast Asia has been heard to say, "The Japanese aggression was bad enough, but we would be hopeless if we were ever faced with an aggressive China."

The central government of China has become aware of the value of its people and its assets abroad. For fifteen centuries, China forbade emigration and officially branded emigrants as traitors to their ancestors' graves. Without official protection of any kind, the Chinese overseas took any sort of job that would enable them to eke out a living. They depended upon their own devices for their political and social well-being. They banded together in local groups, maintained their own schools, and organized secret societies as they had in China from time immemorial. Without any qualms about the families they left behind, they intermarried with local women. They never worried about citizenship or problems of dual allegiance. Their children might become part of their adopted country, but the older generation never lost their nostalgia for China. Above all things, they wanted to return to their old homes to die.

Since the advent of the Republic, Chinese overseas have developed a keen interest in Chinese politics. They wrote about them in their local newspapers; they joined the Communists or the Kuomintang; they sent delegates to the government and party meetings in China; and they remitted huge cash subscriptions to China through the local consulates or party headquarters. Overseas Chinese used their chambers of commerce as spokesmen when they were without diplomatic representation. They took sides in China's international problems. They fanned the flames of anti-imperialism and organized effective anti-Japanese boycotts. When the war broke out they volunteered for defense service, but the colonial governments hesitated to arm and train them. Later, they cooperated with the guerrillas and became leaders in the resistance movement.

Postwar China has been handicapped in its overseas activities, but it has indicated its intention of protecting the vested interests of Chinese against discrimination by local governments or, if need be, against violation by the colonial powers. China has sought new treaties covering questions of friendship, commerce, personal and property rights, and immigration. At the Asian Conference in New Delhi in 1947, the Chinese delegate demonstrated the diplomatic skill for which China's diplomats are justly famous. He immediately took the forum to berate the powers for their attitude toward the Chinese, instead of waiting for them to air the practices of the Chinese which had led to the discriminatory acts.

The successes of the Communists in China have posed new problems. The enthusiasm for "unity" in China has waned since it appears that this would mean unity under the Communist aegis. Communist gains in China have strengthened the hands of Communists working among the Chinese abroad, but those same victories have deepened the fears and sharpened the efforts of enemies of communism. China as a nation is not feared in Southeast Asia as long as it is weak, divided, and permeated with peaceful intentions. But it will be dreaded beyond measure if it threatens to become strong, united, and a possible tool of Moscow. Fears will generate new discriminatory and protective acts.

Differences about communism will increase the fissions in the already divided opinions of Chinese overseas. The Kuomintang-Communist split will give way to Stalinist-Trotskyite, nationalist-internationalist, and native Communist–Chinese Communist divisions. Their arguments can easily spread into bloody uprisings. More Chinese Communist leaders are infiltrating into the South; but more refugees from the Communists are also moving in. The result is likely to be an intensification of local problems, with Chinese in more pronounced roles on both sides. As the new national governments or the colonial governments necessarily take firmer steps for the preservation of internal stability, they will risk more frequent diplomatic clashes with China. And China can be expected to exert more influence abroad as its stability increases at home. China is a potential giant in the international relationships of Southeast Asia.

India has the same potentialities, if she overcomes her domestic difficulties. She intends to take over where Japan was knocked out as the leader of the East. The violence of the first days of freedom has subsided. Experienced leaders of India and Pakistan are putting into effect many existing plans for agricultural expansion and the development of their abundant natural resources. India is suppressing communism as well as all other troublesome political movements with forthright sternness. She is determined to tolerate no political sabotage, lest the discontent of the poorly housed, poorly clothed, and sparsely fed millions should erupt.

India looks upon a firm alliance with Great Britain as plain common sense. India needs British capital goods, machine tools, and technical skills. She would be unwise not to take advantage of long British experience in guarding the inner Asian frontiers and the long Indian coast line. India has no intention of becoming involved with Great Britain or any other country over questions of minority status. Nehru bluntly told his followers in Malaya that India could not extend extraordinary protection to her sons who chose to remain in an alien land.

Pandit Nehru is one of India's greatest assets. He is a mixture of East and West and understands the intricacies of both. He is determined that the Western world must stop treating Asia like a poor relation. A resurgent Asia intends to be satisfied no longer with a minor or secondary role in world affairs. The previous disdain of Asia and lack of interest in her have resulted from thinking of her as a kind of fringe of Europe. Asiatic problems have been considered only as they related to those of Europe. In Nehru's view, this state of affairs must end, because Europe needs Asia as much as Asia needs Europe.

In 1947 Nehru called a conference of Asian nations to review the position of Asia in the postwar world and to exchange ideas on problems common to all. The meeting was a sounding board for conflicting points of view. It revealed the Asian emphasis on cultural and economic problems, and it further exposed the importance of East and Southeast Asia in the solution of those problems. The delegates from the Soviet territories in Asia remained aloof, or gave patterned, generalized answers to questions directed to them. No one showed an interest in an Asian bloc or any permanent organization outside the United Nations. International cooperation was recognized as being more important than Asia for the Asiatics.

The Arab states disclosed their faith in the Arab League, and the Southeast Asian states served notice that they had no intention of being dominated by either India or China. They reported that in some instances there was more local hostility toward rich Indians and Chinese than toward wealthy Europeans. A Mohammedan's conviction was that "Indian landlords, Chinese merchants, and Japanese generals would all be fagots in a Moslem hell." There was general agreement that Asians should exert unified pressure until all Asia should rid herself of foreign rule. When political freedom was won, Asia should concentrate on economic development, but should never let foreign loans be the opening wedge for the revival of economic imperialism.

India assembled a second conference in 1949 in behalf of the Indonesians. Representatives of nineteen Asian countries, representing half the world's population and one-third of the membership of the United Nations, met in New Delhi. They showed restraint in their deliberations and cautious wisdom in their resolutions. They telegraphed the Security Council their resolution that the Dutch should agree to an immediate settlement with Indonesia and turn over sovereignty in the East Indies before July 1, 1950; and they concluded their telegram with the hope that the Council would realize the strength of the feeling behind it.

The second resolution of the conference pledged the participating governments to continue consultations among themselves on the Indonesian problem until a satisfactory solution was reached. The third resolution recommended that the nineteen nations represented at the conference should "consult among themselves in order to explore ways and means of establishing suitable machinery, having regard for the areas concerned, for promoting consultation and cooperation within the framework of the United Nations."

India's leadership in Asian solidarity opens new vistas for Asia in the game of world politics. In the words of the *New York Times* correspondent who covered the conference, Robert Trumbull:

"This was a conference strictly of Eastern peoples with the conspicuous exceptions of Australia and New Zealand. The participants represented Hindus, Moslems, Buddhists, Christians, and minor religions of half the globe. Races represented were white, black, brown, yellow, and odd mixtures, and the languages run into hundreds of dialects.

"They spoke for many cultures, some very ancient and all now striving to rise from decay. They came from nations far behind the West in industrialization, literacy, and standard of living, yet which supply raw materials like oil and metals without which the West could not maintain its pre-eminent material position.

"The atmosphere of the conference produced heightened awareness of the vast area's industrial potential, its possibilities for consumer expansion and, above all, its strategic position in the current struggle for power between Russia and the West."

In March 1949 Nehru assumed a new leadership in the British Commonwealth of Nations. The United Kingdom representative in India suggested a conference of representatives of India, Pakistan, Ceylon, Australia, and the United Kingdom to discuss the problems of Burma. The United Kingdom delegate whispered discreetly, and Nehru jumped at the suggestion. He took the initiative in suggesting mediation between the Republican government of Burma and the Karen dissidents; and India led in the discussions of a loan to Burma, perhaps as much as $100,000,000, for the salvaging of the vital Burma rice crop. Burma spent its money on suppressing Communists and had none left for its rice farmers. As long as India stayed in the foreground, the United Kingdom could advance the money and still escape the charges of self-interest or imperialism.

Australia and New Zealand have become the lands just south of Southeast Asia instead of the "continents way down under." The revolution in modern communications brought them more intimately into the Asian world, almost marking them as prey for Japanese aggression. The United States would have had a very difficult time retrieving its position in the Pacific had it not been for the friendly and whole-hearted cooperation of Australia. In the words of former Ambassador Nelson T. Johnson, "Some seven and one-half million men and women descended of Anglo-European stock living in a continent that is washed on all sides by the waters of the Orient, a people who as to their fortune and their life are entirely committed to the Pacific and what happens there, are of an abiding interest to us."

Australia is concerned over her thinly populated territory and her difficult defense problems. Weak in herself, she gains strength only as she is backed by Great Britain and the United States. Her foreign policy is a neat balance of independence, empire bonds, and good relations with the United States. She wants major-power or at least middle-power status, and she counts upon expanded immigration and industrialization to build up her own strength. Australia regrets the loss of British prestige, importance, and interest in the Far East, but she aspires to take the place of Great Britain as "the best judge of what is best likely to preserve British Commonwealth interests in this part of the world."

The United Kingdom is not disposed to surrender its interests or the right to protect them; South Africa reserves the right to speak on its own behalf; the two Indian states can claim an important voice on grounds almost as good as Australia's; and Canada insists upon its own freedom of decision and action.

Australia has taken a leading role in the deliberations of the United Nations and its subsidiary organs, and with New Zealand has been the ardent champion of regional arrangements both for security and welfare. She advocates vigorously the rule of law as the only sound principle of international peace. But she ruefully admits that no principle is any good if suicide and ill-will motivate nations. "Awaiting the day when men will cease to behave like creatures possessed, Australia is keeping her powder dry— and heaping it up. Defense now absorbs six and one-half per cent of the national income, three times as much as before the war. Meanwhile she reiterates her principles whenever an opportunity offers, taking pride in small victories achieved along the way."

New Zealand interprets her security primarily in terms of economics. She has a high standard of living and means to safeguard and improve it. She has the highest per capita external trade in the world, and is thus peculiarly vulnerable to fluctuating world economic conditions. If other countries raise their standard of living, their purchases will swell New Zealand's profits. She is interested in the maximum movement of capital to backward areas and favors international cooperation to maximize the flow of trade. On the other hand, she insists upon her right to broaden the basis of her own economy and control her external trade, immigration, and the investment of foreign capital. New Zealand has been accused of shortsightedness for her policies of import selection, state marketing, and imperial preference.

Australia's economic dilemma goes far toward explaining her international policies. She has an uneven balance of trade and buys so much more from the United States than she sells there that she suffers from a critical dollar shortage. She bought capital goods from the United States during the war, and now she must look to America for parts and replacements. She is not willing to co-operate in international economic programs like the International Trade Organization and the International Bank for Reconstruction and Development. She has more faith in imperial preference. She invites American capital, but does not like to contribute substantially to the economic strength of the United States. At some later time she might be a rival of the United States for the markets of Southeast Asia. She has sympathy for socialistic programs of government aid. She is afraid that "free enterprise" is a tool of economic imperialism, and she thinks that whether Americans wish it or not, they might experience a boom or bust that would wreck Australia's economy, or the economy of any other nation depending upon them.

Australia is not sure that the United States is pursuing the correct policy toward Japan. She wishes to see Japan completely stripped of her military potential, particularly since British influence and Dutch prestige have declined. Australia fears the reappearance of Japan's power of aggression, which might "accidentally" come back to life if she attains the position of buffer between the United States and Russia. Australia fails to appreciate the danger of a poverty-stricken Japan. Living next to millions of Orientals, these handfuls of occidentals have a "high and ample standard of living due to the courage and enterprise of our forefathers, the energy and industry of our own people. Our land flows with milk and honey, while they do not know where the next meal is coming from." Considerations like these led Dr. Evatt to explain: "White Australia is not an aggressive but a defensive policy, not political but economic in character and substance."

On June 11, 1947 the *Sydney Sun* remarked: "The resumption of trade relations with the Japanese does not imply the slightest change of heart on our part. There can be no sympathy, no magnanimous forgive-and-forget philanthropy in our new dealings with that barbarous and suavely treacherous race. . . . So, without burying our bitter memories of a dehumanized enemy's monstrous crime, we shall have to resume peaceful trade as a matter of sheer economic necessity."

Australia envisages a peace settlement with Japan that will keep her out of Southeast Asia and back in her own four islands. Japan shall be controlled by a supervisory commission, an Allied police force, and an American army based on some neighboring islands. Industries shall be limited, democracy encouraged, and shipping curtailed. Reasonable reparations shall be demanded, and Japan shall be deprived of all her foreign rights and interests.

Australia maintains a strategic silence on Southeast Asian rela-. tions. She has a general and specific interest in the improved well-being of the people in this area. She has shown unusual sympathy for the Indonesians. Australian dock-workers refused to load Dutch supplies intended for military purposes. Australia brought the Dutch-Indonesian dispute before the Security Council, and the Republic asked Australia to represent it on the United Nations Good Offices Committee. Yet she must remain friendly with the colonial powers. To Australia, Southeast Asia is the "Near North." It is not a remote area where contingent political assets or liabilities may be developed. It is part of the immediate neighborhood. Australia cannot step out boldly; she must remain friendly to both sides.

The Postwar Position of the United States

Millions of Americans who would not have heard of Southeast Asia had it not been for the war have been awakened to the realities of foreign policy. They appreciate what it means to say the "peace is indivisible." The future of civilization as we understand it depends upon the wise use of American power. The American people must be ready to implement their government's decisions and to erase the last vestiges of isolation. They must continue to assume their responsibilities for collective security, and to try to understand the incalculable influence they wield in the Pacific as well as in the Atlantic.

The United States was inevitably given the task of administering occupied Japan. The Potsdam declaration and the Far Eastern Commission's Basic Post-Surrender Policy for Japan fixed the main guideposts. The United States was obliged to interpret "demilitarization, democratization, and decentralization of industry" according to its own lights. It sought to give Japan a "peacefully inclined and responsible government" and make it impossible for Japan ever again to menace the peace of the world. As the months went by without a peace treaty it became necessary to shift the emphasis from the punitive phases of the occupation to the assistance aspects. As expense to the American taxpayer continued, the pressure increased to modify corrective measures and to concentrate on Japan's economic improvement. In spite of the objections of Russia and some of Japan's neighbors, the Americans interpreted their new emphasis as being entirely in line with their efforts in other parts of the world to contribute to general recovery.

At the end of the war the United States had high hopes for a strong, united, and democratic China and conducted its diplomacy toward that objective. It gave up its privileges in China and re-established commercial relations on a reciprocal basis. It negotiated agreements for reciprocal air transport rights, for turning over to China at extremely favorable rates prodigious amounts of surplus property, and for extending military and economic aid without any obligation whatever on the part of China. In spite of Communist allegations, these aid agreements did not enslave the Chinese workers. On the contrary, they brought food and employment to them and preserved the very breath of life for many who would otherwise have starved. Troops and military equipment were sent to China originally to effect the Japanese surrender, and a military mission was dispatched to train the Chinese army, regardless of whether it happened to consist of Communists or Kuomintang Chinese. General Marshall's diplomatic mission was intended to give effect to the traditional American policy of Chinese unity and to prevent an irreparable cleavage between the warring factions.

The American program was carried out with the approval of the Chinese National government, and without serious objection on the part of any great power or any substantial portion of the

American people. As conditions in China changed, however, and as the American-Russian fever mounted, it became necessary to consider a change of tactics. America's basic desires for China—independence from outside tyranny, a strong democratic government, and enhanced welfare—remained constant. But a continuation of the procedures which had been welcomed by the Kuomintang might be interpreted by a new regime as unwarranted interference in the internal affairs of another sovereign state.

While wrestling with the problems of Japan and China, the United States felt obliged to take immediate steps in the Pacific islands in the name of security. It had the strength to annex island bases as it pleased, but it faced deterring factors. At Potsdam, President Truman declared that "though the United States wants no territories out of this war, we are going to maintain the military bases necessary for the complete protection of our interests and of world peace." Still, Americans realized that security required more than military might. What good would it do to acquire military bases if the political irritants thus produced would result in precisely the situation against which we were building defenses?

A strong body of American opinion felt that there were stretches of island shores which should be forever American because they had been bought by American blood and treasure. The House Naval Affairs Committee recommended that the United States should take outright the Japanese mandated islands, and should retain specific and substantial rights to American bases constructed on island territories of Allied nations. The committee apparently wanted everything from Kodiak and Adak to Manus and the Philippines, including the Japanese mandated islands, Iwo and Okinawa.

To some Americans this seemed like "unnecessary imperialism in the name of security." They argued that the proposed new bases would be useless in forestalling aggression or repulsing attack. Tropical bases are likely to prove worthless in a polar war, or in an atomic war where guided missiles might be catapulted from continent to continent.

As a compromise the United States acquired the former Japanese mandates as the Trust Territory of the Pacific Islands. An agreement was negotiated with the United Nations which designated the entire area as a strategic zone and the United States as the administering authority. This arrangement permitted us to operate within our promises that "we seek no aggrandizement, territorial or otherwise," and that "the three great Allies covet no gain for themselves and have no thought of territorial expansion." We paid due deference to the trusteeship system inaugurated in the Charter of the United Nations, and yet by the "strategic area" clause we preserved for ourselves practically every privilege for defense that we would have obtained by outright annexation. We have full powers of administration, legislation, and jurisdiction, but we have agreed to apply the objectives of the trusteeship system to people of the Trust Territory. In effect we supervise the harbors, sea routes, and airways in the whole vast semicircle of the open Pacific Ocean north of the equator. The Stars and Stripes fly over 120 new island units inhabited by 90,000 islanders, who after long experience with the Spanish, Germans, and Japanese are now dependent on Americans for their protection and welfare.

President Truman placed the Trust Territory under the interim administration of the secretary of the navy, largely because the navy was in charge of Guam and Samoa and had carried on military government in the islands after the war. Mr. Harold Ickes objected to the navy rule:

"I sum up the record. The Navy in Guam and Samoa for nearly half a century has prevented the fulfillment of national pledges made and accepted in good faith. It has refused to permit on its own motion, and its effective lobby has prevented Congress from granting, any vestige of a bill of rights to its subject peoples. In its own unrestrained conduct of civilian affairs, it has violated willfully and persistently many of the tenets of the American Bill of Rights. It has scorned every concept of due process of law and almost every principle of democracy. It has ignored the economic problems of the islanders and given them inferior education in segregated schools. It has trampled upon the standards of social policy of the International Labor Office for dependent areas."

The navy pointed to its general high standards of sanitation and medical care and its benevolence in administration, and it adopted an enlightened policy for the Trust Territory. Since assuming its new responsibilities, the navy has trained administrators for specialized jobs and has employed a large number of civilians for the professional positions. It looks to an extension and improvement of the educational systems, and is teaching handicrafts and new agricultural and trade methods in its effort to improve the native standard of living. It emphasizes policies of self-help and self-government and has an ultimate aim of fitting both races for citizenship. The navy, however, can never let its obligations as the administering authority for the islands interfere with its basic mission of guaranteeing the security of the United States.

The United States sought to bolster its security positions in the Pacific by negotiating two agreements with the Philippines providing for American military assistance in the training of the Filipino army, and for the point use of bases for the defense of their respective territories. It was difficult to find a satisfactory formula that would permit the United States to station troops in the Philippines without violating the latter's sovereignty. The magic formula was that *mutual* security demanded *mutual* defense measures. Article II, paragraph 3 of the bases agreement provides that: "In the interest of international security any bases listed in Annexes A and B may be made available to the Security Council of the United Nations on its call by prior mutual agreement between the Philippines and the United States." Article XXV, paragraph 1 states that: "The Philippines agrees that it shall not grant, without prior consent of the United States, any bases or any rights, power, or authority whatsoever, in or relating to bases, to any third power."

The agreement is to remain in force for ninety-nine years. The bases listed include Clark Field, Fort Stotsenberg, the Mariveles Military Reservation, Camp John Hay Leave and Recreation Center, the Leyte-Samar Naval Base, Subic Bay, Olongapo, the Tawi Tawi Naval Anchorage, Sangley Point Navy Base, Mactan Island Army and Navy Air Base, Puerta Princesa Army and Navy Air Base, and the Aparri Naval Air Base. These points cover the entire extent of the archipelago from the extreme south to the extreme north, and they include most of the names that have been familiar in the military history of the United States in the Philippines.

The United States maintains a special interest in the Philippines, which is intangible and beyond the letter of treaty stipulations. Many Americans retain a parental interest in the Islands and would advocate immediate war if they were to be attacked by an outside aggressor. They would certainly feel like doing something about it if the Philippines were to be involved in "dangerous" foreign entanglements, to become embroiled with China or Japan, or to fall prey to alien ideologies. Many GI's have pleasant recollections of Manila, while others have memories which are not so pleasant; but in any case they have a personal attachment that will not let them be indifferent to the fate of the independent Republic.

The welfare policies of the United States which might have a particular bearing on Southeast Asia were outlined by President Truman in Point Four of his inaugural message. He said:

"We must embark upon a bold new program for making the benefits of our scientific advances and industrial progress available for the improvement and growth of underdeveloped areas. . . . The material resources which we can afford to use for the assistance of other peoples are limited. But our imponderable resources in technical knowledge are constantly growing and are inexhaustible. . . . We should make available to peace-loving peoples the benefits of our store of technical knowledge in order to help them realize their aspirations for a better life. And, in cooperation with other nations, we should foster capital investment in areas needing development."

He suggested working through the United Nations and invited the cooperation of private capital, business, agriculture, and labor in a program that would do away with the old imperialism and yet would benefit both the investor and "the people whose resources and whose labor go into these developments." The president concluded by saying:

"Only by helping the least fortunate of its members to help themselves can the human family achieve the decent satisfying life that is the right of all people. . . . Democracy alone can supply the vitalizing force to stir the peoples of the world into triumphant action, not only against their human oppressors, but also against their ancient enemies—hunger, misery, and despair."

It was the president's hope to use material means for a non-material end. His plan would bring to millions a fuller and freer life and would enlist the vast potentialities of private capital and initiative in what had heretofore been a government reserve. He wanted development to be a two-way proposition: attractive for the backward area but profitable for the investor. He would lo-cate factories where there are the skills and the resources to justify them, and not merely where the economic nationalists clamor to have them.

In the postwar period the American devotion to its intangible interests has been complicated by the realities of the antagonism between the United States and Russia. The government of the United States declared that it wanted a defense chain of democ-racies in Southeast Asia; but it announced a kind of middle-of-the-road policy when it declared: "It is not our mission to under-write the declaration of independence of others, nor to assist in the forceful reimposition of the territorial sovereignty of others." It felt obliged to state that it "recognizes alike the natural aspira-tions of the Indonesian people and the legitimate rights and inter-ests of the Netherlands Government." The Indian press labeled this ambiguity as "moral cowardice" and alleged that the Ameri-can sympathy for freedom was only platonic. Many "liberal" elements within the United States would have favored a more forthright declaration in favor of the Indonesian Republic. But the government feared that our European allies needed all the strength they could legitimately muster, and was not content to see the intensification of revolutionary processes in their colonies.

The United States did not mince words in the Security Council in its attitudes toward the Indonesian situation. It accused the Russians of obstructionist tactics and of endeavoring to under-mine the strength of the Republic because of its avowed anti-communism. The American delegate to the Security Council said: "No one doubts that the Communists of Indonesia like the Communists throughout the world are responsive to and act in accordance with instructions from Moscow." He then accused the Dutch of failing to cooperate with the United Nations Good

Offices Committee and asserted: "My government fails to find any justification whatever for renewal of military operations in Indonesia."

The United States suspended its economic assistance program to the Netherlands in Indonesia, even though this might work an unavoidable hardship on the local populace. But it felt that it could take no further positive or punitive measures in view of its requirements with regard to its power position in relation to Russia.

At the end of the war, Russian-American relations in Asia were without friction. Neither coveted the resources of the other, and neither felt that the other had gone back on its military commitments for the winning of the war. Subsequent political and economic antagonisms gave birth to mutual distrust. Each feared the other would try to impose its will and its system on the rest of the world. Public opinions became inflamed. Each strengthened its national defense preparations against the alleged aggressions of the other. In the American view, Russia disturbed the peace of the world in disturbing its peace of mind. Nerves breed temper, and temper strife.

Kipling once remarked that the Russian is a delightful person "until he tucks in his shirt." The implication is that the Russian is at heart an Oriental, and that he becomes unnatural and boorish when he tries to imitate the West. It is certain that the Russian way of life is not separated from that of the Orient by the same distance which divides the United States and Asia. The Russians are closer in many ways to the Orientals than we are. They have an advantage in being able to talk to their Asian neighbors in terms and on conditions that are more intimate than we can employ. It must never be forgotten that Russia approaches Southeast Asia by land, and that its inner Asian frontiers with China are the longest land frontiers in the world. All the sea power the British were able to muster in the last century and all the air power the Americans could thrust at Russia by the short route over the pole would not be able effectively to impede physical, and to a certain extent spiritual, contacts between the Russians and their Asian neighbors.

At Yalta the Big Three came into substantial agreement on

Russia's future role in East Asia. Within three months after the surrender of Germany, Russia was to enter the war in Asia. As her rewards she would receive the Kuriles and southern Sakhalin, a voice in the peace with Japan, the restoration of her old imperial position in Manchuria, and a Chinese recognition of the independence of Outer Mongolia. Russia abrogated her neutrality pact with Japan, declared war on schedule, and negotiated a new treaty with China.

The United States and Russia clashed over Korea, Manchuria, Japan, China, and the spread of communism throughout Asia. In spite of all her altruistic pretensions, Russia fastened her grip on Korea north of the thirty-eighth parallel and re-established herself in Manchuria. By virtue of her treaty of good neighborliness with China, she acquired joint ownership of the Manchurian railways, the reopening of Dairen as a free port, and the exclusive use, with China, of Port Arthur as a naval base. Red troops swarmed across Manchuria, annihilated the scattered remnants of the Kuantung army, and took over the Japanese factories from Mukden to Harbin. They considered all enemy property as legitimate booty to be moved or destroyed. To the Americans, it seemed fantastic that the Russians could protest friendship for China and destroy a substantial portion of her most useful assets; to the Russians, it seemed elementary that they should obliterate all sources of military power which a potential hostile combination of the United States and China might want to mobilize against them.

In Japan, Russia accused the United States of favoring the reactionary elements and utilizing the occupation as a means of constructing an anti-Russian military base. Russia accused us of camouflage in our demilitarization, democratization, and decentralization of industry programs, alleging in every case that we abandoned the original objectives in the interests of lifting up Japan and making her strong again as a pro-American bastion in the Far East. The United States charged the Russians with military designs on their own part—refusing to repatriate the prisoners of war who had been captured in Manchuria. It accused the Russians of refusing to cooperate in effecting true democratic reforms in the interest of supporting their Communist puppets.

Had Russia supported the Communists in China with the same singleness of purpose that we supported the Kuomintang, it would have been difficult to avoid a head-on clash. Russia maintained correct relations with Chiang Kai-shek, and took no official cognizance of the American supplies which were being disposed of with an eye to eventual use against the Communists. As late as the August 1945 treaty Russia agreed to recognize the sovereignty and the territory of China, and agreed not to interfere in her internal affairs. Russia also said that whatever aid was extended to China would be given to the Nationalist government as the central government of China.

Russia's restraint seemed to spring from her own comparative weakness. She needed time and security to rebuild. She could not match the United States in military and economic potential, so she could not register effective opposition to the American policies in Japan, China, the Philippines, or the Pacific Ocean area. However, Russia had effective weapons in propaganda and in the indigenous Communist parties.

As the Communists gained strength in Japan and China, Russia derived benefits. It is to be assumed, from lack of absolute proof to the contrary, that the local Communists were independent and not the tools of Moscow; but it is not to be denied that their relations were cordial and their acts sympathetic. A certain philosophic oneness united the Communists from Vladivostok to Calcutta, although local tactical divergencies characterized their individual procedures. Early in 1948 three international Communist conferences in Calcutta—the New Democratic Youth League, the Indian Communists, and the Southeast Asia Youth Conference—provided occasions for coordination and harmonious timing. No observer has been able to uncover a Red network, but many have reported continuous contacts and communications between Communist cells in Harbin, Shanghai, Hong Kong, Singapore, and Bangkok. Encouragement and perhaps funds are supplied to Communists in Southeast Asia from their party brothers and fellow travelers in China, India, Australia, and overseas.

Much Communist strength derives from local conditions. Intelligent leaders have been able to capitalize on the "double yoke of imperialist exploitation and the tyranny of the bourgeoisie," and have been able to arouse the workers and the peasants. They have resorted to the classic procedures of sabotage and strikes, and they have increased their effectiveness because of the weapons they have procured, the slogans they have learned, and the tactics they have copied from the Japanese. They aim at control of the unions, the army, and eventually the government. They associate themselves with independence movements wherever possible; but it has been noted that "wherever Communists come into the government through the window, independence is kicked out through the door."

Ninety per cent of their followers may not have the slightest idea what communism is all about, but they make effective supporters in the Communist program. Any attempt to suppress them by force only drives them underground and lends color and strength to their arguments. "Oppression" and "exploitation" are their favorite words. Their propaganda is directed not only against their own colonial overlords, but against America as well as the chief pillar of the capitalistic system. One writer says: "A lynching in Mississippi will be sung about in Singapore tomorrow. 'Dixieland' has become an enchanted legend in Southeast Asia. But the Dixie they sing about is not the hospitable old south of banjo-plunking and watermelon cracking. It is the Dixie of the Georgia road gangs and strange fruit hanging from Southern trees."

According to Communist propaganda, the United States is the world capital of discrimination and exploitation, while only in the USSR are all men equal regardless of color. Their propaganda is comparatively meaningless and ineffective when it tries to paint pictures of the paradise of the Soviet Union. But it is provocative when it aims its darts at social abuses that Southeast Asians have themselves smarted under and rebelled against.

The numbers of admitted Communists mean little in interpreting the strength of the movement. The factors that are important are the interest of the Soviet Union in the Communists; the astute policy of identifying themselves with popular, liberal political and economic movements; and the continuation of conditions that make it possible for the seeds of communism to grow.

In Indonesia the Communists have not succeeded in gaining

control of the Republican government. They have not known whether to try direct action against the Republican leaders (as they have done unsuccessfully in the past); whether to play into the hands of the Dutch by non-cooperation with the government of the Republic; or whether to cooperate with the Republicans by following a united front, nationalistic policy against the Dutch. The Communists control sufficient following in the Peoples' Democratic Front, the Central Labor Union, and the Peasants' Front to prevent united Republican action without them. Yet their vacillation and ambition for power are major factors in confounding confusion, strengthening the arguments of the Dutch, and alienating the sympathy of the Western world.

The Communists have least strength in the Philippines because the postwar situation was returned most quickly to normal there, and because American largess extracted the teeth of the Communist propaganda campaign. Ho Chi Minh has least need of his classical Communist training, because French maladroitness has driven so many Annamites to revolt. Even if Ho were not a Communist, he would be a popular leader of a strong independence movement in Indochina.

In Malaya, the Communists were unable to cope with the intelligent measures of the British Labor government, which were designed to attract workers into a moderate and constructive trade-union movement. Gangs of Chinese Communists, however, have burned plantations and terrorized the countryside.

In Burma the Communists have been divided. The Red Flags, or extremists, have been operating underground. The White Flags, less radical, have joined forces with the dissident Karens. They have wrecked the country's finances and spread the civil war to the environs of Rangoon. In Siam, the Russian embassy has been suspected of being the party headquarters for all Southeast Asia. Communists have been blamed for Siam's continuing emergency condition. However, Phibun is not above magnifying the danger of the Communists in order to curry Western favor and make more palatable his dictatorial position.

All the governments in Southeast Asia are anti-Communist. That does not mean they are pro-democratic. There is no such thing as "pure communism" or "pure democracy." Like every other region Southeast Asia will have to find the optimum mixture "which will best suit its people, the time, and the circumstances." One writer suggests that perhaps the British compromise will prove most beneficial—with essential industries nationalized, risk capital otherwise encouraged, and the land not collectivized but taken from the feudal owners and redistributed in the hands of the peasants.

It is folly to interpret all social unrest in terms of United States-Communist rivalry, and all liberal or leftist inclinations as "communistic." Radicals are often looked upon as troublemakers, but ultraconservatism can be equally chaotic. "In the story of the Mississippi steamboat which exploded, was the trouble with the stoker who overheated the boilers, or the skipper who refused to open the safety valve?" Democratic strength lies on the side of progress, not on the preservation of the *status quo*. The United States stands to gain in assuming world leadership in support of democratic governments and economic development schemes. Hungry people do not make good democrats. Edmund Burke offered good advice:

"Let the peoples of Europe and Asia and Africa always keep the idea of their civil rights associated with your government; they will cling and grapple to you, and no force under heaven will be of power to tear them from their allegiance. . . . Slavery they can have anywhere. It is a weed that grows in every soil . . . but until you become lost to all feeling of your true interest, and your national dignity, freedom they can have from none but you. This is the commodity of price of which you have the monopoly."

International Organization in Southeast Asia

The postwar community of nations has insisted that its rights be respected in the midst of the conflicts between nations and peoples. The United Nations is the postwar development of the League of Nations. It has been given authority by its members to take action whenever disputes or situations threaten international peace and security. It has been charged with the tasks of international cooperation for economic and social improvement, on the grounds that enhanced welfare will put down or avoid local unrest and will eliminate one of the basic causes of war.

The United Nations is no substitute for the ordinary channels of diplomacy. It is another platform where grievances can be aired, another clearinghouse where ideas can be exchanged. It is only as good as its members make it. The problems of international organization are not those of constitutions, charters, or forms. They are problems of the will to compromise, the determination to curb forces in conflict, and the desire to contribute to the establishment of conditions in which peaceful procedures and orderly processes will be looked upon as a matter of course.

The League of Nations wrestled in vain with problems of disarmament. The United Nations copes with the additional problem of the atomic bomb. The League had no machinery for enforcing its decisions. The United Nations hopes to have an international police force, which will be able to act swiftly wherever and whenever a threat to peace arises. In practice the nations have not been able to agree on the makeup of such a force. It is certain that they would have the greatest difficulty in calling it into service.

The mutual use of bases is a step forward in the enforcement of collective security. The most menacing features of the Australian base at Manus, the British bases at Ceylon, Singapore, and Hong Kong, the French bases at Noumea and Camranh, the Dutch bases at Amboina and Surabaya, and the American bases in the Philippines are nullified by agreements for mutual use, or by an expressed willingness to put the bases at the disposition of the Security Council. No nation is willing to relinquish sovereignty over its territory, nor limit the use of its facilities to any particular power. But no nation can find valid excuse to deprive the United Nations or its agents of the use of any base that would be vital to the enforcement of the peace.

Chapter VIII, Articles 52, 53, and 54 of the United Nations Charter permit the existence of regional arrangements or agencies for dealing with international peace and security. A general agreement covering all questions in the entire Pacific area, or even in Southeast Asia, would be too broad to be effective. But limited regional arrangements for security or development might prove very beneficial. They might provide useful machinery for consultation and collaboration and for the coordination of native interests with those of the supervisory power. They might extend the idea "in union there is strength" beyond the limitations of national boundaries.

In January 1944 Australia and New Zealand signed the Canberra Agreement. They agreed to "act together in matters of common concern in the Southwest and South Pacific areas, within the framework of a general system of security." On July 29, 1948 the South Pacific Commission came into force. It is a consultative and advisory body consisting of representatives of the United States, the United Kingdom, France, the Netherlands, Australia, and New Zealand. It studies all matters of social and economic welfare, provides the participating governments with technical assistance, and promotes cooperation with other governments or private agencies. It has a permanent secretariat and a research council, and holds a periodical conference where native peoples and representatives of metropolitan powers meet to thresh out their problems. At present regional organizations deal exclusively with economic and social problems; but if hopes are fulfilled they might extend their scope into the political and even the military realm.

Chapter XI of the Charter, the Declaration Regarding Non-Self-Governing Territories; Chapter XII, the International Trusteeship System; and Chapter XIII, the Trusteeship Council—all have a direct bearing on international relationships in Southeast Asia. By these obligations the members of the United Nations which have responsibilities for the administration of territories whose people have not yet attained a full measure of self-government recognize the principle that the interests of the populations of these territories are paramount. They accept as a sacred trust the obligation to promote the well-being of the inhabitants by insuring their protection, their cultural advancement, and their development toward self-government. The United Kingdom, the Netherlands, and France all accepted these obligations for their dependent peoples.

The Economic and Social Council has unusual opportunities for contributing to the welfare of Asian peoples. In 1947 it set up, as its principal agent for Asia, the Economic Commission for Asia and the Far East (ECAFE). ECAFE surveyed the war devastation and reconstruction needs of Asia and launched a series of meetings to devise ways and means to solve its tremendous problems. It was handicapped by two basic facts: any international program would have to be subordinated to national programs; and the United States was already so deeply committed to Europe that it had little left over to use for the recovery of Asia. ECAFE discussed a five-year industrialization program which contemplated the expenditure of thirteen billion dollars. The American delegate was obliged to say very forcefully that although his government was fully sympathetic with the needs of Asia, it did not have the resources for a Marshall Plan for Asia. The appalling magnitude of Asia's development programs, as studied and analyzed by ECAFE, contributed to the crystallization and pronouncement of President Truman's Point Four.

Southeast Asia stands to gain directly from the activities of some of the specialized agencies that are either a part of or affiliated with the United Nations. Among these agencies are the International Labor Office (ILO), the Food and Agriculture Organization (FAO), the World Health Organization (WHO), the International Bank for Reconstruction and Development (the Bank), the International Monetary Fund (the Fund), the International Refugee Organization (IRO), and the United Nations Educational, Scientific, and Cultural Organization (UNESCO).

The FAO has set up an International Rice Council which will strive to bring about cooperative action on the production, conservation, distribution, and consumption of rice. The Bank has extended a loan to the Philippines, and the IRO has been granted temporary refuge for 6,000 European refugees in the ex-navy installations at Samar. Up to the end of March 1948, the IRO had returned 4,166 overseas Chinese from China to their prewar homes in the Philippines, Malaya, and the Netherlands Indies. UNESCO is dedicated to the development of cultural resources, and the ILO is seeking to attain in Asia the social objectives that it has sponsored in Europe and the Americas. It has called general attention to the need for providing employment for excess agricultural population, for the expansion of agricultural production, for the fairer distribution of agricultural income, and for fairer terms of exchange for the export of primary products.

The role of international organizations is perhaps symbolic of a more hopeful era in international relations. Imperfect as it is, it focuses the spotlight on areas of conflict and on the causes of war; and in its new procedures, it shifts the emphasis from the old imperial struggles for prestige and profit to new objectives of improved welfare for all concerned.

Suggested Reading

Annals of the American Academy of Political and Social Science. *Southeast Asia and the Philippines.* Vol. 226. March 1943.

Ball, W. MacMahon. "Reflections on Japan," *Pacific Affairs.* March 1948.

———. *Japan—Enemy or Ally.* New York. 1949.

Dennett, Tyler. *Americans in Eastern Asia.* New York. 1922.

DuBois, Cora. *Social Forces in Southeast Asia.* Minneapolis. 1949.

Evatt, Herbert. *Foreign Policy of Australia.* Sydney. 1945.

Fairbank, J. K. *United States and China.* Cambridge, Mass. 1948.

Fisher, H. H. *The United States and Russia in the World Community.*

Hailey, Lord. "The Aims of British Colonial Administration," *The World Affairs Interpreter.* Winter 1949.

Institute of Pacific Relations. *Far Eastern Survey* and *Pacific Affairs.*

Isaacs, Harold. *New Cycle in Asia.* New York. 1947.

Keesing, Felix. "The South Pacific Commission Makes Progress." MS.

Lasker, Bruno. "Southeast Asia Enters the Modern World." MS.

Lattimore, Owen. *Solution in Asia.* Boston. 1944.

———. *Situation in Asia.* Boston. 1949.

Levy, Roger. *L'Indo Chine et ses Traites.* Paris. 1946.

Pannikar, K. M. *The Future of Southeast Asia.* New York. 1943.

Payne, Robert. *The Revolt of Asia.* New York. 1947.

Royal Institute of International Affairs. *The Political and Strategic Interests of the United Kingdom.* London. 1939.

Sharp, Lauriston. *Books to Read on Southeast Asia.* Pamphlet issued by The Institute of Pacific Relations.

United Nations Department of Public Information. *Everyman's United Nations.* 1949.

Vincent, John C., and others. *America's Future in the Pacific.* New Brunswick, N.J. 1946.

Index

4776 018